THE DAY

ALTERNATIVE

MUSIC DIED

*Dylan, Zeppelin, Punk, Glam, Alt, Majors, Indies, and the
Struggle between Art and Money for the Soul of Rock*

Adam Caress

New Troy Books 2015

Manufactured by CreateSpace
Book design by Adam Caress
Primary cover illustration by Kathleen Fulton

Includes bibliographical references and index
ISBN-13: 978-0692438152
ISBN-10: 0692438157

Library of Congress Control Number:
2015907017

New Troy Books
P.O. Box 1184, Montreat, NC 28757

for Jay, Gail, Josh, Jordan, and Alex

with very special thanks to Annie, James, Henry, and Lizzie

TABLE OF CONTENTS

PART III – CORPORATE CONSOLIDATIONS AND CRITICAL REVISIONS

PART IV – ROCK MUSIC FOR A NEW MILLENNIUM

Introduction

The Day Alternative Music Died: April 5, 1994

I was nearing the end of my freshman year of college when I heard the news that Kurt Cobain had died, and for people of my generation—especially music fans—his suicide was a pretty devastating event. For many of us, news of Cobain's death even approached the generation-defining "I remember where I was when…" territory typically reserved for political assassinations and terrorist attacks. Two decades later, however, I realize it's harder to understand the shock. For starters, there was more than a little writing on the wall, even for casual fans; Cobain's heroin issues were public knowledge, as was his stormy relationship with wife Courtney Love, and there were the occasional cancelled shows and whispers about chronic stomach pain and rehab. But it's important to remember that these were the days before the internet and the 24-hour news cycle. Yes, we had some inkling of Cobain's personal demons, but we weren't constantly reminded of them every day in the speculative percolations of the Twittersphere. The personal lives of celebrities may not have been exactly personal—we had *Inside Edition* and *The National Inquirer*, after all—but they were still private enough that we could be surprised by a rock and roll casualty, rather than resigned to its inevitability.

It's also worth remembering that, at the time of his death in the spring of 1994, Kurt Cobain was one of the most recognizable pop culture icons on the planet. "Smells Like Teen Spirit" had been *everywhere*. And not in the way a band like Arcade Fire is everywhere. More like the way Taylor Swift is everywhere. At the time of Cobain's death, Nirvana had sold 5 million copies of *Nevermind* in the U.S. alone. Even a "mainstream" indie band like Arcade Fire has never sold even 1 million copies of any of its albums in the U.S. Nirvana, on the other hand, was a cultural phenomenon. "Smells Like Teen Spirit" got play on mainstream pop radio. Kurt Cobain was recognizable to everyone from square suburban parents to the most obscurantist music snobs. And so the experience of Cobain's death was shared in a way that no rock casualty could be today. The new millennium has yet to produce a rock music figure to approach the kind of mainstream recognizability that Cobain had. Only rock oldsters like Bono or Mick Jagger are that recognizable. But even their loss would be different than the loss of Kurt Cobain; part of the shock of Cobain's death was his youth. He was only 27.

And beyond his sheer recognizability, Kurt Cobain *meant something* to people, a lot of different kinds of people. For casual rock fans tired of the canned posturing of hair bands and metal ballads, "Smells Like Teen Spirit" had opened the door to an entire universe of new and exciting music. For an aging generation of rock critics, Cobain's outsider status had signaled a welcome return to what they perceived as rock's countercultural roots. And for the serious indie music devotees who had followed Nirvana since their independent label beginnings, the mainstream success of *Nevermind* was perceived as a validation of the obscure, decade-long toilings of an entire scene. As indie journalist Gina Arnold succinctly put it, when Nirvana hit, "We won."

But for teenagers like me, Kurt Cobain wasn't burdened by the baggage of rock's history, mainstream or indie. He was simply the lead singer in one of the biggest and most important bands of the time. And his band's success belonged to *my* generation. I didn't inherit the experience of Nirvana from my parents like I did The Beatles or Dylan, or from my older friends and cousins like I did U2 or R.E.M. Nirvana was the first rock band that I had personally experienced "hitting it big," making that miraculous jump from seeming non-existence into the shared cultural consciousness. They quickly became the standard by which I measured all subsequent rock acts. And it wasn't just me. When I arrived at college in the fall of '93, the *Nevermind* CD was displayed on the shelves of seemingly every dorm room I entered, often prominently, either as part of a conscious attempt to display one's individual *coolness* or in an attempt to fit in with what everyone else was doing.

Nevermind was that rare album that could do either; it had achieved both substantive artistic credibility and staggering commercial success. However, at the time of Kurt Cobain's death, I had little understanding of the extent to which the tensions between his competing aspirations to create authentic art and to achieve popular success had torn him apart. Because Nirvana had been the first rock band I had witnessed ascending to pop superstardom, I guess I assumed that the creation of substantive art for a popular audience was the most natural thing in the world.

But on the heels of Cobain's death, those of us who were invested in the music of the alternative scene from which Nirvana had sprung were dismayed to see the way the mainstream music industry seemed to first inflate and then plunder his legacy. The phrase "Spokesman of Generation X"—which had been shelved following the disappointing sales of Nirvana's second major label album *In Utero*—was revived and used again and again. Commemorative images of Cobain began to leer from the t-shirt racks in shopping malls around the country (often sporting an obligatorily extended middle finger). It felt like we were in the midst of some sort of legend-making marketing machine, especially when the angst Cobain and Nirvana had embodied began to be re-packaged and sold to us via second-rate grunge knock-off bands like Candlebox, Seven Mary Three, and Silverchair. We no longer felt like idealistic music fans; we felt like a target market, and we began to cynically suspect that cash registers must be lighting up somewhere.

As it turns out, we were right. In the year following Kurt Cobain's death, 10 million Nirvana albums and videos were purchased, compared to just 7 million during Cobain's entire lifetime. And overall, more albums were purchased in 1994 than ever before: over 900 million in America alone, a staggering figure that would become the norm for the rest of the decade (eventually peaking in 1999 when U.S. album sales topped the 1 billion mark). But even as the music industry was achieving unprecedented sales, it was hard to ignore the extent to which rock music was becoming increasingly homogenized. To me, one of the attractions of the alternative scene from which Nirvana had emerged was that it had been so musically diverse. In addition to grunge-rockers like Nirvana and Pearl Jam, the alternative scene that stormed the charts in the early 90s had included a dazzling array of performers who didn't sound anything like grunge, from emotive singer-songwriter Tori Amos to downbeat crooner Morrissey, from lighter melodic bands like The

Cranberries and The Sundays to the heavier industrial music of Nine Inch Nails, from the female-fronted post-punk of Belly and The Breeders to the emotionally charged roots-rock of Counting Crows. All of these acts had scored their first gold records in the wake of Nirvana's breakthrough. But after Cobain's death in early 1994, the term "alternative" became increasingly synonymous with angsty, male-fronted bands like Green Day, Bush, Sponge, Candlebox, Collective Soul, Tool, Live, The Offspring, Everclear, Foo Fighters, Better Than Ezra, Seven Mary Three, Silverchair, Matchbox Twenty, Sister Hazel, Eve 6, Korn, Fuel, Lit, Creed, Three Doors Down, Nickelback, and on and on. "Alternative music"—which had once described a *scene* that contained countless styles of music and was defined only by its lack of mainstream success and loose affiliation in independent record stores and on alternative radio—was increasingly coming to describe a very specific stylistic *genre* of music, a homogenous sound and attitude chosen specifically for its perceived marketability and modeled on its most iconic band: Nirvana. And we were getting hit over the head with it.

The blatant commercialization and homogenization of alternative music was particularly painful to watch for someone like me who had come of age in L.A.'s vibrant alternative scene. After all, didn't the calculated packaging of music purely for financial profit go against everything Kurt Cobain and his fellow alt-scenesters stood for? The answer to that question is surprisingly complicated, and it points to a tension in rock music between art and money that goes all the way back to the first flowering of the rock music industry half a century ago. Since the mid-1960s, when Bob Dylan first introduced poetry and politics into rock music and major record labels began scooping up countercultural icons like The Grateful Dead and The MC5, there has been a tension between the idea of rock music as a uniquely substantive artistic pursuit and the idea that rock is just another part of the commercial entertainment industry. This tension became exacerbated in the 1970s when the increasingly commercial rock star culture of bands like Kiss was countered by the rebellious idealism of punk bands like The Clash. The same tension continued through the 1980s as legions of artistically adventurous rock acts coalesced into an "alternative" scene that wanted nothing to do with the ridiculous rock star posturing of the hugely popular glam metal bands. But the pull between the competing impulses towards artistic independence and commercial success was perhaps best embodied in the person of Kurt Cobain, who, according to biographer Michael Azerrad, "would vainly try to resolve both impulses within himself."

In years following Cobain's death, the relationship between rock's artistic and commercial aspirations would change dramatically. From the mid-1960s to the mid-1990s, popular rock music had been a vast playing field where artistic and commercial aspirations continually battled each other for supremacy. But the unprecedented corporatization that engulfed the mainstream media industry in the 1990s decisively shifted the balance of power in favor of commercial interests. Never in human history had there been such a vast corporate media complex dedicated to the production of commercial entertainment product, and once the alternative music scene was gobbled whole by the newly corporatized mainstream music industry, artistic aspirations have never again rivaled commercial aspirations in mainstream rock.

Over the past two decades, rock music's absorption into the corporate mainstream has slowly stripped it of the artistic credibility which had given rock its unique gravitas among the competing styles of popular music. And having lost that gravitas, rock music has all but lost its seat at the popular music table. After dominating the popular consciousness from the 60s through the 90s, rock music has drifted into the cultural background. Over the first decade of the new millennium, only *six* of the top fifty selling music acts were rock acts. And beyond just the sales figures, signs of rock's fading mainstream relevancy have become apparent everywhere. MTV's evolution from (predominantly rock) music videos to reality shows was greeted by no pickets or petitions. Rock clubs all over the country have been closing or transitioning to DJs. Formerly iconic rock radio stations like Chicago's Q101 and Boston's WFNX have been dropping like flies. And, slowly but surely, rock music has gone from being the popular music status quo to being a niche taste.

While this shift has had profound cultural consequences, I'd like to stress from the beginning that this book is not some woeful meditation on rock music's popular demise—a development which has clearly produced both positive and negative results. Rather, by grafting the untold story of the rise and fall of alternative music into a larger rock music narrative, this book attempts to shed some light on a number of crucial developments in rock and popular music which remain widely misunderstood, even as they continue to have far-reaching implications for the future of music creation, consumption, and criticism. And I hope this book will provide some engaging and useful insight into what it means to be a music fan, artist, and critic here in the 21st Century.

Preface

In The Beginning...

One of the most glaring problems with the prevailing narratives concerning the history of rock music is that they attempt to draw a straight line from rock's birth in the 1950s to the present day. In doing so, they assume that rock music was born fully-formed, possessing all of its essential characteristics from the very beginning, and that those essential characteristics have remained constant since its inception. For instance, this assumption has led those who believe that rock music is an *important* art form to assume that rock has *always* been an important art form, and that whatever made rock music important during a given era was the same thing that has always been important about it. Conversely, the same assumption about rock's essential continuity has led those who believe that rock is inherently *un*important—that it is, for instance, just another style of popular music—to assert that it has *never* been important, and that any importance it ever seemed to have was imagined by overwrought romantics. But both of these views tend to oversimplify a musical form which has always been in a state of flux. Rock music has been revolutionized and co-opted on multiple occasions, and it has been used by different people at different times to convey very different things for very different reasons with very different results. The fact is, no single narrative could ever hope to capture all of the diverse elements that have coalesced over the last 60 years into what we call rock music. And this is why I have chosen to tell a very specific story: the story of the tensions between the competing aspirations to substantive artistry and commercial success within rock music. Like any story, it has a specific beginning, but deciding *where* to begin was a tricky business, and where this story begins may seem controversial to some. I could spend multiple chapters explaining that choice, but if I were to devote that much time and space to explaining the story before getting on with the story itself, I'd run the risk of bogging us down before we even got to the story proper, and I tend to believe that if you're going to tell a story it's generally best to get the hell on with it. And so this (thankfully brief) preface will have to suffice as an explanation of why this story begins in 1965, even though by that time rock music had already been around for over a decade.

Let me begin by saying that I love Elvis. I love those old Ed Sullivan and Milton Berle clips. I love the pathos of the "Comeback Special." I'm a sucker for the ridiculous audacity of the Vegas-era "American Trilogy." I'll even sit through an entire Elvis movie if it catches me at the right time. Elvis Presley was one of those larger-than-life figures whose every move seemed to be amplified. A subtle wink and four girls would faint in the front row. A twitch of the hip and a TV censor's fingers would move towards the "abort" button. His mammoth charisma even made his human moments—a spontaneous guffaw or a jumbled lyric—seem *more human* by contrast because *he was Elvis Presley* being human. *That was The King* approvingly patting guitarist Scotty Moore on the butt. *That was The King* trying his hand at surfing or karate. When I was in college, my roommates and I invented a game called "Elvis Poker" because the photos on a randomly-purchased deck of Elvis playing cards were so compelling that we had to create a whole new set of poker rules to accommodate them. Elvis was the best. And it's difficult for me to imagine a world where people don't know who he is. I miss him even though I have no memory of a time when he was alive.

But the truth is, Elvis Presley never aspired to be a substantive musical artist. His greatest talent wasn't the creation of art; his greatest talent was simply *being Elvis*. And the vast majority of both his music and film careers were spent coasting on that fact. This is a guy who released an album called *50,000,000 Elvis Fans Can't Be Wrong*, and then later released another one called *Having Fun with Elvis On Stage* which was entirely made up of between-song stage banter and contained no actual songs. He also starred in over 30 movies, but he was basically just playing himself in those, too. And what he said to *Parade* in 1962 about his movie career could just as easily be applied to his music career as well:

I've had intellectuals tell me that I've got to progress as an actor, explore new horizons, take on new challenges, all that routine. I'd like to progress. But I'm smart enough to realize that you can't bite off more than you can chew in this racket. You can't go beyond your limitations. They want me to try an artistic picture. That's fine. Maybe I can pull it off some day. But not now. I've done 11 pictures, and they've all made money. A certain type of audience likes me. I entertain them with what I'm doing. I'd be a fool to tamper with that kind of success. It's ridiculous to take it on my own and say I'm going to appeal to a different type of audience, because I might not. Then if I goof, I'm all washed up, because they don't give you many chances in this business. If you're doing all right, you better keep at it until time itself changes things.

This sentiment shouldn't come as a surprise given Elvis's well-documented aspirations to be a *popular entertainer*, to have a career in "showbiz;" he never set out to be the kind of ideologue that John Lennon or Bob Dylan would later become. And his limited aspirations were shared by his early rock contemporaries—Little Richard, Jerry Lee Lewis, Chuck Berry, Buddy Holly, etc.—all of whom aspired to careers as popular entertainers, nothing more, nothing less, even those of them who, unlike Elvis, wrote their own songs. According to Chuck Berry's account in the 1987 documentary *Hail, Hail, Rock and Roll*:

> Working for my father in the white neighborhoods, I never heard Muddy Waters. I never heard Elmore James. I heard Frank Sinatra. I heard Pat Boone… Then I said, 'Why can't I do as Pat Boone does and play good music for the white people and sell as well there as I could in the neighborhood?' And that's what I shot for writing 'School Days:' nice, nice music. And it caught on. I wrote about school, and half of the people have cars so I wrote about cars. And mostly all of the people, if they're not now, they'll soon be in love. And those that have loved and are out of love remember love, so write about love. So I wrote about all three and thought I hit a pretty good capacity of the people.

In other words, Chuck Berry aspired to write popular songs. So did Buddy Holly, and Lieber and Stoller, and Fats Domino, and all the other leading rock songwriters of the 50s and early 60s. Rock was shaped by its commercial aspirations from the very beginning. The whole reason Sun Records' Sam Phillips had been looking for a "white Southern boy" to sing black rhythm and blues music was to sell more records. That's not to say that music created with commercial aspirations can't have cultural value, but it was rock's commercialism—*not* its counterculturalism (as is widely assumed)—that most distinguished it from its stylistic ancestors in the various American folk music traditions: Delta blues, Appalachian folk, Southern gospel music, etc. Sure, there had been performers in these traditions who had made their living playing music, but each of those individual traditions had existed for centuries prior to the advent of the modern popular music industry, and each had developed organically as an art form apart from the influence of aspirations to mass commercial success. Indeed, it was rock's blatant commercialism that caused traditional music purists to look down their noses at it. As Peter Yarrow (of the folk group Peter, Paul, and Mary) put it, "People adored Elvis Presley; they never wanted to know what his opinion was."

But it wasn't just folkies who dismissed rock music. Prior to the mid-60s, very few people took rock music seriously. There was no such thing as serious rock criticism. Rock was covered in the teen fan-mags like *Dig* and *Modern Teen*, and it was largely—and in most cases, *correctly*—dismissed by serious types as teenage bubble-gum fluff. Few cultural critics took an interest in rock, and when they did, it was usually only to ridicule it. For instance, *Tonight Show* founder Steve Allen had a running bit during the late 50s where he would read the lyrics to popular rock songs with a tinkling piano in the background, in the style of many poetry readings of the day. He would assume a straight face, look meaningfully into the distance, and then begin, "Bee bop a lu la, she's my baby…" And the crowd would immediately burst into laughter, recognizing the absurdity of treating rock lyrics like poetry.

This patronizing view of rock would hold sway until the mid-60s, even *after* the arrival of The Beatles, whose early songs like "Love Me Do" and "I Want to Hold Your Hand" did little to dispel the notion that rock was simply vapid pop music for teenagers. Most intellectuals shared the view of the *New Yorker*, who gently dismissed the initial popularity of the four lovable mop-tops as "a benign infection, perhaps incurable." But again, this shouldn't be surprising given that The Beatles, like Elvis before them, initially aspired to be (and became beyond their wildest dreams) *popular entertainers*, not substantive artists. According to their producer and collaborator George Martin (who also signed them to their first major record deal in 1962) in the PBS documentary *Rock & Roll*:

It wasn't that they were great musicians or great singers or great performers or great songwriters; it was that they had enormous charisma... The first stuff that I heard from Paul and John was not very good. 'Love Me Do' was the best song I could find. [But] once we had a #1 hit, that gave them the inspiration and the urge to do more and to write better. And each time it got better and better. It was terrific. And they were all kind of songs that were of a mode. They were songs designed to be quick, instant, almost forgettable—but not—but certainly able to get over to the public very, very easily and very quickly. They weren't deep songs.

The reason the story I'm telling begins in 1965 is that, prior to that, there was no tension in rock between aspirations to substantive artistry and commercial success. Before 1965, none of the major figures in rock—from Elvis to Chuck Berry to The Beatles—aspired to create substantive art; they all aspired to be commercially popular entertainers. The idea of rock music aspiring to substantive artistic *depth* can be traced directly to Bob Dylan's arrival on the rock scene in 1965. And after rock was subsequently adopted by both the socio-political counterculture and the underground drug culture as their lingua franca in the late 60s, the idea that rock music was *important* became commonplace for an entire generation of music fans, which in turn led to those fans having the (entirely new) expectation that rock performers should be substantive artists in addition to being popular entertainers.

From 1965 on, rock's pendulum has been constantly swinging back and forth between artistic and commercial aspirations. And since that time, what has made rock a uniquely important musical genre has been its potential to be both artistically substantive *and* commercially popular at the same time. Or to put it another way: rock music has had both the potential to *have something to say* and the potential for what it has to say to be *heard by the masses*. It is the *combination* of these potentialities that has distinguished rock music from both the cultural irrelevance of its high-minded contemporaries in the avant-garde musical underground and the shallow frivolity of its many rivals in the popular music arena. But the marriage between goals as divergent as art and money has come with inevitable tensions. And this book is the story of those tensions: from the *meaning* that rock music held for the countercultural zealots of the 60s, to the *betrayal* felt by many rock fans and critics when rock "went commercial" in the 70s, to the *alienation* from popular rock music expressed by punk and alternative music in the late 70s and 80s, to the *tortured psychosis* that resulted from Kurt Cobain's competing desires for both artistic credibility and mass popularity, to the gradual relief of those tensions when major record labels began getting out of the business of recording and marketing artistically substantive rock music in the late 90s, and finally the renewed debate about the tensions between art and commerce spawned by the advent of digital music in the 2000s.

And so, with all due respect to Elvis, the appropriate place to begin this story is *not* when rock was born in the mid-50s, but rather when it was *re-born* in 1965 (at which time Elvis was starring in *Harum Scarum*, a movie in which—as we learned from our Elvis playing cards—"Elvis brings the Big Beat to Bagdad in a riotous rockin' rollin' adventure spoof!!").

PART I

ART AND MONEY
IN ROCK MUSIC: 1965-1991

Chapter One

Art on the Jukebox

Bob Dylan, Rock Criticism, and Rock's Initial Artistic Aspirations

Bob Dylan and the Advent of Rock as Art

On March 27, 1965, Bob Dylan released his fifth studio album, *Bringing It All Back Home*. While his performance at the Newport Folk Festival later that summer is commonly cited as his "electric debut," it was *Bringing It All Back Home* that first introduced Dylan to audiences as a rock performer. Side one of the album features seven tracks performed with a full rock band, while side two features four solo acoustic tracks. *Bringing It All Back Home* hit #6 in the U.S. and its opening track—the rollicking, stream-of-consciousness rocker "Subterranean Homesick Blues"—was Dylan's first song to crack the *Billboard* singles chart, peaking at #39. But the album was even more popular in England, where it went to #1 and turned Dylan into a popular phenomenon rivaling The Beatles. When members of both The Beatles and The Rolling Stones attended Dylan's May 10 performance at Royal Albert Hall in London, they only fanned the flames of Dylan's growing legend and influence. But what was that influence, exactly? As Fred Goodman points out in his 1997 book *The Mansion on the Hill*:

Rock went through a dramatic transformation in the mid-sixties. The folk-rock movement brought a new artistic, social, and political intention to the music that the early rockers did not have. Chuck Berry, Little Richard, Elvis Presley, Jerry Lee Lewis—all were extraordinary and inventive performers, but they aspired to show business careers, not to creating lasting art. The same is true of the early Beatles, and it was folk artists—and Bob Dylan in particular—who changed the music's parameters and aspirations to include a quest for legitimacy, values, and authenticity...

Nothing like Dylan's "Subterranean Homesick Blues," "It's Alright Ma (I'm Only Bleeding)," or "Mr. Tambourine Man" had ever been heard in rock music. A simple juxtaposition of the lyrics on *Bringing it All Back Home* with the lyrics of any pre-1965 Beatles tune (for instance "Love Me Do" or "I Want to Hold Your Hand") clearly illustrates the quantum leap in substantive depth Dylan's arrival heralded for rock music. Even the love songs on *Bringing It All Back Home* like "She Belongs to Me," "Love Minus Zero/No Limit," and "It's All Over Now, Baby Blue" introduced a new level of maturity and complexity into a genre that had, to that point, largely been dismissed as "teenage music." But in Dylan, here was a combination of Rimbaud, Blake, Eliot, the Beats, *and* Elvis. Here was substantive art. As poet Allen Ginsburg has noted, Dylan took popular rock music from "moon/June/spoon/I love you—high school romance stereotypes—to psychological investigations into the nature of consciousness itself." Ginsburg saw the popularization of art via rock music, "art on the jukebox" he called it, as "quite a cultural advance."

This shift took center stage in America when "Like a Rolling Stone"—the first single from Dylan's next album, *Highway 61 Revisited*—went to #2 in the *Billboard* singles charts in August of 1965. According to Goodman in *The Mansion on the Hill*:

> 'Like a Rolling Stone' resounded like a rifle shot from radios across the country and announced a musical revolution... It was not a two-minute-and-thirteen-second rock and roll single like those made by Chuck Berry or Little Richard or The Beach Boys or even The Beatles. It wasn't about dancing or driving or teenage love lost and found. This was an electric epic, simple in its music but remarkably complex and ambitious in its scope. Its length, subject matter, and performance were totally at odds with what constituted a hit single. 'Like a Rolling Stone' erased every rule of pop music... Rock music,

it was now apparent, was capable of far more than almost anyone had imagined.

However, many fans of Dylan's folk albums were outraged by his attempt to apply the serious artistic and social intentions of folk to the blatantly commercial rock medium. According to folk concert promoter Harold Leventhal, "We felt he was going away from the political consciousness that we all had. One can attribute that as going commercial… and that bothered us." After the audience booed Dylan's electric rock performance at the 1965 Newport Folk Festival, folk critic Paul Nelson decided to leave the popular folk magazine *Sing Out!* in protest, explaining his decision to side with Dylan over the folk purists in no uncertain terms, "Those who booed chose suffocation over innovation. I choose Dylan. I choose art. I'll bet my critical reputation, such as it is, that I am right." What the folk purists had trouble seeing—and what is clear in retrospect—is that Dylan wasn't compromising his art by moving to the more commercial rock medium; he was following his own unique artistic vision. As he told *Playboy*'s Nat Hentoff in 1966:

> Contrary to what some scary people think, I don't play with a band now for any kind of propaganda-type or commercial-type reasons. It's just that my songs are pictures and the band makes the sound of the pictures… It's very simple in my mind. It doesn't matter what kind of audience reaction this whole thing gets. What happens on stage is straight. It doesn't expect any rewards or fines from outside agitators. It's ultra-simple, and would exist whether anyone was looking or not… It's not a complicated thing. My motives, or whatever they are, were never commercial in the money sense of the word… I never did it for money.

And Dylan backed up his words with his actions. Even after the negative reaction to his Newport performance, Dylan still decided to recruit a little-known Canadian blues band called The Hawks (who would later change their name to The Band) to be his backing band for a world tour showcasing his new rock approach. According to David Espar in his 1995 documentary *Rock & Roll*, "The fusion of Dylan's poetic vitriol and The Hawks' aggressive blues created a new rock and roll experience. Never had something so scathing and complex been presented to an audience weaned on the sincerity of folk and the simplicity of pop." Indeed, it is hard to imagine the legions of rock fans

3

accustomed to tunes like "(Please Let Me Be Your) Teddy Bear" and "Love Me Do" wrapping their minds around Dylan's complex lyrics without some confusion and difficulty. But even when fans—incited by angry folk devotees—began booing at the shows, Dylan continued to follow his artistic muse and play his music the way he wanted, regardless of how many fans or how much money it was costing him to do so. According to his guitarist Robbie Robertson, "While we thought we were getting somewhere, it's quite shattering on the confidence when people are throwing banana peels at you and booing... Most people would have said, 'Well, I guess they're not going to accept it.' But he didn't give up. And we went all over the world. They booed us everywhere we went."

There were also those who felt Dylan was risking more than just his commercial future. Fellow performer Phil Ochs worried in *Broadside* magazine about Dylan's safety in the face of the growing hostility at his concerts. "I wonder what's going to happen," said Ochs in late 1965. "I don't know if Dylan can get on the stage a year from now. I don't think so. I mean the phenomenon of Dylan will be so much that it will be dangerous... Dylan has become part of so many people's psyches—and there are so many screwed up people in America, and death is such a part of the American scene now." The threat was real enough to scare keyboardist Al Kooper out of Dylan's touring band. "I played The Hollywood Bowl, and then I left the organization," says Kooper in Martin Scorsese's 2005 documentary *No Direction Home*. "I actually was frightened, when I got the tour itinerary, to see that we were going to play Dallas, where they had just killed the President. And I thought, 'If they didn't like that guy, what are they gonna think of *this guy*?' And I didn't want to be the analogy to John Connelly. I didn't want to be the guy next to him." Drummer Levon Helm left the tour after just a few American dates due to similar fears. But Dylan kept touring. And his refusal to compromise made it clear that his artistic vision, not money or popular acceptance, was the driving force behind his music. When the 1965-66 world tour was over, Dylan opted to retreat from the limelight rather than try to capitalize on his fame; he and his wife moved to the tiny rural town of Woodstock, NY to raise a family. He would not tour again for over eight years.

But before retreating from the public eye, Dylan had completely revolutionized rock music, transforming it into a musical style capable of being substantive art, a style capable of being a vehicle for individual creative visions as opposed to a purely commercial popular genre. The primacy of Dylan's artistic aspirations resonated with rock musicians around the world and signaled a sea change from the "hit record" mentality of rock's early pioneers to something far more unique and important. And where the public reaction to Dylan's live performances had been complicated and mixed, his impact on other rock musicians was clear and immediate. On April 12, 1965, L.A. folk-rockers The Byrds released a cover version of "Mr. Tambourine Man" as their first single, just two weeks after Dylan had released his original version on *Bringing It All Back Home*. That June, The Byrds' version of "Mr. Tambourine Man" went to #1, sparking a craze that lasted the rest of the decade. Seemingly everyone in rock—from The Turtles to Jimi Hendrix, The Band to Van Morrison, Johnny Cash to Simon & Garfunkel—covered Bob Dylan songs in the second half of the 60s. When The Byrds' *Greatest Hits* came out in 1967, it included *four* Dylan-penned songs. The Dylan craze also led to countless knock-off imitations like Barry McGuire's "Eve of Destruction" and Sonny & Cher's "I Got You, Babe."

In addition to these more superficial indicators, Dylan also inspired an entire generation of rock songwriters to rethink the way they wrote songs, to take them more seriously, to approach their songs as *artists* rather than pop songsmiths gunning for the top of the charts. His impact on The Beatles, particularly on John Lennon's songwriting, is well documented. Neil Young, Paul Simon, Van Morrison, Joni Mitchell, and Lou Reed were also profoundly affected by Dylan. But in a larger sense, beyond just his direct sphere of influence, Dylan changed what a rock song could be, and in turn, how it was perceived. His groundbreaking work of 1965-66 paved the way for rock music to become the social, moral, political, philosophical, spiritual, and intellectual language and conscience of young America. As Jackson Browne would later write of Dylan on his debut album:

> The great song traveler passed through here
> And he opened my eyes to the view
> And I was among those who called him a prophet
> And I asked him what was true

Thanks in large part to Dylan's influence, rock music became the platform from which rock artists could inform the public consciousness with their unique creative visions. And as a result, rock music and lyrics became something that could be taken seriously as art. Rock music—and, by extension, rock artists—were, for the first time, widely perceived as *having something to say.*

In Martin Scorsese's *No Direction Home*, painter and Dylan cohort Bob Neuwirth describes how he, Dylan, and their circle of friends assessed music in the mid-1960s, "Artistic success was not dollar driven; those were simpler times. If you had something to say, *that* was the way people were rated. They'd say, 'Have you seen [jazz musician] Ornette Coleman? Does he have *anything to say?*' It was the same with Bob [Dylan] or anybody else; did they have anything to say or not?" This "something to say" implied wisdom to impart, enlightenment to be had, perspective to be gained, some sort of truth to be glimpsed, be it by way of the music or the lyrics. As a result, rock music as a whole would begin moving away from the purely commercial aspirations that had characterized its first decade and into the centuries-old Western artistic tradition—a tradition in which aspirations to transcendence, plumbing the depths of the human condition, and the apprehension of truth and wisdom were seen as essential components of the artistic endeavor. And these traditional artistic standards would increasingly be applied to rock music in the late 60s through a brand new medium: rock criticism. By the time a provocative photo of John Lennon in military garb appeared on the cover of the first issue of *Rolling Stone* on November 9, 1967, rock music was a far more serious and influential player in American culture than it had been just a couple of years earlier. According to *Rolling Stone* founder and Editor-in-Chief Jann Wenner in the magazine's debut issue:

> We have begun a new publication reflecting what we see are the changes in rock and roll and the changes related to rock and roll... Because the trade papers have become so inaccurate and irrelevant, and because the fan magazines are an anachronism, fashioned in the mold of myth and nonsense, we hope we have something here for the artists and the industry, and every person who 'believes in the magic that can set you free.'

Rock criticism had been born.

Rock Criticism: Taking Rock Music Seriously

In late January 1966, as Bob Dylan was touring the world with his new rock band, a seventeen-year-old freshman at Philadelphia's Swarthmore College named Paul Williams printed 500 copies of a rock music "magazine" while visiting a friend in New York City. The first issue of *Crawdaddy!*—printed on light-brown mimeographed paper—was only 10 pages long and consisted of reviews of a few new singles, as well as one full-length album review: Simon & Garfunkel's *Sounds of Silence*. Williams spent a few days distributing as many copies as possible throughout the city before hitchhiking back to Swarthmore with the remainder of the copies in a cardboard box under his arm. It was a less than auspicious beginning for American rock criticism. But shortly after arriving back at school, he received a call in his freshman dorm room from Paul Simon himself, who invited Williams to meet him and Art Garfunkel on his next trip to New York. Simon made true on his promise and soon brought Williams along to a concert and radio interview. The rest, as they say, is history.

One of the reasons that Williams' approach to rock music caught on— "taking it seriously, wanting others to take it seriously," as he would later describe it—was that, just as the public perception of rock music was beginning to change, so too was the self-perception of rock performers themselves. The reason Simon picked up the phone to call the 17-year-old publisher of a homemade rock "magazine" was that he saw Williams' serious take on his music as validation of his own artistic aspirations, and he went out of his way to tell Williams that his review of *Sounds of Silence* was the first "intelligent" thing he had read about Simon & Garfunkel's music. This same self-perception was shared by the other performers at the head of rock's late 60s transformation. For instance, The Beach Boys' Brian Wilson traded in the teenage simplicity of early 60s hits like "Surfin' U.S.A." in order to aspire to what he called "artistically stimulating and interesting" music on the band's 1966 album *Pet Sounds*. "The album was artistically set out in front of other albums," said Wilson in the liner notes for *Pet Sounds*' 1990 re-issue. "It was the first time I used more traditional and inspired lyrics which emitted feelings from my soul and not the usual 'Beach Boys' approach." Meanwhile, a friend of another early rock icon would soon comment, "Neil Young thinks he is the

7

modern Shakespeare." While more formal orchestral composers had thought of themselves as serious artists for centuries, this kind of attitude was something completely new among rock performers.

Paul Williams continued to run *Crawdaddy!* for the rest of his collegiate career, fielding calls from the likes of Bob Dylan in his dorm room at Swarthmore. When Williams left to write books about rock music in 1969, the magazine went on a brief hiatus before re-launching in 1970—with Williams' blessing, but without the exclamation point in its name—as a mass market magazine. By that time, *Crawdaddy* had been joined in the rock criticism fray by San Francisco-based *Rolling Stone* (November 1967) and Detroit-based *Creem* (March 1969). The launch of these magazines ushered in a golden age of rock criticism, creating an outlet for now-legendary writers like Lester Bangs, Dave Marsh, Hunter S. Thompson, Cameron Crowe, Robert Christgau, Greil Marcus, Nick Tosches, Richard Meltzer, and Jon Landau (among countless others), many of whom wrote for two—or even all three—publications. Coupled with longstanding British music publications like *New Musical Express* and *Melody Maker*, as well as the increased space being devoted to rock music in arts newspapers like New York's *Village Voice* and the feature-length rock articles and interviews in men's magazines like *Playboy*, there was no shortage of serious rock criticism available on American newsstands.

Rock's newfound artistic credibility may have been the initial catalyst for its growing cultural influence, but there were many factors which developed in the late 60s that affirmed the perception of rock music as a serious artistic medium, especially among young people. The first contributing factor was rock's increasing association with the burgeoning drug culture. Prior to the mid-60s, rock had generally been dismissed by the hipsters of the day as safe, mainstream, bubble-gum pop music for teenagers. The Beats had gravitated instead to the underground jazz scene, where marijuana had been a staple for decades and had contributed to jazz's rebellious outsider status. But when Bob Dylan introduced The Beatles to marijuana at their first meeting in late 1964, The Beatles' subsequent albums, in the words of journalist Al Aronowitz, "began reeking from the aroma," and the association with the illegal drug began to give the most popular band in the world an air of underground street credibility. The Beatles may have been popular, but all of a sudden they were also *in the know*. And by the time they released *Revolver* in the summer of

1966, they had moved on to psychedelics as well, a fact that was not lost on discerning listeners. According to Grateful Dead bassist and vocalist Phil Lesh in the 1995 PBS documentary *Rock & Roll*:

> I don't know where you were the first time you heard 'Tomorrow Never Knows' [off of *Revolver*]. Someone pulled us in off the street… in the Haight, it was 1966, I think. They pulled us right off the street into a record store and said, '*You've got to hear this.*' It was 'Tomorrow Never Knows.' So we felt very strongly at that time that The Beatles were on the same wavelength as we were. In fact, [the same wavelength] everybody in San Francisco was [on] at that time.

While LSD casualties like Pink Floyd's Syd Barrett are now routinely cited as cautionary tales about the inherent dangers of psychedelics, 60s activists like San Francisco-based author Ken Kesey saw psychedelics at the center of a new social order based on what was still idealistically referred to as "mind expansion," one in which rock music would play a significant part. And in December of 1965, when Kesey hired a then-unknown rock act called The Grateful Dead to provide the background music for his communal "Acid Tests," the tie between rock and psychedelics in San Francisco was cemented. The combined association of Dylan, The Beatles, and the San Francisco scene with drug use helped rock music as a whole become increasingly and intimately tied to the growing underground drug culture. And, because of the increased sense of *significance* that drug use granted to even the most mundane experiences, the association between drugs and rock exponentially increased the sense among drug users of rock music's importance. For those who have come up in a post-"War on Drugs" world, it can be difficult to grasp the extent to which drug use in the late 60s was embraced as more than just a recreational hobby, but as an all-encompassing *philosophy*, a *way of life*. And whether or not one used drugs became the dividing line between those who were in the know about that philosophy and those who weren't, with those on the outside being categorically dismissed as "straight" or "square." In that climate, rock songs like The Byrds' "Eight Miles High" and The Beatles' "Lucy in the Sky with Diamonds" were seen by both performers and listeners and as more than just clever plays on words intended to slip drug references past censors; they were coded ambassadorial invitations to a new age, a new society, a new culture, a new way of thinking, a new way of being. And by 1967, nothing captured that spirit better than rock music's legions of faithful fans, performers, and critics.

Another factor that gave rock music an added sense of importance was the widespread exploration of spiritual meaning by the era's countercultural and musical icons. For many in the counterculture, drug experimentation and spiritual exploration were two interrelated components of a larger quest for *meaning*. For instance, San Francisco-based poet and countercultural spokesperson Gary Snyder spent a decade splitting time between studying Zen Buddhism in Japan and advocating its tenets within San Francisco's countercultural scene. Meanwhile, The Beatles supplemented their trend-setting drug experimentations with highly visible and influential trips to India to study Hinduism and its meditative offshoot Hare Krishna. And countless countercultural searches led hippies through the psychedelic experience and into the Christian communes of the "Jesus People" movement.

It was not surprising, then, that much of the era's most iconic rock music reflected these spiritual explorations. Critic Lester Bangs described Van Morrison's 1968 album *Astral Weeks* as a "mystical document," part of what Bangs called "the great search, fueled by the belief that through these musical and mental processes illumination is attainable. Or may at least be glimpsed." Beatles songs began to reflect the band members' varying spiritual explorations: the George Harrison-penned "Within You Without You" (1967), Paul McCartney's "Let it Be" (1970), John Lennon's "Instant Karma" (1970), and Harrison's "My Sweet Lord" (1970). And Bob Dylan's ongoing personal explorations of mystic spiritual themes in songs from "Mr. Tambourine Man" (1965) to "Desolation Row" (1965) to "Visions of Johanna" (1966)—along with his relentless use of biblical imagery in songs like "Gates of Eden" (1965), "Highway 61 Revisited" (1965), and "I Dreamed I Saw St. Augustine" (1967)—solidified the idea that rock music was a place for serious, "consciousness-raising" explorations of spiritual meaning. And this conflagration of rock music and spiritual exploration gave rock an almost religious significance for many of its fans.

Meanwhile, another factor that contributed to rock music being taken seriously by among young people was its perceived embodiment of *authenticity*, which contrasted sharply with the growing commercial mass media establishment. As David Foster Wallace pointed out in his 1991 essay "E Unibus Pluram," "The television of lone-gunman westerns, paternalistic

10

sitcoms, and jut-jawed law enforcement circa 1960 celebrated what by then was a deeply hypocritical self-image... TV was a hypocritical apologist for values whose reality had become attenuated in a period of corporate ascendancy, bureaucratic entrenchment, foreign adventurism, racial conflict, secret bombing, assassination, wiretaps, etc." The "phony" hypocrisy of the mainstream media—including the increasing pervasiveness of its mind-numbing jingles and other crassly commercial advertising appeals—helped give rise to a vague dissatisfaction among young people, a sentiment perhaps best expressed in The Rolling Stones' 1965 breakout hit, "(I Can't Get No) Satisfaction:"

> *When I'm drivin' in my car*
> *And that man comes on the radio*
> *And he's tellin' me more and more*
> *About some useless information*
> *Supposed to fire my imagination...*
>
> *I can't get no satisfaction...*
>
> *When I'm watchin' my TV*
> *And that man comes on to tell me*
> *How white my shirts can be*
> *But he can't be a man 'cause he doesn't smoke*
> *The same cigarettes as me*
> *I can't get no, oh no no no*
> *Hey hey hey, that's what I say*
>
> *I can't get no satisfaction...*

The appeal of The Stones themselves was rooted in their perceived visceral, embodied, sensual, and material *realness*, and this gave them an air of authenticity which contrasted sharply with the ubiquitous banality of typical 60s advertising slogans and campaigns. Against the backdrop of the mainstream media's first clumsy, probing forays into commercial mass marketing, the perceived authenticity of rock artists created a level of trust and devotion among rock fans that can be hard to fathom here in the 21st century.

But perhaps the most visible factor that contributed to the perception of rock music as a serious medium was its increased association with a certain brand of iconoclastic socio-political opinion. What is often dismissed today with terms like "hippie utopianism" was seen by many in the counterculture as a very real political movement, a serious attempt to detach itself from a mainstream society that had clearly gone awry, as evidenced by racism and violence in the American South, worldwide nuclear proliferation, the assassinations of JFK, MLK, and RFK, the Vietnam War, and Richard Nixon's culminating breaches of democracy. And again, Dylan was at the center of rock's increasing politicization. According to Newport Folk Festival stage manager Joe Boyd, "People were going south to register black voters, they were politically engaged, partly inspired by Dylan. Bob Dylan was the pied piper, the troubadour, the hero. And by 1965 he was, along with The Beatles, the biggest star there was."

Even though Dylan had left behind overt political statements before making the move from folk to rock, his early Civil Rights anthems like "Only a Pawn in Their Game" and "Blowin' in the Wind" and politically charged classics like "Masters of War" and "The Times They Are A-Changin'" became hugely influential on subsequent rock acts. And as a result, rock became more and more intertwined with the politics of the era. Socio-political rock anthems like Barry McGuire's "Eve of Destruction" and Buffalo Springfield's "For What It's Worth" began popping up everywhere. Crosby, Stills, Nash & Young's hit "Ohio" was a response to the killing of four protesters at Kent State University and Young's "Southern Man" was a criticism of racism in the American South. As a result of this politicization, the opinions of rock performers were increasingly being sought on social and political issues. And thanks to rock's increased artistic credibility, they were beginning to be taken seriously. Unlike previous pop stars—from Frank Sinatra and Glenn Miller to Elvis and Chuck Berry—whose political opinions remained largely their own, The Beatles were suddenly being asked for their opinions on American involvement in Vietnam. Where Steve Allen had ridiculed early rock music on *The Tonight Show* just a few years earlier, he now fawned over Bob Dylan, respectfully reading from Dylan's reverential press clippings while Dylan sat— visibly embarrassed—waiting to perform. "Genius makes its own rules, and Dylan is a genius," read Allen, "a singing conscience and moral referee, as well as a preacher." The infusion of rock's newfound artistic credibility and serious

12

subject matter into popular music had turned rock artists into a whole new type of pop star: one whose opinion on socio-political issues mattered.

It was the combination of all of these developments in and around rock music which culminated in the advent of serious rock criticism. Rock music criticism did *not* arise thanks to a newfound belief that all popular music or all commercial entertainment was suddenly worthy of serious criticism. Rather, rock criticism came into being because its devotees believed that rock music, specifically, had become a serious and important art form on par with the other artistic disciplines which merited serious criticism: literature, film, visual art, classical music. Given the way that "rock music criticism" has slowly become synonymous with "popular music criticism" over the past fifty years, this is an important distinction to make. Rock's early critics, like the critics from other mediums in whose mold they fashioned themselves, saw themselves as arbiters of artistic taste and cultural values, not as panderers to the commercial record industry or advocates of disposable pop trends. That kind of pandering and advocacy already existed in the superficial fan magazines and industry trade papers, and rock critics saw themselves as something very different.

Due to the charged cultural atmosphere into which rock criticism was born, its template was imbued from the beginning with an implicit understanding that rock music was something to be taken seriously. *Crawdaddy, Rolling Stone,* and *Creem* all saw themselves as part of the emerging counterculture—the leading distinguishing characteristics of which were quickly becoming rock music, drug use, and left-leaning political activism. The new magazines were often blatantly supportive of drug experimentation; early articles in *Rolling Stone,* for instance, contain a staggering number of both explicit and implicit drug endorsements, and drug use was an encouraged part of the everyday culture at the magazine's headquarters. Blatant political advocacy was also a key ingredient at *Rolling Stone*; as *Rolling Stone* biographer Robert Draper points out, the magazine's early staffers saw their jobs as vital cultural obligations and published each issue "as if nothing less than society itself hung in the balance." According to *Rolling Stone* founder Jann Wenner, "The music…carried a lot of content and meaning and was central to people's emotional and spiritual lives." And as *Crawdaddy*'s Robert Smith put it, "It seemed, for a time, that to write about rock and roll was to carry on your shoulders an aesthetic and set of values about the entire counterculture." By the time Woodstock rolled around in

August 1969, many devotees believed in rock music's transformative power to change hearts and minds and—as far-fetched as it may now seem—the world itself.

However, not everyone within rock's emerging critical establishment was thrilled with the way that rock music was suddenly being taken seriously as an art form. For instance, *Rolling Stone*'s Jon Landau insisted that the introduction of "serious" artistic sensibilities into rock music in the late 60s was "one of the most misleading and destructive" things that could happen to rock. In a July 1968 *Rolling Stone* article, Landau argued:

> It must be realized that the core attitude of rock...and the core attitude of formal art were antithetical. Rock was not intended to be reflective or profound... Yet over the last two years, the artiness cult has grown within the rock community. More and more people expect of rock what they used to expect of philosophy, literature, films, and visual art. Others expect of rock what they used to get out of drugs. And in my opinion, rock cannot withstand that kind of burden because it forces on to rock qualities which are the negation of what rock was all about in the first place.

Throughout the piece, Landau's tone conjures that of conservatives of all stripes as he pines for the earlier, simpler era of Chuck Berry's odes to high school, cars, and teenage romance. And he just can't bring himself to accept the fact that rock's "core attitudes" themselves had clearly changed. Moreover, these attitudes hadn't been "forced" onto rock from the outside, as he argues. Rather, rock's move toward substantive artistry had followed the creative visions of individual artists—from Bob Dylan to John Lennon to Paul Simon to Lou Reed to Van Morrison to Neil Young to Joni Mitchell—whose art was clearly both "reflective" and "profound." In later articles, Landau would call those who appreciated rock's artistic qualities "elitists," but in reality it was Landau—just like the folk music purists who had booed Dylan at Newport— who was placing himself above the artists of the era by attempting to bend their individual creative muses to his own abstract conception of what rock music was supposed to be about.

Even though similar attitudes about rock's allegedly inherent simplicity would continue to be echoed periodically by subsequent critics, Landau's conservative nostalgia for the good old days of Elvis and Chuck Berry proved

14

to be a blip on the radar screen in the context of rock's artistic flowering in the years between 1965 and 1970. During that time, any of Landau's readers could easily disprove his claim that "rock and roll musicians are banal, amateurish, and insipidly stupid when they try to express their philosophy of life in the context of popular music" by simply picking up and throwing on the turntable his or her copy of *Highway 61 Revisited, Astral Weeks, The Velvet Underground & Nico, Blonde on Blonde, Abbey Road, Let It Bleed, Bridge Over Troubled Water, After the Gold Rush, Ladies of the Canyon,* or *American Beauty.* By the end of the 60s, rock music's creative vistas had been irrevocably expanded, and Landau's conservative view of rock music's potential was in the distinct minority among rock devotees. Fans and critics everywhere were taking rock performers seriously as artists. And following behind them was an unlikely group who would prove surprisingly willing to take rock artists seriously: music business executives.

Chapter Two

Sex, Drugs, and Rock & Roll

Geffen, Zeppelin, Kiss, and the Ascendancy of Rock Star Culture

The Birth of the Modern Music Industry

Even though rock had been part of the popular music milieu since its birth in the mid-50s, the vast majority of rock music from the mid-50s to the mid-60s had been recorded for small independent labels rather than the big major labels. Virtually all the early rock acts had recorded for small independents: Elvis Presley, Jerry Lee Lewis, Johnny Cash, Carl Perkins, and Roy Orbison for Sun; Fats Domino for Imperial; Ray Charles and The Drifters for Atlantic; Chuck Berry for Chess; Little Richard and Sam Cooke for Specialty. The independent label dominance of rock music during its first decade was largely due to the fact that major labels had deemed dealing in the low-brow rock genre as beneath their dignity, and they had been notably slow to sign rock performers to recording contracts. Their aversion to rock went so far that Capitol Records initially balked at releasing The Beatles' singles in America, even though the band had already achieved unprecedented popular success in England. But as rock music began to dominate the American pop charts in the mid-60s, major labels began sniffing around the rock scene for a way to cash in on rock's growing commercial appeal. And once they got an inkling of how much money they might be able to make in rock music, they were quick to change their tune.

16

According to Columbia Records staff producer David Rubinson in the PBS documentary *Rock & Roll*:

> I took the president of Columbia Records to the Haight [in San Francisco] with his chief honchos... And I walked him down Haight St. and all he could see was dollar signs... And I said, 'Look, this is really happening, but you have to understand what's going on here; this is your dough.' And he said, 'Sign anybody you want. *Sign anybody you want.* These people [gesturing to his entourage]? Tell them they can sign anybody they want.' He just saw the cash registers going off right away.

But the initial major label forays into signing, packaging, and marketing rock acts were almost comically clumsy. For instance, when MGM failed to sign any of the up-and-coming San Francisco bands, they decided to sign a handful of Boston-based bands and bill what they dubbed the "Bosstown sound" as San Francisco's east coast equivalent. Critic Jon Landau, who was living in Boston at the time, recognized what was up and skewered MGM's blatant marketing gambit in *Rolling Stone*. "The question is not *whether* there is hype," he wrote. "The question is whether or not there is anything *beneath* the hype." All four of MGM's Boston-based signings proved to be flops.

Warner Brothers was nearly as clumsy in its initial forays into the rock market. After making a big splash in the rock community by singing The Grateful Dead to a record deal in early 1967, Warner Records executives Joe Smith and Stan Cornyn attended the San Francisco release party for the Dead's debut album in matching navy-blue blazers with the Warner Records "WR" emblazoned over the breast pockets. When Smith took the stage during a break in the concert to say, "I just want to say what an honor it is for Warner Brothers Records to be able to introduce The Grateful Dead and its music to the world," he drew only a scattered, bemused applause from the long-haired, bearded, and beaded Dead fans who had packed the hall. But when guitarist Jerry Garcia grabbed the mic from Smith and replied, "I just want to say what an honor it is for The Grateful Dead to introduce Warner Brothers Records to the world," the crowd went crazy. The event marked the end of the "blue blazers" era at Warner Records company events.

Within the rock world, Garcia's remark about The Grateful Dead introducing Warner Brothers wasn't far off. At that point, Warner was still best known for crooners like Frank Sinatra and Sammy Davis, Jr. and comedy records by Bill Cosby and Bob Newhart. Their most notable rock signings had been an over-the-hill Bill Haley and the clean-cut duo The Everly Brothers back in the late 50s. But in the late 60s the label made a commitment to rock music that would soon pay off; within a few short years Warner Brothers would win the trust of rock artists and fans to become the world's leading rock label. This was due in large part to President Mo Ostin's savvy recognition that the major labels were no longer dealing with vapid pop stars and that they had to amend their business philosophy in order to trust the artist's vision. Part of that trust meant changing the entire philosophy of how rock acts would be recorded and marketed, shifting its focus to the more artistically expansive full-length album format from disposable singles. A new underground FM radio format emerged—which would slowly evolve into the Album Oriented Rock (AOR) format—to play rock songs that weren't necessarily released as singles, and by 1968 full-length album sales outstripped singles for the first time since *Billboard* had begun documenting music sales in the mid-50s.

But Warner Brothers' trust in its artists went beyond simply changing its focus from singles to albums. According to Ostin (who signed Neil Young, Frank Zappa, and Paul Simon, among many others), "If you believe in the artist, if you believe in his talent, if you believe he speaks the truth, then you have to be supportive of him... You have to encourage the artists to do whatever they think is right." Such a philosophy would have been unheard of in the pop music world of the 50s and early 60s, but such was the artistic gravitas that rock artists had accumulated by the late 60s.

While Mo Ostin's Warner Brothers may have been the first major label to scratch the surface of rock music's new artistic and commercial potential, another young executive named David Geffen would come to embody the ethos of the new rock music industry. More than any of his peers, Geffen realized how central the creativity of individual artists had been to rock music's surge in popularity. According to producer Bones Howe in *The Mansion on a Hill*:

> [Geffen] had a total faith in their abilities. He had a description—he said these people are 'significant artists.' The significant artist is the artist who creates their own music, records it, and produces it. As opposed to pop artists, who use other people's work and it's all fabricated. These people create and craft themselves. And he was fascinated with that process. And was smart enough

to know that his best contribution was to make the ground ready and fertilize it and then step away.

Geffen's admiration of the artistic process was central to his vision, first as an agent and manager, then as head of his own independent record label, Los Angeles-based Asylum Records. As Geffen told the BBC's *Old Grey Whistle Test* in 1973:

> I like music. Whatever strikes me as good is something that I want to record. I don't think that every record we make is a hit or that every artist we record is going to be a star, but I think that all the music we put out is very valid and that all the people making these records are making good records. And I think that's what's important. They get a free opportunity to make these records, and if we believe in them we'll stick with them whether they make it or not. We're not going to drop an artist if they don't sell. That isn't the kind of company this is.

Geffen's trust in his artists' creative vision won him the absolute trust and loyalty of his early clients, who included Crosby, Stills & Nash, Neil Young, Joni Mitchell, Jackson Browne, Tom Waits, and The Eagles. According to The Eagles' Glen Frey in the PBS documentary *The Making of David Geffen*, "At the time, most of us, we would do anything to be with David Geffen. We didn't even ask any questions. 'Here, sign this, it's gonna be fine.' 'Here, I'm gonna get you a publishing deal, sign this.' 'Here, I'm gonna get you to record for me; I'm gonna be your manager.' I didn't care. I wanted David Geffen to be involved in as many aspects of my career as possible." According to fellow Asylum artist Jackson Browne, "[Geffen] supported them for a long time while they practiced and became The Eagles, and he kept them together while they learned to sing the way they sing." "David said to me, 'Just worry about the music, I'll take care of everything else,'" says Frey. "He put me on a small salary so I could pay my rent and get a car."

The Eagles aren't generally considered a leading example of artistic aspirations in rock, but the commercial aspirations which would eventually become central to their career reflected the other side of the David Geffen equation. In addition to trusting and nurturing his artists, Geffen was also a cutthroat business executive who would go to the mat for his clients, and for a brief period in the early 70s he was able to make Asylum the prime example of a label capable of both nurturing its artists' creativity and having huge commercial success. By 1973, the percentage of albums that Asylum released that were profitable was higher than any record company in the world. But once that financial success came, the family atmosphere that Geffen had helped nurture at Asylum began to disintegrate. The first cracks in Asylum's familial business model appeared when Geffen and his business partner Elliot Roberts sold a majority interest in Asylum to Warner Brothers in a deal that netted them each $2 million in cash and $5 million in Warner stock. According to The Eagles' Don Henley, "There was no phone call. There was no warning. We just woke up one morning and read about it in the paper. After all this talk about how much he cared about artists and how much he was nurturing their careers, and this, that and the other, to be sold like a commodity, like pork bellies and soy beans, didn't sit too well with us."

Geffen stayed on as president of Asylum through the end of 1975, but things weren't the same after the sale to Warner Brothers. The label had started as an idealistic enterprise, "We were all at the beginning of our careers," says Geffen in *The Making of David Geffen*. "We were all excited about the possibilities, and wherever we went there was another talented person… And I couldn't believe that none of them had [record] deals, that they were all available." But eventually, according to Asylum's co-founder Elliott Roberts, "The dream that we have of Asylum being this familial company, we saw didn't have the merit two years down the line, once it actually became successful."

Even as music moguls like David Geffen and Mo Ostin's belief in rock artists was leading to financial rewards, it was clear that financial motives, not artistic ones, were the driving force for a music industry that remained—in Mo Ostin's words—"a purely pragmatic business." At most major labels, respect for the artistic visions of rock artists was only going to last as long as rock album sales continued to flourish. And flourish they did. Rock music was the catalyst for an explosion in album sales between 1965 and 1973, when overall American album sales hit the 400 million mark for the first time.

However, the increasing commercial success of rock music was beginning to draw suspicion from many of those with countercultural roots who saw the millions of dollars being made in rock as antithetical to their core anti-commercial values. According to critic Fred Goodman in *The Mansion on the Hill*, "Monetarily, the marriage of the music and the music business was an extraordinary success. But artistically and socially, it was a complete reversal of the values that had spawned the music. The underground scene started in earnest when rock assumed the mantle of meaning and intent from folk music, and it was founded on a search for authenticity and an explicit rejection of consumerism and mainstream values."

But as the 70s wore on and the countercultural social and political movements that had helped shape rock's transformation into a serious medium began to crumble, the idea that rock music was intrinsically tied to "a search for authenticity and an explicit rejection of consumerism" became less and less prevalent. And it soon became possible for younger critics to raise the possibility that rock's perceived seriousness had been little more than the drug-induced delusions of the baby boomers' utopian socio-political agenda. Some of these younger critics even began to wonder if rock's seriousness had *ever* been tied to any actual substantive artistic merit. For young critic Tom Carson, the whole idea of taking rock music seriously at all began to look anachronistic. In his contribution to *Stranded: Rock and Roll for a Desert Island*, Carson argued that rock's seriousness in the late 60s had been "inextricably tied up with the utopianism of the counterculture; the possibility of revolution was the only thing that gave *Sgt. Pepper* and the flood of pretentions in its wake credibility. When the countercultural dream died, it turned all that visionary artiness into pure sludge—icing with the cake shot out from under it."

Meanwhile, skepticism about rock music's artistic seriousness was being reinforced by the changes taking place in rock music itself during the early 70s. Rock industry pandering to the emerging personality cults of "rock star" culture was increasing exponentially, and the fan-artist relationship was coming to be epitomized by vacuous celebrity worship—even as it was becoming apparent that the biggest rock stars of the time had little, if anything, of substance to say. Carson would later look back and call the first five years of the 70s "the worst years in rock 'n roll history." And no band symbolized rock's move from the countercultural artistic aspirations of the late 60s to the commercial rock star culture of the 70s more than a dynamic quartet from England that was quickly becoming rock's most popular act.

Led Zeppelin and the Elevation of the "Rock Star"

In July of 1973, the band Led Zeppelin filmed three concerts at Madison Square Garden in New York that would become the basis of their concert film *The Song Remains the Same* (which would eventually be released in 1976). "The film," writes critic Cameron Crowe in the original liner notes, "is much more than a movie of Led Zeppelin in concert; it is a rare series of glimpses into the visions and symbolism of the men who make the music. Fulfilling a long-held desire to express themselves in a cinematic setting, each band member and manager Peter Grant have contributed their own 'fantasy sequence.' For the first time, one can view the images in Page's mind during 'Dazed and Confused,' see life breathed into 'Stairway to Heaven'…" And on it goes—no one can accuse Cameron Crowe of failing to take rock music seriously. But the critical consensus at the time of the film's release was that Led Zeppelin lacked the substance to merit the kind of serious treatment accorded them by starry-eyed fans like the nineteen-year-old Crowe. This may seem surprising given Led Zeppelin's subsequent canonization among the rock immortals, but a simple viewing of *The Song Remains the Same* makes it pretty clear why critics skewered it.

The mythology that has grown up around rock music—and around Led Zeppelin in particular—over the last 40 years can obscure just how ridiculous the band captured in *The Song Remains the Same* appeared to many viewers at the time. And it was this ridiculousness that the critics skewered: Robert Plant's oh-so-low-riding jeans, skimpy shirt/vest, and inane finger-twirling ("Does anybody remember *laughter?*"); Jimmy Page's sequined jumpsuit, double-necked guitar, and extended "violin bow solo;" John Paul Jones' medieval-period-piece hairdo/wig; John Bonham's *nine minute* drum solo; manager Peter Grant's brutish grandstanding; the kaleidoscopic camera tricks and the superfluity of crotch shots (as well as the accompanying shots of the eagerly ecstatic women in the audience). Taken out of context, it is the stuff of high parody, yet it is delivered without a hint of irony. Even *in* context, much of the movie still smacks of parody-waiting-to-happen, especially the "fantasy sequences:" the opening depiction of Grant as a Mafioso boss, Plant's turn as a Tolkien-esque medieval knight (which includes a choreographed sword fight), and Page's disturbing transformation into some sort of dark pagan lord (via a not-so-realistic-looking bolt of lightning).

Taken as a whole, the movie depicts a band that has lost touch with a conventional sense of reality, which—to be sure—is part of the point. The members of Led Zeppelin were consciously enlarging the scope of rock showmanship, and a good part of their appeal was their larger-than-life image. But the band's lack of touch with reality went beyond just their over-the-top stage antics. By the time of the filming of *The Song Remains the Same*, Led Zeppelin was—thanks in part to manager Peter Grant's notoriously hard-nosed business tactics—quickly becoming the wealthiest rock band in the world; the 1973 tour which had provided the footage for the film was the most profitable rock tour to date. And the band portrayed in the film—from Plant's sprawling country estate to Bonham's vintage hot-rod collection—was just about as far removed from their adopted Mississippi Delta Blues roots as humanly possible. By the early 70s, Zeppelin was travelling in a private jet called "The Starship"—which was outfitted with custom velvet couches, a full bar, and private bedrooms to facilitate groupie encounters—and making grandiose requests like insisting their 1973 show in Atlanta be referred to in the press as "the biggest thing to happen to the city since *Gone With the Wind*" (a request that was fulfilled when the band's reluctant PR team falsely attributed the quote to Atlanta mayor Sam Massell). Meanwhile, crazy stories about the band's prodigious groupie indulgences circulated, including a notorious 1969 incident—cited in the Zeppelin biography *Hammer of the Gods* and immortalized by the Frank Zappa song "Mud Shark"—in which the members of the band and their road crew stuffed pieces of dead sharks into the bodily orifices of some groupies in Seattle. And at the time of *The Song Remains the Same*'s filming, Jimmy Page was dating a 15-year-old groupie named Lori Maddox, whom he had begun dating over a year earlier…when she was 14. Conventional societal rules simply didn't apply to bands like Led Zeppelin.

This new breed of opulent rock star lifestyle had very little in common with the lives of typical rock fans, making any sort of legitimate connection between fan and artist—other than hero-worship—nearly impossible, and that lack of connection was beginning to show in the music of the era. As critic Lester Bangs would say in a *New Musical Express* feature, "It's no news by now that the reason most of rock's establishment have dried up creatively is that they've cut themselves off from the real world as exemplified by their

23

fans." And the album that Led Zeppelin was touring on at the time of the filming of *The Song Remains the Same*—1973's *Houses of the Holy*—was widely panned by critics. From Gordon Fletcher's *Rolling Stone* review, June 7, 1973:

> For me, Led Zeppelin began as the epitome of everything good about rock: solid guitar work, forceful vocals and rhythmic backing, devotion to primal blues forms, and most of all, thunderous excitement on stage and vinyl. But as superstardom came to them, so too came the gradual evaporation of those qualities from their sound... *Houses of the Holy* is one of the dullest and most confusing albums I've heard this year... Two songs are naked imitations, and they're easily the worst things this band has ever attempted [while] the truly original songs on *Houses of the Holy* again underscore Led Zeppelin's songwriting deficiencies. Their earliest successes came when they literally stole blues licks note for note, so I guess it should have been expected that there was something drastically wrong with their own material... One would think that the group that stole 'Whole Lotta Love,' et al., might acquire an idea or two along the way, but evidently they weren't looking... Page and friends should realize their limitations and get back to playing the blues-rock that moves mountains. Until they do, Led Zeppelin will remain Limp Blimp.

Critics had never favored Led Zeppelin. According to former Zeppelin PR man Danny Goldberg in his 2008 memoir *Bumping Into Geniuses*, "It seems inconceivable to the younger people who put Zeppelin in the upper levels of the rock pantheon that in 1973, in the collective mind of the critical clique, Led Zeppelin was not only not cool, they were distinctly uncool." Or, as critic Steven Hyden recently put it, "Before Led Zeppelin was *the* Led Zeppelin, Led Zeppelin was Nickelback." Part of the critical disdain for Zeppelin was a reaction to their music, what *Rolling Stone*'s review of their debut album called the band's musical "excesses," their "weak, unimaginative songs" and Robert Plant's "strained, unconvincing shouting." But it also had to do with the perception that the band's massive popularity had been the result of music industry hype. Shortly after their formation in 1968, Zeppelin had signed a lucrative record deal—one that included an unprecedented $200,000 advance—with Atlantic Records, which had just been bought by the corporate conglomeration that would become Warner Brothers Communications. The new major label umbrella meant that there was added pressure for Atlantic's acts to produce commercially, especially one with as much money sunk into it as Zeppelin. But because the band's self-titled debut had been panned by critics and didn't have the kinds of songs that were likely to get play on Top 40 AM radio, Atlantic was forced to try a new kind of marketing campaign. And thus Led Zeppelin became the first act ever to be hyped by a major label to the newly emerging network of "underground" American FM rock radio stations.

Because FM rock DJs prided themselves on their countercultural refusal to be bought by major labels, Atlantic couldn't simply pay them to play Led Zeppelin. So Atlantic hype man Mario Medious was forced to come up with a new approach: bribing FM rock DJs with drugs and hip conversation rather than sacks of cash. According to Medious in *Bumping Into Geniuses*, "I'd go by the station, sit up with them all day, smoke weed with them and beg them to play the record." After months of laborious door-to-door advocacy on behalf of Led Zeppelin—including multiple trips to Boston's influential WBCN in order to sway program director and noted Zeppelin enemy Al Perry—Medious overcame initial DJ resistance to the band and helped the British quartet's debut album become a staple on the country-wide network of "independent" FM stations. And in July of 1969, more than 6 months after its release, *Led Zeppelin* was finally certified as a gold record in America.

Atlantic's success in breaking Led Zeppelin without the benefit of critical acclaim or a hit single immediately shifted the balance of power in the fledging rock scene. After an exceedingly brief period during which artistically-minded critics had been the deciding factor in making or breaking album-oriented rock acts, Atlantic had proved that a savvy major label marketing campaign could overcome even the most universally negative critical consensus, even within the supposedly anti-commercial "underground" rock market. Though rock critics would remain influential throughout the 70s, from the launch of Led Zeppelin on it would be major labels, not rock critics, who would be the primary gatekeepers of rock's commercial success. Following his success with Led Zeppelin, Atlantic's Mario Medious would become a legend within the industry, spawning imitators at every major label as the "underground" hype man—with his trunk full of good weed and free records—became a 70s fixture at FM radio stations across America. And according to Danny Goldberg in *Bumping Into Geniuses*, "The record that made Mario an indispensable player in the rock business was Led Zeppelin's self-titled debut album." But while Atlantic's hype campaign had given

Zeppelin's career an unprecedented jump start, many critics never forgave the band for becoming enormously popular without their blessing.

But it wasn't just Led Zeppelin who was coming to be seen by critics as a creature of rock's emerging commercial establishment. As many of the late 60s most iconic bands—The Who, Pink Floyd, The Rolling Stones, Crosby, Stills & Nash—moved through the early 70s, it was clear that they, too, were losing touch with their countercultural roots. All of them were increasingly being caught up in a new form of adulation, one that had little to do with artistic substance or socio-political ideals. If the "Cult of the Rock Star" had been invented by Elvis and The Beatles, it was perfected by the mega-bands of the 70s. Jimmy Page, Mick Jagger, Pete Townshend—along with countless lesser known performers—came to embody the hedonistic larger-than-life persona of the newly coined phrase "Sex, Drugs and Rock & Roll," making substance abuse, groupies, and excessive self-importance the norm. And throughout the 70s, these extra-musical exploits were quickly becoming rock's leading ethos, one perfectly captured by the lyrics to one of 1973's most popular songs, Grand Funk Railroad's #1 hit "We're an American Band:"

Out on the road for forty days
Last night in Little Rock, put me in a haze
Sweet, sweet Connie was doin' her act
She had the whole show and that's a natural fact...

Booze and ladies, keep me right
As long as we can make it to the show tonight

We're an American band
We're an American band
We're comin' to your town
We'll help you party it down
We're an American band

Four young chiquitas in Omaha
Waitin' for the band to return from the show
Feelin' good, feelin' right and it's Saturday night
The hotel detective, he was outta sight

Now these fine ladies, they had a plan

They was out to meet the boys in the band
They said, 'Come on dudes, let's get it on!'
And we proceeded to tear that hotel down

We're an American band
We're an American band
We're comin' to your town
We'll help you party it down
We're an American band

From the reference to well-known Little Rock groupie Connie Hamsy to the ransacked hotel rooms in Omaha, Grand Funk Railroad's idea of what it meant to be in a rock band was miles away from Fred Goodman's countercultural assertion that rock music was embodied by "the search for authenticity and an explicit rejection of consumerism." The tens of millions of dollars that successful rock bands were earning made it virtually impossible to see them as anything other than part of the commercial mainstream. And rock's skyrocketing financial fortunes would soon attract a new crop of performers who would proceed to take the excesses of rock star culture to yet another level.

The New Rock Ethos: Shock Rock

In the early 1970s, as the mantra "Sex, Drugs, & Rock and Roll" was coming to encapsulate the entirety of the mainstream rock ethos, a new rock derivation called "shock rock" was emerging. However, unlike Led Zeppelin's members, who had still managed to present themselves as real people (albeit real people with a fleeting grasp of reality), shock rockers like Alice Cooper, Kiss, and Ozzy Osbourne of Black Sabbath were almost completely fictional characters. As Osbourne explained in a 1982 *Night Flight* interview, "Ozzy Osbourne and John Osborne is [sic] two different people. John Osbourne is talking to you now, but if you want to be [he takes a maniacal tone] 'Ozzy Osbourne' it takes over. To be Ozzy 24 hours a day [would be] kind of heavy. People expect you to bite the heads off things." Like Osbourne's performances with Black Sabbath, most shock rock shows weren't just out of touch with reality; they had no aspirations to reality. Performers like Osbourne and Kiss's Gene Simmons were more like actors playing the part of rock stars, and as such they took rock star posturing and stylization to its logical extreme.

They also completely rejected the notion of rock's artistic aspirations. Since the mid-60s, even rock performers as commercially successful as Led Zeppelin had thought of themselves as artists and had aspired to create something of substantive artistic value in their music. But according to Kiss's Gene Simmons, rock had nothing at all to do with art. As he told Danny Goldberg in *Bumping Into Geniuses*, "It was more like professional wrestling than art." And in a 2002 NPR interview he explained his rock philosophy to Terry Gross:

> Gross: "Are you interested in music, or is the goal of being in a rock band to have sex a lot?"
> Simmons: "I believe in my heart that anyone who gets up there and says what they're doing is art is on crack, and is delusional, and that in point of fact... it was to get laid and make lots of money. And anybody who tells you otherwise is lying to you. The reason we all wanted to pick up instruments initially, you know, publicly, anyway—I will grant you there are those people who really love music and simply want to do it as a private pleasure... but as soon as you get up publicly and want other people to hear it, it seems that we really get off on the notion that the opposite sex, the fairer sex—that's you—like what we do... If I'm in a rock band, I've got a better than average chance of bedding you down than if I was a dentist. I didn't make those rules."

Even so, the onstage antics that 70s shock-rockers used to woo "the fairer sex" seemed to spring from the imagination of a socially inept 12-year-old boy: pretending to bite the heads off of animals, wearing super-hero makeup, populating the stage with costumed monsters, engaging in mock devil worship, dressing like action figures, filling the arena with pyrotechnics. It was not surprising, then, that shock rock's principal fanbase was made up of teenage (and pre-teen) boys; it was nothing if not an ode to male adolescence. And in contrast to the fatherly role of attempting to prepare boys for the realities and responsibilities of inevitable adulthood, bands like Kiss fed the illusion that the rock and roll fantasy they embodied was somehow applicable beyond adolescence. As lead singer Paul Stanley routinely said, "Kiss is a way of life."

It was also a calculated marketing scheme. No rock band had ever been as brazenly commercially-minded as Kiss; between the sales of action figures, lunch boxes, Halloween costumes, comic books, and seemingly anything else they could think of, Kiss made $100 million in merchandise sales alone between 1977 and 1979. In contrast to their late 60s forbears, who saw commercialization as antithetical to rock's countercultural ideals, the members of Kiss had no qualms about creating their music and stage personas for purely commercial ends. Even the entire idea of appealing to adolescent boys to the exclusion of girls was a calculated marketing decision. "You don't want a large female audience," said Simmons in 1995. "If you depend on women to buy your records, you end up going the way of New Kids on the Block. Female audiences tend to be unfaithful." Ozzy Osbourne's persona, too, was largely calculated for financial gain, "It's all showbiz, you know? I wanted to be recognized. I mean, I've gotta be truthful about this. I milk it to a point. You have to. Otherwise I'm some kind of a fucking dummy. I wanna make dough. I like making lots of dough."

And the extent to which bands like Kiss recoiled from any pretense of rock's substantive seriousness was exceedingly clear. As Simmons told Gross in 2002, "What does it all mean? Nothing! It means for two hours we're going to make you forget about the traffic jam, and the fact that your girlfriend is whining, or whatever else is going on in your life, and for two hours we give you escapism, that's what it means." By the late 70s, the ideological divide between shock-rockers like Kiss and their late 60s forebears was pronounced to say the least, but while the vast majority of rock critics panned heavy metal bands, there was one group of people who took them *very* seriously: their fans. As Charles M. Young described the Kiss experience in a 1977 *Rolling Stone* profile, "It is pagan religion for adolescents."

Even though 70s shock-rockers had no aspirations to artistic seriousness or substantive depth, the young fans who flocked to their shows had nevertheless inherited the idea that rock music was *important* from their countercultural predecessors. And so, even while mainstream rock music was devolving into blatant commercialism and empty posturing, heavy metal fans everywhere were taking shock rock's frivolous adolescent spectacle seriously. For these fans, Kiss's commercially motivated image had become, in accordance with Paul Stanley's motto, *a way of life*. And rock star hero-worship reached a new level of devotion with the "Kiss Army," which boasted over 100,000 registered members in the late 70s. In the process, rock star adulation was finally severed completely from any relationship to substantive artistic content. As a result, an entire generation of aspiring mainstream rockers—many of whom would come to prominence in the glam metal bands of the 1980s—came of age believing in the adolescent rock and roll fantasies lived by Led Zeppelin and preached by Kiss, with little regard for the countercultural notion of rock as substantive art. The "cultural advance" hailed by Allen Ginsburg when Bob Dylan had introduced real artistic sensibilities into popular rock music had completely regressed back to the commercial frivolity of the pre-Dylan era. Only now, the possibilities for commercial exploitation had increased exponentially. But as mainstream rock spiraled deeper and deeper into a caricature of itself, it was only a matter of time before a new counterculture would emerge to challenge mainstream rock's bloated corporate vapidity.

Chapter Three

A New Counterculture

Punk, KROQ, Indies, and the Birth of Alternative Music

Punk

For many countercultural purists in the late 60s, the idea that there could even be such a thing as a "rock music industry" would have seemed paradoxical. When countercultural icons like The Grateful Dead had signed with major labels, they idealistically maintained that they would infiltrate and change the music industry itself rather than let the industry change them. But while The Dead really did seem to remain largely unaffected by their interactions with the music industry, the same could not be said of most of their rock peers. And by the mid-70s, it was becoming possible to question whether the obscene opulence of rock star culture was compatible with substantive artistry; the billions of dollars that were now up for grabs in the rock market had helped commercial aspirations completely overpower artistic aspirations as a creative principle for rock acts. But as rock continued to become less and less countercultural—and more and more financially profitable—a new counterculture would arise to challenge the rock mainstream. However, the challenges to mainstream rock mounted by what became known as the "punk" music scene were not monolithic; they came from many different—and sometimes contradictory—directions.

A NEW COUNTERCULTURE

It was no accident that the punk scene grew up around a New York City rock club, CBGB. Much of the music that influenced punk had been born in New York: The Velvet Underground, The New York Dolls, The Dictators. However, even though the bands that got their start at CBGB in the mid-70s all came to be classified as punk music, they were wildly different from one another. There was the back-to-basics pop simplicity of The Ramones, the complex rhythmic and melodic textures of The Talking Heads, the groundbreaking guitar-rock of Television, the visceral pop sensibility of Blondie, the neo-nihilism of Richard Hell and the Voidoids. But when most cultural critics look back at New York punk, they tend to represent it as a far more monolithic scene than it actually was.

The Ramones represented one of punk's many prevalent notions: the idea that mainstream rock had gotten too damn pretentious and complicated for its own good. In Tom Carson's review of The Ramones' *Rocket to Russia*, he correctly points out that their music signaled "a return to the basics." But he also notes the band had added a new twist in that their music "was both deliberately primitive and revisionist at the same time, a musical and lyrical bluntness of approach which concealed a wealth of complex, disengaging ironies underneath." The power of this nuanced approach soon became apparent. On the surface, The Ramones' overt simplicity was a clear indictment of 70s rock's pretentions that echoed critic Jon Landau's conservative pining for the earlier, simpler time of Chuck Berry's pop ditties. But the introduction of irony into their vision of early rock allowed them to also be implicitly critical of that earlier era as well. Their music may have sounded like a return to rock's basics, but where Berry had been at least tacitly sincere in his celebration of the simple joys of cars, school, and teenage romance, The Ramones ironic treatment of the same subject matter cast it in a totally new light. According to Carson, The Ramones saw Berry's songs and subject matter as "trash music for a trash culture." However, "If that was a depressing truth, The Ramones were cocky enough, and heretical enough, to say that it was ridiculous too; and even to say that it was not without its appeal. Their reveling in the trashy vitality of such an overwrought atmosphere was a life affirming manifesto." Yet, if the idea of celebrating "trash culture" seems like a rather depressing manifesto—one uniquely suited to the 1970s New York City ethos—it was nothing compared to another NYC punk icon's bleak outlook on life.

While some saw The Ramones as the torch-bearers of the punk attitude, there were others who saw Richard Hell's nihilistic hedonism as the epitome of punk. The title of Legs McNeil and Gillian McCain's definitive oral history of punk—*Please Kill Me*—is a reference to the words scrawled on the infamous t-shirt Hell routinely wore around New York in the mid-70s. Hell's nihilism made The Ramones ironic celebration of trash culture seem sunny by comparison. When he wrote and performed songs like "Who Says (It's Good to be Alive)?" he wasn't just rebelling against mainstream rock because its pretentions seemed empty; he saw mainstream rock's empty posturing as just another piece of evidence that *any* attempt at meaning in life or music was doomed to failure. "I don't have anything to live for," Hell told Lester Bangs for a 1978 *Gig* article. "For me rock 'n' roll is the frontier of consciousness, the place where you face the unsentimental question of whether the struggle to remain alive is greater than what you derive by being alive... I can very dispassionately and confidently imagine sticking a pistol in my mouth and pulling the trigger." "What would stop you?" asks Bangs. "Habit. Just habit," responds Hell.

But Hell's nihilistic point of view—he quotes Nietzsche at multiple points during his interview with Bangs—was by no means shared by everyone associated with punk. For instance, Bangs—whose writings on punk forbears like Lou Reed and Iggy Pop had made him an authoritative voice within the emerging punk scene—flatly contradicts Hell's dark view of life in the same 1978 *Gig* article:

> I look at it so differently that I was at a loss for words... I would like it known by anybody who cares that I don't think life is a perpetual dive. And even though it's genuinely frightening, I don't think Richard Hell's fascination with death is anything else but stupid... It's a person's duty to the potentials of his own soul to make the best of it. We're all stuck on this often miserable earth where life is essentially tragic, but there are glints of beauty and bedrock joy that come shining through from time to precious time to remind anybody who cares that there is something higher and larger than ourselves... I am talking about a sense of wonder about life itself and the feeling that there is some redemptive factor that you must at least *search* for until you drop dead of natural causes. And all the Richard Hells are chickenshits who trash the gift too blithely... In other words, he's got a great grasp of the *problems* of being alive in the 70s, but his solutions suck.

Bangs would soon find a more attractive solution to the ills of the 70s in the punk scene exploding across the pond in London. While many hailed The Sex Pistols as London's leading punk iconoclasts, perceptions of their authenticity varied wildly among punk purists; some saw them as iconoclastic symbols of anti-corporate artistic freedom, while others saw them as opportunistic pawns in manager Malcolm McLaren's financially motivated hype machine. And so it would remain for their heirs apparent in The Clash to offer an authentically affirmative philosophical alternative to The Ramones ironic celebration of trash and Richard Hell's bleak nihilism. Unlike Hell's defeatist view of the power of music—"There's nothing to win by this sort of outcry," Hell sings in "Who Says (It's Good to be Alive)?"—Clash singer-songwriter Joe Strummer's credo was explicitly life-affirming: "I don't have any message except 'Don't forget you're alive!'" And his unabashed idealism was reminiscent of the 60s counterculture in a way that would have been anathema to both Richard Hell and The Ramones. "People began to kick hippies around," Strummer reminisces in the documentary *The Future is Unwritten*. "But quite frankly, I'm a hippie! I wanna be a hippie!" And through The Clash, Strummer was able to synthesize the raw power and disillusionment of the punks with the idealism of the 60s counterculture, reviving the perception of rock as a substantive art form capable of effecting real cultural change.

In doing so, The Clash also revived the idea of rock music's capacity for *authenticity*, which was essential to their artistic credibility and stood in stark contrast to mainstream rock's increasingly ridiculous rock star posturing—in much the same way The Rolling Stones' visceral authenticity had stood out against a backdrop of the vapid 60s commercialism over a decade earlier. After meeting The Clash in 1977, Lester Bangs wrote a feature article for *New Musical Express* in which he explained his particular affection for the band. "A process of escalating admiration for this band had begun for me which was to continue until it broached something like awe," writes Bangs. "See, because it's easy to *sing* about your righteous politics, but we all know actions speak louder than words, and The Clash are one of the very few examples I've seen where they would rather set an example by their personal conduct than *talk* about it all day." Later in the same article, after relating a story about The Clash inviting fans back to their hotel bar after a gig to hang out—even allowing a dozen or so of them crash on their hotel room floors—Bangs continues:

Now, dear reader, I don't know how much time you may have spent around bigtime rock 'n' roll bands—you may not think so, but the less the luckier you are in most cases—but let me assure you that the way The Clash treat their fans falls so far outside the normal run of these things as to be outright revolutionary. I'm going to say it and I'm going to say it slow: most rock stars are goddamn pigs who have the usual burly corps of hired thugs to keep the fans away from them at all costs, excepting the usual contingent of lucky (?) nubiles who they'll maybe deign to allow up to their rooms for the privilege of sucking on their coveted wangers, after which often as not they get pitched out into the streets to find their way home without even cabfare. The whole thing is so sick to the marrow, and I could not believe that any band, especially one as musically brutal as The Clash, could depart so far from this fetid norm... And that for me is the essence of The Clash's greatness, over and beyond their music, why I fell in love with them... The everlasting and totally disgusting walls between artist and audience must come down, elitism must perish, the 'stars' have got to be humanized, demythologized, and the audience has got to be treated with more respect. Otherwise it's all shuck, a ripoff, and the music is as dead as The Stones' and Led Zep's has become.

Bangs indictment of 70s mainstream rock was echoed by the punk rockers themselves. According to The Clash's Paul Simonon, "I don't have to hear Led Zeppelin—just looking at their record covers makes me want to throw up." Then there was Sex Pistols lead singer Johnny Rotten's iconic "I Hate Pink Floyd" t-shirt, which wasn't a criticism of Pink Floyd's music as much as it was a condemnation of everything rock star culture stood for. And the fact that some people found the shirt shocking was only evidence of how sycophantic 70s rock star hero-worship had become. In that kind of environment, The Clash stood out all the more. According to Tom Carson in his review of The Clash's 1979 album *London Calling* for *Rolling Stone*:

By now, our expectations of The Clash might seem to have become inflated beyond any possibility of fulfillment. It's not simply that they're the greatest rock & roll band in the world—indeed, after years of watching too many superstars compromise, blow chances and sell out, being the greatest is just about synonymous with being the music's last hope. While the group itself resists such labels, they do tell you exactly how high the stakes are, and how urgent the need. The Clash got their start on the crest of what looked like a revolution, only to see the punk movement either smash up on its own violent momentum or be absorbed into the same corporate-rock machinery it had meant to destroy. Now, almost against their will, they're the only ones left.

As Carson's review points out, by the end of the 70s it was clear that punk's attempt to overthrow the rock mainstream had failed, and for many critics and musicians who had been sympathetic to the punk movement, the failure of punk's frontal assault on the music industry seemed to signal the end of rock's artistic relevance. As a new decade loomed, popular rock continued to be dominated by the cliché-driven posturing of bands like AC/DC and Van Halen who had picked up where Led Zeppelin had left off, and it was looking like rock was in danger of becoming just another popular music genre, no more artistically or culturally important than any of its competitors in the pop charts. But punk's descendants in the underground music scene that would develop in the 80s refused to admit defeat, and as long as there was rock music to be played they would continue to buck mainstream rock's single-minded commercialism. Only, instead of emulating punk's attempt to topple the mainstream, they would create an *alternative* to the mainstream, waging a clandestine war designed to win fans by the dozens rather than by the millions, all the while following their diverse creative muses in the face of mainstream obliviousness.

KROQ and the Birth of Alternative Music

In 1976, a failed Los Angeles rock station with the call letters KROQ (pronounced "K-Rock") was ordered by the FCC to return to the airwaves or surrender its broadcast license. Lacking a strict format and having very little organizational structure, the station's handful of DJs were empowered to play the music that they liked. One DJ in particular, L.A. scenester Rodney Bingenheimer, was sick of the Album Oriented Rock (AOR) format that dominated the FM airwaves. He could hear Led Zeppelin and Pink Floyd anywhere; he wanted to play new music by new artists. Bingenheimer's personal tastes leaned towards punk and new wave music and he made a name for himself and the station in the late 70s by being one of the first American DJs to play music by the first wave of punk bands. "I would play demos—all the early punk stuff: The Sex Pistols, The Germs," says Bingenheimer. "I'd show up with a stack of records: The Ramones, The Damned, Blondie." Due to KROQ's limited following it was hardly a revolution, but the station developed a reputation for being willing to play music by unknown, underground artists. As Eric Himmelsbach would later write in the *L.A. Times*, "By the late 1970s, most FM stations…shoved demographic-driven homogenization down listeners' unsuspecting throats. Which was fine, if you wanted to hear Boston's 'More Than a Feeling' on the hour. But Blondie? The Clash? X? Forget about it. Only L.A.'s own renegade station KROQ dared play the revolutionary new sounds emanating from London, New York, and Southern California with any regularity." KROQ's unique format began to garner some listeners, but a cult following did not equal solvency, and most of the staff quit between 1978 and 1979 as the fledgling station was unable to pay its employees. Bingenheimer was one of the few who stayed. "It was so unlikely that a station would start out playing nothing but weird music and become successful," says longtime KROQ DJ Jed "The Fish" Gould. At the time, it would have been impossible to predict that KROQ would soon become the most influential rock radio station in America.

In late 1978, KROQ's fortunes changed forever when it brought in seasoned program director Rick Carroll, who quickly went about creating a cohesive sound for the station. DJs were still allowed some autonomy, but with a new decade on the horizon, Carroll strove to give the station an identifiable image and he put a premium on new music by new artists. The first casualties were the AOR giants—Led Zeppelin, The Who, The Rolling Stones, Pink Floyd—who some DJs were still mixing into their rotations. Safe sounding pop-rockers in the Genesis, Journey, and REO Speedwagon vein were also out. Cutting edge punk bands like The Clash and The Ramones were in, as was the new wave of Devo, The Police, The Pretenders, Elvis Costello, The Go-Go's, The Cure, and Adam & the Ants. The electro-pop of British bands like Depeche Mode and New Order was another key ingredient. And Bingenheimer was allowed to continue mixing in some local underground post-punk acts like Social Distortion and X. Carroll dubbed the new format "The Rock of the 80s."

Carroll's desire for new music was perfect for Bingenheimer, who is credited with breaking The Sex Pistols, The Runaways, Duran Duran, The B-52's, The Smiths, Nena, and Siouxsie & The Banshees (among many, many others) during the early years of his late night show, "Rodney on the ROQ." Many of the artists he played would go on to become KROQ staples throughout the 80s, and the legend of Bingenheimer's show spread throughout the country as a way for unknown bands to put themselves on the map. Bingenheimer further extended his influence by releasing an annual compilation album featuring his favorite underground bands, many of whom were too raw or abrasive to catch on, even at KROQ. The underground bands anointed by Bingenheimer on his compilations included Black Flag, Social Distortion, The Minutemen, and The Circle Jerks. According to Blondie's Debbie Harry in the 2003 Bingenheimer documentary *Mayor of the Sunset Strip*, when it first started out, "KROQ was not a very powerful radio station." But as it grew in size and influence, "[Bingenheimer] was very creative and influential in dictating their style… He was very influential in actually creating, I think, what became alternative music." Like many of the bands he broke, Blondie became friends with Bingenheimer, even giving him a guitar and bringing him on stage to mime guitar parts during their live set when they visited L.A.

By 1982, KROQ had become one of the leading rock stations in L.A. That same year Carroll was hired as a consultant to bring his "Rock of the 80s" format to KQAK ("The Quake") in San Francisco and San Diego's (Mexico-based) XETRA-FM. At 6pm on January 12, 1983, XETRA made the switch, playing Led Zeppelin's "Stairway to Heaven" one last time as a symbolic goodbye to the AOR format. In fact, one of the side-effects of Carroll's "Rock of the 80s" format was that it necessitated the creation of a new radio format for rock music that had come out prior to 1980; the new format was dubbed "classic rock." Carroll would go on to consult on format changes at KYYX in Seattle, KEGL ("The Eagle") in Dallas, KPOP in Sacramento, WIFI in Philadelphia, WRQC in Cleveland, and WYDD in Pittsburgh. All of these stations took their cues from KROQ, though in keeping with the KROQ model, they each brought their own local flair and preferences to the format. By 1985, Carroll had so many consulting offers that he left KROQ in order to be a full-time consultant. By that time, KROQ had already spawned dozens of "Rock of the 80s" stations across the country.

One of those was Boston FM station WLYN, which switched over to a KROQ-inspired "Rock of the 80s" format in 1982. The following year, *The Phoenix*, Boston's leading alternative arts newspaper, purchased the station and dubbed it WFNX. Their format continued to borrow heavily from the KROQ template, but in a nod to its alt-newspaper roots, the station's format was routinely called "alternative." WFNX was particularly influential on the Boston area's numerous college radio stations, many of which adopted its "alternative" format. The same thing began to happen at college radio stations across the country and by the mid-80s the "Rock of the 80s," "alternative," and "college radio" formats were virtually indistinguishable from each other. Together, they formed a growing network of stations playing punk rock, post-punk, new wave, and electro-pop. And they began to create small but rabid fanbases for new underground bands in little pockets all across America. These fanbases were continually augmented by an independent record store here and a fanzine there until, by the mid-1980s, a vast underground network of alternative venues had emerged.

While megastars like Bruce Springsteen, Prince, and Madonna toured arenas and stadiums, alternative bands in the 80s played CBGB in New York, Maxwell's in Hoboken, The Paradise in Boston, The 9:30 Club in D.C., The 40 Watt in Athens, The Exit/In in Nashville, The Metro in Chicago, First Avenue in Minneapolis, The Whiskey in L.A., The I-Beam in San Francisco. The history of these clubs (along with many, many others) and the bands who played them is a virtual who's who of 1980s and 90s alternative bands. U2, R.E.M., and The Cure cut their teeth on the emerging alternative club circuit long before they had songs in the *Billboard* pop charts. Many of the shows at these venues were sponsored by the local radio stations themselves. Others were showcases for one of the many new independent record labels popping up all across the country.

An identifiable national scene began to emerge around the growing number of alternative radio stations and venues. Though, as the decade wore on, the limiting tag "Rock of the 80s" began to lose its freshness, and the term "alternative" was increasingly used to describe the radio format shared by stations across the country, from KROQ to WFNX. The alternative tag was an effective way to differentiate the format from the "mainstream rock" format that mixed in hits by Bruce Springsteen and Huey Lewis with the glam metal of Bon Jovi and Def Leppard. The tag also differentiated the format from "hard rock" format which included the more abrasive metal of Metallica and Slayer with harder glam bands like Guns N' Roses. However, finding a defining stylistic characteristic within the diversity of alternative radio playlists remained virtually impossible.

A NEW COUNTERCULTURE

What Was Alternative Music, Anyway?

By the second half of the 80s, "alternative" was a loose umbrella term used to define a certain group of bands, venues, music fans, and—above all—radio station formats. The term was not associated with a particular musical style, as evidenced by a quick look at KROQ's playlists. For instance, KROQ's Top 20 songs of 1989 included the operatic pop drama of The Cure, the danceable retro-kitsch of The B-52's, the earnest anthem-rock of U2, the British synth-pop of Depeche Mode, the leftover new wave of Tears for Fears, the slick neo-soul of Fine Young Cannibals, the southern-tinged Americana of R.E.M., the offbeat genius that was The Pixies, the punk-influenced hard rock of Dramarama, the electro-dance pop of New Order, the endearingly over-educated quirkiness of XTC, the primal hard-edged funk of Red Hot Chili Peppers, the pop balladry of Elvis Costello, and the newly polished post-punk of The Replacements.

In retrospect, the fact that these bands were so different stylistically makes it hard to see what they had in common, but the most obvious connection between them was the shared influence of punk music, either stylistically or philosophically (or sometimes both). The punk phenomenon had signaled a departure from the increasingly commercial mainstream rock industry, and it was generally seen as a victory for creative freedom. As Michael Azerrad pointed out in his 2001 book *Our Band Could Be Your Life*, the enduring lesson of punk was "Think for yourself." Whether or not this was actually what punk had always been about, 80s alternative bands—on both indie and major labels—valued that motto, and it showed in the diverse musical styles which exploded during the decade.

The diversity of styles within alternative music contrasted noticeably with monolithic "hair metal" or "glam" sound of mainstream rock that was coming to be typified by bands like Bon Jovi and Poison, who seemed to operate as if the punk movement had never happened at all, instead taking their cues from 70s mainstream rockers like Led Zeppelin, Kiss, and Aerosmith. Alternative radio stations were united in their refusal to play either classic rock or glam bands, neither of which was deemed to have the requisite artistic credibility. Another point of commonality among alternative radio stations was their willingness to play bands on independent labels in addition to those on major labels. Throughout the 80s, bands on indie labels like The Smiths, X, The Replacements, The Pixies, New Order, and Social Distortion got play alongside major label acts like U2, Talking Heads, Pet Shop Boys, and Jane's Addiction. There were also "in-between" bands who recorded for independent labels that were distributed by majors; these included R.E.M., The Go-Go's, Midnight Oil, The Cure, and Depeche Mode.

But the most obvious factor that distinguished the 80s alternative music from the popular rock of the era was the extent to which the alternative scene existed outside the cultural and commercial mainstream. For instance, in 1989, none of the songs in KROQ's year-end Top 20 countdown made *Billboard*'s year-end Top 20 singles chart. KROQ's #1 song that year, The Cure's "Lovesong," came in at #68 on the *Billboard* list, below entries by glam rockers Skid Row, White Lion, Def Leppard, Great White, Bon Jovi (twice), Warrant, and Poison (whose "Every Rose Has Its Thorn" was the #3 pop single that year). Where glam represented rock's most mainstream commercial tendencies and tended to bolster the existing cultural status quo, the alternative scene became a refuge for the freaks and outsiders who existed on the fringes of the mainstream. As R.E.M.'s Michael Stipe would later say of the alternative scene:

> This was a true underground. It was punk rock, but the many bands or musical styles were eclectic. We were a product of a community of youth looking for a connection away from the mainstream. The community built structures outside of the corporate, governmental sphere, independent and decentralized—media connected through the copy machine, a decade before the internet as we know it came to be. [It was] a movement for outsiders: for the fags, for the fat girls, for the broken toys, the shy nerds, the goth kids from Tennessee and Kentucky, for the rockers and the awkward, for the fed-up, the too-smart kids, and the bullied. We were a community.

Even so, for most of the 80s "alternative" remained an umbrella term. The alternative music scene still contained countless subgroups, such as local scenes tied to a geographic area or sub-scenes related to specific styles of music. Perhaps the most influential sub-scenes were those that grew up around the growing number of independent record labels.

SST and the Rise of Independent Labels

By the late 70s, virtually all of the independent labels that had helped launch rock music in the 50s and 60s—Atlantic, Motown, Chess, Specialty, Imperial—had been absorbed by the major labels or gone out of business. But for a lot of bands, the idea of creative freedom inherited from the punk movement meant more than simply accepting the varying levels of artistic autonomy being granted by the all-powerful major record labels. Instead, real freedom meant complete autonomy from the entire corporate major label system. For these zealots, signing with an independent label—or starting one themselves—was a way to maintain both creative and economic freedom.

Put simply, an independent (or "indie") label is any label that is not a subsidiary of (or, depending on the strictness of your definition, distributed by) one of the major corporate label groups. For most of the 1980s, there were six major label groups: Capitol/EMI, Columbia, PolyGram, RCA, MCA, and Warner Brothers (as of 2015, further consolidation has left only three major labels: Sony, Warner, and Universal). The bands that signed to indie labels in the 80s had a whole host of different motivations for doing so. Some bands opted for indie labels because they saw avoiding the inherently compromised corporate structure of major labels as a moral or political imperative. There were also bands that simply felt majors were too restrictive creatively. Others saw no chance of catching on with a major and settled for whatever support an indie label could offer. Still others pined for the increased exposure and financial success offered by majors, but signed with an indie as a potential stepping stone to bigger and better things. But whatever their motivations, bypassing the rock music establishment's infrastructure necessarily made it much more difficult for these bands to record, manufacture, market, and distribute their music. And those disadvantages necessitated an entirely different definition of success for bands on independent labels. For instance, when R.E.M.'s debut album *Murmur* sold 200,000 copies in 1983 with major label distribution, it was seen as a disappointment by their label. In contrast, indie icons The Minutemen were happy to sell 15,000 copies of their albums on the independent SST label. It was clear that indies and major labels operated on completely different playing fields. Where major label rock bands typically aspired to rock stardom, indie bands had much more modest goals. As indie band Buffalo Tom's Bill Janovitz explained to *Mule Variations* in 2011:

> When we got on [indie label] SST Records—which at that time was home to Husker Du and Sonic Youth and Dinosaur Jr. and Black Flag—it was like we had been blessed. We felt anointed that we could be on this label. And labels were so meaningful back then: Sub Pop, Homestead, and those types of indie labels. Because, back in '86, '87, '88 when I was up at college, Bon Jovi and hair metal were on the radio, and that was when popular music was at its lowest point for me and my interest level. But that book *Our Band Could Be Your Life* by Michael Azerrad really captured that spirit, 'What we're doing has nothing to do with what's going on in the mainstream, so we have no chance of crossing over'… We just wanted to go out on the road and sleep on people's couches. And so that's what we did… Nobody was in it for money, because there was no chance at making money. So that was the reality. You really just wanted to survive. It wasn't so much about quitting your day job as much as getting a day job that would let you go on tour.

In 1978, guitarist Greg Ginn had started SST records in Long Beach, California in order to release an EP by his band Black Flag. Ginn had a wide range of musical influences, from The Grateful Dead to B.B. King, but due to his limited guitar skills, virtually none of those influences were discernible in his music. Black Flag was a loud, fast, and abrasive punk band, and Ginn tried to make up for his lack of skill with volume, energy, and charisma. Black Flag is often credited, along with D.C.'s Bad Brains, with inventing the "hardcore" genre, and their dark—often grotesquely violent—cover art and concert posters have become the template for legions of subsequent hardcore and metal bands. Breakouts of violence were commonplace at Black Flag shows, especially once the confrontational Henry Rollins became the band's lead singer in 1981. And while financial success wasn't shunned *per se*, the self-limiting commercial appeal of the band itself made mass popularity exceedingly unlikely. But their paltry record sales and limited fanbase belied their surprisingly wide scope of influence, especially among other musicians.

The key factor in Black Flag's enduring influence was Ginn's SST label. It typified the DIY mentality that many post-punks had adopted, and during its most influential years in the early 80s SST united under its banner iconic post-punk bands like The Minutemen, The Meat Puppets, Overkill, and

Husker Du. In the process, SST and the countless tours they sponsored put Black Flag at the center of a small post-punk scene that was slowly spreading nationally. As the self-distributed SST created new channels through which to get independently released albums into record stores, they opened doors for dozens of subsequent indie labels. Indie bands and labels from all over the country—from Sonic Youth in New York to Sub Pop in Seattle—have acknowledged the debt of gratitude they owe Black Flag and SST. Ginn was an indie pioneer.

Some of the bands in the Southern California post-punk scene that had spawned Black Flag saw their music as a political tool as well. While the politics of most early punk bands like The Ramones had been limited to implicit anti-establishment dissatisfaction, post-punk bands like The Minutemen followed The Clash's lead and gave SST an overtly political edge. And much like The Clash, for The Minutemen there was little separation between their music, their politics, and their lives. The way the band played, said bassist Mike Watt, "was the same way we talked about issues. I don't want to separate them so much. We didn't have the political rap and the band rap. They *were* the rap." Like most of the SST bands, The Minutemen came from a working class background and their music reflected the impression that working people weren't getting a fair shake. They were voracious students of history and played overtly political songs with titles like "American History," "Viet Nam," and "Bob Dylan Wrote Propaganda Songs." In "Fake Contest," guitarist D. Boon shouts, "Industry, industry! We're tools for the industry!" Incidentally, none of these songs topped the two-minute mark; most were less than a minute long. And in those short bursts, the band was more interested in posing questions than offering answers. "Music can inspire people to wake up and say 'Somebody's lying,'" Watt told *Rolling Stone*, "This is the point I'd like to make with my music." Needless to say, Watt's motivation for playing rock music deviated sharply from Gene Simmons' insistence that anyone who played rock music did so only "to get laid and make lots of money."

Following SST's lead, a new generation of small independent labels began popping up both in America and abroad, labels like Homestead in New York, Twin/Tone in Minneapolis, Touch and Go in Chicago, Ace of Hearts in Boston, Sub Pop in Seattle, as well as Factory Records, 4AD, Rough Trade, Beggars Banquet, and Mute in the UK. As the influence of these labels spread, one of the shared musical lessons that their bands took from punk music was that you didn't need to be a musical virtuoso or guitar hero to play rock music. Most aspiring punk musicians couldn't relate to the extended solos of Jimmy Page or the lavish soundscapes of David Gilmour. "They were a different class of people or something, like Martians," says Mike Watt. In contrast, when he heard The Clash his first thought was, "We can do this!" The egalitarian punk ethos—the idea that *anyone* with passion and something to say could play rock music—flew in the face of the idea that being in a rock band was something that required countless hours of training and preparation. And the stories of punk and post-punk bands, from The Sex Pistols to The Minutemen to U2, are littered with tales of near novices picking up instruments and forming bands before having much—if any—idea *how to play*. According to Watt, "You didn't have to have choruses, you didn't have to have lead guitar solos, you didn't have to have *anything*." While the preference for simplicity began as a necessity, it soon became a regimented part of the indie post-punk sound. In that insular scene, having the skill to play a triumphant classic rock guitar solo started to become seen as a *dis*advantage, and admiration for the musical intricacies of pre-punk classic rock acts was strictly anathema. According to Sonic Youth guitarist Lee Ranaldo, "I know in the early days of the group, when I would admit to having a thing for The Grateful Dead at one period, it almost felt like a blasphemous thing to say."

These kinds of self-imposed stylistic restrictions fused with the indie scene's anti-corporate zealotry to keep its cultural influence from growing beyond its limited place as a small but important faction under the larger alternative music umbrella. Even with the proliferation of independent labels, indie bands still made up only a small percentage of the music getting play on alternative radio. The vast majority of alternative music was coming from bands on major labels, major label subsidiaries, or indies that had major label distribution. The reason for this was simple; major labels were still granting far more creative freedom to rock artists during the 1980s than they have at any time since.

Alternative Music Becomes Rock's Middle Class

On July 13, 1985, an estimated 1.9 billion people in 150 countries tuned in to watch over 50 of rock's biggest acts perform at "Live Aid," a simultaneous broadcast of two concerts—one at Wembley Stadium in London and one at JFK Stadium in Philadelphia—to benefit victims of the disastrous Ethiopian famine. Between ticket sales, the live telethon that accompanied the concert, and sales of the live album, the event raised nearly $300 million for charity. As a marriage of rock's musical and socio-political ambitions, Live Aid displayed rock music's continuing cultural relevance, showing just how far it had come in the thirty years since Elvis Presley had stumbled into Sun Records to record a song for his mother. While the concert clearly reflected a desire to help starving families in Africa, it also functioned as a collective back-slapping session between the megastars who performed. And why not? Rock music had turned Mick Jagger, Bob Dylan, Paul McCartney, and Eric Clapton into larger-than-life figures that rivaled the mythic Greco-Roman gods. Even the celebrities like Don Johnson, Bette Midler, and Jack Nicholson who introduced the Live Aid acts seemed to be in awe of the iconic rock star status of The Who, Queen, and a reunited Led Zeppelin. The collective star power was overwhelming, and the audience reception at the two concerts—which were attended by more than 170,000 people—bordered on communal orgasmic ecstasy. Rock music had never had more cultural gravitas in Western pop culture.

For many of today's music fans, it's hard to imagine rock music having the kind of cultural relevance it enjoyed throughout the 1980s. It's even more difficult to conjure because today's deteriorating popular music industry is hardly recognizable as a descendant of the thriving industry that existed during that decade. And at the dawn of the 80s, rock music remained central to the mainstream music industry's success. Blondie's "Call Me" was the #1 single of 1980, Pink Floyd's "Another Brick in the Wall, Part II" was #2, and *twenty-five* rock songs were included among the top 80 *Billboard* singles that year (by contrast, only *three* rock songs were among the top 80 singles of 2010). And while major labels still invested time and money in disposable pop acts like Olivia Newton-John and Captain and Tennille, one thing was clear to most music executives: rock music was king. And this perception remained intact as U.S. album sales rose steadily throughout the 80s, from roughly 440 million in 1982 to over 700 million in 1990.

But rock music's cultural importance wasn't only the result of its commercial success. For many of rock's baby-boomer fans, an event like Live Aid affirmed rock's position as a unique musical style capable of achieving both cultural and artistic substance, in addition to mass popularity. Even though glam metal bands were already becoming rock's leading representative on the pop charts by the time of Live Aid, all the necessary evidence for rock's continuing artistic gravitas that most baby-boomers needed was right there on the Live Aid stage: Bob Dylan, Paul McCartney, Neil Young, Pete Townshend, Keith Richards. And rock's unique status among popular music genres, especially among the baby-boomers who were assuming corporate power across America, meant that major label offices in the 80s were filled with rock music fans, many of whom had come of age in a time when rock music—be it Bob Dylan, Pink Floyd, or The Sex Pistols—had *meant* something to them. Because of this, they tended to be interested in looking for the next important rock artist or the next important movement, in addition to their next big payday. And the industry's overall financial success made it possible for major labels to empower their A&R reps to take chances on rock acts whose artistic potential may or may not translate into huge sales. For instance, Warner Brothers Music Group alone was willing to sign critically respected punk and alternative acts like Devo, Jane's Addiction, The B-52's, The Cure, Talking Heads, The Jesus and Mary Chain, The Pogues, The Sex Pistols, Public Image Ltd., The Pixies, Bjork, Echo and the Bunnymen, The Ramones, Television, Tom Waits, Husker Du, The Replacements, Depeche Mode, Billy Bragg, R.E.M., Violent Femmes, Oingo Boingo, and Elvis Costello.

Even though many of the rock acts signed by major labels during the 80s had limited mainstream commercial potential, the state of the industry was such that major labels could afford the luxury of keeping artists on their rosters whose album sales didn't necessarily match the luster of their critical reviews or the passion of their cult followings. One way that a major label did this was by starting, purchasing, or distributing "vanity label" subsidiaries to focus on its artistically credible artists, freeing up the parent company to sully its hands in the mainstream pop world without tarnishing the reputations of its most artistically respected bands (for instance, Warner Bros. has used a number of its subsidiaries as vanity labels over the years, including Sire, Reprise, Elektra, Nonesuch, Atlantic, Capricorn, and Def American). The byproduct of this climate was that major labels were helping to create and support a vast alternative subculture around the artistically credible rock artists who *didn't* make it huge. During the 80s, while Lionel Ritchie, Michael Jackson, and Phil Collins topped the charts, many rock artists who would never approach that kind of mass popular success were allowed to have lengthy, artistically autonomous major label careers, giving them time to grow and develop musically, as well as time to build loyal fanbases. Between the tiny but influential cadre of obscurant indie rock purists and the compromised corporatism of mainstream glam rock, the music industry's overall success was abundant enough to support a burgeoning middle-class of artistically adventurous rock bands. That middle-class—which had established its own growing network of radio stations, venues, and fans—was called "alternative music."

Chapter Four

The Idiot-bastard Spawn of Rock

The Ridiculous Reign of 80s Glam Bands

The Prophetic Genius of Spinal Tap

In late 1978, just as mainstream rockers like Kiss and Black Sabbath were taking their excesses to new and extraordinary levels, a television writer and actor named Rob Reiner was looking to get into directing. His first project was a sketch comedy called *The TV Show*, and one of the sketches for the pilot episode was a tongue-in-cheek performance of a song called "Rock 'n Roll Nightmare" by a fake English heavy metal band called Spinal Tap. The sketch was the brainchild of comedians Michael McKean (who had a recurring role as "Lenny" on the hit show *Laverne & Shirley*), Harry Shearer (who had worked with McKean as part of the L.A. based comedy troupe "The Credibility Gap"), and Christopher Guest (a former roommate of McKean's). As McKean told *The Guardian* in 2000, "Chris had a character, a great cockney guitar-player-rocker character, and the two of us roomed together years ago in college and always talked about how great and funny rock and roll was when it had pomposity that didn't pay off." The pilot for *The TV Show* didn't end up getting picked up by ABC, but Reiner, McKean, Shearer, and Guest had so much fun with the Spinal Tap sketch that they continued to talk about it any time they saw each other. By 1982, they had begun writing, casting and crewing a feature length film called *This Is Spinal Tap*. It wasn't the first rock "mockumentary"—that honor probably goes to *The Rutles*, Eric Idle's 1978

Beatles send-up—but it was by far the most influential. And as the film's popularity spread throughout the 80s, *Spinal Tap* would help change the way an entire generation of musicians and fans viewed the artistic credibility of 80s heavy metal bands, opening their eyes to the genre's outlandish excesses and psychologically paving the way for its popular demise.

One of the reasons *Spinal Tap* was so effective was the mockumentary format itself. By presenting the band as "real," the film avoided the need for excessive exaggeration, instead allowing the actors to understatedly highlight the ridiculousness inherent in actual heavy metal culture. Many of the vignettes in the movie were based on real events. Nigel Tufnel's outlandish backstage demands (at one point in the film, Christopher Guest's Nigel becomes distraught over the size of the bread slices in the backstage spread) were said to be based on Van Halen's similarly ridiculous backstage demands, which included a bowl of M&Ms *with all of the brown ones removed*. The Stonehenge mishap in the film was inspired by Black Sabbath's *Born Again* tour, which was conceived with a life-size Stonehenge monument in mind, only—due to a mistaken notation of meters rather than feet—it was built too large to use on tour. Tap's skull-like mascot "Jim" was based on metal band Iron Maiden's similarly skeletal mascot "Eddie." Many of Spinal Tap's onstage antics—such as Nigel's over-the-top guitar solo in which he plays the guitar with a violin—are lifted directly from Led Zeppelin's *The Song Remains the Same*. Zeppelin's Robert Plant even said of the scene where Spinal Tap gets lost trying to find their way to the stage, "That was us, playing in Baltimore. It took 25 minutes to do the hundred yards from our Holiday Inn through the kitchen to the arena." The death of former Tap drummer Eric "Stumpy Joe" Childs was also based on the death of Zeppelin drummer John Bonham, who—while suffering from alcohol poisoning—choked to death on his own vomit.

This is Spinal Tap's most impressive achievement, however, was its spot-on portrayal of the hilariously vacuous pomposity of heavy metal musicians themselves. For instance, when told that the band's audience is made up of predominantly young boys, Spinal Tap's Nigel insists this is because the females have been scared away by the bulges in their tight pants. "We've got armadillos in our trousers," says Nigel. "I mean, it's really quite frightening, the size. And [the women] run, screaming." Such assertions were indicative of—if not *more modest* than—the pervasive heavy metal posturing on the subject. From Terry Gross's 2002 NPR interview with Kiss's Gene Simmons:

Gross: "Let's get to the studded codpiece."
Simmons: "Oh yes."
Gross: "Do you have a sense of humor about that?"
Simmons: "No."
Gross: "Does that seem funny to you? Are you…"
Simmons: "No, it holds in my manhood."
Gross: [laughs] "That's right."
Simmons: "Otherwise it would be too much for you to take. You'd have to put the book down and confront life. The notion is that if you want to welcome me with open arms, I'm afraid you're also going to have to welcome me with open legs."
Gross: "That's a really obnoxious thing to say."

Ozzy Osboure's clueless-yet-endearing cockney vapidity was also an obvious influence on Spinal Tap. Earnest claims by Tap's David St. Hubbins like "I believe virtually everything I read" have their roots in similar claims by Osbourne—in his Tap-esque British accent—like this exchange from a 1982 *Night Flight* interview:

Interviewer: "Who do you think has influenced your stage shows the most?"
Osbourne: "Adolf Hitler."
Interviewer: [after a long pause] "What do you mean by that, Ozzy?"
Osbourne: "Adolf Hitler had charisma. In a *bad* way. And I kind of admired him. He was a freak; he was a lunatic, but he had something about him, you know? I know it was all bad, what he did. It was terrible what that guy did— he killed all these people and whatever. But it was like… he had something about him, you know? And I admired him… and I suddenly thought, if somebody put that in the *positive* way, for the *good* of mankind… And that's all I'm about."

One can almost hear Rob Reiner asking (in the same way he questions Spinal Tap's Nigel about his amp going to eleven), "But why didn't you find someone with *positive* charisma and choose to admire *that* person?" To which a Nigel-esque Osborne would ostensibly reply, after a long, confused pause, "But I admired Hitler."

The movie also mocks metal performers' propensity to take their own incredibly shallow lyrics seriously. As Spinal Tap's Derek Smalls says of his bandmates, "We're very lucky to have two visionaries in the band. David and

Nigel are both like poets, like Shelley or Byron or people like that. But they're two totally distinct types of visionaries. It's like fire and ice." Later Smalls continues, "We've grown musically. You listen to some of the rubbish we did early on—it was stupid. And now, a song like 'Sex Farm,' we're taking a sophisticated view of the idea of sex and, you know, putting it on a farm." Of course, the lyrics to "Sex Farm" are:

> *Working on a sex farm*
> *Plowing through your bean field*
> *Getting out my pitchfork*
> *Poking your hay*
> *Sex farm woman*
> *I'm gonna mow you down*
> *Sex farm woman*
> *I'll rake and hoe you down*

The lyrics to Spinal Tap songs like "Sex Farm" and "Big Bottom" weren't all that different from the thinly-veiled suggestive wordplay of heavy metal songs like Aerosmith's "Big Ten Inch" and "Lord of the Thighs," AC/DC's "Big Balls" and "Givin' the Dog a Bone," or Led Zeppelin's "Whole Lotta Love" (*"Gonna give you every inch of my love"*), which makes sense because those songs' juvenile notions of sexuality were exactly what Spinal Tap was lampooning. And it was these types of lyrics that left real-life heavy metal bands open to repeated critical attacks. In *Spinal Tap*, the band is accused by critics of "swimming in a sea of retarded sexuality." Similarly, in his review of AC/DC's 1981 album *For Those About to Rock*, critic Robert Christgau wrote, "'Let's Get It Up' is a limited sentiment in any case. But I'd appreciate some indication that [singer Brian] Johnson knows the difference between his dick and the light tower." It was also hard to tell if AC/DC's 1985 song "Sink the Pink" was an homage to Spinal Tap's line in "Big Bottom" ("I'm gonna sink her with my pink torpedo") or if Spinal Tap's creators were so attuned to juvenile heavy metal wordplay that they were actually able to predict its lyrical future.

Either way, the film's authenticity made it difficult for some viewers to tell if Spinal Tap was a joke or a real band. And many of the hard rock icons targeted by the film didn't get the joke, either. In 1997, Aerosmith's Brad

Whitford told *Spin*, "the first time [Aerosmith singer] Steven Tyler saw it he didn't see any humor in it. That's how close to home it was. He was pissed! He was like, 'That's not funny!'" Part of Tyler's anger probably had something to do with the fact that Aerosmith's current album at the time *Spinal Tap* was released, 1982's *Rock in a Hard Place*, featured a picture of Stonehenge on the cover. And according to Gibson guitar magazine, "Eddie Van Halen reportedly watched *Tap* with a highly amused audience, yet personally didn't find much to laugh at. 'Everything in that movie had happened to me,' he groused."

One surprising fact about *This is Spinal Tap*, given the "classic" status it currently enjoys among musicians and music fans, is that the film's initial box office returns were modest at best. It wasn't until the movie was released on video that it took on a new life as it was passed around the underground music circuit. And because it took a while for the movie to trickle into the public consciousness, 80s glam bands were largely oblivious to the way their ridiculous posturing had already been lampooned. *Spinal Tap*'s underground status inadvertently kept the movie relevant all the way through the 80s. While making the movie, *Spinal Tap*'s creators thought they were satirizing, in the words of Tommy the limo driver, "a fad, a passing thing." But the fact that glam metal's mainstream ascension accelerated *after* the film was released meant that increasing numbers of music fans who were "in the know" were chuckling every time a new glam band took Tap-esque posturing and pomposity to new levels. And by the early 90s, it seemed like the only ones who weren't in on the joke were the glam bands themselves.

Spinal Tap-esque Glam Metal Goes Mainstream

At the time *This is Spinal Tap* was conceived and filmed, the term "heavy metal" was still a relatively useful descriptive term, making it possible for the movie to skewer the entire genre in one large swath. But in the early 80s, a clear divide began to emerge between fans of the heavier speed and death metal bands like Metallica and Megadeth and those who preferred the lighter and more accessible glam metal of bands like Van Halen and Motley Crue. While the darker and faster metal would remain relatively underground for most of the decade (Metallica didn't become a mainstream mega-band until the 90s), glam metal would become a hugely profitable staple of the 80s rock mainstream. Throughout the decade, thanks to continual play on mainstream rock radio and MTV, glam bands like Van Halen, Def Leppard, Motley Crue, Poison, Bon Jovi, and Guns N' Roses were everywhere.

The term "glam rock" (short for "glamorous rock") has its roots in early 70s glam icons like David Bowie, T. Rex, and The New York Dolls, all of whom included various forms of cross-dressing in their performances. But where the early 70s glam rockers often used their gender-bending performances to challenge mainstream conceptions of both music and gender, 80s glam rockers were far more likely to ascribe to Gene Simmons' rock philosophy; by and large, they were in rock bands to "get laid and make lots of money." Aside from the name "glam rock," few of the bands that played glam rock in the 80s were directly influenced by Bowie and his contemporaries. As Chuck Klosterman explains in *Fargo Rock City*, his 2001 tribute to 80s glam metal:

> Ground zero for the glam movement can be traced to one singular guy—David Bowie. Yet Bowie does not play a role in this discussion, and here's why: He did not directly influence metal (at least not 80s metal). At best, he's at least one full cultural generation removed. Over the past five years, it's become very chic for hard rockers to credit Bowie as a major influence, and it would have been cool if he had been—but most of these bands are lying. All that adoration is coming retrospectively. When hairspray bands were developing in 1983, Bowie was putting out records like 'Let's Dance' and dressing like a waiter from the Olive Garden. At the time, it was certainly not cool for any self-respecting metal dude to emulate David Bowie (even the old Bowie).

Instead, 80s glam mixed the hard rock sound and rock star posturing of mainstream heavy metal bands like Led Zeppelin with the make-up-and-super-hero rock star fantasies of shock rockers like Kiss. Due to the "glamorous" hard rock lifestyle portrayed in their songs, many consider Van Halen the first glam metal band. But the first band to put together all of the elements that would come to characterize the 80s glam image—hairspray, make-up, songs about strippers and booze—was Motley Crue. The Los Angeles-based Crue were hard-living, porn-star-dating rock star caricatures, and they were revered by the teenage boys who comprised the majority of their audience. Even though the rock star slogan "Sex, Drugs, and Rock & Roll" was nothing new—mega-bands like Led Zeppelin had already codified it by the early 70s—Motley Crue was *defined* by the decadent rock star image, and their music seemed to function as little more than a vehicle for their posturing. According to J.D. Considine's *Rolling Stone* review of the Crue's 1983 commercial breakthrough *Shout at the Devil*:

> Like most self-styled bad-boy bands, Motley Crue look meaner than they sound. With their layers of leather and carefully applied makeup, their look suggests all the implied violence required of teenybopper antiheroes. But the music the Crue use to back up that image is surprisingly mild-mannered. It's loud, sure, but that's about as close to dangerous as it gets; Motley Crue's version of rock & roll is such a careful distillation of Black Sabbath, Kiss and other arena giants that you'd almost think it was developed by MTV's marketing staff... In short, originality is not this group's long suit.

Although lacking in creative originality, the rock star caricature created by bands like Motley Crue sold like crazy to teenage boys across the country, for whom the Crue provided an introduction to the rock and roll world. Thanks to the youth and inexperience of their target audience, Motley Crue's make-up-wearing, tough-guy posturing appeared to embody real danger, and through them the 80s glam image was born.

While Motley Crue was pioneering the 80s glam image, British rockers Def Leppard were busy perfecting the 80s glam sound: loud but accessible arena-ready riff-rock with enough pop sensibility to appeal to a few girls as well as boys. The fact Def Leppard had female fans—coupled with the fact that the band members didn't wear make-up—led to some confusion among glam fans as to whether they even qualified as glam metal, even though their sound was the obvious template for most 80s glam. The preponderance of giddy teenage girls at Def Leppard shows tended to undercut their perceived "toughness" or "dangerousness," which were the key selling points for many young male glam fans. But Def Leppard had realized that at least nodding to a female audience paid off in the form of more money—and more groupies—and by the time Poison and Bon Jovi hit the charts in 1986, courting a female audience was becoming the norm for glam bands.

If Motley Crue invented the 80s glam image and Def Leppard created the 80s glam sound, it was L.A. glam-rockers Poison who perfectly combined the two. Their 1986 debut *Look What the Cat Dragged In* fused Motley Crue's hard-partying, make-up-and-hairspray image with Def Leppard's arena-rock sound. The commercial payoff was immediate, as Poison's debut album soared into the *Billboard* charts, eventually peaking at #3 in May of 1987. In many ways, the summer of '87 was glam rock's high water mark. At one point in June, four of the top five slots in the *Billboard* 200 album chart belonged glam rockers: Motley Crue, Poison, Whitesnake, and Bon Jovi—with U2's *The Joshua Tree* being the lone non-glam holdout. Glam metal was so popular by the mid-80s that even "serious" rock magazines were begrudgingly forced to cover the phenomenon, even if they couldn't see any artistic merit in it. Tim Holmes' 1985 *Rolling Stone* article typified the contemporary critical view of glam metal's artistic merits:

> Heavy metal is the idiot-bastard spawn of rock, the eternal embarrassment that will not die. It's music that doesn't care what you think. Like some mythical beast that's part tyrannosaur—slow-moving and pea brained—and part Hydra—multiheaded and malevolent—heavy metal just keeps forging on, flattening everything in its path... Critics scratch their flaccid quills against the hide of the beast, but even if a head should fall, there are ninety more ready to spring up in its place. Punk seemed to offer the kids an alternative in terms of grunge, incompetence and snotty, nosethumbing attitudes. After all, what was punk rock but a revved-up morass of heavy-metal chords? But punk remains a cult taste; what went wrong? ... Punk rock is just too damn smart for its own good, whereas heavy metal, by virtue of its undeniable stupidity, has a built-in survival mechanism that guarantees its astounding regenerative capacity. How else do you explain the ongoing commercial impact of all these groups that possess the exact same idea of what makes a band?

While a lot of glam's popularity certainly had to do with its major label backing and lowest-common-denominator commercial intentions, its appeal also had a lot to do with what glam fans themselves were looking for. For instance, where punk bands like The Clash—and the fans and the critics who took them seriously—were interested in the artistic substance and authenticity of the music, glam bands and their fans had a different conception of rock and roll, and they were interested in something else entirely. According to glam fan Chuck Klosterman in *Fargo Rock City*, "The concept of rock music being tied to glamour is incredibly predictable and—in some respects—essential. Except for those Sarah McLachlan-esque idiots who insist they 'need' to make music, it's really the only reason anyone gets into rock n' roll." And in his follow-up to *Fargo Rock City*, 2003's *Sex, Drugs, and Cocoa Puffs*, Klosterman states flatly, "The musical component of rock isn't nearly as important as the iconography and the posturing and the *idea* of what we're supposed to be experiencing. If given the choice between hearing a great band and seeing a cool band, I'll take the latter every single time." But even that bias towards posturing over substance couldn't keep a legion of glam fans from taking at least one glam band exceedingly seriously. In 1987, Guns N' Roses released their debut album *Appetite for Destruction*.

Guns N' Roses: Attempting to Take the Glam Ethos Seriously

Even though it may seem like there was little in 80s glam rock for fans or critics to take seriously, there was a small minority of rock critics who had always been attracted to certain aspects of the glam rock aesthetic. Their logic, perhaps best exemplified by Joe Carducci's 1990 book *Rock and the Pop Narcotic*, went something like this:

1) It is a given that rock music is artistically and culturally important.
2) Throughout its history, rock music has been most typified by dominant electric guitars, aggressive rhythms, primal sexuality, cocksure masculinity, and juvenile attitudes.
3) Therefore, the rock music that most closely adheres to these qualities is the most artistically and culturally important.

In this kind of equation, virtually no consideration is given to the substantive depth of a song's lyrics, the creative originality of its musical composition and performance, the cultural influence of its content, etc. All of these kinds of considerations are made subservient to the overriding question, *"Does it rock?"* which Carducci uses throughout his book as a guiding principle. And with this question at the fore, he spends most of *Rock and the Pop Narcotic*'s 500 pages praising what he deems the substantive artistic merits of bands who exemplify what he sees as rock's defining "heaviness" while derisively dismissing rock bands who fail to rock hard enough as "faggots" who make "femmy" music that has little or no artistic authenticity. "Heavy" is here defined, in a description attributed to Ted Nugent, as "allowing one's balls to drag on the concrete." Meanwhile, Carducci attributes any objections to the idea that "heaviness" is rock's most important characteristic to the fact that "the official culture...can no longer deal with a hard cock." The ridiculousness of Carducci's premise and its homophobic/misogynistic vocabulary could be dismissed as laughable if it didn't speak for so many people in both metal and hardcore circles, even though many of those people would be unwilling—or unable—to express themselves as clearly and succinctly as Carducci does.

It doesn't take much imagination to see how this kind of aesthetic sensibility could be turned into an aesthetic defense of glam metal, and Guns N' Roses in particular (even though Carducci himself dismisses the whole of 80s glam as "contrived" rather than "authentic" heaviness, and calls Guns N' Roses "a poor, typically 1980s archetype"). But for most 80s glam metal fans—almost all of whom lacked Carducci's encyclopedic knowledge of underground metal and hardcore bands—Guns N' Roses epitomized "rock out with your cock out" authenticity. The difference between Guns N' Roses and other 80s glam bands was simple: Axl Rose. After a brief flirtation with hairspray in the "Welcome to the Jungle" video, he largely avoided the big hair synonymous with 80s glam, instead opting for the grittier biker-bandana look. In addition, the behavior that came off as posturing from other glam bands seemed like it might actually be an extension of Axl's personality, and his perceived seriousness meant that a whole host of glam fans took Guns N' Roses just as seriously as punk fans took bands like The Clash. Unlike most glam rockers, Rose aspired to more than just money and fame; he clearly thought of himself as a serious artist. But his compositions generally failed to live up to his artistic aspirations, often devolving into blatantly ignorant diatribes. For instance, on "One in a Million" from the *GNR Lies* EP, Axl sings:

> *Police and Niggers, that's right,*
> *Get out of my way*
> *Don't need to buy none of your*
> *Gold chains today...*
> *Immigrants and faggots*
> *They make no sense to me*
> *They come to our country*
> *And think they'll do as they please*
> *Like start some mini Iran,*

Or spread some fuckin' disease
They talk so many goddamn ways
It's all Greek to me...
Radicals and Racists
Don't point your finger at me
I'm a small town white boy
Just tryin' to make ends meet
Don't need your religion
Don't watch that much T.V.
Just makin' my livin', baby
Well that's enough for me...

According to *Rolling Stone*'s 2003 *Album Guide*, "'Million' is unforgivable mostly because it's stupid." And *Village Voice* critic Robert Christgau said, "['One in a Million'] is disgusting because it's heartfelt and disgusting again because it's a grandstand play. It gives away the 'joke' (to quote the chickenshit 'apologies' on the cover) about the offed girlfriend the way 'Turn around bitch I've got a use for you' [from 'It's So Easy'] gives away 'Sweet Child o' Mine.'" The ignorance apparent in many of Guns N' Roses' songs seemed to validate Jon Landau's earlier assessment that "rock and roll musicians are banal, amateurish, and insipidly stupid when they try to express their philosophy of life in the context of popular music." But while "One in a Million" made an easy target for critics, Christgau's review hinted at the larger danger in taking Joe Carducci's misogynistic rock aesthetic seriously.

Glam rock's portrayal of women was never one of the genre's strong suits, but it was certainly one of its defining characteristics. It was no accident that 80s metal was commonly referred to as "cock rock," and accusations of heavy metal's overt misogyny have been around as long as there has been heavy metal. In fact, charges of misogyny were central to Tipper Gore's PMRC campaign in the 80s which sought to get warning labels on rock albums. But as long as such accusations were aimed at glam rock, it was hard to take them much more seriously than the music itself. As notorious glam video director David Mallet put it, "Why did I put the girls in a cage? Girls belong in cages, come on." In the face of such flippancy, crusaders like Gore had trouble gaining any traction; how worked up could anyone *really* get about the patently ridiculous music videos for Van Halen's "Hot for Teacher" or Warrant's "Cherry Pie?" But Guns N' Roses' attempt to turn the glam metal ethos into a substantive artistic statement cast their portrayals of women in songs like "It's So Easy" and "Back Off Bitch" in a different light. In fact, when both Axl Rose's ex-wife Erin Everly and ex-fiancée Stephanie Seymour accused Rose of domestic violence—Everly said that throughout her four years with Rose she had suffered regular beatings that left her bruised, bloodied, and sometimes unconscious—there was a sense in which the accusations gave Rose a measure of misogynistic *authenticity* (after all, Rose's physical abuse of Seymour in the music video for "Don't Cry" was *based on real life*).

Sadly, the centrality of misogyny to the glam metal aesthetic has led even the most seemingly enlightened of the genre's apologists to defend it. According to Klosterman in *Fargo Rock City*:

> Okay, fine. *Heavy metal was sexist*. It's a judgment call and I'm making the judgment. But that raises yet another question: What's the big deal? ... It's either (a) a marketing ploy, or (b) a negative artistic statement. Either way, it's completely defensible. If these groups were making women into whores for the sole purpose of selling records, they are a *reflection* of society—not the problem that's poisoning it. The nature of capitalism is to feed on desire. A commercial entity will take on whatever characteristics it needs to move the product. For 80s rock, that was misogyny. And if you find that 'irresponsible,' you are naïve.

Such a defense falls flat for obvious reasons. Most glam rock was indeed created for commercial rather than artistic reasons, and if one is inclined to dismiss Motley Crue and their blatant commercialism as unimportant, one could perhaps dismiss their misogyny along with everything else. But Klosterman's entire mission in writing *Fargo Rock City* was to rehabilitate glam's *artistic* reputation, which necessitates taking a band like Guns N' Roses seriously as important artists. This is why, for instance, he devotes six pages of the book to a serious critical assessment of the *GNR Lies* EP, including a 1000 word comparison of the four songs on side two to the first four books of the New Testament (in Klosterman's analogy, the overtly racist and homophobic diatribe "One in a Million" is the Gospel of John). Such exercises only serve to illustrate that the music—not to mention its message—doesn't live up to such serious treatments. And this is why, in contrast to Klosterman's take on the band, the prevailing critical opinion of Guns N' Roses in the late-80s sounded more like *Mojo*'s Barney Hoskyns' take in *Fargo Rock City*, "I thought Guns

N' Roses was really tired… I have no idea what anyone ever saw in Axl Rose. It seemed like so many people wanted him to be some kind of subversive voice from a small town, kind of like Kurt Cobain. But he never was Cobain. He never meant anything important."

While the desire among some critics to take glam metal seriously can be attributed to a belief in the primacy of the "heavy rock" aesthetic defined by Carducci, it was also the result of two additional factors. First, there was the legacy inherited from some early rock critics that rock music was an *inherently* important art form worthy of serious treatment. Second, there was the fact that most of the artistically substantive rock music in the 80s was being created *underground*. And these two factors worked together. The first factor encouraged young rock fans to believe in rock's inherent importance, while the second factor meant that millions of American small-town residents—without access to a local alternative or college radio station—could plausibly assume that glam metal comprised the totality of rock music being made at the time. These factors help explain both the importance accorded to lightweights like Guns N' Roses and the obliviousness to the burgeoning 80s alternative scene which Klosterman (who grew up in tiny Wyndmere, North Dakota—population 429) displays throughout *Fargo Rock City* in passages like this:

> [Axl] Rose slowly evolved into the first artist of my generation who showed glimpses of an (ahem) alternative to the larger-than-life fairy tale of poofy-haired metal that was the template for all my favorite bands… Axl did this first, and his tools were hostility and confusion. Cobain came a few years later and he used personal angst and sexual tolerance.

In light of the thousands of bands in the alternative scene that pre-dated Guns N' Roses arrival on the rock scene (including alternative bands like U2 and R.E.M. who had already crossed over into the mainstream), the idea that Rose was rock's first 80s "alternative" to "poofy-haired metal" is far-fetched, indeed. And Klosterman's suggestion that Nirvana was the *first* alternative rock band is equally ill-informed; a much more convincing argument could be made that Nirvana—inasmuch as they signaled the commercial culmination of a decade-long underground movement—was the *last* true representative of the alternative music scene.

THE IDIOT-BASTARD SPAWN OF ROCK

The problem with the rock narratives in under-researched personal memoirs like *Fargo Rock City* is that they present a wildly inaccurate view of history, in this case downplaying the significance of the sea change that occurred when alternative music ousted glam as rock's popular torchbearer, thus obscuring the reasons that such a shift took place in the first place. There were real reasons that Nirvana refused to tour with Guns N' Roses in the early 90s; not least of which being the fact that the testosterone-fueled misogyny that GNR embodied was one of Kurt Cobain's least favorite qualities in anyone, let alone a rival rock band. There were real reasons that, in the wake of the early 90s alternative revolution, glam rock was largely relegated to seedier fringes of cultural respectability: professional wrestling, strip clubs, and other places where the misogyny inherent in the music fit the less enlightened, predominantly male atmosphere. And there were real reasons for alternative music's unprecedented burst of commercial success in the early 90s, which helped spur album sales to record heights and echoed rock's late 60s surge in popularity. When people who have been primarily exposed to insipid musical clichés for years on end are suddenly confronted with a substantive artistic statement, a lot of them will recognize the difference immediately. And in the early 90s, after nearly a decade of being subjected to the lazy, commercially-driven stereotypes that pervaded glam rock, many mainstream rock listeners who were exposed to the alternative scene for the first time immediately heard something different in it. What they heard in alternative music was—at long last—rock music that had *something to say.*

Chapter Five

We Want to Do Something Different

U2, R.E.M., 120 Minutes, and
Alternative Music's Mainstream Insurgency

120 Minutes

By the mid-1980s, the alternative music template pioneered by Rick Carroll and Rodney Bingenheimer at KROQ had spread to countless commercial and college radio stations across the country and was starting to trickle into the mainstream as an identifiable scene. And on March 10, 1986, MTV launched a new weekly program called *120 Minutes* in order to capitalize on the growing alternative market. Prior to *120 Minutes*, alternative music scenes had generally been tied to geography: the local alternative radio station, the local alternative rock venue, the local independent record store, the local indie label. But *120 Minutes* both reflected and helped create an increasingly cohesive national phenomenon, and through its unifying power alternative music fans began to realize that there were like-minded fans all across the country who were sick of mainstream rock's tired clichés. And because there was no definitive alternative music style, local scenes as musically diverse as the ones exploding in Seattle, WA, Athens, GA, and Manchester, England could all be seen as part of the same alternative scene. According to *120 Minutes* creator Dave Kendall's account on the show's farewell episode in 2003, "There were so many different types of music on *120 Minutes*. You had the goth bands and you

63

had the jangle-rock of R.E.M. You had sort of novelty bands like They Might Be Giants. There wasn't any single form of music that alternative represented, just more of an attitude: We want to do something different. We don't want to do the cookie-cutter clichés of the pop mainstream."

Athens, Georgia's R.E.M. was one of *120 Minutes*' flagship bands in the early years. Even though their music was distributed by a major label, they didn't sound anything like mainstream rock. According to Kendall, "R.E.M. were important simply because they defied a lot of the usual expectations for brash, loud, exuberant rock music at that time. They were very understated, very passionate." And unlike the rock star fantasies of mainstream glam acts like Motley Crue, R.E.M. tended to write songs about real people dealing with real life situations. Their first video to air on *120 Minutes* was for a song called "Driver 8," which tells the story of a burnt out, working-class train engineer in the rural south. Even though R.E.M. was distributed by a major label, their understated, southern-tinged passion plays had more in common with the stories of William Faulkner, Walker Percy, and Flannery O'Connor than they did with the fluorescent histrionics of most mainstream rock. And the video for "Driver 8"—which was little more than cobbled-together video footage of trains rolling through the rural American South—was a perfect reflection of that difference. "'Driver 8' was remarkable because it was also kind of an anti-video," says Kendall. "It wasn't like the pop stars doing their thrusting motions on stage. It's just very kind of passive, quiet, ethereal."

The exposure that R.E.M gained on *120 Minutes* helped propel them into the national consciousness. After somewhat middling sales of their first three albums, R.E.M.'s 1986 release *Life's Rich Pageant* was certified as the band's first gold record in early 1987. And just after the release of their next album, *Document*, in September 1987, the *New York Times* was able to say:

> R.E.M. has shrugged off most of rock's accepted ways and means of songwriting and career-building. In the six years since R.E.M.'s first single appeared, the band has built a dedicated audience... R.E.M. has become the model for independent rock bands in the 1980s, proof that a band can follow its better instincts, ignore pop-world indignities and still reach a huge listenership. *Document* is both confident and defiant; if R.E.M. is about to move from cult-band status to mass popularity, the album decrees that the band will get there on its own terms... anyone who listens regularly to pop is

likely to feel [*Document*'s] unfamiliar breaks and recurrences as a subliminal agitation.

Even though the band had continued to follow its own unique creative vision and had continued to buck mainstream trends, *Document* climbed to #10 on the *Billboard* charts—R.E.M.'s first Top 20 album—and it was certified as their first platinum album the following January. Meanwhile, their growing popularity was evidence that there was still an audience for rock music with artistic aspirations. And in the midst of glam rock's popular hegemony, the rock criticism old guard was thrilled to have an American rock band of substance to talk about; in December of 1987, the cover of *Rolling Stone* proclaimed R.E.M. to be "America's Best Rock & Roll Band." While some indie purists decried the band's move to major label Warner Brothers in 1988, both *120 Minutes* and the nationwide network of alternative radio stations stuck by them, continuing to include the band on their playlists well into the 90s. As R.E.M.'s independent attitude and continued musical adventurousness signaled their separation from mainstream rock, their growing sales figures began to signal mainstream acceptance. Eventually, R.E.M. would become popular enough that their videos began to get play in MTV's regular rotation alongside Bon Jovi and Madonna, where they tended to stick out like an understated sore thumb.

In addition to playing American acts like R.E.M., The Pixies, Dramarama, Concrete Blonde, Cowboy Junkies, Soul Asylum, Michael Penn, Camper Van Beethoven, Jane's Addiction, Tom Waits, The Replacements, Lemonheads, and The Violent Femmes, *120 Minutes* also broadened the base for countless British acts whose only previous American exposure had been on the growing underground network of KROQ-inspired alternative radio stations. According to longtime *120 Minutes* host Matt Pinfield, who joined Kendall for the interview on the show's 2003 farewell episode, "One of the things about alternative music and *120 Minutes* is that it was really a showcase for a lot of British bands when they would first come over... The only place they got exposure were alternative [radio] stations, but it was always spearheaded by *120 Minutes*." And so, throughout the late 80s, *120 Minutes* helped introduce a national American audience to British acts like New Order, The Smiths, The The, The Jesus and Mary Chain, James, Public Image Ltd., Siouxsie & The Banshees, Echo and the Bunnymen, XTC, The Stone Roses, UB40, The

Wonderstuff, Pet Shop Boys, Robyn Hitchcock, Talk Talk, The Happy Mondays, The Charlatans U.K., and Billy Bragg, among many others (*120 Minutes* also played videos by other international bands, most notably Australian bands like Midnight Oil, Crowded House, and The Church). But there were two bands in particular who did more than any others during the late 1980s to raise the profile of the British bands within the American alternative scene.

The Cure—much like R.E.M.—recorded for a small independent label that was distributed by a major label, and they, too, had released a string of albums that achieved only modest U.S. sales, even though they were staples on alternative radio. By the mid-80s, they were household names in England, but it wasn't until *120 Minutes* exposed the band to a wider U.S. audience that they entered the national consciousness in the States. Their 1987 video for "Just Like Heaven" went into rotation on *120 Minutes* and helped make the song their first Top 40 single in the U.S. It also helped make *Kiss Me, Kiss Me, Kiss Me* their first Top 40 album. By the time they released *Disintegration* in 1989, they had become one of *120 Minutes'* favorite bands, and their video for "Lovesong" crossed over into MTV's regular programming, helping make *Disintegration* the band's first platinum album in the U.S. But even while The Cure's career arc mirrored R.E.M.'s—both bands were alternative radio mainstays nudged into the mainstream with the help of *120 Minutes*—their images and musical styles couldn't have been less similar. While R.E.M. opted for muted Southern understatement, The Cure's image was anything but understated—Robert Smith's goth make-up and lavish mini-operas seemed like they were from an entirely different continent, which of course they were. But such was the loose umbrella of alternative music that R.E.M. and The Cure could comfortably sit side-by-side in cassette racks and alternative radio playlists across the country.

1987 also marked Depeche Mode's debut in the U.S. Top 40 with their album *Music for the Masses*. Like The Cure, they too had been household names in England and staples on American alternative radio since the early 80s. And their progressive, computer-enhanced beats had helped make their music a dance-club phenomenon. But it wasn't until their videos for "Strangelove" and "Never Let Me Down Again" went into rotation on *120 Minutes* in 1987 that they began to reach a mainstream U.S. audience. Then, on August 29, 1989, Depeche Mode released the single "Personal Jesus" from their forthcoming album *Violator*. The video, which featured grainy footage of the band dressed as cowboys visiting a remote Spanish brothel, was something of a sensation; the controversial juxtaposition of the lyrics—which criticized televangelism— with images of a whorehouse (thus implicitly equating the two) was not lost on American viewers. The success of "Personal Jesus" signaled the fact that *Violator*, which was scheduled for release in March of 1990, was going to be more than just another modest alternative hit. The album's second single and video "Enjoy the Silence" was so popular that it aired on three straight *120 Minutes* episodes in April of 1990, something the show had never done before with a single video. But by that point, "Enjoy the Silence" was already in heavy rotation in MTV's regular daytime programming and *Violator* was becoming a hit album by any standard. The album went platinum within two months of its release, and within a year it had become the first album by any British band played on *120 Minutes* to go multi-platinum in the U.S. Even so, Depeche Mode wasn't the most popular U.K.-based alternative band on the U.S. charts. There was an Irish band whose popular breakthrough predated *120 Minutes* and proved long before Nirvana that it was possible for an alternative band to achieve both universal critical acclaim and massive commercial success, in the process demonstrating that there were millions of Americans willing to buy albums by rock bands that didn't fit the mainstream glam rock mold.

U2: The Alternative Scene's First Breakthrough Band

The shameless commercial pandering of U2's partnership with Apple for the release of their 2014 album *Songs of Innocence*—and the almost universal critical backlash which accompanied that stunt—make it easy to forget that the common conception of U2 as a compromised, corporate mega-band is a relatively recent phenomenon. Prior to the late 90s, they were largely perceived as artistically adventurous trend-setters, as that rare popular band that refused to compromise to corporate pressures; they were challengers of mainstream rock stereotypes, not the embodiment of them. U2's roots were in the first wave of punk that swept the U.K. in the late 70s. They then spent the first half of the 80s as one of KROQ's flagship bands, even before the term "alternative" had gone into wide circulation. When *The Joshua Tree* made them mega-stars in 1987, they were anything but typical of mainstream rock at the time. And even as their popularity skyrocketed, *The Joshua Tree* continued to get play on underground alternative radio stations across the country. Much like R.E.M. and The Cure, U2's popularity didn't alienate them from the alternative scene. Instead, their mainstream success was seen as a victory for alternative music, a sign that artistically substantive rock bands didn't have to sell out creatively in order to reach a wide audience. Even in the early 90s, more than a decade into their career, U2's *Achtung Baby* became an alternative radio staple, getting airplay alongside Nirvana and Pearl Jam as the alternative scene took over mainstream rock from the glam bands. And their ZOO TV tour of 1992-93 was a revolutionary marriage between sweeping artistic experimentation and mainstream size and scope. Had it been Bono, rather than Kurt Cobain, who had met a tragic death in 1994, the legacies of both U2 and Nirvana would be perceived very differently today.

U2 was formed in Dublin, Ireland in the late 70s with schoolmates Paul Hewson (who would later take the stage name Bono) on vocals, Dave Evans (who would take the stage name The Edge) on guitar, Adam Clayton on bass, and Larry Mullen, Jr. on drums. Their initial inspiration was the punk music that was exploding across the Irish Sea in London. According to Bono in 2006's autobiographical *U2 by U2*, "I was very bored with music at the time... I didn't really like heavy rock. I was looking for something different. And then I remember hearing The Radiators from Space. They were Ireland's first punk band... When I heard [them] my ears pricked up... And I said, 'We can play this. We really can play this. And not only can we play it, but this is the kind of shit I like.' So we were off then."

In keeping with the punk and post-punk tradition, the band was formed before any of the members were accomplished musicians. According to Clayton in *U2 by U2*, "We were very unschooled musicians who were just ripe for the energy of punk when it came along. We were just exuberant enthusiasts and who knows where that flame would have gone without punk? Punk opened the door. It created a language. This was 1977, it was just kicking off in England. A neighbor of mine... had the Sex Pistols singles and we would go round to his house and listen to them along with anything else that was coming out: The Buzzcocks, The Damned, Slaughter and the Dogs, The Stranglers, The Clash." The Edge backs up Clayton's assessment in the same collection of interviews, "I suppose a watershed moment would have been seeing The Jam on *Top of the Pops* and realizing that actually not knowing how to play was not a problem, in that music was more about energy and trying to say something and not necessarily about musicianship. So it was a great encouragement to hear these bands were playing very simple stuff."

U2 went on a short hiatus in the summer of 1977 while Clayton worked a job in London, and he returned to Ireland with treasures for the rest of the band from the punk mecca. "I'd buy records in London and bring them back," says Clayton. "So that particular summer I'd bought Patti Smith's *Horses*, Television's *Marquee Moon*, the first Clash album, The Stranglers... and a heavy metal album by a group called Lonestar that did not go down as well. When I came back, I think the rest of the guys had been listening to things like Richard Hell, so everyone latched on to the same kind of music." While the members of U2 were quickly becoming punk devotees, they also gravitated to the puck acts who stood out from the pack, particularly Patti Smith, whose poetic lyrics were inspirational for the young band.

As U2 developed its trademark sound, the band attempted to incorporate punk's energy and urgency with Patti Smith's poetic lyrical approach. And attempts at that combination are evident in their first two albums, 1980's *Boy* and 1981's *October*. While *Boy* was a critical success, *October* was panned by critics and failed to match *Boy*'s modest sales. But their first single "I Will Follow" had managed to make KROQ's year-end Top 25 in 1981 and there was some underground anticipation for their third album, which was released in February of 1983. On the strength of almost universal critical acclaim, *War* became U2's first gold record in the U.S. and "New Years' Day" and "Sunday, Bloody Sunday" got play on the growing number of underground radio stations around America who were following KROQ's lead. J.D. Considine's 4-star *Rolling Stone* review was typical of *War*'s critical reception:

> *Boy* waxed poetic on the mysteries of childhood without really illuminating any of them; *October*, its successor, wrapped itself in romance and religion but didn't seem to understand either. Without a viewpoint that could conform to the stirring rhythms and sweeping crescendos of their music, U2 often ended up sounding dangerously glib. With their third album, *War*, U2 have found just such a perspective, and with it, have generated their most fulfilling work yet. *War* makes for impressive listening... the songs here stand up against anything on the Clash's *London Calling* in terms of sheer impact, and

the fact that U2 can sweep the listener up in the same sort of enthusiastic romanticism that fuels the band's grand gestures is an impressive feat.

The visceral power and political overtones of "Sunday, Bloody Sunday" stood out from the mainstream and echoed The Clash's ability to create sonically powerful rock music that also *had something to say.* "Sunday Bloody Sunday" also kicked off U2's first live album, *Under a Blood Red Sky,* which was released in November of '83. And together with *War,* it marked the band's transcendence of punk minimalism into something uniquely their own. In his January 1984 review of *Under a Blood Red Sky* for *Rolling Stone,* Christopher Connelly raved, "The high point is 'Sunday Bloody Sunday.' It may not be a rebel song, as Bono tells a presumably baffled German audience, but it is practically everything else: an anguished, thoughtful synthesis of religious and political beliefs, backed by the bone-crushing arena-rock riff of the decade. This is 'Stairway to Heaven' for smart people."

The comparison to Led Zeppelin is apt, and it highlights the particular appeal of the alternative scene that U2 was at the vanguard of. In contrast to heavy metal, the band that U2 was becoming was thoughtful as well as loud, substantive as well as anthemic. And in contrast with its members' punk roots, U2 was accessible in addition to being energetic, musically focused in addition to being passionate, willing to incorporate complex musical ideas as opposed to rigidly minimalistic. In the 80s, alternative music—as typified by bands like U2 and R.E.M. and The Cure—inhabited a rock middle ground between obscurantist indie post-punk and the bloated glam mainstream. Alternative music championed the substantive artistic possibilities of rock without holding to the dogmatic assertion that any music that was even mildly popular was, by definition, artistically bankrupt. U2 proved that, even in the midst of the 80s glam metal morass, a band could have mainstream success and still stay true to its artistic vision, and thus the band maintained its credibility with its initial alternative radio fanbase. And U2's next album would be an even greater success, both commercially and on alternative radio.

1984's *The Unforgettable Fire* was U2's first album with the production team of Brian Eno and Daniel Lanois. And through their collaboration, U2 would build on its increasingly distinctive sound, adding keyboards and more studio-based experimentation into the mix. However, the album's anthemic lead single "Pride (In the Name of Love)"—with its soaring vocal and its implicitly political tribute to Martin Luther King Jr.—picked up right where "Sunday, Bloody Sunday" had left off. "Pride" was voted #3 on KROQ's 1984 year-end alternative chart, and it simultaneously became U2's first Top 40 single, while *The Unforgettable Fire* became U2's first platinum album in the U.S. Even so, U2 was not a household name outside of Ireland and the U.K. until their show-stealing performance at Live Aid on July 13, 1985 in front of a television audience of 1.9 billion people. The anthemic bombast of U2's performance of "Sunday, Bloody Sunday" more than filled out Wembley Stadium, and the song's martial beat and political urgency perfectly captured the moral and political ethos of the event itself. When contrasted with many of the other bands playing that day, U2's performance inadvertently exposed the vapidity of much of the concert's rock star posturing. In many ways, U2's Live Aid performance of "Sunday, Bloody Sunday" was the culmination of rock's 1960s aspirations—never had such a pointedly political rock song been performed at such a momentous political rock event. And U2's subsequent performance that day of "Bad" from *The Unforgettable Fire* defied the hero-worshipping template for artist-fan relationships which had been codified by more than a decade of rock star posturing, as Bono broke the invisible wall between performer and audience in order to climb down from the stage scaffolding into the 72,000 in attendance to rev them up and pull out dance partners to join him on stage.

Folk icon Joan Baez—who had performed earlier in the day at the Philadelphia portion of the Live Aid concert—remembered the experience of watching U2 that day in her 1985 autobiography. "[Bono] doesn't fuck the microphone the way rock stars do when they realize that technology has made it possible for them to extend their egos out over a crowd of thousands. No, this young man is deadly serious about something, and is expressing himself with such tenderness it is enough to break my heart…" And in response to Bono's trip into the crowd to pull out dance partners, she wrote, "I can't recall ever having seen anything like it in my life. It is an act, but it is not an act. It is a private moment, accepted by seventy thousand people. The dance is short, sensuous, and heartbreakingly tender… Rock stars can look and be serious, but it is usually about themselves or their inflated vision of themselves. None of us who stand in front of a hundred thousand people hearing our voice (and band) amplified, tampered with, echoed, and smoothed into cosmic velveteen can escape certain grandiose delusions about ourselves. But this Irish lad is involved with something more than self-aggrandizement." Finally, Baez concluded, "Out of the hours of Live Aid that I saw by the end of the day, the high point was witnessing the magic of U2. They moved me as nothing else moved me."

Thanks in large part to their Live Aid performance, U2 had become one of the most recognizable rock bands in the world, virtually overnight. And the anticipation for their next album was therefore higher than expected for a band with such a modest sales history. As *Rolling Stone* said at the time, "The stakes are enormous and U2 knows it."

One of the great misconceptions about *The Joshua Tree* is that it was a safe album, a commercial play, a bland, middling gloss that meshed thematically with the ethos of a decade in which the honest exploration of dark subject matter was publicly frowned upon. In fact, none of those opinions about the album were prevalent at the time of its release. Instead, review after review noted the dark nature of the content on *The Joshua Tree*, its blatant indictment of the dark side of American imperialism, and just how out of step it was with the rest of mainstream rock. And virtually all of those reviews praised the band for its unwillingness to compromise. According to Steve Pond's *Rolling Stone* review on April 9, 1987:

> The title befits a record that concerns itself with resilience in the face of utter social and political desolation… More than any other U2 album, *The Joshua Tree* has the power and allure to seduce and capture a mass audience on its own terms… But if this is a breakthrough, it's a grim, dark-hued one. At first, refreshingly honest romantic declarations alternate with unsettling religious imagery. Then it gets blacker… But for all its gloom, the album is never a heavy-handed diatribe… *The Joshua Tree* is an appropriate response to these times, and a picture bleaker than any U2 has ever painted: a vision of blasted hopes, pointless violence, and anguish. But this is not a band to surrender to defeatism. Its last album ended with a gorgeous elegy to Martin Luther King, Jr.; *The Joshua Tree* closes with a haunting ode to other victims. 'Mothers of the Disappeared' is built around desolate images of loss but the setting is soothing and restorative—music of great sadness but also unutterable compassion, acceptance, and calm. *The Unforgettable Chill*, you might call this album, and *unforgettable* is certainly the right word.

According to Robert Hilburn of the *L.A. Times*, "These are human tales of reaching for your ideals while battling against moments of doubt and despair: drug addiction ('Running to Stand Still'), the death of a friend ('One Tree Hill'), government terrorism ('Mothers of the Disappeared') and social injustice ('Red Hill Mining Town')... The songs are about faith, but—as suggested by such titles as 'Where the Streets Have No Name' and 'I Still Haven't Found What I'm Looking For'—they aren't tidy statements of rejoicing." According to critic Thom Duffy, "*The Joshua Tree* does not find U2 offering th[e] masses glib anthems for the 80s. Instead, in extraordinarily intense rock 'n' roll terms, this LP explores the uncertainty and pain of a spiritual pilgrimage through a bleak and harsh world." And in May of '87, *Rolling Stone*'s Anthony DeCurtis predicted that the album would become "one of the most successful, not to mention most important, albums of the decade... [But] the sheer aural pleasure of *The Joshua Tree* and the awesome, uplifting power of U2's live shows will probably obscure the fact that the album is as foreboding a record as can be imagined." DeCurtis was ultimately proven correct on all counts.

However, even DeCurtis's predictions of success couldn't foretell the popular phenomenon the album would become. *The Joshua Tree* was the fastest selling album to date in U.K. history, selling over 300,000 copies in just two days. In the U.S., the album quickly shot to #1, where it stayed for nine weeks (it would spend 35 weeks in the Top 10). 3 million copies were sold in the U.S. alone in less than two months, on its way to selling over 25 million copies worldwide. The album spawned two #1 singles in the U.S., "With or Without You" and "I Still Haven't Found What I'm Looking For," and a third song, "Where the Streets Have No Name," made the Top 20. Perhaps more surprisingly, given the album's astronomical sales figures, was how popular it remained among alternative radio fans. KROQ's 1987 year-end countdown featured three U2 songs in the Top 20, five in the Top 50, and eight in the Top 100. And the album even garnered praise from the notably obscurantist *Village Voice*'s Robert Christgau, who opined in his review, "Let it build and ebb and wash and thunder in the background and you'll hear something special— mournful and passionate, stately and involved." U2 had managed to become the world's biggest-selling rock band without losing—and instead expanding—its alternative fanbase. In the process, the band shattered the glass ceiling on the success of alternative music, paving the way for the subsequent success of alternative bands from R.E.M. to Nirvana.

As *The Joshua Tree* sat atop the charts, it was noticeably out of step with the other acts who populated the *Billboard* Top 20. For instance, at one point during *The Joshua Tree*'s nine week stint at #1, the other four acts in the Top 5 were all glam rock bands: Motley Crue, Poison, Whitesnake, and Bon Jovi. But it wasn't just U2's music that was out of step with the rock mainstream; the band also deigned to challenge the "Sex, Drugs, and Rock and Roll" fantasy that was the backbone of glam rock. "I don't accept the rock & roll mythology of living on the edge," Bono told *Rolling Stone* in May 1987, just after The Joshua Tree had gone to #1. "I don't accept that. We're all pretty much removed from reality I suppose—the reality of life and death. But rock & roll is even *more* removed from reality. Rock & roll artists who are living on the edge—what can they possibly have to offer? Their songs are written from such a removed point of view." In the same interview, Bono also challenged the notion that U2's spiritual exploration of serious, big-picture questions fell outside the rock and roll purview. "Marvin Gaye, Patti Smith, Van Morrison, Bob Dylan, Stevie Wonder—I don't think there's anyone I like in rock & roll that isn't as screwed up as me in this area. Rock & roll devoid of that spiritual confusion is the rock & roll I don't like anyway. I started realizing, 'Hey, we're not the odd ones out. This shit on the radio is the odd stuff.' It's a natural place to be."

However, in 1987, the "shit on the radio" still had enough of a chokehold on the charts that the time wasn't yet ripe for an alternative music overthrow. And the alternative scene, while growing, was still too underdeveloped to offer much of a commercial threat to mainstream rock. But the success of *The Joshua Tree* had exposed the cracks in glam's popular rock monopoly, and the seeds of a mainstream rock revolution had been sown. By the time U2 finished two world tours on the strength of *The Joshua Tree*, the alternative breakthrough of 1991 was just around the corner. In the intervening years U2 would discover just how hard it was to maintain touch with reality while also being big-time rock stars. After the release of the sprawling tour film *Rattle and Hum* in 1988, questions about U2's continued relevance were beginning to arise among both fans and critics. Had they become the out of touch rock stars they had criticized just a year earlier? Before becoming an active participant in the alternative overthrow of mainstream rock, it was clear that U2 would, in Bono's words, "have to go away and dream it all up again." Their reinvention and re-emergence in late 1991 was unlike anything anyone familiar with their music would have predicted. *Achtung Baby* and the subsequent ZOO TV tour would answer any lingering doubts about the band's artistic commitment or relevance, and—alongside Nirvana—they would play a vital part in the toppling of the mainstream glam rock edifice.

1991: Dispatches from an Alternative Nation on the Brink

Throughout 1991, there was an increasing amount of evidence that alternative music—that great rock music middle class that inhabited the space between indie obscurity and mainstream ubiquity—was primed for a breakthrough. The scene that had its humble beginnings in a failed Los Angeles radio station had grown steadily, forged a unique identity, spread to isolated outposts throughout America, and been unified into a cohesive scene with its own infrastructure, all while maintaining its creative freedom and defying stylistic categorization. Throughout the 80s, sporadic popular flare-ups had demonstrated the popular appeal of alternative music, but in the year prior to the seismic breakthrough of Nirvana's "Smells Like Teen Spirit," the rumblings of seemingly unrelated events taking place around the world were loosening the ground, serving as dispatches from the underground, warning of an impending quake.

. . .

Los Angeles, California—December 1, 1990: KROQ sponsors its first year-end "Almost Acoustic Christmas" concert at the Gibson Amphitheatre in Universal City. The show features a diverse lineup of the alternative radio station's favorite acts, including Dramarama, Social Distortion, Chris Isaak, The Posies, and The Trashcan Sinatras. The "Almost Acoustic Christmas" show is a huge success and goes on to become KROQ's signature concert event.

. . .

Athens, Georgia—March 12, 1991: R.E.M releases its seventh studio album, *Out of Time*. It hits #1 on the *Billboard* charts on May 18, supplanting Mariah Carey's debut album in order to become R.E.M.'s first #1 album. By the end of the year, the album has sold more copies than all of R.E.M.'s previous albums combined, well on its way to over 4 million copies sold in the U.S. alone. The single "Losing My Religion" goes to #4 on the *Billboard* singles charts and the video becomes a staple on MTV, where it is rewarded with the Video Music Award for "Video of the Year." The song is also an alternative radio sensation and finishes #1 in KROQ's 1991 year-end countdown, ahead of Nirvana's "Smells Like Teen Spirit," which finishes #2.

. . .

Essex, England—March 19, 1991: In a telling sign of British alternative music's popularity in America, Depeche Mode's *Violator* is certified double-platinum by the RIAA . The album will go on to sell over 3 million copies in the U.S. alone.

. . .

Seattle, Washington—April 17, 1991: Having recently added new drummer Dave Grohl, a little-known Seattle band called Nirvana debuts a song called "Smells Like Teen Spirit" at Seattle's OK Hotel. It is the band's last live performance before officially signing with Geffen Records on April 30 and departing for Los Angeles to record their major label debut.

. . .

Seattle, Washington—April 17, 1991: Meanwhile, on the very same night that Nirvana debuts "Smells Like Teen Spirit" at the OK Hotel, Cameron Crowe is *across the street* filming a concert by the Seattle band Alice In Chains to be included in his forthcoming feature film *Singles*. Crowe is on location in Seattle, filming in his adopted hometown largely because he feels the city's vibrant music scene will make a great backdrop for the love story he is telling. The film is to prominently feature appearances by Seattle bands Alice in Chains, Soundgarden, and a new band called Pearl Jam, who is already in the process of recording its debut album at Seattle's London Bridge Studios. Crowe had been a fan of the band Mother Love Bone, and chooses to model the look of Matt Dillon's character in *Singles* on former Mother Love Bone (and current Pearl Jam) bassist Jeff Ament, whose clothes Dillon wears throughout the movie. The members of Pearl Jam are also tapped to play the backing members of Dillon's fictional band Citizen Dick.

. . .

Phoenix, Arizona—July 18, 1991: Lollapalooza, a brand new alternative concert tour and outdoor festival, gets off to an inauspicious beginning when its first show, scheduled to take place in Phoenix, Arizona, has to be cancelled due to technical difficulties. However, the festival quickly recovers and successfully tours the country for six weeks. Originally conceived as a farewell tour for Jane's Addiction by frontman Perry Farrell, Lollapalooza also features alternative acts Siouxsie & The Banshees, Nine Inch Nails, Butthole Surfers, Rollins Band, and The Violent Femmes, in addition to Jane's Addiction, who serves as the tour's headliner. The tour is the surprise success of the summer, and additional shows have to be added in Los Angeles, San Francisco, and Boston to meet demand, demonstrating the growing national market for alternative music. Along the way, Farrell begins referring to the festival's attendees as "Alternative Nation."

. . .

Reading, England—August 23, 1991: The three-day Reading Festival kicks off. After being rebranded as an alternative music festival in 1989, 1991's incarnation features twenty-eight alternative bands on the main stage, including The Sisters of Mercy, Ned's Atomic Dustbin, James, Blur, Teenage Fanclub, Iggy Pop, Sonic Youth, and Dinosaur Jr. Over 30,000 people are in attendance for the three-day festival, making it the single largest alternative music event to date. Nirvana—who has finished recording but has not yet released its major label debut—is relegated to a mid-day slot on the festival's opening day, the least well-attended segment of the festival.

. . .

Seattle, Washington—August 27, 1991: Pearl Jam releases its debut album *Ten*.

WE WANT TO DO SOMETHING DIFFERENT

. . .

Dublin, Ireland—September 17, 1991: Mixing of U2's new album concludes at Dublin's Windmill Lane Studios. The following day, guitarist The Edge flies to Los Angeles deliver the completed masters of the album, now titled *Achtung Baby*.

. . .

Los Angeles, California—September 17, 1991: Guns N' Roses release their epic *Use Your Illusion* double-album. The album is a huge commercial success, but it proves to be glam rock's last gasp. Even before the album is released, Guns N' Roses is falling apart, and the double-album will be the band's final album of original music for 17 years. In addition, by the time of *Use Your Illusion*, most of glam's other heavy hitters are also in trouble. Def Leppard has lost its founding guitarist to drugs and alcohol. Bon Jovi is on an exhaustion-induced two year hiatus. Whitesnake has embarked on a four year hiatus. Poison is infighting and in the process of firing its lead guitarist. Motley Crue is on a five year break between original releases and in the process of firing its lead singer. Aside from *Use Your Illusion*, the only remaining defenders of the mainstream glam rock establishment seem to be lightweight ballads by bands like Extreme and Mr. Big. All that remains is for someone, *anyone*, to walk in.

. . .

Seattle, Washington—September 24, 1991: Nirvana releases *Nevermind*.

PART II

ALTERNATIVE NATION

Chapter Six

Everybody Loves Our Town

Seattle: Alternative Music's Unlikely New Epicenter

Seattle: Rocking Out in a Vacuum

> Bands never used to come here because they used to go as far as San Francisco and then not come all the way up to Seattle because it wasn't worth it to play just one show.
> —Nils Bernstein, former Sub Pop Records Publicist

> In 1980, I think bands stopped coming to Seattle.
> —Carla Torgerson, The Walkabouts

> A lot of touring bands totally skipped Portland and Seattle because it was 14 hours north of San Francisco and 32 hours west of Minneapolis. People in the Northwest had to make up their own entertainment.
> —Mark Arm, Mudhoney

In the early 80s, Seattle was about as far from the center of the popular music universe as possible. It was an isolated city in the most far-flung corner of the country, largely cut off from what was going on musically in the rest of America. The resulting isolation encouraged an independent "us-against-the-world" DIY attitude. This attitude would eventually help Seattle become—according to a 1992 *Spin* magazine article—"to the rock 'n roll world what Bethlehem was to Christianity." But at the dawn of the 80s, the "grunge revolution" was a long way off. Seattle was out of the loop, nearly a decade behind America's other big cities in terms of fashion. Starbucks had yet to expand beyond the city limits, and the idea of Seattle as an international—or even national—trendsetter was laughable. Seattle-based producer Steve Fisk described the music scene of the time in the 1996 documentary *Hype!*, "Seattle was really lame. In the early 80s... it had a fake Talking Heads. It had a fake Pere Ubu. It had a fake Killing Joke. It had all the fake Ramones you could shake a stick at. And people from [Seattle suburb] Bellevue singing with English accents."

Prior to the 80s, the last Seattle-based rock movement had been the 1960s garage-rock trend that produced The Kingsmen, Paul Revere and the Raiders, and—perhaps most influentially—the instrumental surfabilly rock of The Ventures. But in the early 80s, a new Seattle rock scene began to form around post-punk bands like The U-Men and Girl Trouble, who mixed the Ventures' surfabilly influence with punk rock, creating a strange hybrid that sounded like something approximating an "evil Elvis." The U-Men, in particular, were central to the new scene, thanks in large part to their imposing lead singer John Bigley, who would prowl the stage during shows, belting sometimes incomprehensible lyrics over the band's surf-punk melodies. Even though the U-Men's unusual sound was never adopted by the core of bands that came to be identified with Seattle, the band was a trendsetter in other ways. For instance, they were the first underground Seattle band of their generation to sign to an out-of-town label—New York's Homestead Records—and they actually embarked on a national tour in 1985. To Seattle's young music fans, what The U-Men were doing was nothing short of revolutionary. As Seattle-based journalist Gillian Gaar told Mark Yarm (not to be confused with Mudhoney lead singer Mark Arm) for his 2011 oral history of grunge *Everybody Loves Our Town*, "I can't remember who said this first, but he put it well: 'It seemed more amazing that The U-Men put a record out and went on tour than it did that Nirvana went to number one.' I mean, how could people get on a record and how did records get out there? It seemed totally unattainable, and you had no idea how to do it. Like nuclear physics or something."

The U-Men were also the initial bridge between the Seattle music scene and the indie-punk ethos, and their motivations for being in a band contrasted sharply with commercially-minded posturing of mainstream glam metal. "I had a lot of personal issues that would have probably fueled some of my attitudes and behaviors," says U-Men lead singer John Bigley in *Everybody Loves Our Town*. "The band was a big deal. It wasn't a *yahoo-let's-have-fun-TGIF-rock-and-roll* experience for me. I was uncomfortable in front of people, so it was…very intense. Every show, that was the real me." Bigley's brooding authenticity became a staple of Seattle's post-punk scene, but the U-Men's aversion to rock star posturing was as much a result of Seattle's isolation from rock success stories as it was a result of some dogmatic anti-commercial philosophy. According to U-Men producer Jack Endino, "The bands that stuck it out did it because they really, really enjoyed playing their music. And that was really the only positive reinforcement anybody got… It wasn't L.A. Nobody was gonna come and sign us."

It's Not Punk and It's Not Metal

One of the most unique things about the Seattle music scene in the early 80s was that it was so far out of the loop that fans of underground punk and mainstream heavy metal weren't aware that they were supposed to hate each other. Due to their cultural isolation, most music fans in Seattle were oblivious to the emerging divide between the perceived creative freedom of post-punk music and commercially-driven mainstream glam metal. And so the idea that a band could emulate aspects of both punk and glam bands at the same time—both musically and philosophically—was commonplace among Seattle musicians. This central contradiction within the Seattle scene has been lost on the many critics who have mistakenly asserted that Seattle "grunge" was an indie-punk movement that completely rejected the more commercial metal scene. It was also lost on the many metal fans who thought "grunge" was simply another metal derivation when they first heard it. Neither of those assessments captures the unique essence of the Seattle scene. In the 1980s, Seattle musicians with wildly varying punk and metal tastes were often friends with each other and even played in bands together. The result was that, while punk/alternative music fans and glam/classic rock fans across America were choosing sides and vilifying each other, Seattle musicians largely avoided that kind of thing. According to Mudhoney's Mark Arm, "Everyone came from different backgrounds. There's no purity test. I think that's retarded."

While the post-punk influence of The U-Men was huge in Seattle, there were also a lot of young Seattle musicians being influenced by the classic rock they heard on the city's popular AOR station, KZOK, which played 70s rock heavy hitters like Led Zeppelin and Kiss. One such musician was Andrew Wood, who started the band Malfunkshun in 1980 when he was just 14. And after seeing a Kiss show, young Andrew's interest in the popular shock-rockers would soon become an obsession. According to The U-Men's John Bigley in *Everybody Loves Our Town*, "One of the first things I remember about Andrew was him telling me, 'If you're ever on Bainbridge Island, let me know and I'll show you my Kiss shrine.' He was deadpan, not clowning around. 'Oh, you're not kidding.' And he starts describing this shrine: 'There's two red bongs and a signed Kiss *Destroyer* jacket'—and he just went on—'and I'd like you to see it.' No, I never saw it – they were still living at their mom's." Captivated by the rock star lifestyle, Wood was soon performing in whiteface, referring to himself as "Landrew the Love God," and could be seen parading around town in a white fur coat, make-up, and white gloves.

Because the scene was so loose and accepting, individual musicians would sometimes combine disparate musical elements in ways that more regimented scenes would have frowned upon. For instance, even though Soundgarden guitarist Kim Thayil was a fan of indie post-punk bands like Bauhaus and Killing Joke, he adopted Black Sabbath's signature drop D guitar tuning, and as a result Soundgarden's sound became a mix of eclectic post-punk and mainstream classic rock. Those kinds of combinations were not uncommon in Seattle during the mid-80s. Like many punks before him, Mark Arm started his first band, Mr. Epp and the Calculations, before knowing how to play an instrument, but the band's members were anything but punk purists. "A lot of [punk rockers] hated us," says Epp singer/guitarist Jeff Smith, "because we didn't have the right signifiers, like mohawks or songs about Reagan." After Mr. Epp disbanded in 1984, Arm and fellow Epp bandmate Steve Turner recruited drummer Alex Shumway, bassist Jeff Ament, and guitarist Stone Gossard to form the band Green River. Not only is Green River considered by many to be the first "grunge" band—the liner notes of their first EP describe their music as "ultra-loose GRUNGE that destroyed the morals of a generation"—but their eventual breakup spawned some of Seattle's most iconic bands. Arm and Turner would go on to form Mudhoney while Gossard and Ament would go on to form Mother Love Bone and, eventually, Pearl Jam.

THE DAY ALTERNATIVE MUSIC DIED

By the mid-80s, Seattle's DIY sensibility and unusual combination of influences had given birth to a small but unique music scene that was developing completely under the mass pop culture radar. In 1986 Chris Hanzek and Tina Casale formed C/Z Records in order to put out a compilation album documenting the newly-bursting Seattle rock scene. The compilation—called *Deep Six*—featured songs from six Seattle bands: The U-Men, Green River, Soundgarden, Malfunkshun, The Melvins, and Skin Yard. The album didn't sell particularly well, but it has become the stuff of legend, largely because bands and musicians on the album represented—either directly or indirectly— almost every major band that would come out of Seattle in the next five years. *Deep Six* is as good a way as any to illustrate the incestuous nature of the Seattle scene in the 80s: Green River's Mark Arm and Steve Turner would go on to play in Mudhoney, while their Green River bandmates Stone Gossard, Jeff Ament and Bruce Fairweather would go on to play in Mother Love Bone (and Ament and Gossard would go on to found Pearl Jam); Malfunkshun's Andrew Wood would go on to join Gossard, Ament, and Fairweather in Mother Love Bone; The Melvins' drummer Dale Crover would briefly play with Nirvana before returning to The Melvins; Melvins bassist Matt Lukin went on to join Arm and Turner in Mudhoney; Skin Yard drummer Matt Cameron would go on to play in both Soundgarden and Pearl Jam; and Skin Yard guitarist Jack Endino would go on to become Sub Pop Records' in-house producer, eventually recording Soundgarden, Green River, Mudhoney, and Nirvana.

Even though *Deep Six* was recorded cheaply and many of the bands repudiated the final mixes, the compilation signaled a new sound, one that reflected the combined influences of both post-punk underground rock and mainstream metal. According to Dawn Anderson's June 1986 review in Seattle's leading music newspaper *The Rocket*:

> [*Deep Six*] proves how thoroughly the underground's absorbed certain influences, resulting in music that isn't punk-metal but a third sound distinct from either. Some of the influences are apparent visually; blatant posing on stage is acceptable again. I've seen all but one of these bands live at least once and a few of the musicians, along with many of their fans, could pass for members of [L.A. glam band] Ratt. Some people find this distracting, as it seems to have little to do with the style of their music. I personally don't mind boys in make-up. If bands today can get by with rifling rock history for any

cheap thrill they can find, I say that's great, because it serves to further break down divisions and discourage snobbery and purism, the worst enemies of rock 'n' roll.

Sub Pop and the Seattle Hype Machine

On the heels of the release of *Deep Six*, Soundgarden was being wooed by two aspiring Seattle music moguls, each of whom wanted to record the band. Instead of choosing between the two moguls, the members of Soundgarden suggested that Bruce Pavitt, who had the wider musical knowledge of the two, join forces with Jonathan Poneman, who had more business acumen—and more disposable income. Although Pavitt and Poneman each fought the idea initially, they eventually agreed that a partnership made sense and Sub Pop Records was born. What they had in common was a larger vision for the Seattle music scene than any of their peers. According to Sub Pop photographer Charles Petersen's account in *Hype!*:

> Up to that time, everyone played it really safe, all the small labels. 'Well, we'll put out a single every three months and, you know, we'll sell a thousand copies of it. And that's cool because I've got my day job.' And Jon and Bruce were having none of that. They said, 'We don't want to work day jobs. We don't want our bands to work day jobs. We want them out there on the road. We want them in the big magazines. We want their records everywhere. It's punk rock, but we don't care. We want to make it bigger than punk rock.' And that's why these two gentlemen are the kings of the scene.

Under Pavitt and Poneman's guidance, Sub Pop came to symbolize the same combination of post-punk creative freedom and mainstream commercial aspirations that were embodied in the larger alternative scene by bands like U2 and R.E.M., while echoing the same intertwined artistic and commercial aspirations of David Geffen's Asylum Records in the early 70s. Unlike other indies such as SST or Homestead, Sub Pop bristled at the prevalent idea within the indie community that indie bands and labels shouldn't seek mass popularity. Pavitt and Poneman had been raised on the music of Motown and Atlantic, independent labels that sought popularity while simultaneously trying to encourage creative artistry. And while the two Sub Pop moguls respected small indie labels like SST and Homestead, their commercial sights were set much higher.

But just as the Seattle scene was asserting its musical diversity via projects like *Deep Six*, Pavitt and Poneman decided to try and distill the scene into an identifiable image and sound that they could market beyond the Pacific Northwest. They began by hiring photographer Charles Petersen to photograph all the bands on the label, and his distinctive black and white photos of live performances created a cohesive mood for all Sub Pop albums and literature. Pavitt and Poneman also chose bands that fit a certain sonic mold, one that mirrored Pavitt's tastes: more punk than metal, more accessible than experimental. And they had all of their bands record in the same studio with the same producer—Jack Endino, who would produce 75 singles, EPs, and albums for Sub Pop between 1987 and 1989—in order to try and create a cohesive sound. The sound captured by Endino and Sub Pop would eventually come to be known as "grunge."

Sub Pop recorded and released Soundgarden's first single and EP, *Screaming Life*, in 1987. They also signed Green River and released their first—and only—full-length album, *Rehab Doll*, in June of 1988, but by that time Green River had already broken up. Tensions between the more mainstream elements of the band and the more punk/underground faction had finally come to the forefront. Mark Arm was afraid that Green River was going to become another sell-out glam band made up of ex-punks, while Jeff Ament and Stone Gossard found the minimalistic punk ethos limiting and were looking for something, according to Ament, "with endless possibilities." Once Green River had broken up, neither faction wasted anytime pursuing their visions. Even before the release of *Rehab Doll*, Arm and Turner had already founded a new band called Mudhoney, while Gossard and Ament had already joined forces with Malfunkshun's charismatic frontman Andrew Wood to form another new band called Mother Love Bone. Mudhoney quickly signed with Sub Pop and released the single "Touch Me, I'm Sick" on August 1, 1988. The single and subsequent EP, *Superfuzz Bigmuff*, quickly established Mudhoney as Sub Pop's flagship band.

One of Pavitt and Poneman's marketing strategies at Sub Pop was to try and break their acts in England, where listeners and tastemakers had no idea how small and isolated the Seattle scene actually was. In England, Seattle was a blank canvas on which Pavitt and Poneman could practically invent an image.

In March of '89, Sub Pop invited *Melody Maker* journalist Everett True to Seattle to check out the scene and showered him with as many free drinks and free shows as he could handle, while feeding him tall tales about Sub Pop's working-class roster made up of uneducated lumberjacks. Pavitt's largely fabricated exaggerations were intended to appeal to British stereotypes of Americans. According to Mudhoney's Mark Arm, "The U.K. was so fuckin' class-oriented. Like if rock is going to be authentic it's gotta come from the lower class." Everett True, for his part, was just looking for a good story, as he explains in *Everybody Loves Our Town*, "Bruce Pavitt and Jonathan Poneman were some of the most charming, eloquent liars that I ever met. I just thought it was hilarious that everybody lied… If they wanted to portray Tad Doyle [of Sub Pop band TAD] as some kind of chainsaw-toting, dope-smoking, backwoods redneck who didn't wash and used to be a butcher… that was cool by me, because why the hell not?" True wrote a *Melody Maker* cover story on Sub Pop and followed it up with a cover story on Mudhoney the following week. But with all the press came some mixed feelings. According to Arm, Seattle musicians generally disparaged British rock music hype, "which was the general feeling among most American underground people of the day—it's all hype, what a load of crap. And next thing you know, *we're* the load of crap." But Sub Pop's marketing strategy had been hugely successful. All of a sudden, tiny Seattle-based Sub Pop was the new hip label in England.

The timing was perfect for Mudhoney. True's article came out in *Melody Maker* just before the band hit the U.K., and the well-primed English audience was the most enthusiastic they had ever played to. Thanks to True's articles and BBC DJ John Peel's endorsement in *The Times*, Mudhoney had become something of a phenomenon in England. And once all the British attention began trickling back to the States, American journalists began inquiring about the Seattle scene—and about Sup Pop and Mudhoney in particular. Pavitt and Poneman were ready for them. One of their greatest skills was making Sub Pop seem like a bigger operation than it actually was. According to Pavitt in *Everybody Loves Our Town*, "Part of our shtick was that we were this huge player on the West Coast, and a lot of people bought into that. In the *Sub Pop 200* compilation there was a picture of the building, and it said, 'Sub Pop World Headquarters.' And so people looked at the picture and were like, 'Wow, they've got this 11-floor office building!' When in actuality we had maybe 50 square feet." Sub Pop's hype machine was not only successful in raising the profile of their label; it was also partially responsible for growing national interest in the Seattle scene in general. By September 1989, *Chicago Sun-Times* writer Michael Corcoran was able to say, "As were Athens, Ga., Austin, Texas, and Minneapolis before it, the newest 'little city with the big music scene' is Seattle... Influential music magazines from Europe to the United States have called 'The Seattle Sound' the best thing to happen to new music since the advent of New York's CBGB's." Seattle was officially on the verge.

In 1988, just as Sub Pop was getting their hype machine going, major labels were starting to show an interest in Seattle bands, most notably Soundgarden, who signed with A&M that year. Shortly thereafter, Mother Love Bone was being courted by major labels, thanks in large part to Jeff Ament and Stone Gossard's reputation from their time in Green River. The combination of singer Andrew Wood's glam showmanship with the rest of the band's post-punk roots was a particularly compelling—yet typically unusual—Seattle combination. But even before the band signed its major label deal with Polygram, there were already concerns about Wood's heroin use. Numerous interventions were staged and there were even a couple of rehab stints, but on March 16, 1990, just days before the scheduled release of Mother Love Bone's debut full-length album *Apple*, Wood OD'd and was rushed to the hospital. Three days later, he was dead.

The Death of a Seattle Icon and the Birth of Pearl Jam

Andrew Wood's death reverberated throughout Seattle music community, and reactions were varied. Some junkies vowed to clean up their acts, while others tried to find out where Wood got the "good stuff" that killed him. But for a lot of his fellow musicians, Wood's death marked the end of the innocence of the Seattle scene. Soundgarden's Chris Cornell had visited a comatose Wood in the hospital, and in 2011 he told Cameron Crowe:

> It's difficult to articulate it, but up to that point I think life was really good for us, just as a group of musicians in a scene making music. The world was sort of our oyster and we supported each other. And [Wood] was kind of this beam of light sort of above it all. And to see him hooked up to machines, that was, I think, the death of the innocence of the scene. It wasn't later when people

surmised that Kurt [Cobain] blowing his head off was the end of the innocence... It was walking into [Andrew Wood's hospital] room.

Cornell—who had once moved in with Wood for a time and had tried to keep him out of trouble—coped with his grief by channeling it into a musical tribute to Wood which would include the members of Wood's old band Mother Love Bone. The album would be called *Temple of the Dog*, after one of Wood's lyrics. Meanwhile, former Mother Love Bone members Jeff Ament and Stone Gossard had decided to put together a new band, and they were already practicing with guitarist Mike McCready and San Diego-based singer Eddie Vedder when they started working with Cornell on his tribute project. According to his account in *Everybody Loves Our Town*, Cornell was blown away the first time he heard Vedder sing:

> When we started rehearsing the songs, I had pulled out 'Hunger Strike' and I had this feeling it was just kind of going to be filler, it didn't feel like a real song. Eddie was sitting there kind of waiting for a rehearsal and I was singing parts, and he kind of humbly—but with some balls—walked up to the mic and started singing the low parts for me because he saw it was kind of hard. We got through a couple choruses of him doing that and suddenly the lightbulb came on in my head, this guy's voice is amazing for these low parts. History wrote itself after that. That became the single...

After finishing the *Temple of the Dog* project, Ament, Gossard, McCready, and Vedder continued to rehearse in the hopes of starting a new band, and they were all immediately struck by the musical chemistry they had together. Ament and Gossard had been playing together for years, but Vedder brought a fresh outsider's perspective to the music. "He was really coming from a different place that I didn't fully understand," says Gossard. "And... it wasn't Mother Love Bone. That was big. We had gotten a few tapes and they were all like Andy kind of tribute things." Coming as he was from San Diego, Vedder wasn't tied to the incestuous punk/metal hybrid of the Seattle scene, and he added a new texture to the music that made for a totally unique sound. Half of what would become Pearl Jam's debut album was written in just a few days, and after just five days of rehearsing the band played their first show. According to Ament, "We thought it was just insane that we were playing a show after just five or six days together."

The connection between the band members was immediate on a personal level, as well, and it added a particularly intense depth to Pearl Jam's first songs. According to Vedder in *Twenty*, "My dad, he passed away before I knew he was my dad. So I grew up with this dad that I thought was my dad, then I found out later that he wasn't. And the guy that *was* my dad had already passed a few years earlier." Vedder's sense of loss mirrored what the other band members were going through in coping with Andrew Wood's death. "In ways we were strangers," says Vedder. "But we were coming from a similar place. And all that came out in our first batch of songs."

One of the songs Pearl Jam performed at their first show was "Alive," which would eventually become their breakthrough single. The song's combination of Vedder's heartfelt angst and the band's ferocious virtuosity was unlike anything else in the Seattle scene, or anything going on in rock in general at the time. Here was a combination of punk roots, metal volume, real rock musicianship, and genuine emotion all wrapped into one package. And thanks to Ament and Gossard's Mother Love Bone pedigree, Pearl Jam had instant access to major labels. As the demos began to circulate, a bidding war ensued, and the band signed with Epic Records after just a handful of shows. Vedder would later say that he wished he had paid his dues on the club circuit before hitting it big, but Ament and Gossard's meandering trials in Green River and Mother Love Bone more than made up for Vedder's inexperience. For them, Pearl Jam's major label deal was the culmination of a journey that had started in Seattle's underground club scene nearly a decade earlier.

Heroin

Andrew Wood had not been the only musician in Seattle dealing with heroin addiction. The notoriously addictive drug was the elephant in the room that no one in the Seattle music scene wanted to talk about, and its prevalence seemed to increase in direct proportion to the scene's growing popularity. By the late 80s, it seemed like every Seattle group had at least one junkie in the band. Mudhoney's Mark Arm struggled with heroin addiction for years, "I OD'd probably five times. If I was alone, I would have been dead for sure." One of the problems for Arm was that, unlike other heroin users whose addiction cost them their jobs, the rock star lifestyle actually enabled his addiction. Mudhoney was making enough money to fund his heroin habit, and Arm saw little incentive to quit. Chris Cornell backed up Arm's assessment in a 2009 Adlercast interview, "If you're about to lose your job and you don't have any other prospects and you don't have any money and you're sleeping on somebody's couch, those are all really hugely motivating factors to cleaning up your act. But if you don't have any of those concerns, what is your motivating factor? Because it's a tough thing to get over." But Cornell also asserts in the same interview that it wasn't just the money that made the rock star lifestyle an enabler for substance abuse, "If the rock star shows up drunk, he's not gonna lose his job. Not only are you not going to lose your job, people kind of expect it and people kind of like it. Because the rock star, you're living sort of vicariously through that person, the danger of that person's lifestyle, and sort of the more tumultuous the better, in a way. It's almost supported. And I think that's where guys like Layne [Staley, lead singer of Alice in Chains] kind of got into trouble."

If The U-Men were at the most "punk" end of the Seattle music spectrum, Alice in Chains were at the most "metal" end. They started out as glam metal fans, but as the band developed, they lost the make-up and hairspray but maintained their metal edge. When the major labels began to descend on Seattle, Alice in Chains was one of the first bands to get a deal, signing in 1989 with Columbia. But enigmatic lead singer Layne Staley was also a heroin addict who was becoming a prisoner of his own invention. By Alice in Chains' second album, *Dirt*, Staley's junkie persona had become central to his lyrics and public image, and it was particularly hard for his friends to watch. "It's fucking heartbreaking to see how disillusioned people get to where that escape is so sought after," says former Alice in Chains manager Susan Silver. And Kelly Curtis—who co-managed Alice in Chains with Silver for a time—adds in *Everybody Love Our Town*, "We had lost Andy [Wood] to heroin, and there was a lot of that going on with Alice in Chains. I just had a little girl, and I remember Layne was holding her once and he nodded out. And I thought, 'I don't want to do this anymore.' He was a great guy—all those guys were great—but there was a dark cloud over them, and it really affected me. I hated it."

But the dark cloud soon spread beyond Alice in Chains. When they went on tour with fellow Seattle natives Screaming Trees, Trees lead singer Mark Lanegan began shooting up with Staley, and soon Lanegan was addicted as well. After years trying to break free of its pull, Lanegan was eventually able to quit heroin, but Screaming Trees never fully recovered, and another young Seattle band's career was cut short. Lanegan later told Mark Yarm:

> [Kicking heroin] was the end of a long nightmare that lasted for years and years... Nobody likes to think they need anybody's help in anything, and the smarter you are—and I'm not smart—or the tougher you are—and at times I thought I was pretty tough—the more trouble you have. The smartest guys I ever met are not around anymore, because they thought they could think their way out of an unthinkable situation, and the tough guys have to just be beaten up repeatedly, and some guys just never do make it out.

One of the guys Lanegan was referring to was Staley, who finally lost his long battle with heroin when he died of an overdose in 2002. Another was the lead singer of yet another promising young Seattle band called Nirvana.

Chapter Seven

They Wanted to be Big

Kurt Cobain and Nirvana: The Band that Ignited the Alternative Revolution

The Rise of Nirvana

The irony is that none of the members of Nirvana were even from Seattle. Even there, they started out as outsiders. Founding members Kurt Cobain and Krist Novacelic came from tiny Aberdeen, Washington, a working class coastal town about two hours southwest of Seattle. And eventual drummer Dave Grohl, who would join the band just in time for its rise to superstardom, was from Virginia. Aberdeen wasn't exactly a punk mecca, and so Kurt Cobain grew up listening to the same mainstream heavy metal bands as his peers—his first rock concert was a Sammy Hagar show—but his musical aspirations changed forever when he caught a free show by local punk band The Melvins behind the local Thriftway when he was 16. As he would later write in his journal, "I came to the promised land of a grocery store parking lot and found my special purpose." Cobain and Krist Novacelic both became die-hard fans of The Melvins, who were from the neighboring small town of Montesano, and the two eventual Nirvana bandmates got to know each other hanging out at The Melvins' practice space and riding into Seattle together to watch them play. Melvins singer Buzz Osborne's dedication to punk was contagious, and by 1987 Cobain and Novacelic had started jamming together in the hope of forming their own band. They went through a number of drummers, including Melvins drummer Dale Crover, who jammed with them for a while before introducing the band to Sub Pop producer Jack Endino, who agreed to record a demo for them. Endino was impressed enough that he took the demo to Sub Pop, but not everyone at Sub Pop loved the recordings. Co-owner Bruce Pavitt thought the demo was too "metal" sounding; he was going for a cohesive sound at Sub Pop, one that was more punk than metal, and Nirvana'a early demos sounded a lot more like the heavy metal they had grown up on than the punks they aspired to be. But Pavitt's business partner Jonathan Poneman loved the demos and was eventually able to convince Pavitt to sign Nirvana.

After releasing the single "Love Buzz" in November of '88, the band began working on a full length album for Sub Pop with drummer Chad Channing and producer Jack Endino the very next month. As the album started coming together, something that was unusual in the Seattle scene was starting to emerge in songs like "About a Girl:" a pop sensibility, a sweetened sense of melody that served as a counterpoint to the twin abrasions of punk and metal which pervaded Nirvana's sound. Still, a chunky, riff-metal sound was the band's dominant characteristic, and their first full-length release was anything but radio-polished. *Bleach* came out in June of 1989—just in time for Nirvana to be included in Pavitt and Poneman's exaggerated publicity push and the English Sub Pop phenomenon. But the backwoods stereotypes being thrown around by the Sub Pop moguls hit a little too close to home for the small-town Aberdeen native Cobain. According to Poneman, "Kurt Cobain protested vigorously later on in his career, saying, 'Those guys portrayed us as a bunch of dumb rednecks.'" But the stereotypes were part of a marketing campaign that had been incredibly effective in getting the attention of the British press. And Nirvana became one of that campaign's biggest beneficiaries when Everett True published a gushing review of *Bleach* for *Melody Maker*, "Nirvana are beauty incarnate. A relentless two-chord garage beat which lays down some serious foundations for a sheer monster of a guitar to howl over." A buzz was starting to build around Nirvana.

On June 9, 1989, Sub Pop threw its inaugural "Lamefest," which doubled as the release party for *Bleach*. The show sold out the 1400-seat Moore Theater, something even the U-Men had never done, and Pavitt dates the concert as the moment grunge "blew up." Of course, "blew up" is a relative term. Even with all the press and the Seattle-based buzz, *Bleach* was still very much an underground phenomenon. The album only sold 40,000 copies from 1989-91 (though after Nirvana hit it big, *Bleach* would become a retroactive hit, with nearly 2 million copies sold to date in the United States alone), and Cobain was starting to feel like they were destined for bigger things. As Poneman told Mark Yarm in 2011, "Kurt got frustrated [and] they started shopping for a new label. He said many times with regard to *Bleach*, 'This record should be selling millions of copies.' And I'm explaining to him what, in retrospect, seems foolish and condescending on my part, that the idea of a band like Nirvana selling between 30,000 and 50,000 records then was amazing." Cobain's desire for bigger things was starting to affect other aspects of Nirvana's career as well. In *Everybody Loves Our Town*, their old mentor Melvins lead singer Buzz Osborne relates his frustration with Nirvana during that time:

> When Nirvana started doing better, we played a show with them in Portland, and that was when the worm had turned. That was before [drummer] Dave Grohl was ever in the band. We just assumed that we were going to play last, and they said that they thought that they should headline, because things were really taking off for them, and then they were really weird about splitting up the money. That was when I knew that things were really not the same with these guys. They had become exactly what I had tried to avoid. This was way before they got popular—that's what people don't get. They lined up for this shit. They put themselves in line to be aligned with horrible people. I blamed them for the whole thing. They got in line to be involved with horrible management, horrible booking agents, horrible everything. They didn't need to do it, but they did it.

While there is certainly some truth in Osborne's assessment, it was also true that Nirvana really did have to make a change. Sub Pop was so broke that Nirvana had to pay for the recording of *Bleach* themselves. And the label also tried to borrow money from the band just to put it out. As Pavitt told Yarm in 2011, "There is a story that is true and it's kind of embarrassing: I called up Kurt and said, 'Can I borrow your money to put out your album?' Which sounds absolutely insane, but that's where we were at financially... He said no. We ended up borrowing $5,000 from a friend to put it out." Given these financial realities, the fact that the band was looking for management and a new label wasn't exactly surprising to Pavitt and Sub Pop.

By 1990, the members of Nirvana—and Cobain in particular—were feeling pulls in opposite directions. On the one hand, Cobain had bristled under Sub Pop's attempts to package and market the band. But on the other hand, the members of Nirvana also wanted to be bigger than they were, and the kind of success they were looking for would necessitate large-scale marketing campaigns. Those two pulls—the impulse towards independent punk individualism, and the impulse towards mainstream rock stardom—would only become harder and harder to reconcile as the band became more popular. And according to Nirvana biographer Michael Azzerad, rather than choosing one impulse or the other, "Kurt Cobain would vainly try to resolve both impulses within himself." He was never able to do so.

Cobain's mentors weren't much help in guiding him towards a resolution of his competing impulses, either. While Nirvana was starting to look for a new record deal, Cobain was going through a period of transition and seeking guidance. He had been aware of punk music since Buzz Osborne had taken him to his first Black Flag concert as a teenager, but he remained self-conscious about the fact that his own music had always sounded more like the riff-heavy metal he had listened to in his youth. For a time, Cobain had seen Calvin Johnson—K Records founder and Olympia, Washington's leading indie-punk zealot—as a potential mentor, even going so far as to get the K Records logo tattooed on his forearm. But Cobain never felt accepted by Johnson or his legion of faithful followers (dubbed "the Calvinists"), and he bristled under the local icon's indie-punk rigidity. However, by 1990, Cobain was starting to meet and tour with indie bands from around the world and learning more about the DIY punk ethos first hand through Nirvana's Sub Pop connections. And he soon found a more willing mentor in Sonic Youth's Thurston Moore, who outlined his own particular version of the indie-punk ethos while on tour with Nirvana in 1991, "When the youth culture becomes monopolized by big business, what are the youth to do? I think we should destroy the bogus capitalist process that is destroying youth culture by mass marketing and commercial paranoia behavior control. And the first step... is to destroy the record companies." Moore was an unusual spokesman for the independent "youth culture;" he wasn't exactly a kid himself—he was already thirty-three in 1991—and his band Sonic Youth had just signed a long-term deal with corporate major label subsidiary Geffen Records. But Cobain loved

Sonic Youth and idolized Moore, and soon—for better or worse—Moore and Sonic Youth were the most important professional influences in Cobain's life.

Sonic Youth: Indie's Unlikely Icons

From its inception, New York City-based Sonic Youth was full of contradictions. For starters, unlike many underground indie bands of the time whose working-class background gave their anti-establishment ethos an air of class-warrior credibility, Sonic Youth founders Thurston Moore and Kim Gordon were both the children of college professors. And in addition to its members' affluent backgrounds, Sonic Youth had another advantage unavailable to most indie bands. According to Michael Azerrad's account in *Our Band Could Be Your Life*, in order to pay for their first full length album, "they borrowed money from a wealthy, somewhat eccentric Swiss couple named Catherine and Nicholas Ceresole, who held a weekly salon for downtown artists and musicians. The Ceresoles went on to bankroll several more Sonic Youth albums and frequently put up the band in their luxurious home on Lake Geneva, just up the road from [French filmmaker] Jean-Luc Godard." From the beginning, Sonic Youth's financial reality was from a different planet than Nirvana's blue-collar roots in Aberdeen, Washington.

Also, unlike the Seattle bands, who had been molded by a combination of underground indie-punk and popular heavy metal, Sonic Youth's members all came from art school backgrounds, and their initial attraction to each other was as a result of a shared interest in New York's avant-garde music scene, which included composers like John Cage, Philip Glass, Rhys Chatham, and Glenn Branca who specialized in minimalism, atonality, dissonance, and—in at least one instance—no sound at all; Cage's most infamous "composition" is called "4'33," in which an entire assembled orchestra sits in silence for 4 minutes and 33 seconds while a conductor flips page after page of empty sheet music. While people's opinions on the merits of such an endeavor vary wildly, such a spectacle—and its attendant pretentions—was just about as far removed from the punk/metal hybrid emanating from Seattle as one could possibly imagine. However, it was Cage's friend Glenn Branca—and his experimental, atonal compositions for the electric guitar—who would become the primary touchstone for Sonic Youth's band members. Sonic Youth guitarist Lee

Ranaldo was playing in Branca's sextet when he met eventual bandmates Moore and Gordon, and all of Sonic Youth's original members, including eventual drummer Bob Bert, would join Branca on stage at one time or another.

The idea of treating rock music like serious art dated all the way back to the mid-60s influence of Bob Dylan and The Beatles. But what had distinguished Dylan and The Beatles from their contemporaries in the underground avant-garde art world was that their chosen artistic medium was a decidedly commercial one, and the structure and simplicity inherent to the rock music form made it possible to convey substantive artistic ideas in a way that was relatable to a wide audience. But Sonic Youth's roots in the avant-garde world's elitist contempt for popular tastes colored their music from the beginning. And the spare, atonal, minimalist playing and occasional sonic outbursts of early Sonic Youth songs like "She Is Not Alone" and "Where the Red Fern Grows" bore a much greater resemblance to New York's avant-garde compositional experimentalism than they did to traditional rock music. And the vocals only added to the dissonance. According to critic Greil Marcus, Sonic Youth's vocals "resembled nothing so much as the sort of chants little kids come up with when they've been sent to their rooms without supper."

In addition, where the straightforward musical simplicity of punk and post-punk bands like The Clash or Black Flag was the result of limited musical ability, the reactionary, minimalist atonality of Sonic Youth was the conscious effort of accomplished musicians. One of the ways Sonic Youth achieved their atonal sound was through the use of dissonant alternate guitar tunings. According to Ranaldo's account in *Our Band Could Be Your Life*, "When you tuned a guitar a new way, you were a beginner all over again and you could discover all sorts of new things. It allowed us to throw out a whole broad body of knowledge about how to play the guitar." The unusual tunings also necessitated the use of upwards of a dozen guitars at each gig, which required extensive tuning time prior to their sets. According to Azerrad, "they'd start tuning on stage. A cheer would inevitably go up as the crowd thought the set was starting. But it soon subsided as Moore and Ranaldo did nothing but methodically tune one instrument after another for fifteen minutes or more, then leave the stage." According to Ranaldo, the alienating effect on the audience was intentional, "It opened up to the audience this notion of what we were all about. They'd see all the guitars and the fact that...they were differently tuned. I always thought it was a cool prelude to the beginning of the set—it was like a briefing." The disdain for the audience that such a spectacle exhibited made wide popular acceptance all but impossible, and by eliminating the possibility of mass popularity, the band also eliminated—at least for themselves—the tensions between the aspirations to artistic credibility and mass popularity that had been with rock since the mid-60s.

With popular acceptance out of the equation, Sonic Youth turned their sights on garnering critical acclaim. "One thing Sonic Youth always did, almost to a gross point, was that they always knew who the hot journalists were and they always became really close," former Sonic Youth drummer Bob Bert told Azerrad in 2001. "You'd go to a party and Kim would know who the *Village Voice* writer was in the corner of the room and she'd make sure she went over there. They were really good at schmoozing in every respect. They always made sure they met as many popular, famous people as they could, whether it be the art world or the music world." Sonic Youth's members were also adept at networking with other bands. After achieving some success in Europe, they were quick to share their success with other bands they liked by bringing those bands on tour with them. The same was true as they started to build a following in the States, and the band's generosity won them countless loyal friends in the indie music community, friends who would serve them well throughout their career.

As Sonic Youth began to garner critical accolades, they also began to build a modest fanbase. And as their popularity grew in underground circles, they found themselves increasingly interested in growing that fanbase. As a result, they chafed under the limitations of each and every indie label for whom they recorded during the 80s; none of those labels were capable of satisfying the band's newfound desire for broader popularity. Shortly after signing their first record deal with Gerard Cosloy—a huge Sonic Youth devotee—at New York's Homestead Records, the band began itching to join the more prestigious SST stable, and they made the jump after just one album with Homestead. Cosloy "wasn't too happy about it," said Moore, "but he got over it." Once they were with SST, they achieved their widest—though still modest— exposure yet, but the band still wasn't satisfied. As Gordon described it in *Our Band Could Be Your Life*, "SST is growing, but not fast enough for us." Sonic Youth's next move was to sign with Enigma, which was distributed by major label Capitol Records. But after releasing their most popular album to date, 1988's *Daydream Nation*, the band was again dissatisfied, and again willing to air their laundry publicly. As Moore told Azerrad, "Enigma was basically a cheap-jack Mafioso outfit, I guess. You can quote me on that, but I'm not sure how truthful that is. That was the impression we were given." Ironically, the members of the most archetypal indie band of the 80s weren't happy until they signed with a major label. Sonic Youth finally found a perfect fit in 1990 when they signed with major label subsidiary Geffen Records, with whom they would stay for 18 years. Their sweetheart major label deal granted them complete creative control over their music, and they were under no pressure to sell any records. Instead, the label shrewdly hoped to capitalize on Sonic Youth's hip standing among other indie bands, enlisting them to apply their greatest skill—schmoozing—on behalf of Geffen Records. The move paid off beyond Geffen's wildest expectations when Sonic Youth helped convince a little-known band called Nirvana to sign with Geffen in 1991. As Nick Terzo, an executive for Geffen's rival Columbia Records, put it in *Everybody Loves Our Town*, "My biggest problem trying to sign Nirvana to Columbia was I didn't have Sonic Youth. Kurt cared about Sonic Youth and being where Sonic Youth was."

The deal with Geffen had brought the members of Sonic Youth full circle, and they spent the early 90s much as they had spent the early 80s: as the beneficiaries of a wealthy patron who allowed them to create the music they wanted without any financial considerations whatsoever. The reason that Moore was able to talk about destroying the record companies at the same time his band was living off the benevolence of a major label was that Sonic Youth was never going to be a hugely popular band. Their music, which had evolved significantly from its intentionally atonal beginnings into a more conventional rock sound, was still too vocally sloppy and sonically abrasive to ever have a widespread mainstream appeal. And the fact that Sonic Youth would never score a gold album (let alone a platinum or multi-platinum album) meant that they were able to maintain their underground indie credibility even though they were on a major label.

Although it was exceedingly unlikely that another indie band would ever find itself in Sonic Youth's enviable situation, the band's career path still functioned as an influential indie paradigm for countless other bands, including Nirvana. But unlike Sonic Youth, Nirvana had Cobain's undeniable vocal power and increasingly deft pop sensibilities working for them, as well as a burning desire to be heard by the masses (*"This record should be selling millions of copies"*). In short, Nirvana had all the necessary ingredients to be big. And even as Moore talked out of one side of his mouth about his anti-corporate desire to "destroy the record companies," he still actively recruited Nirvana to join Sonic Youth under Geffen Records' corporate major label umbrella, feeding the idea that major labels and indie-punk credibility were compatible. Cobain would later learn the hard way that this wasn't always the case.

Before Teen Spirit

Eventually, Moore convinced Cobain and Nirvana to sign with big-time management firm Gold Mountain Entertainment—who managed mainstream acts like Bonnie Raitt, Alannah Myles, Belinda Carlisle, and The Allman Brothers, in addition to Sonic Youth—in order to help them negotiate a record deal. As Gold Mountain's Danny Goldberg said in 2011, "The first meeting I had with Nirvana... I asked at one point if they wanted to stay on Sub Pop. Kurt, who had been quiet up until then, just said, '*No*, definitely not!' He wanted to be big. They committed to us after the first meeting." Kurt Cobain may have wanted to be big, but at the time, no one had any idea just how big Nirvana would eventually be.

However, between signing with Geffen Records in April of 1991 and the release of their major label debut that September, Nirvana was anything but big-time. And in the months leading up to *Nevermind*'s release, their lead singer was—quite literally—homeless. Kurt Cobain had been evicted from his apartment for failure to pay the rent, and when he wasn't on the road fulfilling the band's increasingly rigorous touring schedule, he was crashing at friends' houses or—more often than not—sleeping in the backseat of his 1963 Plymouth Valiant. "I was so bored and so poor," Cobain would later tell Michael Azerrad in an interview that eventually appeared in the documentary *About a Son*. "I mean, we were signed to Geffen for months, and we didn't have any money. We ended up having to pawn our amps and our TV and all kinds of stuff just to eat corn dogs. It just felt really weird to be signed to this multi-million dollar corporation and be totally dirt poor."

It wasn't the first time Cobain had been without a home. His parents had divorced when he was seven, an event his biographer Charles Cross called "the most significant single event in his life," and when alternating attempts to live with his separated parents finally ended poorly while Cobain was in high school, he migrated from his grandparents' house to various friends' houses to a friend's front porch to—as the legend goes—a stint sleeping under a bridge near his mother's house (he would eventually cement this legend in the lyrics of *Nevermind*'s "Something in the Way"). During that earlier homeless stint, neither of Cobain's parents had sought to make sure young Kurt had a place to sleep, let alone seen to it that he graduated high school, a feat he never accomplished. The basic support structure that most Americans took for granted was not shared by Kurt Cobain.

And so later, even as he was internally codifying the anti-mainstream indie-punk ethos of mentors like Buzz Osborne and Thurston Moore, Cobain still yearned for the attention, approval, and acceptance he imagined rock stardom might finally bring him. However, as a result of his internalization of these competing standards of success, any popular approval he did enjoy was more than offset by the guilt he felt for betraying his punk ideals. And to complicate matters further, between the recording of *Nevermind* in May of 1991 and its release that September, he decided to turn his occasional use of heroin into a full-blown daily addiction. As he later wrote in a requisite "drug history" for a treatment program:

> When I got back from our second European tour with Sonic Youth [in August of 1991], I decided to use heroine [sic] on a daily basis because of an ongoing stomach ailment that I had been suffering from for the past five years [that] had literally taken me to the point of wanting to kill myself… I consulted 15 different doctors, and tried about 50 different types of ulcer medication. The only thing I found that worked were heavy opiates. There were many times I found myself literally incapacitated, in bed for weeks, vomiting and starving. So I decided, if I feel like a junkie as it is, I may as well be one.

While Cobain's friends and colleagues have debated whether his drug abuse was an attempt to self-medicate or the actual cause of his mysterious stomach ailment, it is now known that for the entire time from August of '91 until his death in April of '94 Cobain was in varying stages of heroin addiction. That fact, coupled with his lack of a familial support structure, his other physical ailments, and his internal contradictions concerning his own music career, makes it hard to imagine a person less equipped to handle superstardom than Kurt Cobain circa 1991.

And yet, a combination of events taking place around the world were conspiring to create an environment in which it would be possible for Nirvana to become rock's most popular band and Cobain its most recognizable icon, all in the span of just a few short months. But aside from all of the external factors that made Nirvana's rise to superstardom possible, there was something at the core of Nirvana's music that transcended circumstance and hype, and that was Kurt Cobain's singular artistic voice and vision. There were countless disaffected twenty-somethings performing in rock bands across the country, but what set Cobain apart was his ability to distill his own individual dissatisfactions into songs that were undeniably personal and authentic, yet universally relatable enough to appeal to a remarkably wide range of young listeners.

At the center of Kurt Cobain's many dissatisfactions was the fact that he had never had a loving, functional family—or even one that behaved civilly towards each other. As Cobain explained in *About a Son*, "Overall, it's sad that two people can't—if they chose to marry one another and have children—that they can't at least get along. It amazes me that people who think that they're in love with one another can't even pretend—or at least have enough courtesy for their children—to talk to one another civilly when they have to see each other just every once in a while, when they pick the kids up from a visit. That's sad, but it's not my story any more than it's anybody else's." Even as he expressed the hurt and confusion he felt through his songs, Cobain also felt guilty about the hurt he was experiencing. "I'm a product of a fucking spoiled America. When you think of how much worse my family life could be if I grew up in another country or in a Depression. There are so many worse things besides a divorce. I've just been brooding and bellyaching about something I couldn't have, which is a family, a solid family unit… [But] I'm glad that I can share it with kids who've had the same experiences." As Michael Azerrad would later write, "*Nevermind* sold to every abused child in the country… the divorce rate soared to nearly fifty percent in the mid-Seventies, and all those children of broken homes are becoming adults. Including Kurt Cobain."

But even as his angst was claimed by millions, Nirvana's songs were still a reflection of Cobain's individual experience. They were the mournful and angry expressions of an alienated outsider: the boy who had been excluded from sports-centric male bonding, the boy who couldn't relate to the confident machismo of mainstream rock, the boy who had been ridiculed for being "different," the boy who had been routinely called a "faggot" by his classmates because he wore strange clothes and was shy around girls. But his experiences were common enough that it was possible for young fans all around the country to see themselves in Kurt Cobain, to see his songs as expressing their pain and frustration, and to experience catharsis in listening to *Nevermind* at loud volumes. The grittiness of the album's subject matter and the authenticity in Cobain's voice offered a counterpoint to the fantasy world of glam metal; where glam had offered escapism, Nirvana offered understanding and catharsis. And after a decade of escapism, there were millions of teenagers yearning for something different.

Part of the reason so many people of Cobain's generation gravitated to Nirvana's music was that the pain they had experienced as a result of the divorce epidemic among baby boomers was routinely downplayed by the elder generations. For instance, in response to Cobain's suicide in 1994, *60 Minutes* commentator Andy Rooney went on the air and essentially called Cobain and his generation wimps. "What's all this nonsense about how terrible life is? A young girl who stood outside his home in Seattle with tears streaming down her face said, 'It's hard to be a young person nowadays. He helped open people's eyes to our struggles.' Please wipe the tears from your eyes, dear. You're breaking my heart. I'd love to relieve the pain you're going through by switching my age for yours. What would all these young people be doing if they had real problems like a Depression, World War II, or Vietnam?" Attitudes like Rooney's only served to reinforce the guilt young people felt about their pain—note how Rooney's criticisms echoed Cobain's own guilt— yet all of that repressed hurt was lingering just below the surface, looking for an outlet. And Nirvana's music would provide just such an outlet.

But for Kurt Cobain himself, even as his musical goals were being fulfilled one by one—being in a real band, signing with the hippest label in Seattle, winning the approval of the underground indie community, signing with a major record label—he continued to look for relief on each successive rung of the ladder. Until he was at the top, with no relief in sight, and with a mountain of new responsibilities.

Chapter Eight

Smells Like Teen Spirit

The Alternative Takeover of Mainstream Rock

Smells Like Teen Spirit

By the fall of 1991, a whole host of indicators was signaling that the alternative music scene might be primed for a takeover of American mainstream rock. Bands like U2 and R.E.M. had already proved that there was a huge market for alternative music. The alternative scene had built its own infrastructure of radio stations, venues, fanzines, and labels through which alternative bands were being increasingly and actively promoted. The alternative Lollapalooza tour that summer had been a huge hit. And alternative music even had its own foothold at the hugely influential MTV network: the weekly program *120 Minutes*. Not to mention the extent to which glam metal, rock's leading representative on the charts, had worn out its welcome during its nearly decade-long popular run. Even so, no one within the music industry thought the catalyst for a seismic shift in the mainstream rock landscape would be a relatively unknown band from Seattle called Nirvana. The band's own label, Geffen Records, had only modest sales expectations for their major label debut, *Nevermind*. "In the marketing meetings at the time," said Geffen radio promoter John Rosenfelder, "sales of 50,000 were what was planned, since Sonic Youth had sold 118,000 of [their Geffen debut] *Goo*. We figured if it could sell half that, we were doing good."

But from the moment people started hearing the songs from *Nevermind*, the music elicited a reaction that far exceeded those modest expectations. The positive reaction at a Los Angeles industry showcase in August, where Nirvana played the songs off *Nevermind*, led one Geffen vice president to up his sales prediction to 100,000. Then, just before the album's release, after bootleg recordings of the album had leaked throughout Seattle, the line for an in-store meet-and-greet at Seattle's Beehive Records ballooned to over 200 people, hours before the band's scheduled appearance. When Kurt Cobain saw the crowd developing outside the record store, he decided that the band wouldn't just appear and sign autographs, they would set up and play a few songs for the waiting fans, and the impromptu 45-minute set elicited a new kind of reaction for Nirvana. "People were ripping posters off the wall," said store manager Jamie Brown, "just so they'd have a piece of paper for Kurt to autograph." According to biographer Charles Cross, "Kurt kept shaking his head in amazement."

Released on Sept. 24, 1991, *Nevermind* debuted at #144 on the *Billboard* album charts on Oct. 5. And over the next few weeks, it rose steadily—from #144 to #109 to #65 to #35. It may have risen even more quickly had Geffen been prepared for the album's popularity; they had printed only 46,000 copies initially, meaning *Nevermind* was temporarily sold out in many markets. Meanwhile, as the staff at MTV was trying to figure out what to do with the video for "Smells Like Teen Spirit," a 22-year-old staffer named Amy Finnerty made it her personal quest to get Nirvana into the influential network's regular rotation. According to her account in *Everybody Loves Our Town*:

> The 'Smells Like Teen Spirit' video came in at the same time the new Guns N' Roses video came in, and at this point I hadn't worked at MTV for very long. I went to Abbey Konowitch, the head of the programming department at that point, and I said, 'Look, I love this place. I'm having a great time. That being said, this place doesn't really represent my generation. We really aren't playing videos from bands that I'm passionate about. We have something that's come in that I'm extremely passionate about. I'm just saying to you that if you don't play this, I don't feel like there's a place for me here.' I put my job on the line, basically. I believed in it that much. The video world-premiered on *120 Minutes*. Within a week or two, we got it in heavy rotation,

and within less than a month, the face of MTV had started to make a major transition.

Throughout November, heavy play of "Smells Like Teen Spirit" on both MTV and the nation-wide network of alternative radio stations like L.A.'s KROQ (where influential DJ Rodney Bingenheimer was a huge Nirvana supporter) and Boston's WFNX (which had played the whole album from beginning to end the day it came out) was helping to turn *Nevermind* into a bona fide hit. And on November 27 the album was certified platinum by the RIAA, marking the sale of 1 million albums in the U.S., an astounding number given the label's modest pre-release expectations. After a brief December sales plateau, sales were reinvigorated over the Christmas holiday season—reportedly when teenagers returned the albums they had been given as Christmas presents in order to get copies of *Nevermind*—and the album was certified double-platinum on January 7, 1992. When the *Billboard* album charts came out on January 11, *Nevermind* had supplanted Michael Jackson's *Dangerous* as the #1 album in America. According to KROQ's Bingenheimer, "I went home, went to bed, and suddenly they were #1."

Because *Nevermind*'s huge success hadn't been the result of a big, calculated marketing campaign—instead, it had taken most industry insiders off guard (Geffen president Eddie Rosenblatt had told the *New York Times* that his marketing plan for the album had been to "get out of the way and duck")—there was a sense around the music business that the album's rise to the top of the charts had been a grassroots success story. As *Spin* magazine put it in a 1992 profile, "[Nirvana] made it the old-fashioned way—with virtually no record company hype, through word of mouth street-talk, on its own." Soon, *Billboard* magazine was able to say, "Nirvana is that rare band that has everything: critical acclaim, industry respect, pop radio appeal, and a rock-solid college/alternative base." As *Nevermind* continued to sell—it went triple-platinum in early February—the sheer numbers were starting to draw the notice of label executives from across the industry. Where the commercial success stories of previous alternative bands had built slowly—it had taken U2 four albums to go platinum, and it had taken R.E.M. five—it took just eight weeks for *Nevermind* to go platinum. And with the album's sudden, unexpected success, major label executives were finally alerted to the fact that there was a huge untapped market for music which they had been ignoring. From a commercial perspective, if Nirvana could sell 3 million albums with only minimal marketing, how many albums could other bands from the alternative scene sell with focused major label marketing campaigns behind them? The quest to answer that question would change the face of the entire mainstream rock industry, but that change would not take place overnight.

For starters, at the beginning of 1992, the major labels simply didn't have the infrastructure in place to take alternative music into the mainstream en masse. The rock divisions within their A&R and marketing departments had spent nearly a decade focusing on glam bands like Poison, Bon Jovi, and Warrant, and breaking alternative bands would require going after an entirely new demographic and focusing their efforts on a different set of radio stations, record stores, and music publications. Meanwhile, there were still those at the major labels who believed that *Nevermind*'s success was just a blip on the radar—after all, glam stalwarts Def Leppard's 1992 release *Adrenalize* spent more weeks at #1 than *Nevermind* had. And for most major label executives, the biggest story of 1991-92 wasn't Nirvana, it was country music's sudden ascendance to pop chart dominance; of the 52 weekly *Billboard* album charts released in 1992, mega-hit albums by Garth Brooks and Billy Ray Cyrus owned the top spot for 34 of them.

And so, 1992 was fractured a year of transition for the record industry. While Nirvana's success was turning heads, pop acts like Michael Jackson and Boyz II Men continued to sell records, country music was becoming a sales phenomenon, hip hop acts Ice Cube and Kriss Kross both had #1 albums, and leftover glam bands like Guns N' Roses and Def Leppard were still lingering on the charts. Bands from the alternative scene enjoyed more chart success in 1992 than ever before, but only a handful of those bands scored hit albums. Alternative scene veterans Red Hot Chili Peppers notched their first platinum album with *Blood Sugar Sex Magik*, which would go triple-platinum by the end of the year. Fellow alternative mainstays The Cure saw U.S. sales of their 1992 effort *Wish* surpass the U.S. sales of any of their previous releases, eventually going double-platinum. Peter Gabriel's *Us* and R.E.M.'s *Automatic for the People* each debuted at #2 in back-to-back weeks in October; both were quickly certified platinum, and by the end of the year *Automatic for the People* had already gone double-platinum. The growing popularity of the alternative scene also spawned unlikely hits from acts as diverse as 10,000 Maniacs, Nine Inch Nails, and Toad the Wet Sprocket, all of whom scored gold records in

1992. But in the second half of the year, it was another Seattle-based band that would begin to rival Nirvana's popularity.

When the lineup for Lollapalooza 1992 was announced in May, festival co-founder Ted Gardner introduced Pearl Jam to MTV viewers as "a great little band from Seattle, Washington." But by the time the tour wrapped up in September, Pearl Jam had become co-headliners with Red Hot Chili Peppers, and their debut album *Ten* had gone triple-platinum. In addition to the exposure they got on the Lollapalooza tour, Pearl Jam also benefitted—much like Nirvana had—from MTV; the video for their song "Jeremy" debuted on August 1, 1992, went into heavy rotation, and stayed there for weeks. The video's content, which depicted the suicide of a high school boy in front of his classmates, was miles away from the light-hearted sexual innuendo of typical glam videos, and the addition of Eddie Vedder's brooding persona to Kurt Cobain's vitriolic angst signaled a discernible trend-shift in mainstream rock music and set the tone for what would become the "Seattle grunge" phenomenon. By the end of 1992, albums from Seattle-based bands Soundgarden, Alice in Chains, and the Soundgarden/Pearl Jam tribute project Temple of the Dog had joined Nirvana and Pearl Jam in *Billboard*'s year-end Top 100. Grunge moved further into the mainstream when Cameron Crowe's feature film *Singles*—which was set in Seattle and prominently featured performances by Soundgarden, Pearl Jam, Screaming Trees, and Alice in Chains—was released in September. The film's soundtrack hit the 1 million sales mark in October on its way to double-platinum status.

Ever since Bruce Pavitt and Jonathan Poneman's marketing adventures on behalf of Sub Pop Records in the late 80s, hype had gone hand in hand with grunge. As Poneman told the *New York Times* in late 1992, "All things grunge are treated with the utmost cynicism and amusement, because the whole thing is a fabricated movement and always has been." But as the Seattle scene entered the mainstream, the hype associated with the grunge phenomenon was beginning to see some increasingly absurd manifestations, even by Seattle standards. On November 3, under the direction of fashion impresario Marc Jacobs, Perry Ellis unveiled its "Grunge Collection" at New York's fashion week. The line—which would figure prominently in the December 1992 issue of *Vogue*—featured waifish female models wearing Nirvana t-shirts stretched over exposed long underwear and prep-school boys sporting wool caps and oversized flannel shirts and jackets. Most observers were dumbfounded.

"Grunge is about *not* making a statement," said James Truman, then editor of the men's magazine *Details*, "which is why it's crazy for it to become a fashion statement... Buying grunge from Seventh Avenue is ludicrous." Not surprisingly, the line flopped (Jacobs was fired by Perry Ellis the following spring). Then, on November 15, the *New York Times* published a prominent profile by Rick Marin titled, "Grunge: A Success Story." In his eagerness for insight into the newly popular scene, Marin included a "lexicon of grunge speak" attributed to Megan Jasper, a former Sub Pop staffer, which included such hilarities as "WACK SLACKS = old ripped jeans," "FUZZ = heavy wool sweaters," and "SWINGIN' ON THE FLIPPITY FLOP = hanging out." Unbeknown to Marin, Jasper had fabricated the entire thing. According to her account in *Everybody Loves Our Town*:

> Shortly after I got laid off at Sub Pop, there was a UK magazine called *Sky* that called up saying, 'Maybe you can give us some words people in Seattle use?' So I threw out some lies to them and they published this lexicon that they thought was real... Somehow someone at the *New York Times* heard that there was a lexicon that existed... and the reporter called... I kept escalating the craziness of the translations because anyone in their right mind would go, 'Oh, come on, this is bullshit.' I thought we would have a hearty laugh, and he would have to write it off as 15 minutes wasted, but it never happened, because he was concentrating so hard on getting the information right. My favorite was 'swingin' on the flippity-flop'... And a few days later, it was a huge thing on the front page of the Style section.

As the grunge phenomenon began to take on a life of its own, Kurt Cobain grew increasingly uncomfortable with the hype, and spoke out against it whenever possible. While he confidently proclaimed in *Rolling Stone* that *Nevermind* was "better than a lot of the commercial shit that's been crammed down people's throats for a long time," he also insisted that "famous is the last thing I wanted to be." But according to Cobain biographer Charles Cross in *Heavier than Heaven*:

> Kurt whined in interviews that MTV played his videos too much; privately he called his managers and complained when he thought they didn't play them enough... Though Kurt always downplayed his success and made out in interviews that he was trapped by his popularity, at every turn of his career he

made critical choices that furthered fame and success; it was one of the greatest contradictions in his character. The absurdity of a man appearing on MTV and talking about how he hated publicity was lost on many of Nirvana's fans, who preferred to see Kurt as he successfully presented himself—as an unwilling victim of fame rather than someone who had skillfully sought it.

These contradictions came to the fore publicly once Cobain started feeling threatened by Pearl Jam's popularity, and he went out of his way to diss his fellow Seattle natives in the press whenever possible. In the spring of '92, he told *Musician* magazine that Pearl Jam was "corporate, alternative, cock-rock fusion." Then in April he told *Rolling Stone*, "I would love to be erased from my association with that band and other corporate bands... I do feel a duty to warn the kids of false music that's claiming to be underground or alternative." And in May he told *Flipside*, "I have strong feelings towards Pearl Jam and Alice in Chains and bands like that. They're obviously just corporate puppets that are just trying to jump on the alternative bandwagon—and we are being lumped into that category." The comments struck those familiar with the Seattle scene as ridiculous, in part because Pearl Jam's major label debut *Ten* had been recorded and released *before* Nirvana's major label debut *Nevermind*. According to Mudhoney guitarist Steve Turner, "We knew Jeff [Ament of Pearl Jam], and for Kurt to say anything about Pearl Jam not having roots in punk rock—are you fuckin' stupid? Jeff was there from day one of the Seattle thing." According to Ament himself in *Everybody Loves Our Town*, "Kurt was talking shit about us, and we talked a little shit back... My point was: fuck, man, we were putting records out on [indie label] Homestead Records while Kurt was going to Sammy Hagar concerts. At that point I was like, if you want to talk about punk-rock credibility, I can back it up. I was there when it was going down. A couple of times I went up and introduced myself to Kurt and tried to have a conversation with him, but he didn't want to have any part of it." It wasn't until Cobain and Eddie Vedder—neither of whom were exactly sober at the time—were coerced into slow-dancing together backstage during Eric Clapton's set at the 1992 MTV Video Music Awards that September, that the tension was broken and the feud—the public side of it anyway—was laid to rest.

But as the grunge fad was sweeping the nation throughout 1992, Nirvana was conspicuously absent from the rock concert circuit. And in a May

L.A. Times article headlined "Why is Nirvana Missing from a Heavenly Tour Season?" Steve Hochman wrote, "[Nirvana's] low profile has renewed public speculation that singer/guitarist Kurt Cobain has a heroin problem." Amidst rumors of rehab—and even death—word was circulating that Nirvana might cancel their prestigious headlining slot at England's Reading Festival that August. Cobain—who really *had* come to Reading directly from a rehab stint in Los Angeles—decided to play to the rumors and, when the time came for Nirvana's set, he had himself wheeled onstage in a wheelchair wearing a hospital smock. After collapsing out of the wheelchair onto the stage, he immediately hopped up and launched into a spirited version of "Breed" from *Nevermind* to kick off a raucous 25-song set. The audience reaction was electric and Nirvana—for the time being, anyway—remained on top of the rock world.

As the Seattle bands were jockeying for position and attempting to come to terms with their newfound fame, there was another band with roots in the alternative scene—one who had been around the block a couple of times—who was matching Nirvana and Pearl Jam's sales numbers throughout 1992. And the most sweeping artistic statement to come out of the alternative scene that year wasn't grunge; it was a forward-thinking album and revolutionary concert tour by a band whose alternative credentials had been called into question just a couple of years earlier.

ZOO TV

In February 2012, *Spin* magazine named U2's *Achtung Baby* "The Best Album of the Last 25 Years," and in the accompanying article Charles Aaron adds that the album had cemented U2's status as "the emblematic band of the alternative-rock era." This claim goes against the conventional 21st Century wisdom in which Nirvana—and their album *Nevermind*—are typically trotted out as the alternative archetypes. If one is considering only the period of alternative music's 1990s commercial breakthrough and its aftermath, the choice of Nirvana makes perfect sense. But if one is considering the totality of the alternative music era, from the early 80s through the mid-90s, U2 serves as a far better symbol. They had been there since the beginning, when their debut album was getting play in 1981 on the still-fledgling KROQ. And the band's

1991 masterpiece *Achtung Baby* and the subsequent ZOO TV concert tour provided a closing bookend to their decade-long career as an alternative band. For the rest of their post-ZOO TV career, it would be difficult to look at U2 as anything other than a mainstream rock band. But back in 1991, they still had one more countercultural statement to make, and it would be the riskiest of their career.

It is unusual, to say the least, for a popular rock act to completely reinvent themselves at the height of their fame. As Elvis had said all the way back in 1962, "A certain type of audience likes me. I entertain them with what I'm doing. I'd be a fool to tamper with that kind of success." And the few rock artists who *had* managed to successfully reinvent themselves—Bob Dylan, The Beatles, The Rolling Stones—were among the most respected acts in rock history. But after the widespread criticism that had been leveled at *Rattle and Hum*, U2 was disillusioned and in a desperate place. Following three consecutive years of touring, they returned to Ireland as conquering heroes, but they were no longer the same band. According to Bono in the 2012 documentary *From the Sky Down*, when the band got home, "Irish people go... You left here as an interesting post-punk phenomenon. You go to America— fine, we'll run with you on *The Joshua Tree*—but now you've become... self-conscious and overblown." This revelation was a wake-up call for the band. "When we were kids—16, 17 years old—going to see The Clash in Dublin," Bono continues, "this was the enemy. We'd become the enemy."

The members of U2 eventually agreed that a complete reimagining of the band would be necessary if they were going to be able to continue making music together. According to bassist Adam Clayton in *U2 by U2*, "If we hadn't done something we were excited about, that made us apprehensive and challenged everything we stood for, then there would really have been no reason to carry on... If [we couldn't make] a great record by our standards, the existence of the band would have been threatened." But actually walking away from the version of themselves that they had built up over more than a decade proved scarier than they'd thought. According to Bono, "You have to reject one expression of the band first, *before* you get to the next expression. And in between, you have nothing. You have to risk it all."

At first, all the band had was a vague idea about trying to incorporate the electronic dance beats of Europe's burgeoning club scene into a rock form that they could actually execute. And the original plan for writing and

114

recording the album was to set up shop in newly-reunified Berlin's Hansa Studios—a former SS concert hall which had been used as a recording studio by artists from David Bowie to Depeche Mode—and wait for inspiration to strike. While *The Joshua Tree* and *Rattle and Hum* had been hugely influenced by American music and culture, Berlin—on the heels of the fall of the Berlin Wall—seemed like a perfect place to channel the ethos of "The New Europe." But the plan proved to be an unmitigated disaster. "We felt as we walked into this room that it's so full of greatness that greatness will visit with us," recalls Bono in *From the Sky Down*. "So we're there, and greatness is nowhere to be found. Greatness has left the building... At this moment we're a long way, *a long way*, from the madness of ZOO TV. At this moment, we couldn't imagine what we were going to become." Clayton adds, "Berlin was a baptism of fire. It was something that we had to go through to realize that what we were looking for and trying to get to was not something you could find physically, outside of ourselves, in some other city." And so, throughout the months in Berlin, the band was experiencing an acute identity crisis. "It's fraught with danger because you can fail at any moment," adds U2's longtime producer and engineer Flood, although he also saw the band's identity crisis as a unique opportunity. "That's the whole beauty of it, if you're prepared to remove the safety net, and if you're prepared to really expose yourselves. Because your pursuit is after the magic moments, those moments of 'Wow, I would *never* have imagined...'"

Luckily for U2, the band experienced one of those moments just before their scheduled time in Berlin was set to expire. In the midst of an improvised jam session, they stumbled onto the chord progression and vocal melody for "One," the song which would eventually become the centerpiece of *Achtung Baby*. Once the band reconvened in Ireland to finish recording, "One" would set the lyrical tone for the rest of the album, both in its emotional transparency and in its thematic exploration of division and disunity. Song after song—from "So Cruel" to "Acrobat" to "Love is Blindness"—probed the depths of doubt and despair, as the band slowly let go of the redemptive rope that they had clung to throughout their career, even through the darkest moments of their previous albums. Within the context of the album itself, the doubt and pain of *Achtung Baby* remain unresolved; they *might* end in redemption, but then again they might not, and closing the album with a song called "Love is Blindness" seemed to hint which direction things were going. In fact, it was the exposed rawness of the songs themselves that led directly to the ironic posturing which eventually came to typify U2's subsequent live performances for the ZOO TV tour. "If I was going to expose my heart," explains Bono, "I needed the right kind of armor to protect the rest of me."

But the ironic posturing which began as a defense mechanism soon morphed into its own persona—called "The Fly"—which Bono would employ for much of the ZOO TV tour. And as he toyed with the persona in the studio, he even wrote a couple of songs—"The Fly" and "Even Better than the Real Thing"—from the perspective of this newly invented character. "Getting down into that guttural place—*into the gutter*... I could let a whole new vocabulary open up," he explained. The character of The Fly worked on a number of levels. First, what the character had to say wasn't necessarily *untrue*; for instance, from the song "The Fly:"

> *It's no secret that a conscience can sometimes be a pest*
> *It's no secret ambition bites the nails of success*
> *Every artist is a cannibal, every poet is a thief*
> *All kill their inspiration and sing about their grief*

But the *source* of the "wisdom" being imparted, hidden behind his dark sunglasses and black leather pants, was clearly not to be trusted. On this level, The Fly echoed a literary tradition that included Dostoyevsky's "Devil" character (who counsels Ivan in *The Brothers Karamazov*), C.S. Lewis's "Screwtape" character, Umberto Eco's "Simonini" character, and on and on.

The Fly also gave U2 a way to counter the charges of self-importance that had been leveled at their previous album and tour. As Bono put it in *From the Sky Down*, "If we're being accused of megalomania, let's do some judo. Let's use the force of what's attacking us to defend ourselves... Let's give them a 'rock star.' Let's have some fun with this." This development allowed The Fly—and the entire ZOO TV tour—to serve as a commentary on rock stardom itself, and this initial thematic concept was eventually expanded into a commentary on pop culture as a whole: mass commercialism, media technology, and ultimately the very nature of truth and meaning in the postmodern age. "['The Fly'] informed so much," says Bono, "[it] ended up becoming our exploration live of media and the truth, which was ZOO TV."

116

THE DAY ALTERNATIVE MUSIC DIED

The ZOO TV tour was like nothing that has ever been attempted by a rock band—before or since. As *Pitchfork*'s Ryan Dombal would write in 2011, "Even 20 years on, the tour looks like something to behold, a singularly inventive experience that no band—including U2 itself—has been able to really expound upon in a meaningful way." The staging for the tour was centered around multiple "Vidiwalls"—huge TV screens that spanned the stage—and numerous supplemental groupings of smaller television screens that, when combined with the band's music, were capable of flooding the audience with an overwhelming sensory overload. And thus the stage itself became an exercise in performance art. The screens were filled a constant barrage of words which alternated between familiar and bizarre sayings—inspired by New York-based performance artist Jenny Holzer and conceived in conjunction with video artist Mark Pellington and visual artist David Wojnarowicz—which created a subliminal disorienting effect. In the ramp-up to the start of the show, the crowd was pumped up by footage of a Hitler Youth drum corps, as well as manipulated footage of then-President George H. W. Bush saying "We. Will. We. Will. Rock. You." Seemingly every familiar media trick and sensory appeal was taken to a new level—and accompanied by an unsettling subliminal admonition to question that very appeal.

It was the ability of ZOO TV to simultaneously be both an artistic statement and a commentary on artistic statements that caused many observers to dub the tour a "postmodern" phenomenon. And this perception was only heightened by the meta-self-referential nature of the performance. At one point during ZOO TV performances of "Where the Streets Have No Name," as *Joshua Tree*-era footage of the band played on the huge TV screen behind them, Bono would turn to the screen and shout, "Hey you!" and the on-screen Bono would turn and wave back. It was unclear if Bono was mocking or celebrating his previous incarnation's comparative seriousness and naiveté, but the moment was powerful and fascinating, and before it could be further assessed it was gone, swept aside by the music and the next image on the screen. ZOO TV was full of these kinds of moments.

Meanwhile, in the midst of the technological circus on stage, there was a musical performance being given which included U2's most naked and vulnerable lyrics to date. And as the performance veered wildly between the sincere and insincere, the authentic and inauthentic, this unusual dynamic fused with the technological onslaught to create an entirely new rock show experience, one which mined the past and predicted the future but was also intimately tied to its own time and place. ZOO TV is difficult to revisit on film, not only because the limitations of video fail to capture the totality of the live show experience, but because part of the full power of the ZOO TV experience was only possible in real time, in the days before the ubiquity of the internet and hand-held media devices, when the juxtaposition of news, art, and entertainment—the mashing together of footage of Gulf War destruction, weepingly apologetic televangelists, melodramatic soap operas, and the world's biggest rock band—still felt strange, and that strangeness could be drawn out into the open and considered critically. Here in the second decade of the 21st Century, the familiarity of media immersion has rendered this exercise all but impossible, and in the present context the power of ZOO TV is harder to understand. It was a warning that went unheeded about a crisis that has long been forgotten, and because ZOO TV was on the losing side of a cultural debate that no longer seems relevant, its legacy has suffered, even though the questions it was asking about the nature of mass media and truth are every bit as important—perhaps even more so—in the context of today's all-encompassing online world.

Another factor that has obscured the significance of *Achtung Baby* and ZOO TV is that, where *Nevermind*'s commercial breakthrough had been a surprise to industry insiders, *Achtung Baby*'s commercial success—coming, as it was, on the heels of the multi-platinum *Joshua Tree*—was far less surprising. Nevertheless, *Achtung* was a huge album; it debuted at #1 in December of 1991, had sold over 2 million copies in America by the end of January '92, and remained in the top 10 for much of that year, matching *Nevermind* sale for sale. In fact, at the time of Kurt Cobain's death in April 1994, *Achtung Baby* had outsold *Nevermind*, both in the U.S. and abroad. To date, it has sold 18 million copies worldwide. And as the ZOO TV tour played to 5.3 million people around the world throughout 1992-93—more than any other tour in history at that point—its in-your-face artistic experimentation and countercultural questioning of mainstream media expanded the public conception of what mainstream rock music could be, broadening the popular rock music palette and helping to lay the groundwork for the alternative scene's massive 1993 commercial breakthrough.

1993: The High Water Mark of the Alternative Scene

As grunge and ZOO TV slammed their wrecking balls into the mainstream glam rock edifice, more and more holes were opening up through which other artistically adventurous bands from the alternative scene could make their way into the mainstream. And throughout 1993, the alternative scene would trickle into the public consciousness in all of its diversity, finally and decisively eclipsing glam as rock music's popular torchbearer. During the course of the year, over *thirty* albums by bands from the alternative scene would be certified gold (500,000 sales) or platinum (1 million sales) in the U.S., with many more alternative albums released in 1993 well on their way to being certified gold and platinum in early 1994. In a marked contrast with previous years, *every song* in KROQ's 1993 year-end Top 20 countdown was from an album that had been—or would eventually become—certified gold by the RIAA.

In the early part of 1993, the alternative albums hitting the charts tended to be the leftover remnants of the grunge phenomenon. Soundgarden's *Badmotorfinger* rode the grunge wave to platinum status in January. Nirvana's collection of unreleased rarities and B-sides, *Incesticide*, went gold the following month. And *Core*, the debut from San Diego-based grunge wannabees Stone Temple Pilots, was certified gold in April. But the grunge fad quickly dissipated, and as the year went on, the floodgates seemed to open as bands from every slice of the alternative scene's stylistic spectrum began charging into the mainstream. One minute, the hauntingly emotive *Little Earthquakes* by singer-songwriter Tori Amos was crossing over, and the next it was former Jane's Addiction frontman Perry Farrell's quirky new project, Porno for Pyros. Minneapolis-based roots-punk-rockers Soul Asylum rode the success of their single "Runaway Train" into the charts. And as the spring turned into summer, new releases from alternative scene veterans Depeche Mode and Duran Duran quickly went platinum. In August, U2's follow-up to *Achtung Baby*, *Zooropa*, debuted at #1 and immediately went double-platinum. And throughout the second half of the year, a whole slew of gold and platinum records were certified by alternative acts who had never previously gone gold, and these acts displayed widely varying styles: the neo-psychedelic jam-rock of Blind Melon, the ethereal dream-pop of The Sundays, the noisy Brit-rock of Radiohead, the crooning melancholy of former Smiths frontman Morrissey, the emotive punk/metal/classic-rock hybrid of The Smashing Pumpkins, the more polished rock hooks of The Gin Blossoms, the brooding Irish lilt of The Cranberries.

Part of the reason for the sudden breakthrough of all these acts was the increased exposure the alternative scene was getting on MTV; in late 1992, the network had launched a new nightly show called *Alternative Nation*. The show was hosted by former KROQ intern Lisa Kennedy Montgomery, who would take the stage name "Kennedy" and spend the next half-decade spinning the latest alternative videos in between interviews with alternative icons from David Bowie to Trent Reznor, Tori Amos to Marilyn Manson. And throughout 1993, the show helped introduce an entire generation of mainstream MTV viewers to the formerly underground alternative phenomenon, forcing the pre-existing alternative infrastructure to expand in order to handle the new demand. In June of 1993, KROQ held its first "Weenie Roast," a day-long outdoor alternative music festival that has been a Los Angeles summer staple ever since. The inaugural event was a sell-out and included sets from a wide array of alternative acts: The The, Stone Temple Pilots, X, Dramarama, Bettie Serveert, The Posies, Suede, The Lemonheads, The Gin Blossoms. And KROQ's year-end "Almost Acoustic Christmas" concert that December expanded to two nights—both of which were sellouts—and featured a diverse bill stuffed with newly-breaking alternative acts: Smashing Pumpkins, Blind Melon, Cowboy Junkies, Cracker, The Cranberries, 4 Non Blondes, The Lemonheads, Porno for Pyros, Primus, They Might Be Giants, Rage Against the Machine, The Wonderstuff, The Violent Femmes, and former Black Flag frontman Henry Rollins. Lollapalooza's 1993 incarnation was also expanded to include *thirty-two* acts (up from just eleven in 1991), as the festival added a second stage and toured the country to sold-out crowds. And soon new alternative radio stations like Chicago's Q101 began popping up and hosting their own local alternative concert festivals.

The ability of the diverse alternative scene to break through commercially where punk had failed was widely hailed as a victory for punk-inspired creative freedom over the commercial stylistic homogeneity that had typified mainstream popular rock for much of 80s. But for some, the alternative scene's punk roots led to a mistaken *equation* of "alternative" and "punk," even though it was clear that the two movements had many differences. For instance, even as Sonic Youth's Thurston Moore gave his indie-punk spiel about "destroying the record companies" in the 1992 documentary *The Year Punk Broke*—which follows Sonic Youth and Nirvana's 1991 European tour—both bands were signed to major record labels, as were virtually all of the bands at the head of the alternative scene's 1991-93 commercial breakthrough. Clearly, whatever the alternative breakthrough signified, it did not signify a victory for the part of the indie-punk ethos that anathematized major labels and eschewed commercial success of any kind. Neither was the alternative breakthrough a victory for the stylistic simplicity of post-punk minimalism that had been codified by many of the indie bands of the 80s. In fact, the bands that most rigidly adhered to that kind of minimalism—like Sonic Youth and Mudhoney—tended to be the bands who *failed* to catch the alternative wave into the mainstream. Meanwhile, the music that *did* cross over reflected the stylistic diversity which had been a staple of alternative radio playlists throughout the preceding decade. Where the stylistic rigidity of the punk movement had made it possible to distill punk into an identifiable sound, stylistic diversity was a hallmark of the alternative scene; the inclusion of bands as sonically dissimilar as, say, The Sundays and Pearl Jam had been essential to the alternative scene since its inception over a decade earlier.

As alternative music moved further and further into the mainstream, there was an irony to the fact that a music scene which had generally prided itself on its relative lack of commercial success was suddenly enjoying such a widespread sales boom. But while there were some purists who frowned upon alternative music's newfound popular success, most people in the alternative scene embraced its crossover success and the validation that success seemed to provide. "It's great!" Jennifer Finch of L.A.-based alternative band L7 told *Spin* magazine at the time, "It's about time we can walk into a 7-Eleven and hear something cool. It's about time we don't have to listen to crap on the radio anymore." And the effects of alternative music's mainstream breakthrough also trickled down into high schools and junior highs, where alternative music's newfound popularity helped an entire generation of marginalized outsiders achieve a new degree of social credibility. As Arcade Fire frontman Win Butler would later recall to *Time*, "All of a sudden the whole kind of social dynamic at my junior high changed, where these kind of misfit kids who maybe come from a broken home and they're smoking cigarettes in the back and they didn't have money for nice clothes, all of a sudden those kids socially were in a weird way on the same level as everyone else... I was sort of like a weird kid who didn't know where I fit in or whatever and just to have that kind of voice be that big in culture, I feel like that was a magical period of alternative music where we had Jane's Addiction and R.E.M. and Nirvana. It was like seeing these kind of freaks from all the different cities of North America and you're like, oh wow." Or, as indie journalist Gina Arnold succinctly put it, the alternative breakthrough meant "We won." And throughout 1993, alternative music's mainstream crossover was embraced by Lollapalooza concert goers, *Alternative Nation* viewers, and most of the alternative bands themselves, many of whom were enjoying newfound fame and fortune thanks to alternative music's commercial breakthrough. But the question remained: What would mainstream commercial success mean for the artistic freedom and diversity that had been the alternative scene's trademark for over a decade?

Chapter Nine

The Myth of Nirvana

The Death of an Icon and a New Template for Alternative Music

Alternative Music in the Months before Kurt Cobain's Death

On September 21, 1993, Nirvana released *In Utero*, the much anticipated follow-up to the band's breakthrough hit *Nevermind*. Following the rollercoaster ride Kurt Cobain and Nirvana had been on over the previous two years—the rapid ascent to fame, the rumored drug addiction and cancelled shows, the legendary live performance at Reading '92—no one knew what to expect from the new album. But the narrative surrounding *In Utero*'s release would come to be shaped by the fact that both the critical and commercial establishments had been embarrassed by their failure to see *Nevermind*'s success coming, and both were determined not to make the same mistake with *In Utero*. For instance, *Rolling Stone* hadn't even bothered to review *Nevermind* at the time of its release in September of 1991. Only in late November of that year, *after* the album had started to climb the charts, had the magazine published a middling 3-star review—a below average rating compared to the other albums reviewed by the magazine that week—which dismissively referred to Nirvana as "the latest underground bonus-baby to test mainstream tolerance for alternative music." In this context, the gushing hyperbole of David Fricke's 4.5-star *In Utero* review in September of 1993 came across like *Rolling Stone*'s attempt to make up for its failure to predict *Nevermind*'s success. "If Generation Hex is ever going to have its own Lennon," Fricke opines in his *In Utero* review, "Cobain is damn near it."

Nirvana's label Geffen Records wasn't going to be caught off guard this time around, either. Rather, they were going to do whatever they could in order to stack the deck in favor of the new album. When the recordings of *In Utero* were completed, both the label and Nirvana's management insisted that the album be remixed in order to sound more commercially viable. And so, with the approval of the band, the tracks were remixed and remastered in order to sweeten the album's sound, most notably the potential singles "Heart-Shaped Box" and "All Apologies." The label also made sure to give *In Utero* the big-time major label promotional push that *Nevermind* had never received, raining advance copies of the album on the nationwide network of alternative radio stations in the weeks leading up to its release and helping bankroll a $500,000 music video for the lead single "Heart-Shaped Box." And thanks to the band's cache this time around, the new video didn't need the insider advocacy "Smells Like Teen Spirit" had gotten in order to go into immediate heavy rotation on MTV. Commercially, everything seemed to be lining up in the album's favor. Even a potential sales snag was averted when, after Wal-Mart and Kmart initially refused to stock the album due its "potentially offensive artwork" (as well as the inclusion of a song titled "Rape Me"), Kurt Cobain quickly agreed to change the artwork and list the controversial song's title as "Waif Me" so that the huge retail chains would stock the album. "One of the main reasons I signed to a major label was so that people could buy our records at Kmart," Cobain explained to the *New York Times* at the time. "In some small towns, Kmart is the only place kids can buy records."

But in spite of all the critical and commercial efforts that accompanied its release, *In Utero* wasn't able to match *Nevermind*'s runaway success. The album debuted at #1 in the *Billboard* album chart, but its roughly 180,000 first-week sales were widely seen as a disappointment in the midst of a breakthrough year during which over thirty albums by bands from the alternative scene would achieve gold record status certifying 500,000 sales or more. *In Utero* hit the million sales mark in late November, but sales dropped off quickly, and by the end of 1993, *In Utero* was out of the Top 20; it would not achieve double-platinum status until after Kurt Cobain's death the following spring, a huge disappointment in comparison to *Nevermind*'s 5 million U.S. sales to date.

There were countless theories as to why the album failed to catch on commercially. Many of Nirvana's handlers thought the decision to record a more sonically abrasive departure from *Nevermind* had limited the album's commercial appeal. Some blamed the controversial liner notes that had accompanied Nirvana's 1992 B-sides album *Incesticide*, which had taken aim at any of the band's fans who might be homophobes, misogynists, or racists. "Leave us the fuck alone!" read the liner notes. "Don't come to our shows and don't buy our records." In addition, Nirvana had cancelled over 50 shows due to Cobain's various "illnesses" between the releases of *Nevermind* and *In Utero*—twice going more than six months without playing a single show in the U.S.—limiting the band's exposure and alienating fans who had purchased tickets for the cancelled shows. There was also the fact that many of the songs on the new album—such as "Rape Me" and "Radio Friendly Unit Shifter"—focused on Cobain's discontent with the inner workings of the record industry rather than the more relatable subject matter of *Nevermind*. And there were those who simply thought the quality of the songs just wasn't what it had been on the previous album. "It was just this improvisational, atonal stuff, just noisy," said Craig Montgomery, who helped the band record the demos for *In Utero*. "I could tell that Kurt wasn't at one of his creative peaks at all. It was obvious—and he had said to me and others—that he just wasn't really excited about Nirvana anymore and he wanted to do something else. They were struggling to get enough material together for an album." But whatever the reason for the album's disappointing sales, *In Utero*'s lackluster reception made it clear that Nirvana was no longer the most popular band in rock, or the most popular band from the alternative scene, or even the most popular Seattle-based band; all of those titles had been decisively usurped by Kurt Cobain's least favorite rival band, Pearl Jam. And by the end of 1993, it was starting to look like Nirvana might have been a "one-hit wonder."

On October 19, 1993, just a month after the release of *In Utero*, Pearl Jam released its second album, *Vs.* The album received generally positive reviews, but no one anticipated the massive commercial success it would become. Unlike sales of *In Utero*, which had sputtered out of the gate, *Vs.* was an immediate sensation, selling over 950,000 copies in its first week (more than 5 times what *In Utero* had sold), setting an all-time record for opening-week sales and topping the *combined* sales of the rest of the albums in that week's *Billboard* Top 10. By January, the album was certified quintuple-platinum, certifying 5 million albums sold in the U.S., becoming the fastest album to reach 5 million sales since the RIAA had begun keeping records. The popular success of *Vs.* both solidified Pearl Jam's standing as the most popular American rock band and highlighted *In Utero*'s relative commercial failure. By early 1994, Pearl Jam had clearly supplanted Nirvana as the new face of alternative music.

But even as *Vs.* was setting sales records, there was discouraging news for any major label executives who might be looking to base a marketing template on Pearl Jam's success. *Vs.* had achieved its dizzying commercial success in spite of the fact that the band had largely refused to do promotional interviews for the album, had refused to make videos for any of the album's songs, and had been generally hostile to marketing efforts of any kind prior to the album's release. And as 1993 turned into 1994, any potential efforts to codify some sort of alternative marketing template were further discouraged by the continued musical diversity of the breakthrough scene. On January 11, subdued alt-scene veterans 10,000 Maniacs' *Unplugged* album was certified platinum. The next day, the hyped-up angst of Rage Against the Machine's debut album went gold. Tori Amos' new album *Under the Pink* was released at the end of the month, debuted at #1 in the U.K., and quickly went platinum in the U.S. And in the following weeks, these commercial breakthroughs were followed by certified gold records for a wide range of sonically diverse alternative acts: the emotionally charged roots-rock of Counting Crows, the pop-oriented dance beats of New Order, the southern-tinged rock and roll of Cracker, the female-fronted post-punk of The Breeders and Belly.

In the year since the grunge fad had died down in early 1993, the mainstream crossover of alternative music had again exhibited a remarkable range of styles, and thus the alternative scene remained difficult to pigeon-hole stylistically for commercial purposes. Perhaps the most iconic attempt to commercialize the alternative scene during this period was the January 1994 feature film *Reality Bites*. Douglas Coupland's 1991 novel *Generation X* had recently popularized the trendy generational moniker, and the ascendance of its use in popular culture had coincided with alternative music's popular rise, leading to the widespread perception of alternative music as the soundtrack of the burgeoning post-boomer generation. In the case of *Reality Bites*, this meant that, in addition to a soundtrack filled with seminal alternative bands like The Violent Femmes, U2, and Dinosaur Jr., the film also included cameos from alternative music icons like Soul Asylum's Dave Pirner and The Lemonheads' Evan Dando. Ethan Hawke's lead character even plays in an alternative band, and a central plot point turns on Hawke's performance of the Violent Femmes' alternative staple "Add It Up." Though the film clearly overreaches in its attempt to capture a defining generational ethos, *Reality Bites* still serves as a revelatory time capsule exhibiting how sonically diverse the music of the alternative scene remained in the final months prior to Kurt Cobain's death. In fact, the only #1 single by an alternative act during the scene's 1991-94 commercial breakthrough was Lisa Loeb's acoustic guitar-based ballad "Stay (I Missed You)," which, at the time, rivaled "Smells Like Teen Spirit" as the definitive crossover alternative song of the early 90s. "Stay (I Missed You)" propelled the *Reality Bites* soundtrack to gold record status, an honor which it achieved on April 5, 1994—the same day Kurt Cobain committed suicide. Had Cobain lived, it is possible that alternative music would have lived on in the collective memory as the diverse soundtrack for Generation X—much like the baby boomers' association with the diverse palette of 60s rock music—rather than as a specific musical style and attitude. But Kurt Cobain did not live, and the effects of his death on the popular perceptions of both Nirvana and alternative music in general would be immediate and profound.

The Day Alternative Music Died

In the year leading up to his death, Kurt Cobain continued to be plagued by his conflicting impulses towards punk-inspired creative autonomy and mainstream rock stardom. He had hired indie icon Steve Albini—former frontman of the 80s indie band Big Black and producer of The Pixies' influential *Surfer Rosa* album—to produce *In Utero* in an attempt to move away from what he had come to perceive as the "polished" sound of *Nevermind* and to regain some of his indie-punk credibility in the wake of Nirvana's commercial success. If Cobain was looking for a producer who would resist commercial influence, he found his man in Albini. "I couldn't give a shit about commercial pressure," Albini would later say. "None of that mattered to me. It mattered to all the flotsam and jetsam that were attracted to Nirvana, all the shit-box people that were there; their management people, their record label, their fucking hangers-on of all types." But when the finished masters of *In Utero* were poorly received by Nirvana's label and management, Cobain agreed to have producer Scott Litt—best known for his work on R.E.M.'s recent string of platinum albums—come in and remix some of the songs, especially the potential singles. Upset by this decision, Albini complained to the *Chicago Tribune*, "Geffen and Nirvana's management *hate* the record... I have no faith it will be released." But instead of standing by his hand-picked producer, Cobain chose to deny Albini's allegations, and he was so concerned about how the public might perceive the conflict that he had Geffen Records take out a full-page ad in *Billboard* denying that the label had rejected the album. In the end, it was the remixed and remastered Scott Litt version of *In Utero* that was released to the public.

But Cobain hated himself for compromising, and he fantasized in his journal about releasing the Albini version of the album—under his preferred title of *I Hate Myself and Want to Die*, which had been rejected for fear of lawsuits—on vinyl, cassette, and eight-track tape only. However, his journals from the time were wildly self-contradictory, often supplementing his dreams of indie purity with angry rants against indie-punk rigidity. "I made about five million dollars last year and I'm not giving a red cent to that elitist, little fuck [indie icon and one-time mentor] Calvin Johnson," ranted one unsent letter to ex-girlfriend Tobi Vail. "I chose to let corporate white men exploit me a few years ago and I love it. It feels good. And I'm not gonna donate a single fucking dollar to the fucking needy indie fascist regime. They can starve. Let them eat vinyl." Then, just as *In Utero* was about to be released, Cobain bowed to pressure from Wal-Mart and Kmart and agreed to change the album in order to get it into their stores. As Cobain biographer Charles Cross put it, "Once again, when challenged by a problem that might affect the success of his record, Kurt acquiesced to the path of least resistance and greatest sales." But he never felt good about it, and *In Utero*'s #1 debut was—like all of Nirvana's commercial achievements—overshadowed by the guilt he felt for betraying his indie-punk ideals.

Meanwhile, Cobain's problems with heroin had only worsened. He OD'd a dozen times throughout 1993, and each time he was revived and restored to relative physical health. But he was not in a healthy place mentally. Since early 1992, Cobain had been obsessed with watching a bootlegged video he owned of a man shooting himself in the head. "He had this video of a senator blowing his brains out on TV," recalled friend Jesse Reed in *Heavier than Heaven*. "This guy takes a .357 magnum from a manila envelope, and blows his brains out. It was pretty graphic." And Cobain's journal entries from 1993 reveal a desperately lonely man at the end of his rope, pleading in vain for a new group of friends who could rescue him from his loneliness:

> Friends who I can talk to and hang out with and have fun with, just like I've always dreamed... Hey, I can't stop pulling my hair out! Please! God damn, Jesus fucking Christ Almighty, love me, we could go on a trial basis, please I don't care if it's the out-of-the-in crowd, I just need a crowd, a gang, a reason to smile. I won't smother you, ah shit, shit, please, isn't there somebody out there? Somebody, anybody, God help, help me please. I want to be accepted. I have to be accepted. I'll wear any kind of clothes you want! I'm so tired of crying and dreaming, I'm soo soo alone. Isn't there anyone out there? Please help me. HELP ME.

Virtually every interview Cobain gave in 1993 mentioned suicide. Finally, in December of that year, according to his wife, he tried to commit suicide himself, an act that was revealed only to his inner circle. Then on March 8, 1994, while in Rome on tour with Nirvana, he composed a suicide note and downed 60 Rohypnol pills, which left him in a coma for nearly twenty-four hours. The event was publicly proclaimed an accidental overdose, but his longtime friend and bandmate Krist Novacelic wondered if the coma had left him with brain damage. "He wouldn't listen to *anybody*," Novacelic recalled of Cobain's post-coma behavior. "He was *so* fucked up." By the next month, Cobain had decided to employ a more foolproof suicide method, and on April 8—an estimated three days after his death—he was found at his Seattle home, in a room above the garage, dead of a self-inflicted shotgun wound to the head.

The Myth of Nirvana

From the very first public announcements of Kurt Cobain's death, the clock was turned back and, for the first time in months, Nirvana was repeatedly referred to as a band on the rise, as the band at the head of the "alternative revolution." The cancelled shows, the controversial *Incesticide* liner notes, the pre-release disputes over *In Utero*, the album's subsequent commercial failure, the way Nirvana's popularity had been eclipsed by other bands from the alternative scene, all of these elements were removed from the standard Nirvana narrative in the aftermath of Cobain's death. Kurt Loder's live MTV's broadcast on April 8 was typical of how the announcements of his death were framed, "Hi, I'm Kurt Loder with an MTV News special report on a very sad day. Kurt Cobain, the leader of one of rock's most gifted and promising bands, Nirvana, is dead." In a way, this made perfect sense; when a public figure dies, it is only natural to want to focus on the positive aspects of his or her life and career out of respect for the dead, especially given the way that such announcements are generally reduced to just a couple of sentences. But by the time *Rolling Stone*'s commemorative Kurt Cobain issue hit newsstands the following month, a full-fledged mythology was already being constructed around Cobain and Nirvana.

The very first sentence of Anthony DeCurtis' cover story for *Rolling Stone*'s commemorative issue referred to Cobain as "the spokesman of a generation," a phrase that had been bandied about in the heady days after *Nevermind*'s surprise success, but one which had been shelved for months, particularly after *In Utero*'s lackluster popular reception. "Whatever importance Cobain assumed as a symbol," says DeCurtis, "one thing is certain: He and his band Nirvana announced the end of one rock & roll era and the start of another. In essence, Nirvana transformed the 80s into the 90s." Throughout the entire issue, article after article echoed and reinforced that sentiment. Donna Gaines' profile insists, "In Nirvana, Cobain moved a kid's private hell to a generation's collective howl." And David Fricke's closing think-piece declares, "Nirvana's *Nevermind* tore a hole through the *Billboard* album chart at the end of 1991 and broke the death grip of 80s mainstream pomp and bloat on rock & roll." According to Fricke, "Smells Like Teen Spirit" was one of the few songs which "define an epoch," in the hallowed company of Elvis' "Heartbreak Hotel," The Beatles' "I Want to Hold Your Hand," Dylan's "Like a Rolling Stone," and The Sex Pistols' "Anarchy in the UK." *Spin* got into the myth-making game with their commemorative issue as well. "Nirvana... permanently altered the attitudes of record companies toward a new generation of 'alternative' artists," wrote *Spin*'s Eric Weisbard. "It would not be ridiculous, then, to make a second claim: Kurt Cobain's life saved rock 'n' roll."

There was, of course, some truth in all of these characterizations, it was just that they, as rock critics are wont to do, distilled a complicated—and often self-contradictory—narrative into an overwrought and oversimplified myth. Suddenly, inconvenient tidbits like the fact that both U2's *Achtung Baby* and Pearl Jam's *Ten* had outsold *Nevermind* were cast aside in order to paint Nirvana, not as one of many potential emblematic symbols of the alternative scene or Generation X, but as the singular embodiment of both. The way the media was portraying it, the sprawling alternative scene which had predated and nurtured Nirvana needn't have existed at all. It was Nirvana alone who had toppled 80s glam rock. It was Kurt Cobain alone who spoke for an entire generation. Chuck Klosterman discussed this phenomenon at length in his 2005 book *Killing Yourself to Live*:

> The life and death of Kurt Cobain has been (almost without rival) the most poorly remembered cultural event of my lifetime… What I seem to remember are the months just prior to Cobain's suicide, and sometimes I feel like I'm the only person who does. And what I remember were people attacking Cobain at every turn. Everybody had purchased *In Utero* that fall, but not many people seemed to love it; the mainstream, man-on-the-street consensus was that Pearl Jam's *Vs.* was a little better. This is the biggest thing pop historians revise when talking about Nirvana: They never seem willing to admit that, by the spring of 1994, Pearl Jam was *way more popular*. It wasn't even that close. The week of its release, *Vs.* sold over 900,000 copies, a seven-day record that seemed unbreakable at the time. Pearl Jam was seen as the peoples' band; Nirvana was seen as the band that hated its own people. Nirvana dropped off the schedule for Lollapalooza '94 and everyone blamed Kurt (except the insiders, who blamed his wife). Jokes were made when he almost killed himself in Rome. Kids were confused and insulted by his liner notes for *Incesticide*, where Kurt expressed annoyance over uncool people liking his songs. There was just this widespread sentiment that Kurt Cobain was a self-absorbed complainer and that if he hated being famous, he should just disappear forever. Which he did. And then everything immediately changed for everyone… Soon after, the reverse engineering began in earnest. Slowly, the memory of Cobain evolved… The memory of the recent Nirvana backlash completely disappeared; suddenly, Nirvana had always been everyone's favorite band. *Nevermind* was no longer the soundtrack to living in the early 90s—now it was that experience *in totality*.

As a result of the unfolding mythology, Kurt Cobain claimed in death what he had never been able to claim in life; he achieved the unanimous indie-punk artistic credibility he had always craved at the same time that Nirvana became far and away the most commercially successful band in the world. In death, the indie-punk community forgave Cobain for his popularity and embraced him as one of their own, the martyr who had sacrificed himself to bring punk to the masses. "He's the guy that made punk rock commercial," said Cris Kirkwood of underground icons The Meat Puppets in the first *Rolling Stone* issue after Cobain's death. And as time went by and the mythologized narrative was solidified, fewer and fewer critics would dare question the purity of Cobain's punk credibility. Suddenly everyone seemed to agree that Nirvana—their blatant commercial aspirations and mainstream influences notwithstanding— had been a punk band, plain and simple. By 2003, *Pitchfork* would be able to say, "With all the facts laid out, Nirvana begins to look much more like a plain old punk band that happened to exist at the heart of a cultural movement they wanted nothing to do with." The problem with that kind of cut-and-dry assessment, of course, was that it required ignoring quite a few inconvenient facts.

At the same time that Nirvana's punk credibility was beginning to move towards iron-clad status, Kurt Cobain's death immediately turned Nirvana into a more viable commercial entity that it had been at any time during the band's short career. The very same morning Cobain's body was found, Seattle's Sub Pop Mega Mart store was besieged by customers. As Kerri Harrop, who opened the store that day, recalls in *Everybody Loves Our Town*:

> I went over across the street to the store, and already there were people waiting outside, which was something that never, ever happened. Ten people followed me into the store, which automatically packed the place. And the first guy in, some twenty-something, asks, 'Do you have any Nirvana vinyl?' I was so sickened at the thought… if you didn't have *Bleach* on vinyl by now, why the fuck do you need it now? It was so gross to me. Within like 10 minutes, the store is a madhouse…

However, the mounting consumer desire for anything and everything Nirvana soon became a full-fledged merchandising binge, typified by the way Kurt Cobain's image came to dominate the t-shirt shops at malls across America—

often sporting an obligatorily extended middle finger. But nowhere was Nirvana's growing commercial appeal more apparent than in the sales of the music itself. Sales of *In Utero* were immediately revived—the album jumped from #72 to #11 on the *Billboard* chart in the two weeks following Cobain's suicide—and it was certified double-platinum on April 11 and then triple-platinum the following month, turning an album that had once been perceived as a commercial failure into a bona fide hit. The band's back catalog was also reinvigorated; *Nevermind* sold another 2 million copies in the year following Cobain's death, and *Bleach* and *Incesticide* each went platinum. Then there were the posthumous releases. *MTV Unplugged in New York* was released in November of 1994 and sold 3 million copies in less than two months. And the concert video *Live! Tonight! Sold Out!!* was released two weeks later and quickly sold a million copies. By the time April of 1995 came around, more Nirvana albums and videos had been purchased in America in the year since Cobain's death (10 million) than had been purchased during his entire lifetime (7 million).

The timing of Kurt Cobain's death and the ensuing commercial bonanza meant that, just as the major labels had finished re-making their rock divisions in an alternative mold in order to wring every last cent out of alternative music's mainstream crossover, the Cobain mythology was profoundly changing both the public and industry perception of what "alternative" meant. To the extent that Kurt Cobain was coming to be seen as the be all and end all of the alternative style and ethos, Nirvana was quickly becoming the definitive alternative template: a style, a sound, and an attitude that audiences, advertisers, radio programmers, and corporate major label shareholders could all easily recognize and understand.

PART III

CORPORATE CONSOLIDATIONS
AND CRITICAL REVISIONS

Chapter Ten

The End of the Record Business

Mergers, Acquisitions, and the
Ultra-Corporatization of the Major Labels

Warner Bros., Geffen, and the Record Business "Status Quo" of the 70s and 80s

On March 19, 1958, Warner Brothers Pictures launched its own record company: Warner Brothers Records. Warner Bros. president Jack Warner had always been extremely wary of the record business, and so in its first few years Warner Records focused primarily on safe projects like Warner Pictures movie soundtracks and novelty albums by Warner Television stars, a strategy which—not surprisingly—proved less than profitable. But within a few years, the label started to branch out and Warner Bros. began to score some popular hits in the early 60s with albums by a wide array of acts: comedians Bob Newhart and Bill Cosby, squeaky-clean rockers The Everly Brothers, folk singers Peter, Paul & Mary, and pop crooners Sammy Davis Jr. and Frank Sinatra (whose personal label Reprise was purchased by Warner Bros. in 1962). Then, when rock music began to dominate the pop charts in the late-60s, Warner Records' relative youth and lack of established stylistic identity allowed it to embrace rock music more quickly than its rival major labels, and by the end of the decade Warner Bros. had become the major label whose fortunes were most tied to rock's commercial success or failure.

THE END OF THE RECORD BUSINESS

The years 1967-70 were tumultuous ones for Warner Records. As the label was shifting gears and moving to capitalize on the expanding rock music market—a move which included the purchase of the iconic independent labels Atlantic and Elektra—parent company Warner Pictures was in the process of being sold, first to Seven Arts Productions in 1967, then to Kinney National Services in 1969. The resulting media conglomerate was dubbed Warner Communications Inc. (WCI) and was headed up by former Kinney CEO Steve Ross, an ambitious young executive who had come a long way in a relatively short time. The son of Brooklyn-based Jewish immigrants, Ross had married into the funeral parlor business in the early 50s, an advantage which he parlayed into a small fiefdom of rent-a-car, parking garage, and cleaning companies, which he then consolidated into Kinney National Services and took public in 1962. By the late 60s, Ross was looking to remake Kinney into an entertainment company and engineered the purchase of the iconic Ashley Famous talent agency, which was quickly followed by the stunning takeover of the entire Warner Bros. media empire. When the dust settled from all the corporate maneuvering, Ross found himself sitting astride one of the world's foremost media conglomerates at the age of forty-two. If his competitors were tempted to underestimate the one-time mortician's media business savvy, they were quickly reproved when Ross went on to oversee the revitalization of Warner's film studio, the visionary purchase of Atari, and the expansion of its cable television holdings (including the creation of MTV and Nickelodeon) as piece by piece he built WCI into America's most powerful media empire.

But the financial engine that powered the growth of Steve Ross's WCI was its music division. Soon after taking control of Warner Bros., Ross created Warner Music Group, an umbrella under which three distinct record companies would operate almost independently: the newly-acquired Atlantic Records under the leadership of its founder and longtime president Ahmet Ertegun, newly-acquired Elektra Records under its founder Jac Holzman, and Warner Bros. Records (which included the Reprise imprint) under longtime Warner and Reprise executive Mo Ostin. Ross was a staunch believer in finding, empowering, and rewarding executive talent, and because each of the three labels had been successful prior to their consolidation under the Warner Music umbrella, he was willing to allow each label a great deal of latitude and independence. This basic structural arrangement would remain in place for the balance of WCI's two-decade run—and would pay off handsomely as Warner

Music Group's revenues skyrocketed from $200 million in 1969 to over $3.2 billion in 1992, when Ross's untimely death finally ended his run at Warner.

In spite of their independence, what all three Warner labels initially had in common was a focus on rock music. In the early 70s, Elektra was home to The Doors, Queen, Bread, and Carly Simon (among many others); Atlantic was home to Led Zeppelin, The Rolling Stones, The J. Geils Band, Yes, Bad Company, and Crosby, Stills, & Nash; and Warner Bros. was home to Neil Young, Van Morrison, The Grateful Dead, America, Alice Cooper, and The Allman Brothers. Together, the three labels controlled a formidable piece of the rock music market.

That piece would expand in late 1972 when David Geffen's Asylum Records was added to the fold, bringing with it Jackson Browne, Tom Waits, Joni Mitchell, Linda Ronstadt, and The Eagles. Steve Ross's eye for executive talent had made Geffen's label a uniquely attractive commodity; Ross was at least as interested in acquiring the services of Geffen himself as he was in acquiring Asylum's recording artists. And when Asylum and Elektra were merged into one entity following the purchase, Ross made the 29-year-old Geffen the head of the newly-consolidated Elektra/Asylum imprint, moving the more experienced Elektra founder Jac Holzman to WCI's technology division (where he ended up thriving). Ross's confidence in Geffen was rewarded as Elektra/Asylum's sales boomed. The Eagles soon became the best-selling act of the decade, and Geffen even managed to sign Bob Dylan to Elektra/Asylum during Dylan's brief reunion with The Band—which produced Dylan's first #1 album in America, *Planet Waves*, as well the hugely successful double-live album *Before the Flood*. But having owned his own management firm and label, Geffen began to chafe under the confines of being someone else's employee. And in 1975 Geffen asked for—and received—a position in WCI's film division, hoping the new medium would enliven his life as an employee. But his stay at Warner Pictures was brief and undistinguished, and when his five-year contract with WCI ran out in 1978 Geffen left the entertainment business altogether, a semi-retired millionaire in his mid-30s.

The commercial success of Warner Music Group—and rock music in general—in the 1970s had affirmed the pragmatic bet Warner Records president Mo Ostin had made on the commercial value of rock artists' creativity. "My feeling was always follow the artist, follow the music," Ostin told *The New York Times* in 1995. "It will lead you to the money." But as the

70s went on, "following the artist" required fewer and fewer concessions on Ostin's part. The rise of rock star culture was making commercial success an acceptable goal for rock artists, and their aspirations were moving closer and closer to Ostin's sales-minded pragmatism. By the late 70s, the anti-commercial zealotry of the 60s counterculture was a distant memory, and what exceptions there were to rock's growing commercialism tended to be short-lived and financially inconsequential. For instance, punk music—though vital to tens of thousands of underground devotees—was little more than a blip on the mainstream commercial radar. Punk bands like The Ramones, The Sex Pistols, and The Clash had all aspired to challenge the commercial status quo, but each failed to score even a gold record—let alone a platinum or multi-platinum record—during punk's late 70s heyday. And as the 80s dawned, rock's commercial status quo seemed to stretch towards an infinite future, as the unabashed commercial aspirations of mainstream rock acts—from Kiss to AC/DC to The Rolling Stones—were meeting with less and less overt resistance.

Between the 1970s and 1980s, very little changed within the structure of the mainstream record business; the years 1972-1988 were an extended period of relative stability. For that entire time, the music industry would be dominated by the same six major record labels: Warner Bros., EMI/Capitol, Columbia, RCA, MCA, and Polygram, all of whom continued to enjoy relative independence within their parent media corporations. And this independence would only be buttressed by the steady growth in album sales throughout the 80s, both in America—where sales grew from roughly 440 million in 1982 to over 700 million in 1990—and abroad, where an international market for Western popular culture was expanding exponentially. And rock music remained sacred in major label boardrooms where the majority of executives owed their positions to rock music's commercial success.

One of those executives was David Geffen. He had returned to the music business in 1980 when he partnered with WCI to create his own record label, Geffen Records. After the success that Geffen's previous label Asylum had enjoyed under the Warner umbrella, Steve Ross was eager to partner with Geffen again, and Ross agreed to provide the startup capital for Geffen Records—$25 million—in exchange for a 50% stake in the company. But Geffen's new label would prove to be different from Asylum in many ways. At Asylum, Geffen had signed acts whose music he personally liked, which gave the label an identifiable sound: laid-back, West Coast, singer-songwriter-based rock acts like Jackson Browne, Joni Mitchell, The Eagles, and Linda Ronstadt. But from the beginning, Geffen Records was intended to be a big tent record label which would mix in music from all popular genres; in short, style was subservient to sales potential. And instead of building his new label on unknown talent like he had at Asylum, Geffen wanted to announce his return to the business by landing as many big name stars as possible, and he quickly signed John Lennon, Elton John, Donna Summer, and Neil Young to lucrative recording contracts. But Lennon's untimely death ended his time with Geffen Records after just one album, and all of Geffen's other high-profile signings proved to be on the downside of their greatest commercial successes. All in all, Geffen ended up with little to show for his labor during the first couple of years at his new label. Even Steve Ross seemed to lose confidence in Geffen, and in 1984 Ross sold WCI's share of Geffen Records back to Geffen in exchange for the label's foreign distribution rights. The sale was a vote of no confidence in Geffen Records that Ross would later come to regret when Geffen's label rebounded in the second half of the decade.

Geffen Records' recovery in the second half of the 80s was made possible by an unprecedented boom in music industry profits. The advent of the compact disc invigorated sales as music lovers sought to update their album collections in the shiny new medium, contributing to a 60% increase in American album sales between 1982 and 1990. And not only that, the inflated list price of CDs—which ranged from $14 to $18, roughly twice the list price of a vinyl album—meant that each additional sale included a greater profit margin, a margin which would only increase as the manufacturing of CDs became less and less expensive. The end result was that annual record industry profits more than doubled in less than a decade.

The runaway profits major labels were enjoying allowed them to sign and develop dozens of artistically substantive rock acts from the growing alternative scene, in addition to their more mainstream oriented acts. Geffen Records was a case in point. After turning the corner towards profitability in the second half of the 80s on the strength of hit albums by Whitesnake, Sammy Hagar, Don Henley, Guns N' Roses, Cher, and Aerosmith, Geffen Records continued to release albums by modest-selling alternative artists like XTC, Siouxsie & The Banshees, The Sundays, Sonic Youth and—eventually— Nirvana. The same was true at the other major labels, particularly those within the Warner family. Throughout the 80s, Warner Music Group was willing to sign and distribute albums by critically respected alternative acts like Devo, Jane's Addiction, The B-52's, The Cure, Talking Heads, The Jesus and Mary Chain, The Pogues, Public Image Ltd., The Pixies, Bjork, Echo and the Bunnymen, Tom Waits, Husker Du, The Replacements, Depeche Mode, Billy Bragg, R.E.M., Violent Femmes, Oingo Boingo, and Elvis Costello.

However, there was a sense in which the record business had become too successful for its own good. The record-setting profits being generated at the major record labels were making them—and by extension their parent media companies—attractive assets for takeover by the multinational corporate conglomerates that were beginning to dominate the international business landscape. And the coming years would witness a spree of corporate takeovers involving the media industry that would turn the record business on its head, completely reorganizing its internal business structure and instituting a new corporate philosophy, a philosophy which would eventually lead the major labels away from the business of signing, recording, and marketing artistically substantive rock acts.

Mergers, Acquisitions, and the Corporatization of the Music Industry

From its pre-rock origins all the way through the late 80s, there was a distinct entity called "the record business." It was notoriously exemplified by cigar-chomping moguls, doctored books, mysterious sacks of cash, and performers who didn't always get paid their fair share. When rock stars were introduced into the equation in the late 60s, the record business caricature was expanded to include drugs, groupies, and other worldly indulgences. Though the sleazy reputation of the record business may have been an exaggeration, there was an undeniable seediness and borderline illegality about the whole enterprise. But in spite of its obvious shortcomings, the record business was not without its own unique charms. There is a popular quote, often attributed to legendary *Rolling Stone* columnist Hunter S. Thompson, which goes something like this:

> The music business is a cruel and shallow money trench, a long and plastic hallway where thieves and pimps run free, and good men die like dogs. There is also a negative side.

Though Thompson never uttered these exact words, they reflect what was once a surprisingly popular sentiment within the industry. Part of the record business's affection for its own ethos was due to the fact that, in spite of its shadiness, or perhaps *because* of it, the music business was a place—much like the Wild West—where eccentrics and outcasts of all stripes, aspiring artists and moguls alike, might find a home and strike it rich. For instance, it is hard to imagine Atlantic Records founder Ahmet Ertegun, son of Turkey's first ambassador to America—with his refined tastes and tailored European suits, his Old World charm, an appetite for drugs and women that rivaled his artists, and a business sense that relied almost exclusively on his gut instincts—achieving the same legendary success in any other walk of life. The same can be said for Led Zeppelin's rough-and-tumble manager Peter Grant, the former sheet-metal factory worker whose brutish strong-arm tactics re-wrote the rulebook for rock management and helped make Zeppelin the richest band in the world. But there was room in the record business world for both Ertegun and Grant's outsized eccentricities, and together the two men would form an unlikely partnership that helped mold Led Zeppelin into the 70s most profitable rock band.

Record business executives tended to be eccentric, and they prided themselves on their independence from the rest of corporate America. Many—like Ertegun, Mo Ostin, and Jac Holzman, the initial heads of the three Warner Music labels—had been involved in inventing the business in which they worked; they had forged their own unique paths to success and made their own rules along the way. This was why WCI's Steve Ross had been the perfect corporate overseer for the record business. As long as his label chiefs made their numbers, they were generally left to make their own creative decisions, and they were rewarded handsomely when those decisions paid off. Having worked for years with the nuts and bolts of the industry—including the signing, recording, and promotion of their artists—the Warner Music label heads had an intuitive feel and respect for the artistic process, and no amount of financial success could ever fully separate them from that respect. Thus, the prosperous financial times of the 70s and 80s also meant the steady expansion of artist rosters and budgets, with an eye towards cultivating critically respected artists in addition to the more blatantly commercial pop stars. Maintaining artistic credibility played to the record moguls' self-perception as more than just money men; they were cultural patrons and savants, privy not only to the financial rewards of business success, but also to the special respect afforded cultural curators—as well as the social and sexual perks afforded to those who traveled in the company of rock stars.

All of this would change in the late 80s and 90s, as the absorption of five of the six major record labels into international corporate conglomerates meant that their budgets and independence would be determined by outside factors like stock prices, IPOs, and the performance of the other businesses within those conglomerates. For the heads of major record labels, success would no longer mean simply making their numbers; it would also mean keeping investors happy, projecting a clean and successful image to Wall Street, and conforming to official corporation-wide policies and standards. Not surprisingly, this shift would lead to the departure of the music industry's old guard, and with them "the record business" as an entity distinct from the rest of the international corporate world.

For Warner Music Group, the first crack in the old business model came in 1983, when the collapse of the video game market plunged WCI subsidiary Atari, Inc. into losses of close to $500 million for the year, triggering immediate budget cuts throughout WCI, including the music division. In order to make the cuts, Steve Ross hired Robert Morgado, the former chief of staff to New York governor Hugh Carey (for whom Ross had been a major fundraiser). "Morgado was a hatchet man," said longtime Warner executive Sheldon Vogel in Fred Goodman's 2010 book *Fortune's Fool*. "His job was to fire enough people for us to stay in business." Though the record chiefs bristled at the intrusion, the cost-cutting was necessary to WCI's survival, and Morgado performed well enough at his task that Ross decided to keep him in the WCI fold, even after the crisis had passed. This decision would have long-term implications for Warner's record division when Morgado was named president of Warner Music Group in 1985, a position from which he would eventually dismantle the entire Warner Music empire. But that was still a few years off; throughout the 80s, the individual presidents of the Warner record labels still reported directly to Ross, who had no interest in tampering with a business model that had shown steady growth for nearly two decades. However, fundamental changes were just around the corner.

On March 4, 1989, a $14.9 billion merger between Time Inc. and WCI was announced. But shortly after the announcement of the merger, Paramount launched a hostile bid to acquire Time, forcing a complete restructuring of the

Time-Warner merger in order to ward off the takeover, delaying its consummation until early 1990 and necessitating a litany of complex corporate machinations that would take years to sort out and implement. These tasks would end up occupying Steve Ross's undivided attention from the time the merger was announced until his death from cancer in December of 1992. Meanwhile, the upshot for Warner Music was that, thanks to the merger, it needed to show immediate short-term growth in order to satisfy its new corporate partners. And Robert Morgado, as the titular head of the entire music operation, took advantage of the power vacuum left by Ross in order to flex his newfound muscle in an attempt to raise profits by increasing efficiency. But Morgado soon met an unexpected obstacle: his own complete lack of understanding of what actually took place in the day-to-day operations of a record company. "He was convinced that there were patterns to be managed," said former Warner executive Danny Goldberg in *Fortune's Fool*. "He tried to take the risk out of the business, and that doesn't work." Morgado's attempts to set and maintain rigid release schedules and sales projections confounded the record industry veterans who worked under him. Warner executive Howie Klein recalled his first conversation with Morgado in *Fortune's Fool*, "He doesn't even say hello—he just starts yelling, 'Where's the Ministry album?' I said the lead singer hadn't turned it in yet. 'What!? It's on the sheet.' So I explained that the guy was in rehab. Morgado says, 'What do you mean?' I said, 'Drugs.' 'What? Is that what you're dealing with?' I said, 'Hey, we're not selling shoes here.'"

The communication breakdown between Morgado and his senior executives plunged the Warner offices into a nasty power struggle between the old-school record business types and their new corporate masters. And during the protracted struggle, no one at Warner Music butted heads with Morgado more conspicuously than Elektra president Bob Krasnow. A record business throwback who made no secret of his recreational drug use, Krasnow was also incredibly successful; since taking over Elektra in 1982, he had increased the imprint's percentage of Warner Music's sales from 7 percent to 28 percent. And in 1991, when Morgado ordered him to close Elektra's London office— which had brought the label a string of successful acts like The Cure, Simply Red, and Howard Jones—as a cost-cutting measure, Krasnow simply refused. Meanwhile, as Krasnow was openly defying Morgado, Warner Bros. Records president Mo Ostin was ignoring him, refusing to take Morgado's calls and routinely sending subordinates to meetings. Ostin assumed that, in accordance with the rules of the old record business, as long as he hit his numbers he was untouchable. But Morgado responded to Krasnow and Ostin's executive insubordination by increasing the profile of Doug Morris, who had taken over as chairman of Atlantic Records when founder Ahmet Ertegun had accepted the position of "chairman emeritus" and gone into semi-retirement. And by 1994, Morris had become enough of an executive anchor that Morgado finally felt comfortable enough to force the resignations of both Krasnow and Ostin, effectively ending Warner Music Group's executive ties to its own iconic legacy.

However, Morgado's move backfired when Morris replaced the deposed label heads with loyal executives who banded together with him to lobby for Morgado's firing. And under the consolidated pressure coming from his entire music division, new Time Warner CEO Stanley Levin obliged by giving Morgado his walking papers—and a reported $50 million severance package. But Morris's victory ended up being just as short-lived as Morgado's had been. Levin, who saw the entire music division—especially all its corporate maneuvering and backstabbing—as an unwanted headache, decided to clean house completely, and soon Morris and his loyalists were also shown the door. By the time the dust settled in 1995, a year when the international music industry was achieving record-breaking sales and Warner Music held the largest share of those sales, Time Warner had managed to fire nearly every key executive who had helped build the company's success—and had handed out over $150 million dollars in golden parachutes to its ousted executives in the process. Without those key executives, Warner Music Group would see its music industry market share fall drastically over the next six years—from 25 percent to 13 percent—so that by 2001, when Time Warner completed its historic merger with America Online (AOL), Warner Music Group was a shell of its former self.

The corporate revolution was hardly confined to Warner Music. In 1986, the German multinational corporation Bertelsmann had acquired record industry pioneer RCA, rechristening its new label group BMG Music and setting off a chain reaction of corporate consequences. Then, in 1989, Japan's Sony Corporation purchased Columbia Records, and longtime Columbia Records president Walter Yetnikoff, who had presided over the iconic label's steady growth since 1975, was summarily shown the door. Not to be outdone,

Sony's Japanese rival the Matsushita Corporation (which would eventually change its name to Panasonic) purchased MCA Records in 1990. But Matsushita soon had a change of heart and sold MCA to Canada's Seagram's liquor company in 1995. Seagram's had also purchased Universal Studios and its subsidiaries that same year, and changed the name of its record operation to Universal Records Group. Then, in 1998, Universal purchased major label Polygram Records, reducing the number of major labels from six to five, and making Universal the world leader in music market share virtually overnight.

Seagram's foray into the entertainment business was instructive as to how external corporate influences would come to dictate day-to-day record business operations. When Seagram's purchased MCA Records from Matsushita in 1995, Wall Street investors frowned on the purchase, dropping Seagram's stock from $44 a share to $37 a share, which resulted in a staggering $3 billion loss for Seagram's and triggered a round of severe budget cuts within MCA itself that had nothing whatsoever to do with its performance as a record label. Then, in order to sell Seagram's subsequent purchase of Polygram Records to the Seagram's board—which was still wary of anything music related after the disastrous results of the MCA purchase—Seagram's CEO Edgar Bronfman, Jr. promised to eliminate $300 million in salaries and expenses, which meant firing 20 percent of the newly-consolidated record company's staff and dropping over 200 acts from its artist roster. At a time when both record sales and record company profits were at an all-time high, tallying roughly a billion U.S. album sales annually and nearly $27 billion in worldwide revenue, the industry's new leader in market share was firing employees and slashing its artist roster, the exact *opposite* of what one would expect from the leader in an industry reaping massive profits.

These kinds of shortsighted decisions were increasingly typical of a world in which corporate demands were dictating day-to-day business decisions. And corporate pressures on the music industry would only increase in the coming years. In 2001, AOL consummated a $164 billion merger with Time Warner, creating the largest media conglomeration in history. But Wall Street didn't like the merger, and AOL Time Warner stock plummeted. The huge losses forced the company to sell off its entire music division—the once-iconic Warner Music Group—to a group of private investors headed by former Seagram's CEO Edgar Bronfman, Jr. And just like when his previous company had purchased Polygram, Bronfman's first orders were to slash the budget—to

147

the tune of $225 million dollars and 30 percent of Warner's already shrunken artist roster. Again, these budget cuts had little to do with the actual financial performance of the label or its roster. Rather, the cuts were instituted in order to provide a quick cash return to the investors—including Bronfman himself—who had just purchased the company. Within a year, the investors had recouped their initial cash investment in full, but as a result the label's artist roster had been deeply gutted. By that time, the old Warner Music Group of Steve Ross, Mo Ostin, and Ahmet Ertegun was little more than a distant memory.

Chapter Eleven

Nirvanawannabees

Grunge, Green Day, Bush, and the Co-opting of Alternative Music

Transforming the Alternative Scene into the Alternative Genre

As timing would have it, the corporatization and consolidation of the music industry in the 1990s coincided with alternative music's rise to prominence. The alternative revolution had begun under the old guard, where Mo Ostin's admonition to "trust the artist" still held sway. For instance, as much as Kurt Cobain bellyached about his corporate masters, Geffen Records had still granted Nirvana a great deal of artistic freedom. In the summer of 1993, in the midst of the debate over which version of the Nirvana album *In Utero* would be released, Nirvana's manager Danny Goldberg had taken Cobain to David Geffen's house in Malibu. As Goldberg recalled in *Bumping Into Geniuses*, Geffen told Cobain, "Don't think about the radio. And don't pay any attention to what anyone else says or thinks. Give us the record that you like. Our job is to sell it." In the end, the decision to release the more radio-friendly version of *In Utero* had been Cobain's, not his label's. But Geffen's artist-friendly attitude was becoming increasingly rare, even at Geffen Records itself. The meeting with Cobain was one of David Geffen's last substantive acts on behalf of Geffen Records before shifting his full-time attention to a new project: DreamWorks Studios, his new multi-billion dollar collaboration with Steven

Spielberg and Jeffrey Katzenberg that would solidify Geffen's position as one of the most powerful moguls in all the entertainment business.

By the time of Kurt Cobain's death in 1994, the old guard was on its way out of the music business, and the task of curating the ongoing alternative revolution was falling to the new crop of corporate managers like Warner Music's Robert Morgado. Morgado may not have understood the nuts and bolts of the record industry, but he and his fellow corporate managers certainly knew how to assess sales trends, and by 1993 the trend in rock music was clear. That year, bands from the alternative scene had scored over thirty gold or platinum records, while glam bands had tallied just five. A changing of the guard had clearly taken place, and it was obvious where the money in the rock business was being made. Meanwhile, the iconic status that Cobain's death had bestowed on Nirvana provided the new executives with a definitive alternative template. Where the alternative music *scene* of the 80s and early 90s had been too diverse to fit into an easily marketable mold, the major labels would now begin creating an easily identifiable alternative music *genre* which would come to exhibit a very specific Nirvana-inspired style, sound, and attitude.

Warner Bros. executive Danny Goldberg had never been an alternative scenester. Prior to founding Gold Mountain Entertainment—which managed alternative icons Nirvana and Sonic Youth—Goldberg had been a PR man for mainstream rock acts like Led Zeppelin and Kiss, and he hadn't even been aware that the alternative scene existed until relatively recently. According to his account in his memoir *Bumping Into Geniuses*, "In 1989 I had married music business attorney Rosemary Carroll, who was a fan of punk and postmodern rock and who focused my attention on the fact that there was an entirely new generation of rock fans for whom the only credible rock and roll was that which came from this alternative culture." And so, when Goldberg was hired by Warner subsidiary Atlantic Records' A&R department on the heels of Nirvana's big breakthrough, he was far less interested in fidelity to the underground alternative scene than he was in signing acts who might be able to duplicate Nirvana's commercial success.

Goldberg's first signing for Atlantic was the San Diego-based rock band Stone Temple Pilots, whose songs were such naked imitations of Seattle grunge that the band's debut album *Core* became a joke throughout the Seattle scene. "I remember Mark [Arm, of Mudhoney] saying he figured they hadn't really made it because there was no fake Mudhoney song on the first Stone

Temple Pilots album," said former Arm bandmate Jeff Smith in *Everybody Loves Our Town*. "Beavis and Butt-Head were like... 'What, this *isn't* Pearl Jam?' It had a fake Alice in Chains song, a fake Nirvana song. That record is almost like a best-of-Seattle." But *Core* was a huge hit, and within a year Goldberg was named president of Atlantic Records. Under Goldberg's direction, Atlantic signed the band Collective Soul in 1993 on the strength of their song "Shine," which was also a transparent grunge imitation (the song's guttural "Yeah!" became almost shorthand for grunge imitations). Their debut album for Atlantic was released in the spring of 1994—just as the Kurt Cobain mythology was beginning to redefine alternative music—and the lead single "Shine" became an instant runaway hit. Goldberg was soon named president of Atlantic's more prestigious sister label, Warner Bros. Records, and in the two years following Cobain's death Warner Music Group enjoyed a string of platinum-selling hit albums which followed Nirvana's loud, angsty, male-fronted mold: Green Day's major label debut *Dookie*, Bush's major label debut *Sixteen Stone*, Stone Temple Pilots' second album *Purple*, Seven Mary Three's major label debut *American Standard*, Green Day's follow-up *Insomniac*, Matchbox Twenty's debut album *Yourself or Someone Like You*, Bush's second album *Razorblade Suitcase*.

And efforts to create an identifiable alternative genre soon extended beyond just Warner Brothers. On the heels of Kurt Cobain's death in April of 1994, the entire mainstream music industry began jumping on the angsty, Nirvana-inspired bandwagon. Gary Gersh, the Geffen Records A&R rep who had signed Nirvana, was named president of Capitol Records in 1994 and immediately signed California-based angst-rockers Everclear and Nirvana spinoff Foo Fighters (former Nirvana drummer Dave Grohl's new band). On the strength of the single "Self-Esteem"—perhaps the most blatant "Smells Like Teen Spirit" rip-off of the era—The Offspring's 1994 album *Smash* became a surprise hit for the punk label Epitaph. Sony subsidiary Epic Records likewise enjoyed multi-platinum selling hits in late-1994 from angsty newcomers Live and Korn (and then struck pay dirt again in 1995 when grungy teenage hard-rockers Silverchair's debut album *Frogstomp* went double-platinum). The second half of 1994 also provided one last hurrah for some of the original Seattle grunge bands. In addition to the posthumous commercial success of Nirvana's entire catalog, Alice in Chains' EP *Jar of Flies* went double platinum, Soundgarden's album *Superunknown* quickly became the band's best-selling album, and Pearl Jam's *Vitalogy* extended the band's record-breaking commercial success, selling almost 900,000 copies in its first week and nearly matching *Vs.* sales records. Even Seattle-based grunge knockoffs Candlebox enjoyed multi-platinum success in the second half of 1994. The cumulative effect was transformative; in the months immediately following Kurt Cobain's death, the alternative music *scene*—which had long contained countless stylistic genres of music and had been defined only by its lack of mainstream success and loose affiliation in independent record stores and on alternative radio—was being calculatedly transformed into a homogenous stylistic *genre*, a sound and attitude modeled the most iconic alternative band, Nirvana, and chosen specifically for its perceived marketability.

The national network of alternative radio stations was quick to embrace the new alternative genre, and by the end of 1994, *every song* in the KROQ year-end Top 10—which had always been notable for its diversity of musical styles—was in the grungy post-Nirvana mold. The same was true at Chicago's Q101, Boston's WFNX, San Diego's XETRA, and other influential alternative radio stations across the country. And in the midst of this increasingly homogenized alternative radio environment, most of the veteran bands from the alternative scene who managed to hang on commercially did so by following the trend and beefing up their sound. For instance, The Cranberries traded in the jangly, melodic sound of their debut single "Linger" for the angry distortion of their late-1994 hit "Zombie." Similarly, R.E.M. left behind the muted Southern understatement which had been their trademark in favor of the muscular electric guitars that defined their 1994 album *Monster*. Both albums went platinum that December.

Meanwhile, the alternative acts who didn't fit the newly codified angsty-male alternative template paid the price commercially. Despite almost universally positive reviews, alt icon Morrissey's 1994 release *Vauxhall and I* failed to approach the American commercial success of his previous solo albums. Radiohead's decision to release the acoustic-based ballad "Fake Plastic Trees" as the first U.S. single for their March 1995 release *The Bends* led to disappointing radio play and sales, and the critically-acclaimed album remains the iconic band's lowest selling album to date. And in spite of great reviews and a spot on *Rolling Stone*'s cover, Belly's February 1995 release *King* failed to garner any significant alternative radio play; the rules had changed drastically since their 1993 hit *Star*, especially for female-fronted acts, and the band soon folded in the wake of *King*'s commercial failure. The masculine sensibility of the new alternative genre also led to diminishing commercial returns for other female alternative acts like Tori Amos, whose first two albums *Little Earthquakes* and *Under the Pink* had gone multi-platinum. But without the alternative radio airplay which had helped put Amos on the map, none of her subsequent albums would ever again attain multi-platinum status.

Sometimes the makeover of alternative music went to absurd lengths. When a ballad called "The Freshman" by Michigan natives The Verve Pipe began to get some modest alternative radio airplay, the band was quickly signed by major label RCA and asked to re-record a louder, beefier version of the song for release as a single. The gentle, nuanced vocal delivery of the original version was replaced by a scratchier, angrier approach that fit the zeitgeist of the times, in the process obliterating whatever simple, world-weary charm the original version had possessed. For the subsequent video, lead singer Brian Vander Ark even got a new haircut and bleach-job that echoed one of Kurt Cobain's many looks. RCA's re-packaging efforts paid off when the grungier version of the song was added to alternative playlists around the country and shot to #1 on the *Billboard* modern rock charts and #5 overall.

Eventually, alternative radio's grungy homogeneity began to draw critics. As Radiohead's Ed O'Brien would say of the new mid-90s trend in alternative radio, "[Alternative] is such a stale format. As far as I can work out—and we as a band can work out—is that the music they put on these stations isn't for the people. It's to satisfy the advertisers. It's completely reactive as opposed to proactive." According to bandmate Thom Yorke in the documentary *Meeting People Is Easy*, "When you're driving around and around, and you have the alternative stations on in the background, or in your hotel room, it's just like a fridge buzzing. That's all I'm hearing. I'm just hearing buzz." And as the *New York Times* put it in 1997, "Alternative rock hasn't lost its meaning: it has developed a very specific one. When the term came into being in the 1980s, it defined itself in opposition to mainstream rock. Alternative bands made rock-based music that wasn't influenced by the reigning pop forms of the time (heavy metal ballads, rarefied new wave, high-energy dance anthems). Nor did their music aspire to mainstream status. Today, a very different definition of alternative rock is in use: it is a term used to denote hard-edged rock distinguished by brittle, 70s-inspired guitar riffing and singers agonizing over their problems until they take on epic proportions."

While the stylistic diversity of the alternative scene was being weeded out of alternative radio playlists, the angsty, male-fronted bands that typified the new alternative genre were starting to get exposure beyond just the alternative radio universe. Glam rock's demise meant that mainstream rock stations were looking for new material and starting to play alternative bands. At the same time, the hard-edged sound of the new alternative genre meant that these bands were now also getting play on hard rock stations, too. And so, throughout the second half of the 90s, alternative genre rock songs were getting play on alternative, mainstream, and hard rock radio stations—all at the same time—leading to a level of ubiquity that could only end in backlash. And as the new millennium approached, the two-dimensional, cookie-cutter sound and attitude of new alternative genre bands like Sister Hazel, Eve 6, Fuel, Lit, Creed, Three Doors Down, and Nickelback only added to the growing resentment of the alternative genre. Never in its history had the sound of popular rock music been so homogenized.

The Disappearance of the Alternative Scene

One of the reasons the repurposing of the term "alternative" met with such little resistance was that, even as Kurt Cobain's death and the ensuing Nirvana mythology were helping mold the new alternative rock genre, the alternative scene from which Nirvana had emerged was quickly disappearing, and the vast infrastructure which had sustained the scene for over a decade was crumbling. Writers for local alt-newspapers and independent fanzines were being poached by bigger magazines like *Rolling Stone*, *Spin*, and *Blender*. The increased availability of alternative albums at Sam Goody or Tower Records superstores (or through Columbia House mail-orders) was significantly diminishing the demand for independent record stores, which began disappearing en masse in the mid-90s.

But the most significant blow to the alternative infrastructure was the loss of the independent record labels, which had been both an essential artistic refuge for alternative bands unwilling to conform to mainstream expectations and a crucial developing ground for bands who would eventually move on to major label careers. In the first half of the 90s, as indie label offices and rosters were gutted by the major labels, most of the influential independent labels which had risen to prominence in the 80s either folded or were purchased by majors. Twin/Tone (which had been home to The Replacements, Soul Asylum, and The Jayhawks, among many others) closed up shop in 1994. SST (Black Flag, The Minutemen, Husker Du) went into hibernation in the mid-90s, becoming little more than an outlet for founder Greg Ginn's personal projects. Homestead Records (The U-Men, Sonic Youth, Dinosaur Jr.) and I.R.S. Records (R.E.M., Concrete Blonde, Oingo Boingo) both folded in 1996. And by the mid-90s, U.K. mainstays Rough Trade Records (The Smiths, Buzzcocks) and Factory Records (Joy Division, New Order, Happy Mondays) had gone out of business as well. Most of the indie labels that did survive, both in America and abroad, did so by making deals with major labels. 4AD (The Pixies, Red House Painters, Belly) made a deal with Warner Brothers in 1992. Matador (Pavement, Guided by Voices, Liz Phair) partnered with Warner subsidiary Atlantic in 1993 before eventually selling a 49 percent interest in the label to Capitol Records in 1996. Similarly, Sub Pop (Nirvana, Soundgarden, Mudhoney) sold a 49 percent interest to Warner Brothers in 1994. Mute Records (Depeche Mode, Erasure) was eventually sold to EMI. Seemingly overnight, the grounding indie label backbone of the alternative scene had disappeared.

Meanwhile, the expectations for alternative bands on major labels had changed drastically. Throughout the 80s, alternative bands on major labels had often been vanity projects, there to give the label artistic credibility while glam rock paid the bills. But with the ascendance of alternative music and the demise of glam, alternative bands were now expected to be the commercial bread winners for their rock divisions, driving sales rather than simply living off the sales of others. No longer was there room on major label rosters for artistically adventurous alternative bands who failed to produce hit albums. According to former Island Records and Sony Records executive Glenn Boothe in the 2009 book *Our Noise*, "When I started at major labels in 1990, the watchword was always 'artist development.' During the 80s, bands like The Cure, and R.E.M., and U2 started slow, but by 10 years later, they're the biggest acts on the label... But all that really changed with Nirvana. All of a sudden, the bands who could have been the future R.E.M.s and Cures and U2s were expected to do it in two years, not ten years."

Back in 1992, while Nirvana's *Nevermind* was still atop the charts, Sub Pop Records co-founder Jonathan Poneman had wondered aloud what it would look like if an alternative revolution actually took over the mainstream music industry. "No one ever asked what would happen if it succeeded," mused Poneman to the *Seattle Times*. "By demolishing the old establishment, you automatically become the new one." Within two years of Kurt Cobain's death, Poneman's prediction had come true: the alternative scene was no longer a distinct entity that was easily discernible from the mainstream. Just a few short years after its triumphant rise to commercial prominence, the alternative music *scene* had almost completely ceased to exist, while the new alternative *genre* which had supplanted it was becoming the face of corporate mainstream rock.

Green Day, Bush, and the New Alternative Ethos

One of the key factors in the commercial success of the alternative genre was that the new crop of "alternative" bands themselves didn't have the same aversion to commercial aspirations as their predecessors; in fact, most of them had completely abandoned the anti-commercial convictions of their punk/alternative pedigrees. For instance, California-based rockers Green Day employed all of the recognizable "punk" signifiers—loud three-chord rock, the spiked hair, the piercings, the eyeliner, the anti-authority posturing—but where these signifiers had originally been *anti*-commercial statements, Green Day was shrewdly repurposing them in the interest of commercial success. And so it was fitting that "Woodstock '94" ("The Commercial Woodstock," as the 25th anniversary event came to be known) would function as Green Day's coming out party. Even though Green Day's repurposing of the punk ethos for commercial ends was lost on many fans, the members of the band themselves were very aware of what they were doing. As lead singer and songwriter Billie Joe Armstrong told *Rolling Stone* in 2013, "We came from such a punk rock background—'rock star' was a four-letter word. [But] I loved watching the crowds getting bigger, the excitement of people singing every word… Coming from Gilman Street and the *Maximum Rock N Roll* era of bands, which was basically a socialist mentality, what we did was straight-up blasphemy: becoming rock stars."

While Green Day and subsequent "pop-punk" acts like No Doubt and Blink 182 were detaching punk signifiers from their founding anti-commercial ethos, it was becoming debatable whether the term "punk" still carried any artistic or cultural significance beyond its obvious usefulness as a commercial marketing tool. For Green Day, this debate would become almost moot when the band proved willing to abandon even their trademark punk sound in order to score their biggest selling single, the ubiquitous 1997 release "Good Riddance (Time of Your Life)." And the song's ultra-trite lyrics and hackneyed melody opened the band to a whole new host of critical attacks. "We got backlash more than all those other bands together," Armstrong recently told *Rolling Stone*. "I firmly believe that." However, Armstrong's opinion notwithstanding, Green Day's Warner Music label mates Bush received their fair share of backlash, as well.

By December of 1994, the Nirvana-inspired alternative genre was already starting to dominate mainstream rock. Nirvana, Pearl Jam, Green Day, and The Offspring all had albums in the Top 10, and the major label machine was putting all of its financial and promotional power behind the new genre. In short, the timing was perfect for the London-based alt-rockers Bush to release their debut album *Sixteen Stone*. On the strength of the hit singles "Everything Zen," "Comedown," and "Glycerine," *Sixteen Stone* would sell over 5 million copies in America alone in just 18 months, displaying just how commercially successful a new alternative genre act could be with a focused major label promotional campaign behind it. But thanks to the hype campaign which accompanied *Sixteen Stone*'s release and the blatantly derivative nature of the band's material, critics had a field day. An April 1996 *Rolling Stone* cover declared, "Three million albums, five hit singles… Why won't anyone take [Bush lead singer] Gavin Rossdale seriously?" This leading question was answered in part by the accompanying photo of a shirtless Rossdale lying on a bed, languidly biting his finger for the benefit of the camera. The rest of the answer to the question was summarized by the title of the cover story itself: "Nirvanawannabees." Where critics had seen Nirvana's success as a grassroots success story, Steven Daly's *Rolling Stone* article described Bush's Rossdale as "quite the genetically engineered 90s pop star" and summed up Bush's critical reception as "almost unanimously portraying [Rossdale] and his band as *arrivistes* feeding off a scene with decade-deep underground roots. According to this view, R.E.M., Sonic Youth, and The Pixies did not slog around the 80s

157

college circuit in unheated vans to make the world safe for a bunch of MTV confections like Bush (or, for that matter, Candlebox, Better Than Ezra, Collective Soul, Sponge, and Silverchair)." As an early 1997 *Independent* article titled "The Great Pretender" summed up:

> The reason that Bush do so well in America is that they sound like Nirvana. Whether or not it's calculated—Rossdale says not, of course—the fragmentary lyrics, the aching groan, the punk rock guitars and the sudden, Pixies-influenced dynamic switches are all Seattle trademarks. Except that they don't quite convince. They don't have the passion or the power. They don't have the... grunginess. As for Rossdale himself, the elfin figure hunched on the chaise-longue in front of me looks like a fashion magazine's idea of a grunge star. Okay, there's a brown zip-up cardigan over a white T-shirt, but where are the rips and holes? The fading black jeans are okay, but I'm not sure about those teddy-boy creepers. And he is too handsome, too fine-featured, his streaked brown hair too carefully styled. To quote the man who discovered Bush, Rossdale has 'a look which [is] very favourable for marketing and selling records.'

The fact that Rossdale insisted on lying about his age—even when presented with contrary evidence—didn't endear him to *The Independent*, either. Nevertheless, the negative critical reaction to the commercial posturing and aspirations of bands like Green Day and Bush was, in many ways, the last gasp of a dying journalistic breed. As commercial aspirations increasingly became the status quo among rock acts throughout the 90s, critics began to give them a pass. Eventually, calling out a band for "selling out" would become so passé that a recent *Grantland* article about the 1990s found it necessary to remind its readers, "You have to remember that 'selling out' and 'being independent' and 'having principles that you didn't want compromised by corporations' were still ideas that people actually talked about and took seriously." But even as the critical consensus was moving towards accepting commercial aspirations among alternative acts, one unlikely alternative act would prove willing to openly rebel against the increasing corporatization and commercialization that was engulfing the music industry.

Pearl Jam Rebels

> That's probably why you create in the first place, because of the freedom. You can do whatever you want. You can lay whatever you want on tape. But again, commerce is involved. And as soon as it starts going through those channels, those money-making channels, everything changes.
> —Pearl Jam lead singer Eddie Vedder in the documentary *Hype!*

In the early 90s, many alternative scenesters thought Nirvana's breakthrough meant that the battle against corporate commercialism had been won, once and for all. Even as late as Kurt Cobain's death in 1994, *Spin*'s Eric Weisbard felt free to write that "Nirvana... permanently altered the attitudes of record companies toward a new generation of 'alternative' artists." But that "permanence" had proved fleeting. In the wake of Kurt Cobain's death, it had taken only a few short months for the major label system to gobble up the alternative scene and rebrand "alternative" as a blatantly commercial mainstream genre. And while most alternative bands in the 90s accepted—or were oblivious to—the industry's growing corporate commercialism, Pearl Jam would repeatedly show a willingness to question and criticize the increasingly commercial industry status quo.

Pearl Jam's rise to the top of the rock world had been dizzying. After releasing their debut album *Ten* in August of 1991, the band had gone from playing clubs to headlining arenas and festivals in a matter of a few months. By the summer of 1993, *Ten* had sold 5 million copies in America alone. In less than two years, Pearl Jam had risen from virtual anonymity to take their place among the world's most popular bands. Along the way, the members of the band had tried to maintain a direct connection to their fans in a number of ways: recording live concert broadcasts that they would distribute free to radio stations, playing a series of unadvertised fan-club-only shows, scheduling vinyl album releases a week before CDs and cassettes shipped to stores, offering moderately priced concert tickets. But the promotional machine which had grown up around them was becoming increasingly difficult to control. The first of many wake-up calls came in the fall of 1992, when the band felt obligated to play an MTV-sponsored promotional party for the release of the movie *Singles*, even though the party was scheduled for one of the few off-days in the midst of a grueling tour schedule. They played the party, but the band members—

particularly lead singer Eddie Vedder—decided to drown their exhaustion and frustration in alcohol, and the result was a disastrous performance in front of an influential crowd full of L.A.'s media elites. As guitarist Stone Gossard explained in the 2011 Pearl Jam documentary *Twenty*, "Because we had waited so long for anyone to ask us to do something, we were saying, 'Yes. Yes. Yes.' That was a moment where it was really evident that there was always going to be one more thing they were going to want you to do. At some point, you had to say no. That was the birth of no."

Pearl Jam's first significant "no" would come soon after the *Singles* party. After the way the video for their song "Jeremy" had been plastered all over MTV for months, the band decided not to make a follow-up video for the song "Black," and they refused to allow their label Epic to release the song as a single, either. Even as the pressure from Epic mounted, the band held firm. "Some songs just aren't meant to be played between 'Hit No. 2' and 'Hit No. 3,'" Vedder explained to *Rolling Stone*'s Cameron Crowe in 1993. "You start doing those things, you'll crush it. That's not why we wrote songs. We didn't write to make hits. But those fragile songs get crushed by the *business*. I don't want to be a part of it. I don't think the band wants to be a part of it." For Vedder, especially, an aversion to commercial exploitation went to the core of why he had joined Pearl Jam in the first place. In *Twenty*, Vedder describes his first conversations with his eventual Pearl Jam bandmates, "I don't know if it was first contact. It must have been. It was with [bassist] Jeff [Ament]. I do remember there being a real connection made on the phone, talking about artwork, about how… it's not a rock star thing. It's about music. It's about art."

When the time came for the band to make decisions about the release and promotion of their much-anticipated sophomore album *Vs.*, the members of Pearl Jam made the controversial decision not to make music videos for *any* of their songs—a decision which was virtually unprecedented at the time for a rock band of their stature. As Ament explained to Crowe in 1993, "Ten years from now, I don't want people to remember our songs as videos." There were aspects of their label's promotional campaign for *Vs.* which they had no control over, but on anything they *did* have control over—like interviews and TV appearances—the band pulled in the reins as tightly as possible. And unlike the commercial compromises Nirvana had made around the release of *In Utero* (allowing the album to be re-mixed for radio, changing the artwork and song titles for sale at Wal-Mart and Kmart, doing a big-budget video for the single "Heart-Shaped Box"), the members of Pearl Jam stuck to their guns.

But in spite of Pearl Jam's virtual media blackout, when *Vs.* was released in October of 1993, it quickly became the fastest-selling album of all-time, selling over 950,000 copies in its first week—and over 5 million in just three months in America alone. And according to an industry insider quoted in *Spin* in 1994, *Vs.* record-setting sales would have been twice as big if Pearl Jam had played ball and made just one video for MTV. By any commercial measure, they were now the most popular rock band in the world, and in the midst of the frenzy, the band members came to realize just how little control they had over their own careers. A week after *Vs.* was released, *Time* published an unauthorized story on the band and put a photo of Vedder on the cover alongside the caption "All the Rage." The article—which, among other things, refers to Pearl Jam as an "alternative-metal band" in its opening—drew the particular ire of the band's members. "*Time* magazine was your parents' magazine, or the magazine you read in the doctor's office," explained Vedder in *Twenty*. "And I just thought, 'Wow, we've been swallowed up by the mainstream. *No one*'s going to want to listen to us.'"

The band members' most persistent frustration, however, was their inability to control skyrocketing ticket prices for their own shows. Not only were promoters pressuring the band to raise ticket prices in order to increase promoter revenue, but Ticketmaster—the ticketing giant which held a virtual monopoly on sales for large concerts—was charging exorbitant fees for each ticket purchase, no matter how low the band was able to keep the list prices, meaning that the fees could approach 50% of the face value of the ticket itself. In attempting to circumvent the fees, the band soon found that virtually all the large venues and promoters in the country had exclusive contracts with Ticketmaster, making it all but impossible to eliminate—or even reduce—the ticket fees their fans were being charged. But that was just the tip of the iceberg. When Pearl Jam tried to arrange a free show for Seattle fans in late 1992, Ticketmaster demanded a $1 fee for each free pass the band distributed. Then, in October of 1993, Pearl Jam made arrangements with Ticketmaster for both the band and the ticketing agency to each donate $20,000 in revenues from a series of upcoming Seattle shows to a local charity for impoverished children. But at the last minute, Ticketmaster informed the band that they would be raising fees $1 per ticket in order to collect their $20,000, essentially recouping their promised donation from Pearl Jam's fans. In response to the fierce objections of the band, Ticketmaster scrapped the additional $1 surcharge and ended up donating $14,000 to the charity, but the incident further strained relations between the band and the ticketing giant. These were just a couple in a long series of disputes between the two parties, and by the spring of 1994 Pearl Jam had reached its breaking point with Ticketmaster and was in the process of looking into booking a summer tour of alternative, non-Ticketmaster venues.

In their attempt to build a tour that circumvented Ticketmaster, the band encountered wariness and resistance from both venues and promoters who claimed to have been told by Ticketmaster that crossing the ticketing giant and hosting Pearl Jam concerts would have serious consequences. Finally, on May 6, 1994, Pearl Jam filed an official complaint, alleging that Ticketmaster exercised a national monopoly over ticket distribution and was using its influence with promoters to boycott Pearl Jam's planned low-priced tour that summer. The complaint triggered a Justice Department civil investigation into possible anti-competitive practices in the ticket distribution industry, and on June 30 a congressional hearing was convened at which Pearl Jam members Stone Gossard and Jeff Ament testified. For their part, a Ticketmaster press release called the band "petulant young children who ascribe to business anarchy" and dismissed the band's complaints as a "brilliant marketing ploy." Nevertheless, the band received encouragement from none other than the President himself. "The White House is impressed by Pearl Jam's commitment to its fans," said George Stephanopoulos, then a senior adviser to President Clinton. "We want to make it very clear that we can't judge the merits of the band's allegations against Ticketmaster or prejudge the Justice Department action in any way. But that said, we think the goal of making concert ticket prices affordable is a laudable one. It's something we believe in." And Michigan Congressman John Conyers also delivered a compelling case for the band's rights. "When art is successful, it unavoidably becomes a business," said Conyers at the congressional hearing. "The question, then, is whether artists have an inherent right to control the limits of their business and how it relates to the growth of their art. The answer, I am convinced, is that artists do have a right to that control."

But despite the widespread support and political endorsements, the Justice Department quietly dropped its investigation of Ticketmaster in 1995.

In the meantime, Pearl Jam's continued efforts to circumvent the company led to countless ticketing problems and cancelled shows, effectively keeping the band off the road for nearly two years. Finally, in 1996, amidst growing complaints from fans unable to see them perform, Pearl Jam resumed their use of Ticketmaster in order to maintain a regular touring schedule. Their boycott was widely seen as a failure, in that no other major artists joined the boycott and Ticketmaster was able continue business as usual, but along the way they won the vocal admiration of many fellow artists, including R.E.M., The Grateful Dead, and Neil Young.

Neil Young had had his own well-documented run-ins with music industry commercialism, and having read about Kurt Cobain's internal struggles with the pressures of the industry, Young was heartbroken when he heard of the young Nirvana frontman's suicide in 1994. Compounding Young's heartbreak was the fact that Cobain's suicide note ended with a quote from Young's song "Hey Hey, My My (Into the Black)." "I don't have the passion anymore," wrote Cobain. "And so remember, 'It's better to burn out than to fade away.'" In the 2011 documentary *Twenty*, Young said of Cobain:

> I was trying to call him because I read something he said, that he couldn't keep it real. And I just wanted to tell him, 'Listen, you don't have to do anything anybody fucking tells you. Just stop fucking playing. Cancel all your shows. Don't do anything.' I had a whole thing I was going to tell him but I never got the chance.

And so when Young heard about Pearl Jam's ongoing battles with the industry, he made a point of reaching out to the band in order to offer any help and advice he could. Young soon became Pearl Jam's most trusted mentor, touring extensively with the younger musicians and employing them as the backing band on his 1995 album *Mirrorball*. At a time when the band was at a career crossroads, Young provided much-needed guidance and support, helping them make sense of their strange reality and serving as an inspiring example of what an independent career in music could look like. "I'm glad I've finally got an adult in my life who leads by example," said Vedder of Young. "I've had some crazy adults in my life. So it's about time I got one that inspires me."

By the second half of the 90s, Pearl Jam's refusal to make videos and engage in publicity campaigns had significantly diminished their commercial potential. Where their 1994 release *Vitalogy* had been a huge hit, selling roughly 900,000 copies in its first week of release (second only to their previous album *Vs.* in all-time opening week sales), their 1996 album *No Code* sold just 367,000 copies in its first week of release. Even though *No Code* debuted at #1 on the *Billboard* charts and would have been considered a huge commercial success by virtually any other band's standards (it more than doubled the opening week sales of Nirvana's *In Utero*), Pearl Jam's lofty sales history meant that the album was widely seen as a commercial failure. But the band saw it differently. As Eddie Vedder told the *L.A. Times* in 1996:

> I guess what has happened to us with this record shows that promotion really does matter, just like everybody told us. If you don't operate in that framework, which we don't, it's obvious that you won't sell as many records. And that's fine. We expected this to happen much sooner than it has. To us, it's about choices and lifestyles. Do you want to spend your time on the road and doing promotion, or do you spend your time making [new] music and living your life? At the end of the day, what is most important? To us, I'd like to think it's our music and the quality of our lives.

As the band continued to limit the marketing around their subsequent albums, sales predictably declined. *Vitalogy* proved to be the band's last multi-platinum album in America, and 1998's *Yield* was their last platinum album. But the band continued to make the music they wanted, secure in the knowledge that whatever music they made was the result of their own unique creative vision and not the result of corporate commercial influence. By the turn of the millennium, what had once been the most commercially successful rock band in the world had achieved a remarkable level of indie credibility. And their efforts along the way helped inspire a whole generation of musicians to re-think the relationship between their art and the commercial music industry. Vedder's advice to up-and-coming musicians in 1996's *Hype!* would, for many, come to symbolize Pearl Jam's legacy:

> It's nothing to strive for, this kind of success, or trying to fulfill this kind of hype. It can destroy everything. It can destroy what's real, which is music... or what's real, which is your life. It can destroy. It can make it a commodity. At whose cost? Yours. Your life, your music. They'll take it all away from you. And you're supposed to be happy about it because you're 'successful.'

Chapter Twelve

A New Music Industry Regime

Alanis, Limp Bizkit, and the Hyper-Commercialization of Rock Music

Art and Commercialism under the New Music Industry Regime

In the second half of the 90s, all of the corporate restructuring and consolidation of the music industry—the mergers and takeovers, the power struggles, firings, and budget cuts—were beginning to have a real impact on the nuts and bolts of how the music itself was being created, recorded, and marketed at major labels. According to media critic Mark Crispin Miller in the 2001 PBS documentary *Merchants of Cool*, this was no surprise, "When you've got a few gigantic transnational corporations—each one loaded down with debt—competing madly for as much shelf space and brain space as they can take, they're going to do whatever they think works the fastest and with the most people. Which means they will drag standards down."

Once upon a time, record executives like Mo Ostin and David Geffen had believed that nurturing the creative visions of individual artists was the key to commercial success in the record business. And this pragmatic belief in the value of art had set the music business on a course that resulted in more than two decades of steady growth in both sales and profits. But as a new corporate culture became increasingly dominant at major labels in the 1990s, record executives became less and less likely to value the creative visions of individual artists. Where Mo Ostin had said, "Follow the artist, follow the music. It will lead you to the money," the new generation of music moguls followed a different leader: market research. This was a huge and fundamental shift. According to cultural critic John Seabrook in an interview for *Merchants of Cool*, "[Music] that's based on market research and on the cynical manipulation of consumer tastes just in order to move product is not art." In contrast, said Seabrook, music based on the creative visions of individual artists was "trying to get a difficult emotion, or just something that's glimpsed out of the corner of the eye that they're not really sure what it is, and trying through the work to bring that into focus, share that with the audience, and articulate an emotion or an idea that has never really been thought or felt before. And *that* is art."

Seabrook's opinion notwithstanding, what market research revealed in the late 90s was a startling fact: there were more teenagers in America than ever before—32 million by the end of the decade, even more than when the baby boomers had been teens—and they were responsible for $150 billion in annual spending. Teenagers had always been a target market for the music industry, but the revelation of the size and scope of their buying power would dictate a complete reorientation of major label rosters and budgets towards capitalization on the teen market. In other words, it was no accident that the late 90s became the era of Spice Girls, Britney Spears, Backstreet Boys, Christina Aguilera, and 'N Sync; the focus on teen-oriented pop idols was the clear directive of all the leading market research. And this new focus would have an immediate effect on how major labels signed, developed, recorded, and marketed music.

For years and years there had been two distinct approaches to developing artists within the music industry, one approach for traditional pop acts and an entirely different one for rock acts. For decades, pop-oriented acts—from Frank Sinatra to The Osmonds to Madonna—had been signed by major labels according to their voice and/or look (and sometimes their dancing ability) and then the label would provide songs for them to perform and record, songs which had been written by professional songwriters according to tried and true commercially successful formulas. The artist would then be paired with a group of in-house studio musicians and producers with whom he or she would record the songs, and then be paired with a different group of hired musicians in order to develop a live show. The more popular artists among them—like Sinatra or Madonna—could, if they so chose, use their popularity as leverage to lobby for more creative control of the music they performed, but this only tended to happen in the rarest of cases, and the extent to which the songs that pop artists performed had any correlation at all to their individual artistic visions was murky at best. "Artist," in this case, was almost a misleading term; "entertainer" or "performer" was far more accurate.

However, in the wake of the trend-setting influence of 60s rock artists like Bob Dylan and The Beatles, a different developmental model soon grew up alongside the traditional pop model. Because the new generation of rock acts wrote and performed their own songs, the perceived quality of a given rock artist's creative vision was essential to whether or not a major label decided to sign and develop that artist. And keeping a rock artist on the label meant trusting and following his or her creative vision. This is why the president of the world's leading rock label, Warner Brothers' Mo Ostin, was able to say, "If you believe in the artist, if you believe in his talent, if you believe he speaks the truth, then you have to be supportive of him... You have to encourage the artists to do whatever they think is right." Within the music business, this had been a truly revolutionary attitude, and it had drastically shifted the industry's balance of power in favor of artists.

The difference between these two approaches was well-recognized within the industry, even if it was lost on most casual music fans. For instance, moguls like David Geffen perceived independent-minded rock artists very differently than their pop counterparts. According to producer Bones Howe in *The Mansion on a Hill*, "[Geffen] had a description [of rock artists]—he said these people are 'significant artists.' The significant artist is the artist who creates their own music, records it, and produces it. As opposed to pop artists, who use other people's work and it's all fabricated. These people create and craft themselves. And he was fascinated with that process." But not all label executives were as fascinated by the artistic process as Geffen. For many major label executives in the late 1990s, one pleasant side effect of the market research-mandated return to the old pop music paradigm was that it relieved executives of the hassle of having to deal with independent artists. Where headstrong rock artists like Neil Young or Kurt Cobain could be difficult, eccentric, and—above all—unpredictable, the pop idol machine was nothing if not efficient and predictable. Songs were patterned on market-tested formulas and crafted by an insular group of professional songwriters and producers whose livelihoods and stature within the industry depended solely on commercial success (for instance, the ASCAP Awards which honor professional songwriters are based primarily on sales figures). The aspiring pop artists themselves were typically young, fame-obsessed, and willing to be molded into whatever image a label's market research suggested would sell. And if they balked at their suggested molding, there was always another aspiring pop idol in waiting. Many of the pop stars who rose to prominence in the late 90s had been groomed for popular exploitation since childhood; for instance, Britney Spears, Christina Aguilera, and 'N Sync's Justin Timberlake and J.C. Chasez had all been child actors on Disney's *Mickey Mouse Club*. Unlike the many rock artists who—thanks to their countercultural or punk pedigrees—maintained a healthy dose of skepticism concerning commercial aspirations, the pop idols of the late 90s had come of age in an environment where aspirations to stardom and commercial success were as natural as breathing itself.

At the same time, even in the midst of staggering industry-wide sales and profits, corporate consolidation was triggering budget cuts which were forcing the major labels to slash their artist rosters. And the new focus on teen-oriented pop music allowed them to jettison countless rock acts and double-down on the remaining pop acts on their rosters. In fact, one of the overlooked factors surrounding the record-breaking multi-platinum pop hits of the late 90s and early 2000s was just how much money was poured into promoting them. For instance, Sony spent a staggering $14 million launching actress Jennifer Lopez's debut album *On the 6* in 1999. With that kind of promotional budget, it was no surprise that the album sold 8 million copies worldwide.

However, even huge promotional budgets didn't always guarantee success. MCA famously spent $2.2 million recording and promoting the 2001 debut album *Ultimate High* by pop singer Carly Hennessy, which went on to sell exactly 378 copies. This was the danger in betting on aspiring pop stars. Unlike rock artists—who often spent years touring and building a grassroots fanbase before being signed to a major label—when pop artists flopped, they flopped huge; there was no grassroots fanbase to lighten the blow. In fact, of the 6,455 albums distributed by major labels in 2001, only 112 of them sold 500,000 copies or more (the number which music executives said an album needed to sell in order to break even). According to that math, major labels lost money on 98% of the albums they released in 2001, meaning that the remaining 2% had to be big enough hits to make up for all of those losses. Even if executives were exaggerating the number of copies an album needed to sell in order to break even, it was still clear that major labels were losing money on the vast majority of releases; in 2001, only 417 albums—less than 7% of those distributed by major labels—sold even 100,000 copies. In that kind of climate, big multi-platinum blockbusters by Britney Spears or 'N Sync weren't just pleasant bonuses; they were absolutely essential just to keep major labels afloat. And the artists who didn't produce those kinds of numbers were becoming increasingly expendable.

Labels Start Using the Pop Artist Development Model to Develop Rock Acts

Much like Britney Spears, Christina Aguilera, and Justin Timberlake, Canadian-born singer Alanis Morissette had gotten her start in the entertainment business as a child-actor, snagging a recurring role on Nickelodeon's *You Can't Do That on Television* in 1986 at the age of 12. After her television run ended, Morissette began working with local Ottawa talent manager Stephan Klovan, with an eye towards auditioning for the popular American TV program *Star Search*, the era's closest approximation of *American Idol* (Spears, Aguilera, Timberlake, and Beyoncé Knowles all gained early exposure as *Star Search* contestants). Morissette's audition performance of The Osmonds' hit "One Bad Apple" failed to garner her a coveted slot as a *Star Search* contestant, but in the process of rehearsing the song she met writer/producer/musician Leslie Howe, who partnered with Klovan to try and help secure the young singer a record deal. The managerial duo spent thousands of dollars of their own money creating a promotional video for a Morissette/Howe composition titled "Walk Away," which would eventually appear on her debut album. And in 1990, Klovan and Howe scored a record deal for Morissette with the Canadian arm of major label MCA. She was just 16 years old.

Morissette's debut album *Alanis* (1991) drew comparisons to American teen sensations Tiffany and Debbie Gibson, even though the album's dance beats and highly choreographed videos were actually more in the style of former Los Angeles Laker cheerleader-turned-pop-star Paula Abdul, whose sophomore album *Spellbound* hit the charts that same year. On the strength of the hit singles/videos "Too Hot" and "Feel Your Love" (both of which make for amusing viewing on YouTube), *Alanis* was certified gold in 1992 by the Canadian Recording Industry Association, denoting 50,000 copies sold. And at the 1992 Juno Awards (the Canadian equivalent of the Grammys), Morissette was nominated in three categories: Single of the Year, Best Dance Record, and Most Promising Female Vocalist—the latter of which she won. However, disappointing sales of her follow-up album *Now Is the Time* (1992) left Morissette in debt to MCA, and the label eventually let her go. In an attempt to salvage her career, an executive named John Alexander at MCA Publishing—which still owned Morissette's publishing rights—introduced Morissette to Scott Welch, the agent/manager who had launched Paula Abdul's career, hoping Welch would agree to help get Morissette's first two albums released and promoted in the U.S. Welch agreed to manage the young singer, but argued that she should be re-packaged as a more adult-oriented artist and suggested that Morissette begin working with professional industry co-writers in order to cultivate a new, edgier style and image.

After countless trips to Los Angeles and Nashville to write with roughly 100 different professional songwriters, Morissette finally developed a rapport with veteran Los Angeles writer/producer Glen Ballard, best known for co-writing and producing songs for the pop group Wilson Phillips—including the huge international hit "Hold On," which had helped make Wilson Phillips' self-titled debut album the best-selling album by a female group to that point in history. Morissette soon moved to Los Angeles to continue working with Ballard on the songs that would eventually comprise her next album, *Jagged Little Pill*. The songs that emerged from the Morissette/Ballard collaborations possessed Ballard's trademark pop sensibilities, but—this being 1994, amidst the first commercial flowering the alternative rock genre—they were more rock oriented than anything either collaborator had previously written, especially the angsty confessional "You Oughta Know." Once the demos were finished, Welch, Alexander, and Ballard's extensive connections gave them instant access to major labels, and in early 1995 Warner Music subsidiary Maverick Records—which had struck pay dirt with alt-rockers Candlebox the previous year—signed Morissette to her second major label deal just prior to her 21st birthday.

170

THE DAY ALTERNATIVE MUSIC DIED

The final tracks for *Jagged Little Pill* were recorded by veteran session musicians and produced by Ballard himself. In an attempt to distance Morissette from her dance-pop past and capitalize on the angsty alt-rock trend, Maverick chose "You Oughta Know" as the lead single, and the album was slated for a July 1995 release. Then Morissette and Maverick got two huge breaks. First, on May 13, 1995, Timothy White—editor of *Billboard*'s trade magazine, which was hugely influential on industry insiders—wrote an editorial praising *Jagged Little Pill* and predicting its commercial success (White would later convince *Spin* to give Morissette her first major cover story). Then, just three days later, after Maverick's Abbey Konowitch had hand-delivered a copy of "You Oughta Know" to KROQ's program director, Morissette gained a timely shot of credibility when the influential alternative radio station—which by now was fully in thrall to the new alternative genre—put the angsty grunge approximation in heavy rotation, sometimes six or seven times a day, opening the door to the vast nationwide network of alternative stations who followed KROQ's lead. With Morissette's alt credibility firmly established, Maverick followed up "You Oughta Know" with a string of less edgy singles—"Hand in my Pocket," "Ironic," "You Learn," and "Head Over Feet"—intended for AAA radio (Adult Album Alternative, a new radio format pioneered in recent years by Eric Clapton's multi-platinum *Unplugged* album and artists like Sheryl Crow and Hootie and the Blowfish), which targeted an older, mellower, more mature audience than the alternative format (which was now almost exclusively comprised of angsty alternative genre music). And the pop sheen of Ballard's production made for easy inclusion on Top 40 radio, as well, helping Maverick and Morissette score a trifecta: a hit on three different popular radio formats. Morissette was also a hit on MTV, where her videos showcased the singer's quirky, endearing personality, and by the end of 1995, *Jagged Little Pill* was a runaway commercial success.

From start to finish, Alanis Morissette's development as an artist had followed the old pop developmental model rather than the rock model. As with any music made under the pop model, the extensive involvement of industry insiders in *Jagged Little Pill*'s conception and creation meant that it was impossible to determine how much of Morissette's music and image was the result of her individual artistic vision and how much was the calculated result of corporate formulas and market research. This fact contributed to widespread critical skepticism, even among the album's greatest champions. For instance, when *Rolling Stone* included *Jagged Little Pill* in its decade-end list of the 100 best albums of the 90s, they seemed to almost resent having to do so, saying, "Proof that the gods of rock are unfair bastards: A former TV moppet from the not-so-dirty North hooks up with Wilson Phillips' producer and makes an opportunistic angst-rock platter that not only sells 13 million copies—it *doesn't suck.*" *Rolling Stone*'s back-handed compliments echoed the assessments of numerous reviewers, including critic Robert Christgau's assessment of the album, which concluded, "Privileged phonies have identity problems too. Not to mention man problems." But for others, *Jagged Little Pill*'s calculated genesis made it simply unpalatable. Pioneering female rock icon Joni Mitchell distanced herself from comparisons to Morissette, telling *Details*, "I'm a musical explorer and not just a pop songwriter or an occasional writer of a song or half a song, like these other women. Alanis Morissette writes words, someone else helps set it to music, and then she's kind of stylized into the part." Meanwhile, others pointed out that the songs on *Jagged Little Pill* weren't exactly profound, especially the album's highest charting single "Ironic," which drew the particular ire of linguists everywhere. As Richard Leiby wrote in the *Washington Post*, "Ironic" described "a series of events that qualify as annoying or unfortunate, but wouldn't pass for ironic in most freshman English courses."

Eventually, however, *Jagged Little Pill*'s staggering commercial success—33 million worldwide sales—would sweep away all but its most steadfast detractors. And within major label offices, the album's success was proof that artistic visions which originated outside of the industry's corporate machinery were superfluous to the creation of popular music. The successful development of Alanis Morissette would have a profound effect on the way major labels would develop and market subsequent artists—especially female artists—for years to come, from Meredith Brooks' calculated "You Oughta Know" knock-off "Bitch" through the continuing string of "edgy" female artists developed within the major label system, from Pink and Avril Lavigne all the way through newer acts like Lorde and Haim who were signed in their early teens and groomed for success within the confines of the corporate major label machinery. It is possible to trace all of their roots to the music industry's success in developing and marketing Alanis Morissette. In the end, few factors contributed more to the eventual meaninglessness of the term "alternative" than the development and commercial success of *Jagged Little Pill*. But for all its calculated artifice, Alanis Morissette's career path was still a familiar one—it was just that it had been transplanted from the pop world to the rock world. However, an entirely new breed of artist development was coming, one made possible by a specific set of corporate circumstances new to the late 90s.

Nothing Alternative about Alternative

By the late 90s, three decades of purchases, takeovers, and consolidation meant that the five remaining major record labels comprised the operations of what had once been *eighty-nine* distinct record labels, and they owned shares in dozens more. But music industry corporatization and consolidation went far beyond just the record labels. MTV—along with its sister station VH1—had fought off its aspiring competitors to maintain a chokehold on the music TV market. Ticketmaster had achieved a virtual monopoly in ticket sales for large concerts. And the Telecommunications Act of 1996 had completely revolutionized the radio industry, allowing a small handful of companies to purchase and operate the majority of American radio stations. For example, within three years of the act's passage, a Texas-based company called Clear Channel had gone from owning 50 American radio stations to owning over 1,200, meaning that one single company was suddenly responsible for programming up to 8-10 different radio stations in each of the larger U.S. markets. The speed and scope of consolidation across the entire media industry was extraordinary. In 1983, the media industry had been controlled by roughly 50 large companies; by 2000, that number has shrunk to less than 10. According to author and media critic Robert McChesney in an interview for the 2001 PBS documentary *Merchants of Cool*:

> What's happened in the media in the United States in the past 10 or 15 years—especially since about 1994 or 1995—has been an unprecedented concentration of ownership... The entertainment companies—which are a handful of massive conglomerates that own four of the five music companies that sell 90 percent of the music in the United States—those same companies also own all the film studios, all the major TV networks, all the TV stations in the ten largest markets. They own all or part of every single commercial cable channel... They're huge conglomerates, and this is really a new thing. It used to be the largest media companies 20 or 40 years ago only produced newspapers, they only made movies, they only had a TV network. Now

they're dominant players in each of these markets. They're highly non-competitive. They don't have to worry about a newcomer coming in. The barriers to entry, as economists talk about, are so high that basically it's a private club, a gentleman's club of like a half-dozen, seven or eight companies that really rule the thing. And they're closely linked. I mean they know each other. They have deals together, and what they're able to do with this tremendous power between them is hyper-commercialize their content without fear of competitive retribution... And that's the reigning logic behind the entire system. It's based on concentration and hyper-commercialism. So they look at music as just one small part of it. They aren't music companies; they're money-making companies. And music is a weapon that generates money for them.

For most of the 80s, and even into the early 90s, the alternative music scene had been a lonely skeptic in the midst of an increasingly commercial music industry. But by the late 90s, the alternative scene had been almost completely devoured by the mainstream, and the "alternative" tag was now being applied to "nu metal" rock acts like Korn, Limp Bizkit, and Linkin Park for whom massive commercial success was a completely acceptable—and oftentimes primary—goal. As British music critic Tommy Udo pointed out in his 2002 book *Brave Nu World*, "The key to their success is their willingness to get their hands dirty making singles, doing videos for MTV, allowing corporate sponsors to get involved." Meanwhile, the corporatization and consolidation of the media industry were making it possible to synergize and amplify old-school hype campaigns across entertainment mediums and corporate borders in order to manufacture the era's most commercially successful rock bands from virtually start to finish. Limp Bizkit's engineered rise was a case in point.

In July of 1997, Limp Bizkit released its debut album *Three Dollar Bill Y'all* to little fanfare and nearly universal critical disdain. With sales still stagnant in early 1998, the band's label—Interscope Records, a subsidiary of the world's largest record label, Universal Music Group—decided to launch a massive promotional campaign on the band's behalf which would position Limp Bizkit as an "edgy" pop alternative to the boy band trend which was beginning to dominate the pop charts. At the center of the plan was new twist on the age-old record company practice of paying radio stations to play songs. Only this time around, in order to be completely legal and transparent, each play was to be preceded by an announcement that it had been "sponsored" by

Interscope Records. This was the arrangement when Interscope paid Oregon radio station KUFO $5,000 to play the Limp Bizkit song "Counterfeit" 50 times, preceded each time by the disclaimer, "Brought to you by Flip/Interscope." The disclosure of this arrangement landed both band and label on the front page of the *New York Times* in an article titled "Pay-for-Play Back on the Air But This Rendition Legal."

It may have been legal, but it was only part of Interscope's Limp Bizkit campaign. The label also partnered with MTV to arrange for the video for "Counterfeit" to debut on MTV's video show *Total Request Live* (*TRL*). How, one might ask, could Interscope and MTV "arrange" for a video to appear on a show whose content was determined by viewers' votes? As explained by then *New York Times* music critic Ann Powers in 2001's *Merchants of Cool*, "I guess you could say that *Total Request Live* is democratic [but] the field of candidates is very small, and there are organizations behind them… who are deciding which candidates get promoted. So, in other words, you can't just be Joe Fabulous who's releasing your little indie record and get on *Total Request Live*." Or as John Seabrook put it in an interview for the same documentary, "What you're seeing [on *TRL*] is supposedly all about the audience, what the audience wants. But, in fact, MTV is using that platform as a way of introducing videos that they want to put into heavy rotation, of having hosts that they think are future MTV stars, and doing it all under the umbrella of, 'This is what the audience wants.'" Following Limp Bizkit's *TRL* debut, MTV and Interscope arranged a follow-up live performance of "Counterfeit" on MTV's highly-rated "Spring Break '98" broadcast, and then, a few months later, an appearance on MTV's New Year's Eve special. Essentially, if you watched MTV at all, Limp Bizkit was virtually inescapable.

In the wake of the radio payoffs and the MTV hype campaign, slowly but surely, *Three Dollar Bill Y'all* began to sell, and it was finally certified both gold and platinum by the RIAA in the spring of 1999, nearly two years after the album's release, and just prior to the release of the band's follow-up album *Significant Other*. But Limp Bizkit would not become a household name until the massive public outcry in reaction to "Woodstock '99," where Limp Bizkit's anger-fueled performance was blamed for inciting a violent, festival-ending riot and numerous sexual assaults, including the gang-rape of a teenage girl during the band's set, just yards from the stage. All the negative publicity had a two-fold effect for the band. First, it granted Limp Bizkit the elusive "outsider" status which they had always craved, and now gladly accepted. "It's easy to point the finger at us and we kinda like that," said Bizkit lead singer Fred Durst in the midst of the controversy. "We like that it's your easiest way out. I'll be your scapegoat." Second, all the publicity brought the band torrents of new notoriety; within three weeks of their Woodstock '99 performance, *Significant Other* was certified triple-platinum by the RIAA. As public fury over the riot and sexual assaults intensified, Interscope came under criticism for signing and promoting Limp Bizkit, to which the label's founder Jimmy Iovine had the gall to insist that Interscope's association with the band was simply the result of populist demand. "There's no way to stop a movement in popular culture," said Iovine in *Merchants of Cool*, as if he were unaware of the massive hype campaign that had been necessary to get people interested in the band. "There's no way to stop it. It's going to happen with or without you. There's absolutely no way to stop that train." And by the time Interscope released Limp Bizkit's next album, it was clear that the band's bad-boy infamy was enhancing rather than deterring sales. In October of 2000, Limp Bizkit's third album *Chocolate Starfish and the Hot Dog Flavored Water* sold 1,054,511 copies in its first week of release, eclipsing Pearl Jam's *Vs.* as the fastest-selling rock album of all time.

According to Tommy Udo in *Brave Nu World*, "To some extent the success of the nu metal school, particularly Korn and Limp Bizkit, has as many similarities with ever-growing franchise brands such as Starbucks or Gap as it does with any previous generation of rock and roll." The band Korn was famously sponsored by Adidas, and fulfilled its end of the bargain by featuring an ode to the shoemaker titled "A.D.I.D.A.S." on its second album, 1996's double-platinum *Life Is Peachy*. Then, in the best tradition of corporate America, the band abruptly ditched Adidas in favor of Puma when the latter company made them a more lucrative endorsement offer. However, unlike earlier rock critics who would have instantly branded the nu metal bands as sellouts, Udo actually praised such behavior as examples of the "can-do" American work ethic, attributing any objections to Korn and Bizkit's behavior to "some redundant hangover from punk or hippy days." And he dismissed other current bands' resistance to commercialism as "self-defeating," arguing, for instance, that Radiohead's refusal of corporate sponsorship for their *Kid A* tour in 2000 was the result of "a strain of elitism that has always run through pop culture; bands become embarrassed by their own popularity… This elitism in rock and roll, this sneering cooler-than-thou attitude that pervades both performers and punters alike, is a trait that is absent from most of the nu metal bands; yet the fact that Fred Durst is wealthy, a workaholic, and has many activities outside the band seems to draw the ire of critics."

According to Udo's logic, the bands being recorded, bankrolled, and marketed to the point of ubiquity by the world's most powerful corporations were "populist," whereas the bands who wished to avoid commercial entanglements and let their music stand on its own merits were "elitist." Blatant logical contradictions notwithstanding, Udo's reasoning was understandable in the midst of the ongoing millennial celebration of commercial success, which had become all but synonymous with "The American Dream." After all, Bill Gates and Steve Jobs were universally hailed for their commercial ambition in other media industries. What was any different about Fred Durst—who would go on to parlay Limp Bizkit's success into a seat on the Interscope board and his own major-label funded vanity label, Flawless Records—carving out a niche for himself as a turn-of-the-millennium captain of the music industry? Nothing at all, at least from a purely commercial point of view. However, this was precisely the issue at stake. Udo's logic required an assessment of music according to purely *commercial*, rather than *artistic* standards, which explains why he conspicuously fails to mention Durst's lack of discernible artistic talent as a possible reason for all the critical ire.

In addition to failing to account for artistic talent or quality, purely commercial assessments of rock music also intrinsically valued the winner over the loser, the popular over the outcast, the powerful over the weak, the mainstream over the alternative. And in nu metal's specific case, this meant valuing the white over the black, the male over the female, the heterosexual over the homosexual. In other words, it was no coincidence that Limp Bizkit's music had been the background music for Woodstock '99's sexual assaults. As female alt-rocker Corin Tucker of Sleater-Kinney put it later that year, "1999 saw a lot of ugly changes in rock, particularly a backlash against the success that women have had in rock. For example: the rapes and sexual assaults that happened at Woodstock, along with signs from the audience like 'Show me your tits' or the popularity of bands like Insane Clown Posse or Limp Bizkit that have misogynist lyrics. In a way, I see it as a more blatant power struggle for recognition within the corporate world." Hard-rocker Marilyn Manson more succinctly described Fred Durst as "one of the illiterate apes who used to beat you up at school for being a fag." But in a more general sense, it was clear that alternative music's descendants were no longer on the side of the outsider or the underdog, a fact that nu metal artists and fans seemed painfully oblivious to. As *Salon*'s Joey Sweeney's pointed out in 2001:

> Nu metal has done well with the seemingly always-fledgling modern rock radio format. This, in a lot of cases, might cause some of the bands mentioned here to be identified as the new sound of what was called alternative music. But make no mistake: There is nothing alternative about it. You can't swing a dead freshman these days without running into this sub-Bizkit band or that one. In fact, the influence of Limp Bizkit throughout just about all of modern rock these days is nothing short of epidemic; it's not even worth quibbling over what exactly lead singer Fred Durst and the boys are angry about. [But] if kids today are supposed to be so smart and media-savvy, why can't they see through all this showbiz rage and know that they're being played by bad poets, overweight DJs, and clueless hessians?... Check out this gem, from [nu metal band] Fear Factory's 'Shock:'

> *I will be the power urge*
> *Shock to the system*
> *Electrified, amplified*
> *Shock to the system.*

> Dude, I got a shocker for you: You are the system. And you're as expected as rain.

By the dawn of the 21st century, commercial aspirations were completely overpowering artistic aspirations in mainstream rock music. Even the term "alternative," which had been coined by an artistically adventurous scene in order to differentiate itself from the corporate mainstream, was now being used almost exclusively to describe commercially aspirant mainstream acts. For bands whose aspirations were more commercial than artistic, this reality presented few problems. But for any rock act hoping to follow in the long tradition of rock music that was both popular *and* artistically substantive—as well any casual rock fans continuing to look to popular rock for artistically credible music—the list of rock acts on *Billboard*'s year-end rock charts for the year 2000 was thoroughly depressing: Linkin Park, Creed, Three Doors Down, Fuel, Incubus, Disturbed, Limp Bizkit, Stone Temple Pilots, Papa Roach,

Godsmack, Green Day, Nickelback, Lit, Everclear, Eve 6, Vertical Horizon, Bush, Kid Rock, Korn, Staind, Collective Soul, P.O.D., Good Charlotte, System of a Down, and on and on. It was becoming clear that in the new millennium rock artists who wanted to make artistically substantive music would have to do so outside of the corporate major label system.

Chapter Thirteen

Rock for Rock's Sake

Rolling Stone, the Rock Hall of Fame, and the Mythologizing of Rock

The Rise and Fall of Rolling Stone

As the mainstream rock music industry was experiencing a period of unprecedented corporatization, commercialization, and homogenization, rock criticism was also undergoing a profound transformation. In the three decades since rock criticism's first appearance, the medium which had gotten its start as a countercultural adversary of the establishment had become something of an establishment itself, complete with its own territory to protect and power to perpetuate. Because of this shift, the critical establishment was becoming more and more concerned with constructing a rock mythology which would expand rock music's legend and influence, and becoming less and less concerned with providing an independent critical voice. By the 1990s, the opening of the Rock and Roll Hall of Fame and Museum and the ubiquity of sycophantic "History of Rock and Roll" documentaries were indicative of this ongoing shift, but perhaps nothing symbolized rock criticism's shift from underground insurgency to establishment mythology more than the evolution of *Rolling Stone* magazine.

From its first issue in late 1967, San Francisco-based *Rolling Stone* magazine had been firmly aligned with the counterculture. Its writers and editors saw themselves on one side of a clear cultural divide, with the mainstream political, military, and commercial power structures on the other. And in its early years, the young magazine's sensibility mixed the ideological counterculture politics of Bay area tinder box UC Berkeley with the burgeoning psychedelia of Haight-Ashbury's drug-centered hippie scene. This meant that scathing criticisms of arch-establishment adversaries like Richard Nixon and then-California governor Ronald Reagan were printed alongside offers for free roach clips with *Rolling Stone* subscriptions. It proved to be a potent mix, and part of founder and editor Jann Wenner's genius was recognizing rock music as the shared cultural touchpoint between these two amorphous countercultural constituencies. As the 21-year-old founder wrote in his opening editorial, "*Rolling Stone* is not just about music, but also about the things and attitudes that the music embraces... To describe it any further would be difficult without sounding like bullshit, and bullshit is like gathering moss." Within mere months of its launch, *Rolling Stone* was already being widely referred to as "the voice of the counterculture."

This is not to say that *Rolling Stone*—or rock criticism in general—was categorically opposed to popularity or commercial success; after all, many of the countercultural rock icons whom *Rolling Stone* praised had already achieved mass commercial success by the time the magazine arrived on the scene. But even if *Rolling Stone*'s early writers weren't obscurantists, they still strived to assert their editorial independence from the commercial music industry establishment whenever possible, and for a time they managed to wield more influence over the major record labels than vice versa. Atlantic Records senior executive Jerry Wexler became a *Rolling Stone* subscriber after the magazine's second issue. By 1968, Columbia Records president Clive Davis had made the magazine required reading for the entire Columbia staff. And because of this influence, *Rolling Stone*'s rock critics maintained the independence necessary to pan many of the most popular rock albums of the day, even those put out by the major labels that advertised in the magazine. According to *Rolling Stone* biographer Robert Draper:

> *Rolling Stone* could be expected not only to see through industry hype but to point it out whenever it materialized... It took a lot of nerve. Here was a magazine whose very existence depended on record company ads, whose record store distribution was handled by A&M Records (later by CBS), whose

high editorial quality owed much to the industry's good graces...yet *Rolling Stone* seemed to bite every feeder's hand. It reviled the bands on which the record companies heaped the most money... When a new ultra-commercial band starring an unknown singer named Olivia Newton-John was announced by Monkees creator Don Kirshner, the magazine's news article described the press conference as 'the greatest barrage of promotional bullshit in many years'... *Rolling Stone* even went so far as to insult, in print, the advertisements Columbia Records placed *in the magazine*, declaring these 'The Man Can't Bust Our Music' ads insincere, and ultimately causing [Columbia president] Clive Davis to scuttle the whole campaign.

In addition to the "Us vs. Them" mentality which attracted many of *Rolling Stone's* early editors, the magazine's editorial independence was also a result of the way in which writers and critics initially came to *Rolling Stone*. These were not, by and large, seasoned journalists tied to the values of what was commonly referred to in the counterculture as "the straight press." In fact, most of the album reviews published in the magazine's first couple of years had been mailed to its San Francisco headquarters in response to a simple recurring advertisement: "Rolling Stone is interested in receiving record reviews, movie reviews and book reviews from interested writers or those who would like to write. Any such reviews printed will be paid for. If you would like to give it a chance—and we are most interested in finding new reviewers—please send your manuscript..."

When Jann Wenner's old Berkeley friend Greil Marcus became *Rolling Stone's* first music reviews editor in 1969, he soon realized that the magazine was receiving as many as ten to fifteen reviews a week from a twenty-year-old women's shoe salesman from suburban San Diego named Lester Bangs. Marcus printed two of these reviews back to back in his first section—one panning the self-titled debut from San Francisco-based band It's a Beautiful Day and the other praising experimental rocker Captain Beefheart's *Trout Mask Replica*—and the career of a legendary rock critic was born. According to Draper, early *Rolling Stone* critics "did not want jobs so much as a chance to speak and be heard on a subject that meant something vital to them... for them music was miraculous, like language and fire, proof of magic and thus maybe, eventually, of hope." This was certainly true of Bangs, whose reviews ranged from the bizarre to the profound as he passionately searched within rock music for some glimpse of enlightenment, hope, truth, magic, *salvation*. From his opening review of Captain Beefheart, Bangs insistence on rock's substantive artistic possibilities helped set the tone for a whole generation of critics. "Captain Beefheart, the only true dadaist in rock, has been victimized repeatedly by public incomprehension and critical authoritarianism," writes Bangs. "What the critics failed to see was that this was a band with a *vision,* that their music, difficult raucous and rough as it is, proceeded from a unique and original consciousness... Thus it's very gratifying to say that Captain Beefheart's new album is a total success, a brilliant, stunning enlargement and clarification of his art." Bangs goes on to compare the album's rhythms and melodic textures to free jazz pianist Cecil Taylor, and concludes by declaring that the album "may well be the most unusual and challenging musical experience you'll have this year." Ultimately, what was important wasn't his specific assessment of Captain Beefheart—whose music remains as polarizing today as it was then—but rather the larger idea that rock music could be assessed according to the same kinds of artistic standards employed by critics in other artistic fields such as jazz music, classical music, literature, film, or visual art. These artistic standards would remain the basis for rock criticism well into the 1970s.

Rolling Stone's template for rock criticism changed little during the magazine's first decade. Reviews were serious-minded if not always serious, and the expansive "Records" section often included upwards of 20-30 album reviews per issue, ensuring that music reviews remained an integral part of the magazine's identity. Along the way, *Rolling Stone* developed a hard-earned reputation as a serious journalistic magazine, thanks not only to its music-related content, but also to award-winning features by the likes of Hunter S. Thompson, Tom Wolfe, and Joe Ezterhas on topics ranging from political campaigns to nightclub fashion to police corruption, all while maintaining a knowing tone of left-leaning countercultural sentiment. In 1990, former *Newsweek* and *Rolling Stone* publisher Porter Bibb was able to look back at the magazine's 1970s zenith and proclaim that *Rolling Stone* founder Jann Wenner "had attracted more talent than any other magazine publisher in this century. Furthermore, it doesn't matter what editors you name: nobody had a better understanding of what was going on in this country in the sixties and seventies than Jann Wenner. And I don't think anybody's ever going to put together a journal that is as accurate a reflection of what's going on in the country as he did in *Rolling Stone*'s heyday." As *Rolling Stone* biographer Robert Draper put it, "By the end of 1969, Jann Wenner's two-year-old *Rolling Stone*...was generally accepted as the most authoritative rock & roll magazine in the land. By 1971, *Rolling Stone* was what *Esquire* had been in the sixties and the *New York Herald Tribune* had been a decade before that: a breeding ground of explosive New Journalists... Two years later, the magazine began to make money. Three years after that, it helped elect a President... It thus became a generation's voice—perhaps the only trustworthy voice... From 1970-77, no magazine was as honest or imaginative as what Jann Wenner called his 'little rock & roll newspaper from San Francisco.' Greater truths were its aim. That meant toppling false idols of every denomination—from Nixon, the FBI and the Nuclear Regulatory Commission to Woodstock, Charles Manson and the Symbionese Liberation Army."

By any measure, what *Rolling Stone* achieved in its first decade was impressive, the heady stuff of legend. But it was from these heights that the magazine would experience a gradual but unmistakable decline, and the coming decades would see a steady erosion of both its editorial quality and cultural relevance. There were many reasons for this decline, but beginning in the late 70s the most glaring problem for a "countercultural" magazine which based its identity on rock music was that, by that time, rock music as a whole was anything but countercultural; in fact, rock was the commercial force driving many of America's most successful mainstream media corporations, from Warner Communications to CBS. And *Rolling Stone*, too, was quickly becoming a mainstream media company itself; by 1976, the "little rock & roll newspaper" had secured a war chest of roughly $2 million. The following year *Rolling Stone* moved its headquarters from the countercultural outpost of San Francisco to New York City, the belly of the commercial beast. According to *Rolling Stone* biographer Robert Draper, "Jann Wenner's magazine changed almost overnight. Writers and editors left—gradually at first; then in droves... By the end of 1981, not a single writer or editor from San Francisco remained in the New York office." The magazine's changing priorities were soon evident everywhere. With the move to New York, the bill for the company's office space jumped from $500 a month to $27,500 a month. The magazine began to be known for its lavish parties which attracted the city's hip cultural elite. Wenner bought himself a Rolls-Royce. Within mere months of the move, *Rolling Stone* was firmly entrenched as part of the New Establishment.

THE DAY ALTERNATIVE MUSIC DIED

The recognition that rock—and rock criticism—had lost some of its countercultural mojo was one of the reasons so many rock critics fell so hard for punk music in the late 70s; here, at last, was a rock movement that rekindled the countercultural spirit which had given birth to *Rolling Stone* and rock criticism in the first place. Younger *Rolling Stone* critics like Tom Carson and Charles M. Young were intent on pushing the punk agenda, but Young's 1977 cover story on The Sex Pistols produced a noticeable drop in newsstand sales. The message this sent to Jann Wenner was clear: punk didn't sell. Wenner had been willing to give punk a chance, to throw The Sex Pistols on the cover and see what happened, but as a businessman, the issue's sluggish sales made his decision easy. "Once that happened," said managing editor Jim Henke, "Jann's mind was pretty much made up about punk." Rather than focus the magazine's critical attention on championing music that most of its core readers had little awareness of or interest in, Wenner opted instead to continue to focus *Rolling Stone*'s music coverage on the tried and true baby-boomer rock acts who had always been the magazine's bread and butter, even as those acts began to fade further and further from artistic and cultural relevance. At a time when L.A.'s KROQ was pioneering the "alternative" radio format—eventually necessitating the creation of a new format called "classic rock" to play music by older rock artists—*Rolling Stone* chose to throw its hat in with those older artists rather than champion the small but artistically adventurous post-punk alternative scene. Practically, this decision meant ignoring much of the music being made by the younger generation of rock acts, and thus the magazine became increasingly cut off from the younger cutting edge of both music and culture. From the late 70s onward, *Rolling Stone* would cease to be the voice of countercultural youth; it would instead become a pop culture "lifestyle magazine" for an aging generation of baby-boomers.

As the 70s turned into the 80s, *Rolling Stone* embraced its association with the baby boom generation, many of whom, as they drifted into middle-age, found themselves taking straight jobs, buying into mainstream American consumerism, and—gasp!—voting for a Republican presidential candidate. Countercultural policies like refusing ads from cigarette companies, perfume companies, and even the military were dropped one by one, as those kinds of ideological stands became less and less important to the magazine's readership. Throughout the 80s, *Rolling Stone*'s covers came to be dominated by the faces of mainstream baby-boomer entertainment icons like Don Johnson, Bruce

Willis, and Michael Douglas, as well as over-the-hill rock icons like Paul McCartney, Robert Plant, and The Rolling Stones. Meanwhile, throughout the entire decade of the 1980s, only *two acts* from the alternative scene graced the magazine's cover: U2 and R.E.M., neither of whom were granted the status until they had achieved platinum-selling crossover success. And by the end of the 80s, the once-prominent "Records" section was routinely publishing less than ten album reviews per issue. As a result of all of these developments, fewer and fewer young music fans were looking to the once-influential music magazine to discover new and interesting music.

Rolling Stone, the Rock Hall of Fame, and the Mythologizing of Rock Music

In 1983, Atlantic Records founder and president Ahmet Ertegun created the Rock and Roll Hall of Fame Foundation (acts would begin being inducted into the Hall in 1986 though the physical Rock and Roll Hall of Fame and Museum would not open in Cleveland until 1995). One of the foundation's founding members was *Rolling Stone* founder Jann Wenner. He would eventually become co-chairman with Ertegun, and then, upon Ertegun's death in 2006, sole chairman of the Rock and Roll Hall of Fame Foundation. The partnership between Ertegun, whose major label subsidiary Atlantic Records had long symbolized rock's *commercial* aspirations, and Wenner, whose magazine *Rolling Stone* had been a pioneering champion of rock's *artistic* aspirations, seemed on the surface to be an odd match. But once the two men had reached the pinnacles of wealth and power in their respective fields, their interests had become increasingly similar; the businesses with which Wenner and Ertegun had become synonymous were now both dependent on rock music's continued commercial success and popular relevance. And so it was not surprising that one of the primary qualifications for induction into the Rock and Roll Hall of Fame became—according to the official Hall of Fame induction guidelines— how much an act furthered the "perpetuation of rock and roll."

      The idea that the Rock and Roll Hall of Fame would reward those who had contributed to the "perpetuation of rock" made all the sense in the world; the Rock Hall of Fame was—like any other Hall of Fame endeavor—inherently prone to self-congratulatory myth-making. The problem came when *Rolling*

Stone magazine also began adopting the Rock Hall of Fame's "perpetuation of rock" standard as its own guiding standard for critical assessment. Since its inception, *Rolling Stone* had fulfilled a very different function than a Hall of Fame; the iconic magazine had been rock music's leading critical voice, trusted to provide an assessment of rock music according to artistic standards that were independent of commercial success or rock mythology. In fact, according to founder Jann Wenner's mission statement in *Rolling Stone*'s inaugural issue, the magazine had been founded specifically to combat the "myth and nonsense" of the sycophantic fan magazines and commercial trade publications of the time. But in the 1980s, *Rolling Stone* was in the process of becoming a leading oracle of rock mythology rather than an independent critical voice.

The reason for this shift was easy to trace. By the time the Rock and Roll Hall of Fame Foundation had begun inducting acts in the late 80s, rock's popular dominance was being challenged not only by pop performers like Michael Jackson and Madonna, but also by the skyrocketing popularity of hip hop music and a revitalized country music industry. This was bad news for rock-centric *Rolling Stone*, and the magazine began to see panning a popular rock album as something akin to criticizing a member of its own team. And so, in the ensuing years, *Rolling Stone* would help lead rock's critical establishment away from trying to delineate between good and bad rock acts in order to begin creating a mythology in which rock music itself was celebrated as *inherently* artistically and culturally valuable. This shift would necessitate relaxing the artistic critical standards which had defined the influential magazine's formative years in in order to embrace even the most artistically vapid popular rock acts. This review from the November 3, 1988 issue was representative of the ongoing shift:

> Bon Jovi's new album, defiantly titled *New Jersey*, is so purely commercial that it's practically beyond criticism (it would be more appropriate to evaluate its sales potential)... The relatively savage 'Lay Your Hands on Me' kicks off *New Jersey*, but sugar-metal outings like 'Wild Is the Wind,' which are veiled in a smoke screen of distortomatic guitars, are the album's true heart. *Slippery When Wet* has sold 13 million copies, and the temptation to repeat a tried-and-true formula evidently proved too great... *New Jersey* has all the virtues and drawbacks of a popular record, hitting all the marks yet remaining thoroughly unidiosyncratic... Bon Jovi's trick is to use heavy-metal chords and still sound absolutely safe. Rock & roll used to be rebellion disguised as

> commercialism; now so much of it is commercialism disguised as rebellion. Bon Jovi is safe as milk...

The scathing copy of Michael Azerrad's review reads like vintage *Rolling Stone*, but this being the late 80s rather than the late 60s, the magazine saw fit to award *New Jersey* with a 3-star, or "Good," rating (the same bet-hedging star rating, incidentally, that the magazine would soon award Nirvana's *Nevermind*). In Bon Jovi's case, the reason for *Rolling Stone*'s punch-pulling was clear: Bon Jovi helped *Rolling Stone* sell magazines. By the release of *New Jersey*, the pretty boys of metal already had one puff-piece *Rolling Stone* cover story under their belts, and another was just around the corner. For the magazine, jeopardizing such a cozy relationship with a commercially successful band would have been bad business. But *Rolling Stone*'s unwillingness to out-and-out pan a sure-to-be-popular rock album contrasted sharply with its formative era, when it still had the courage to brazenly slam popular rock bands like Led Zeppelin and Black Sabbath. *Rolling Stone*'s credibility as a critical voice had largely been built on its willingness to criticize the commercial establishment, and pandering to rock bands who were commercially successful in order to boost newsstand sales was clearly at odds with that tradition. Eventually, however, *Rolling Stone* would part ways with its own heritage and begin retroactively applying its new, more relaxed standards to earlier rock acts, a project that would necessitate a re-assessment of rock's entire history.

Rolling Stone's initial foray into codifying a rock "canon" had come in 1979 with the publication of *The Rolling Stone Record Guide*, in which the magazine's editors took on the task of rating roughly 10,000 albums on a scale of 5-Stars ("Indispensable"—or "Classic" in later iterations) to 1-Star ("Worthless: records that need never, or should never, have been created"). It was a bold undertaking, and the initial 1979 *Record Guide* attempted to apply the rigorous artistic standards that *Rolling Stone* had been known for in its early years. The guide went so far as to classify its 5-Star albums as "record[s] that must be included in any comprehensive collection," echoing traditional critical assertions about the longstanding canons in other artistic mediums, the kinds of assertions which had populated textbooks and university syllabi for decades. However, subsequent editions of the *Record Guide*—which appeared in 1979,

1983, 1992, and 2003—would reveal just how drastically *Rolling Stone* was relaxing its standards in order perpetuate a sycophantic rock mythology.

For instance, in *Rolling Stone*'s original 1973 review of Led Zeppelin's *Houses of the Holy*, Gordon Fletcher had dubbed the album "one of the dullest and most confusing albums I've heard this year" thanks to its "naked imitations" and "songwriting deficiencies." But by 1983 (the same year the Rock Hall of Fame Foundation was founded), the *Record Guide* had upgraded *Houses of the Holy* to 4-Star, or "Excellent" status. And on the heels of Zeppelin's induction into the Rock Hall of Fame, 2003's *Album Guide* (as it was now called) finally gave *Houses of the Holy* a "Classic" 5-Star rating. By that time, the *Album Guide* had no qualms about reveling in the very "myth and nonsense" that Jann Wenner's inaugural *Rolling Stone* editorial had cautioned against, unabashedly attributing *Houses of the Holy*'s 5-star status to the fact that Led Zeppelin "had the largest crowds, the loudest rock songs, the most groupies, the fullest manes of hair." Such were the revised standards of rock criticism.

The impact of these revised standards on the development of the rock "canon" extended far beyond just Led Zeppelin. For instance, the 1983 version of the *Record Guide* had given *all eleven* of Black Sabbath's existing albums 1-Star (or "Worthless") ratings, explaining succinctly that "these would-be Kings of Heavy Metal are eternally foiled by their own stupidity." But by 1992, the *Album Guide* had relaxed its standards enough to grant all of those same albums at least 2-Star ratings, with a few even achieving 3-Star status. And by 2003, a complete reversal had taken place; Black Sabbath's first two albums were now 5-Star "Classics," with *five* additional 4-Star ratings among the same eleven albums which had been granted 1-Star status two decades earlier. Of course, not one note of the band's music had changed during that time, just *Rolling Stone*'s standards of assessment. And similarly complete critical reversals were evident in the changing assessments of a whole slew of artistically challenged but commercially popular classic rock acts. In 1979, the inaugural *Record Guide* had given all of AC/DC's existing albums the 1-Star treatment and described them as "an Australian hard-rock band whose main purpose on earth apparently is to offend anyone within sight or earshot. They succeed on both counts." Yet by the early 2000s, AC/DC's music had been deemed canon-worthy. Ditto for Judas Priest, whose reputation had been rehabilitated from a similarly damning initial assessment as "grunting, flailing

Seventies hard rock, as vulgar as its name, but less euphonious. For lovers of recycled Led Zeppelin riffs only."

By the time *Rolling Stone* unveiled its list of rock's "100 Greatest Acts"—"The Immortals," as they were dubbed—in 2004, it was now clear that either perceived artistic substance *or* commercial success was enough to merit inclusion in the canon of rock greatness. Throughout the list, short-selling critical darlings like The Velvet Underground and Gram Parsons were set side-by-side with once-dismissed commercial behemoths like Led Zeppelin and Black Sabbath, but the list's biases now clearly favored commercial success over artistic substance. For instance, R.E.M., who the magazine had once proclaimed "America's Best Band," failed to make the list at all, while vacuous classic rockers like AC/DC and Aerosmith made the cut. These kinds of decisions were obvious reflections of the influence of the rock establishment's ongoing myth-making campaign. In fact, by the time *Rolling Stone* released its list of "Immortals," the magazine's assessments had become virtually identical with those of the Rock and Roll Hall of Fame. All told, of the 100 acts "immortalized" by *Rolling Stone* in 2004, *ninety-five* have been inducted into the Rock Hall of Fame (and three of those not inducted simply aren't yet eligible). Such universal overlap between these two "independent" canons was not surprising considering Jann Wenner's leadership of both organizations, not to mention the conspicuous number of *Rolling Stone* writers who have also been members of the Hall of Fame nominating committee. In reality, the rock canon was being determined by a remarkably small group of industry insiders bent on the "perpetuation of rock."

Throughout the 1990s, *Rolling Stone*'s venerable influence helped legitimize a wholesale mythologizing of rock that was being actively cultivated by The Rock and Roll Hall of Fame, a new spat of sycophantic "History of Rock and Roll" documentaries, and new myth-affirming TV franchises like VH1's *Legends* and *Behind the Music*. The combined effect of this myth-making apparatus would profoundly re-shape popular perceptions of rock's history. As the *Legends* series lumped The Clash and The Bee Gees into the same exalted category and *Behind the Music* presented John Lennon, R.E.M., Motley Crue, and Kiss as equally worthy subjects of serious documentary treatment, the tensions which had once existed between artistic and commercial assessments of rock music began to be blurred beyond recognition. Upstart publications like *Spin* magazine might have been expected to challenge the rock establishment's compromised criteria, but instead they exaggerated it. When *Spin* revealed its first list of "The Greatest Albums of All Time," ultra-obscure but artistically respected albums like Tom Waits' *Swordfishtrombones* and The Minutemen's *Double Nickels on the Dime* were honored alongside commercially popular but artistically trivial albums like George Michael's *Faith*, begging the question: Under what criteria could all of these albums be judged as "great?"

Circling the Wagons

In the midst of this evolution, rock acts who dared to challenge the newfound coziness between rock's artistic and commercial aspirations began to be branded as traitors by the rock establishment. For instance, in October of 1996, on the heels of Pearl Jam's fight against Ticketmaster and amidst the band's general rejection of commercial marketing, *Rolling Stone* published a long-winded cover article smearing the band's outspoken lead singer. The feature, titled "Eddie Vedder: Who Are You?" is filled with quotes from anonymous sources from his record label (not exactly a sympathetic ear for criticisms of industry commercialism) who, in turn, brand Vedder as a "master manipulator," a "hustler," and a "control freak." The article rips the singer for sins as various as his "unwinnable war against Ticketmaster," the lack of "arena anthems" on Pearl Jam's latest album *No Code,* and his "bemoan[ing], endlessly, the burdens of his fame and success." In addition, a series of unnamed high school acquaintances are trotted out to testify that Vedder had been a "popular" member of his high school drama troupe in order to create the impression that the frustrations and dissatisfactions evident in the singer's lyrics and persona were the result of calculated invention rather than authentic sentiment. In implying that Vedder's childhood trials—his broken home, for instance, and his confusion about his father's identity—weren't sufficiently tragic circumstances to warrant legitimate feelings of anger and estrangement, *Rolling Stone* was echoing Andy Rooney's callous charge that the struggles which led Kurt Cobain to suicide had been small potatoes. "What's all this nonsense about how terrible life is?" Rooney had quipped about Cobain. *Rolling Stone* was now asking essentially the same question of Vedder.

There were those who recognized a smear-job when they saw one and rallied to Vedder's defense. In a short but potent "Letter to the Editor," R.E.M.'s Michael Stipe wrote, "Limbo, limbo, limbo. How low can they go? Can the kibbles and bits—this is cat box journalism at its lowest. Eddie Vedder, Pearl Jam, and the readers of *Rolling Stone* deserve better." Kurt Cobain's widow Courtney Love sent her own scathing letter to the magazine which read, "So wait... You're trying to tell me that Eddie is deserving of a brutal press rape because: 1) He won't talk to you. 2) He stood up against a huge corporation when everybody else told him not to. 3) He wanted to be in a band. He sounds more like Abraham Lincoln to me." And another reader added, "I can't believe *Rolling Stone* has stooped to interviewing anonymous high-school buds to 'prove' that Eddie Vedder is what? A poseur? Calculating fame seeker? Maybe he is; I really don't know or care. But it blows my mind that anyone would try and pick apart a man who encourages the kids to resist materialism, shrug off the easy buck, and show a little peace, love, and empathy. Back the hell off, *Rolling Stone*."

But Pearl Jam's reputation within rock's critical establishment was damaged beyond repair, and the question "What's wrong with Pearl Jam?" soon became a popular topic for mainstream rock critics. Within weeks of *Rolling Stone*'s damning Vedder feature, the cover of the *L.A. Times* calendar section proclaimed: "Has Pearl Jam turned to Jelly? They were alternative rock's brightest stars, but this year the band's record sales were way down, they didn't tour much, and Eddie Vedder was very public in his pouting. Are they worried?" In the accompanying feature, senior *L.A. Times* music critic Robert Hilburn cites *Rolling Stone*'s article as evidence that Pearl Jam is "in crisis." And he quotes a slew of anonymous industry "insiders" who line up to criticize the band's resistance to commercial aspirations. "They've got to rethink the way they promote themselves," says one source. "The way it is now, they are cutting themselves off from their fans." However, the same source implies that the industry would welcome Pearl Jam back with open arms if they would only amend their prodigal ways, "With some changes...they could be as big as ever. It's their choice." Another source adds hopefully, "One of the concerns was they didn't want to do anything that would explode their fame even further. Some of that pressure is off now and that makes it liberating. I wouldn't be surprised to see them do a few more things, even a video at some point." To which Hilburn answers, "That could be good news for Epic Records stockholders." *Stockholders*? In a bizarre reversal of rock criticism's countercultural beginnings, rock's most respected critics were now openly functioning as willing mouthpieces for rock's commercial—rather than its artistic—interests.

It was also during this period that the idea of Nirvana as legendary artists and Pearl Jam as also-rans began to be codified. For instance, *Rolling Stone*'s 1996 Eddie Vedder profile characterized Pearl Jam as "little more than a cuddlier, more MTV-friendly version of the genuinely anarchic and dangerous Nirvana." Such an assessment was odd, considering that it was Pearl Jam who had refused to make videos for MTV while Nirvana had repeatedly proved willing to play ball and compromise with the commercial industry establishment. In fact, part of the reason the rock establishment was able to canonize Nirvana among the rock immortals was the fact that Kurt Cobain was no longer around to complain about the hype. Whereas the members of Pearl Jam were not only alive, but consistently challenging the entire mainstream rock edifice, making them prime targets for the scorn of the rock establishment. And so it was not surprising that when *Rolling Stone* announced its list of 100 "Immortal" rock acts in 2004, Nirvana was granted the #27 slot—in the company of rock royalty like U2 (#22), Bruce Springsteen (#23), The Who (#29), and The Clash (#30)—while Pearl Jam was left off the list entirely. Such were the penalties for challenging the rock establishment.

Meanwhile, at the same time that *Rolling Stone* was slamming Pearl Jam for resisting commercial pressures, the magazine was more than happy to help promote the cash-grab reunion tours that popped-up throughout the 90s: The Eagles, Page & Plant, Fleetwood Mac, Bruce Springsteen & The E Street Band. One result of the rock establishment's legend-making machine had been the creation of a fertile market for "legacy acts," rock bands who could convert their stature within rock's burgeoning mythology into staggering profits. As a new millennium dawned, a slew of reunited acts would join longtime touring veterans like The Rolling Stones, Kiss, U2, Bon Jovi, and Aerosmith on the "legacy circuit," where they could ride into a golden sunset playing thirty-year-old hits to stadium crowds.

However, by the year 2000, the obvious problem for the rock establishment's "perpetuation of rock" strategy was the glaring lack of *new* rock acts on the *Billboard* charts, which were coming to be dominated by decidedly non-rock acts like Britney Spears and The Backstreet Boys. This fact presented a particular problem for mainstream rock critics. According to former *Rolling Stone* and *Village Voice* music critic Tom Carson in 2001, "More and more, you can see even working critics giving up, just saying, 'Screw it, I'm going to go on pretending that knowing something about Paul Simon is information worth sharing with you people, because I'll go insane if I have to wake up every morning telling myself I care which one in N'Sync is Justin.'" And so some critics went on lauding their old heroes, despite the fact that celebrating the current work of rock's baby-boomer icons was becoming more and more of a stretch. In August of 2002, *Rolling Stone* went so far as to declare Bruce Springsteen's horribly clichéd *The Rising* "the first 5-Star album of the year" (even as the *Village Voice* mockingly pleaded with The Boss "not [to] rhyme 'Waitin' on a sunny day' with 'Gonna chase the clouds away,' especially not in a chorus. I mean, can you tell him how to get, how to get to Sesame Street already?").

In addition, there were still those within the rock establishment's old guard who continued to trumpet belief in rock music's mythological regenerative powers, insisting that rock's inevitable return to popular dominance was just around the corner. As longtime *Rolling Stone* critic (and *Almost Famous* writer/director) Cameron Crowe told Charlie Rose in 2000, "Rock gets passionate and important every couple of years. In '92 we had Nirvana, Pearl Jam, and that was just a year after everyone was saying rock was dead. They said rock was dead then. They say rock is dead now. I'm dying to see what song is being written in a garage right now that's going to bring it all ragingly back." "And are you convinced there is?" asked Rose. "Oh, definitely," replied Crowe, "*definitely.*"

But by 2002 the rock old guard was starting to get antsy; it had been over a decade since "Smells Like Teen Spirit" had ignited rock's last popular movement, and artistically credible popular rock music made by young artists was becoming harder and harder to come by. And so, with no new popular rock movement forthcoming, *Rolling Stone* decided to see if it could create one of its own with a good old-fashioned hype campaign. The magazine's September 19, 2002 cover boldly declared that "ROCK IS BACK!" alongside the subheading "Meet The Vines: with The Strokes, The White Stripes, The Hives." Somewhat predictably, all four bands being hyped by the magazine were "rock revivalists" who fit neatly into rock's mythology. The most prominent common traits between them seemed to be an ability to regurgitate tired rock clichés and a flair for self-promotion. All were adept at playing the part of rock stars—The Vines with their omnipresent drunkenness and penchant for destroying backstage rooms, The White Stripes with their red-and-white-only wardrobe and fabricated backstory, The Strokes with their image-conscious recycling of 70s New York chic, The Hives with their matching outfits and unabashed recycling of the entirety of the 1960s "British Invasion"—but all of them seemed to have precious little of substance to say. *Rolling Stone*'s cover story on The Vines led with the brash proclamation that "[Vines frontman] Craig Nicholls has all the makings of a rock star: good looks, great songs, serious mental problems," in spite of the fact that the magazine itself had given The Vines' debut album a middling 3-Star review just two months earlier, saying it "suffers from retro fever." But even with major label-level marketing support behind all four acts, *Rolling Stone*'s hype campaign couldn't turn any of their current albums into platinum-selling hits. Their failure to do so was a clear demonstration of the magazine's loss of influence, and it would prove to be the last time *Rolling Stone* would attempt to manufacture a new rock movement. Instead, the magazine was headed in a new direction.

Many date the official end of *Rolling Stone*'s relevance to Jann Wenner's hiring of Ed Needham—the former editor of *FHM* (*For Him Magazine*, best known for its annual "100 Sexiest Women in the World" issue)—to helm the struggling magazine in the summer of 2002. However, even as it bemoaned the hiring of Needham, the *L.A. Times* noted that *Rolling Stone* hadn't been particularly relevant for some time, "The magazine is now like a guy who knew he was cool in the 60s, rebelled in the 70s, got rich in the 80s, stagnated in the 90s, and finally has decided: It's time for a tuck." *Salon*'s Sean Elder was even less gracious, "[*Rolling Stone*] has been a shadow of its former self for so long that most of us have forgotten what its former self looked like... Most of its subscribers are probably unaware that they still get it." Nevertheless, it pained Elder to see the once-great magazine suffer the indignity of becoming just another magazine putting a "nearly-naked Natalie Portman...(or Kirsten Dunst or any other beautiful young actress) on the cover." Instead, Elder had a different suggestion for Jann Wenner. "Why not do something altogether more radical? Why not shut the mother down? ... [*Rolling Stone*'s sister publication] *Us* is doing fine without a thought in its head. Let's hope that if *Rolling Stone* gets the same lobotomy, Wenner will have the decency to smother it with a pillow."

By the early 2000s, the rock establishment's relentless perpetuation of rock mythology had produced a slew of unintended consequences. Initially, the critical establishment's move to accept commercial success as evidence of "greatness" in rock had been undertaken in order to preserve and perpetuate the idea of rock as a vital genre. But rather than aiding the perpetuation of rock, rock criticism's abandonment of artistic standards had slowly stripped rock of its unique gravitas within popular music. Meanwhile, the rock establishment's myth-making machine had had a leveling effect, tidily packing up the entirety of rock history and folding it into an all-encompassing "old" which could be easily dismissed en masse by younger music fans. By the turn of the millennium, rock's fading artistic gravitas and overbearing mythology had helped encourage the perception that rock music had never been anything other than just another commercial popular music genre, no more artistically substantive or culturally relevant than any other style of popular music. And in trying to perpetuate its own relevance, rock's critical establishment had unwittingly helped set the stage for the wholesale discrediting of rock criticism itself.

Chapter Fourteen

The End of Rock Criticism

Radiohead, Rockism, and the Toppling of Rock Mythology

OK Computer

In May of 1997, at the height of the rock establishment's myth-making campaign, the English band Radiohead released its third studio album *OK Computer* to nearly universal critical acclaim. Britain's venerable *New Music Express* gave the album a rare 10/10 rating and proclaimed *OK Computer* to be "both age-defining and one of the most startling albums ever made. Here are 12 tracks crammed with towering lyrical ambition and musical exploration; that refuse to retread the successful formulae of before and instead opt for innovation and surprise; and that vividly articulate both the dreams and anxieties of one man without ever considering sacrifice or surrender. In short, here is a landmark record of the 1990s, and one that deserves your attention more than any other released this year." Fellow Brits *Q* called the album "a landmark on every latitude… an emotionally draining, epic experience. Now Radiohead can definitely be ranked high among the world's great bands." In America, the upstart online music mag *Pitchfork* also gave *OK Computer* a 10/10 rating and called it an "album of unadulterated genius." And *Rolling Stone* gave the album 4 Stars (later upgraded to a perfect 5 in its 2003 *Album Guide*), declaring the album "a stunning art-rock tour de force." The critical acclaim for *OK Computer* was so great, in fact, that critic Tim Footman was eventually able to say, "Not since 1967, with the release of *Sgt. Pepper's*

Lonely Hearts Club Band, had so many major critics agreed immediately, not only on an album's merits, but on its long-term significance."

Radiohead had come a long way since its 1993 debut single "Creep," an undeniably catchy song which had suffered from an overwrought sense of self-deprecation and seemed destined for "one-hit-wonder" status. Radiohead's second full-length album, 1995's *The Bends,* had revealed a first-rate rock band firing on all cylinders, but—even though many critics would retroactively deem it one of the best rock albums of the decade—it failed to capture the popular or critical imagination at the time of its release; *Rolling Stone* hadn't even bothered reviewing *The Bends,* and *Spin* panned it with a dismissive 5/10 rating. The critical reaction to *OK Computer* would prove to be an entirely different animal.

There were many factors which contributed to *OK Computer's* rapturous reception. One was the anemic state of popular rock at the time of the album's release. In 1997, amidst of the deadening homogeneity of hits from Bush, Matchbox Twenty, Sister Hazel, and Eve 6, *any* popular rock album exhibiting an original artistic pulse was bound to stand out from the pack. Another factor was *OK Computer's* subject matter, which tapped into a pervasive undercurrent of pre-millennial uneasiness about the dizzying acceleration of technological immersion and the seemingly boundless expansion of corporate encroachment (and the widespread acquiescence to both). The experience of this uneasiness is harder to understand in retrospect, but when the album was released there was a sense in which *OK Computer* achieved "zeitgeist of the time" status. As Dai Griffiths would later write in the "33 1/3" entry for *OK Computer,* "You want to know what 1997 felt like? *OK Computer*: tracks six-eight."

In the end though, as much as *OK Computer* may have tapped into a collective uneasiness, at its core was a singular artistic expression: a blatant and emotional plea, a nakedly open indictment that defied purely sociological explanations. The album's lyrics are at turns pleading, scathing, and exhorting, achingly delivered by singer Thom Yorke's powerfully emotive voice and lushly packaged in a diverse musical landscape that both nodded to the greats of rock's past (Pink Floyd, Joy Division, The Cure, *Achtung*-era U2) and stretched the rock genre's artistic boundaries. In short, it was everything a classic album was supposed to be. Like *Highway 61 Revisited, Sgt. Pepper,*

198

London Calling, and *Nevermind* before it, *OK Computer* was poised to inform the collective consciousness, challenge the status quo, *change the world*.

Except that it didn't. And, ironically, the rock establishment's attempt to instantly canonize the album was one of the factors which limited its potential impact. While the content of *OK Computer* was indeed countercultural—inasmuch as it openly and passionately questioned mainstream commercial consumerism and the unimpeded march of depersonalizing technology—its countercultural sentiment was expressed using traditional rock forms and song structures which were easily recognized and appreciated by the rock establishment, making it possible for *OK Computer* to be quickly grafted into mainstream rock mythology. And this process allowed critics within the rock establishment to universally praise the album without actually grappling with its unflinching content. The reaction to *OK Computer* clearly demonstrated that, within the confines of rock mythology, "great" rock albums were no longer the stuff of transformative, truth-seeking, consciousness-raising immersion that had the potential to actually inform one's life. Instead, great rock albums were to be objects of detached reflection, embalmed, encased, and enshrined alongside the other "Great Album" relics of the past.

Regardless of what the gushing copy of *OK Computer*'s reviews claimed, the truth was that most mainstream rock critics no longer believed in rock as a potentially transformative artistic medium. Back in the heady days of rock criticism's first flowering, albums like Van Morrison's *Astral Weeks* had been sought by critics like Lester Bangs as potential beacons of *enlightenment* or *illumination*, as expressions of a unique artistic *truth* capable of informing the way one lived his or her life. The same was true of punk and post-punk albums by The Clash or The Minutemen. And even as late as 1991, provocative rock albums like *Nevermind* and *Achtung Baby* (and its accompanying ZOOTV tour) had been seen by listeners and critics alike as having something to do with the way people lived their day-to-day lives. But by the late 90s, mainstream critics were no longer looking to an album like *OK Computer* for greater truths that might actually have real-life implications. Few, if any, critics reacted to *OK Computer*'s bold criticisms of consumerism and technology by talking about canceling their credit cards or throwing their newly-purchased cellular phones into the nearest river. Instead, *OK Computer* was being granted admission to the rock pantheon according to its artistic substance—according

199

to widespread critical assertions of the "truth" and "timeliness" of its message—even as the actions of critics themselves failed to testify to those same truths. Mainstream rock criticism had become an essentially disingenuous process, a cultural coping mechanism used to ease a collective conscience troubled by the growing distance between perceived truth and personal action. This was the function of the "Great Album" in the post-Rock Hall of Fame era, to be safely enshrined rather than actively engaged, accepted as "important" and reverentially referred to as such, even as its content was quickly dismissed and forgotten.

Needless to say, this arrangement was not acceptable to the members of Radiohead. "Fucking rock music sucks. I hate it," said Thom Yorke in a 2001 interview. "It's not really the music. It's not sitting on a stage playing guitar, drums, and singing. That's not what I'm talking about. What I'm talking about is all the mythology that goes with it. I have a real fucking problem with it… In a way, it negates the work." From the band's perspective, *OK Computer* had been a sharp indictment of everything the corporate rock industry stood for, and yet here were the shills for the rock establishment lining up with smiles on their faces to pat them on the back and say "Well done!" before going back to business as usual. It was an implausible—and severely disorienting—situation for the band to be in. In the *OK Computer* tour documentary *Meeting People Is Easy*, Thom Yorke expresses his feelings about the disorienting nature of the reaction to the album, "Last year we were the most hyped band. We were #1 in all the polls, and it's *bollocks*, man, *it's bollocks*… It's just a head fuck. It's a complete head fuck. Isn't it?" And later in the same documentary, he continues:

> It's like a supply and demand thing. It's like, this is what they want you to do, this is what they want to hear? 'Oh, I'll do more of this. This is great and they love me.' And suddenly the people start giving you cash as well. Suddenly you've got money and you get used to this lifestyle. And you don't want to take any risks because they've got you by the balls. You've got all this baggage you're carrying around with you everywhere and you can't let go. You've got all these things you've bought and you're attached to. And if you start spending all this money, 'That's how they get ya.'

In short, even the most scathing criticism of commercialism that Radiohead could conjure had been co-opted by the commercial rock establishment. This reality would inform everything about the creation and release of the band's next album *Kid A*. Unlike *OK Computer*, which had provided one last opportunity for consensus among rock's critical establishment, *Kid A* would split that consensus, revealing the cracks in rock criticism's mythological artifice while helping to create the necessary space for a widespread rejection of rock mythology itself.

Kid A

Thanks to a severe case of writers block suffered in conjunction with the *OK Computer* tour, Radiohead singer Thom Yorke's lyrical approach to the songs that would eventually become *Kid A* was as much the result of necessity as calculation. According to a 2001 interview:

> The reason I'd had such terrible [writer's] block [was] because I felt that I'd lost control of any element of my life—or any element of anything that I was involved in—and ultimately being so incredibly angry it was inexpressible… What I tried to do with the writer's block thing was have all the things that didn't work and stop throwing them away—which is what I'd been doing before—and keeping them and cutting them up and putting them in this top hat and pulling them out. And that was really cool because it managed to preserve whatever emotions were in the initial writing of the words, but in a way that I'm not trying to emote. Because the words are just part of what's going on.

This lyrical approach led to an entirely different kind of indictment of the culture's commercialism and technology. Instead of employing traditional narrative techniques in order to form a linear commentary on the culture, as the lyrics for *OK Computer* had done, the fragmented, half-crazed nature of the emotional sentiment expressed in *Kid A*'s lyrics ended up *embodying* Yorke's impressions of fractured millennial life. And once the rest of the band got a hold of Yorke's lyrics and began working with him to capture the spirit of their emotion, it was clear that *Kid A* was not going to sound anything like its predecessor.

The opening track "Everything in its Right Place," with its minimalist keyboard refrain, sporadic loop sputters, and dissonantly simple vocal melody, immediately announces that this isn't going to be another guitar-based album in the traditional rock mold. From there come the unsettling, computer-distorted vocals of "Kid A" and the repetitive bass riffing (and saxophones!?) of "The National Anthem." The haunting "How to Disappear Completely" employs a more traditional approach, but the self-defeating lyrical refrain "I'm not here/This isn't happening" is anything but reassuring. The ambient instrumental "Treefingers" is followed by the more traditionally arranged "Optimistic," but again the pointed lyrics undercut any sense of easy comfort. "In Limbo" employs a rolling, oddly-timed rhythm beneath Yorke's gentle insistence that "you're living in a fantasy." This is followed by "Idioteque," the album's most powerful combination of Yorke's fragmented lyrical approach and the band's idiosyncratic instrumentation. The song's insistent refrain "everything all of the time" perfectly captures the mood of the album thus far, not to mention the mood of the technology-saturated millennial West. And "Idioteque's" equally insistent computer-enhanced beat plods forward as Yorke's voice reaches a new level of intensity for the lyrics "We're not scaremongering, *this is really happening*," which functions as the wake-up call from the self-deluded sleep of "How to Disappear Completely." In the wake of the naked intensity of "Idioteque," "Morning Bell" is almost anticlimactic, but its melodic baseline, unadorned vocals, and more traditional rock dynamics provide a short respite before its psychedelic climax trails off into the closing track, "Motion Picture Soundtrack." The final song on *Kid A* opens with a mournful pump organ, which is soon joined by Yorke's beautifully pained voice, which by this point seems almost resigned to the unfortunate fate intimated by the preceding songs. But just as the listener is settling into the spare beauty of the simple melody and arrangement, the second verse explodes in a dazzling orchestral burst of whirling harp flourishes which circle around Yorke's voice and organ like a swirl of fireflies. The harp is joined by a theremin-like vocal chorus before giving way to Yorke's naked delivery of the line, "I will see you in the next life," which trails off into a silence which lasts for roughly a minute. One more flourish of sound appears before subsiding again into the two minutes of silence which close the album. It is a stunning and confounding end to a singularly confounding album.

From an artistic perspective, the fragmented lyrics and experimental music made for a far more honest articulation of the band's creative temperament than a more straightforward "rock" effort could have. Even if the band had wanted to make an easily digestible follow-up to *OK Computer*, doing so would have meant denying the reality of their situation; as artists, making *Kid A* was, in a sense, their only option. In addition, releasing an album full of fragmented lyrics and experimental music made it harder for critics to interpret, classify, and safely tuck *Kid A* away in the museum of rock mythology. This result was surely satisfying to Yorke and the band, and they virtually assured critical confusion by only allowing critics to listen to the album in controlled environments before writing their pre-release reviews; critics weren't even given physical copies of the album to take home with them. Needless to say, *Kid A* was not an album that lent itself to easy classifications on the strength of one or two listenings.

Even so, the critical controversy surrounding the release of *Kid A* was unprecedented in rock history, and in one fell swoop Radiohead managed to splinter the mainstream critical consensus which had been forged throughout the 90s by the rock establishment's mythmaking campaign. As the *Village Voice* put it, "With *Kid A*, they've given their core constituency the biggest, warmest recorded go-fuck-yourself in recent memory." At one end of the spectrum of critical reaction were those within the rock establishment who flatly rejected the album, typified by cultural critic (and *High Fidelity* screenwriter) Nick Hornby's October 2000 *New Yorker* article, whose title "Beyond the Pale" found it necessary to place *Kid A* beyond the agreed standards of acceptable human decency. Hornby opens by stating that rock music's admonition that we "trust the artist" had caused "an awful lot of trouble and disappointment"—most notably, according to Hornby, in the more "experimental" albums of rock artists like Lou Reed (*Metal Machine Music*), Neil Young (*Arc*), and Bob Dylan (*Self Portrait*). As the article continues, Hornby essentially argues that any piece of art that is "challenging" is by its very nature "pretentious," and thus *Kid A* is both "pretentious" and "self-indulgent" because "you have to sit at home night after night and give yourself over to the paranoid millennial atmosphere as you try to decipher elliptical snatches of lyrics and puzzle out how the titles might refer to the songs." This, according to Hornby, is simply unacceptable amidst the "competing demands for his time" as a hard-working modern adult. *Kid A*'s principal sin is that—unlike Radiohead's easily decipherable breakthrough single "Creep," of which Hornby is a big fan—it requires the "patience of the devoted," which becomes a scarcer commodity "once you start picking up a paycheck." Thus, in reaction to Radiohead's artistic experimentation on *Kid A*, Hornby bluntly and angrily replies, "Shut up! You're supposed to be a pop group!"

Nick Hornby's screed was the kind of reaction the members of Radiohead had been expecting from the rock establishment in response to *OK Computer*, but it had taken *Kid A*'s rejection of traditional rock forms and song structures in order to burst through the confines of rock mythology and arrive—according to Hornby's assessment anyway—"beyond the pale." Echoing some of Hornby's objections, his British counterparts at *New Music Express*, *Q*, and *Mojo*—all of whom had waxed rhapsodic over *OK Computer*—flatly dubbed *Kid A* a "disappointment." However, not everyone in the rock establishment panned the album. While Greg Kot's *Chicago Tribune* review allows that the album "will be written off by some as a fascinating failure, by others as a self-indulgent mess," Kot nevertheless lauds the album as "a stream-of-consciousness tone poem that yields its charms with a subtlety miraculous by today's instant-gratification standards." *Rolling Stone* also praised the album, giving *Kid A* a positive 4-Star review, though a positive assessment of the album had become almost obligatory once *OK Computer* had vaulted Radiohead into the pantheon of rock greatness; after all, who was *Rolling Stone* to question the work of "Immortals?" But the failure of the mainstream critical establishment to universally embrace *Kid A* the way it had *OK Computer* left the door open for an alternative critical voice to stand out from the pack by wholeheartedly embracing Radiohead's defiant statement of artistic independence.

Unlike mainstream stalwarts like *Rolling Stone*, *Spin*, and *Blender*, the upstart online music magazine *Pitchfork* had little invested in rock mythology. Not only that, after struggling along in obscurity during the five years since its debut, it had nothing to lose. And so the fledgling magazine was free to unabashedly embrace *Kid A* in a way that traditional publications weren't. *Pitchfork*'s brash 10.0/10.0 rating for *Kid A* contrasted with the back-and-forth squabbling in mainstream criticism, and the unorthodox first-person, quasi-stream-of-consciousness approach of Brent DiCrescenzo's accompanying review echoed rock criticism's late 60s attempt to distance itself from the existing rock music coverage in "the straight press." But beneath the sometimes distracting descriptive flourishes was what turned out to be a prophetic assessment:

Kid A... completely obliterates how albums, and Radiohead themselves, will be considered... *Kid A* makes rock and roll childish. Considerations on its merits as 'rock' (i.e. its radio fodder potential, its guitar riffs, and its hooks) are pointless. Comparing this to other albums is like comparing an aquarium to blue construction paper. And not because it's jazz or fusion or ambient or electronic. Classifications don't come to mind once deep inside this expansive, hypnotic world... This is an emotional, psychological experience. *Kid A* sounds like a clouded brain trying to recall an alien abduction. It's the sound of a band, and its leader, losing faith in themselves, destroying themselves, and subsequently rebuilding a perfect entity. In other words, Radiohead hated being Radiohead, but ended up with the most ideal, natural Radiohead record yet.

Not only did DiCrescenzo's review echo early rock criticism's belief in the transcendent experience of art, *Pitchfork* was virtually alone at the time in recognizing how decisively *Kid A* had burst the bubble of rock mythology. Over time, the artistic assessments which had marked rock criticism's initial flowering had been replaced by assessments according to calcified, rock-centric touchpoints—"radio fodder potential...guitar riffs...hooks"—which *Kid A* exposed as being entirely inadequate for artistic assessments of any music that dared to step outside rock's traditional boundaries. In fact, it had been Nick Hornby's desire for a traditional rock album that blinded him to what DiCrescenzo called the "emotional, psychological experience" of actually immersing oneself in *Kid A*. And in the end, DiCrescenzo's verbal flourishes proved far more adept at describing that experience than the tired clichés of millennial mainstream rock criticism. "The experience and emotions tied to listening to *Kid A*," he writes in the review's closing paragraph, "are like witnessing the stillborn birth of a child while simultaneously having the opportunity to see her play in the afterlife on Imax."

Pitchfork's *Kid A* review became something of a sensation, boosting the online magazine's circulation from what founder Ryan Shreiber called "negligible" to over 5,000 hits a day. And what new readers discovered when they clicked away from *Pitchfork*'s *Kid A* review to peruse the rest of the site was a brash independence sorely lacking in mainstream rock criticism. For instance, where *Rolling Stone* had decided to bite its lip and embrace the commercially popular yet artistically challenged music of post-alternative hardcore bands like Incubus, P.O.D., Slipknot, System of a Down, and Tool—

all of whom had albums in *Rolling Stone*'s year-end "Best of 2001" list— *Pitchfork* was free to irreverently skewer hardcore's dumbed-down rock aesthetic. Brent DiCrescenzo's tongue-in-cheek "review" of Tool's 2001 album *Lateralus*—which *Rolling Stone* had awarded 4-Stars (the same rating it had given *Kid A*)—was published under the heading "My Summer Vacation, by Crispin Fubert, Ms. Higgins' Eng. Comp." and written from the point of view of a die-hard 14-year-old Tool fan:

> It's the best Tool record because it's the longest... The packaging is also cool, since it has this clear book with a skinless guy, and as you turn the pages, it rips off his muscles and stuff. Tool's music does the same thing. It can just rip the muscles and skin off you. I think that's what they meant... Tool know about space and math, and it's pretty complex. 'Saturn ascends/ Not one but ten,' he sings. No Doubt and R.E.M. sang about that, too, but those songs were wimpy and short. Maynard shows his intelligence with raw stats. I think there's meaning behind those numbers, like calculus. He also mentions 'prison cell' and 'tear it down' and 'controlling' and 'sinking deeper,' which all symbolize how he feels... [There's also a] song called 'Reflection' since it's quieter and slower and sounds like it's from India, where people go to reflect... In conclusion, there is more emotion on that album than would be on 30 Weezer albums. At the very least, there's 2.5 times as much. Like I said, it's messed up, like the world, which makes it very real.

DiCrescenzo's mock review was accompanied by a sardonic 1.9/10.0 rating and became another viral internet sensation. By celebrating independent idiosyncrasies and skewering—or, more typically, ignoring—lumbering mainstream rock, *Pitchfork* would both tap into and help define the growing scene developing around a new generation of indie labels, positioning the online magazine such that it could grow in conjunction with the burgeoning indie scene. While the fracturing of rock's critical consensus was already manifesting itself in the proliferation of thousands of online music blogs, the loyalty that *Pitchfork*'s brash independence generated in the first years of the new millennium would allow it to become the flagship indie music site, one-stop-shopping for those looking to keep their finger on the pulse of the trends in indie music without having to scour dozens of music blogs on a daily basis. And throughout the 2000s, as the circulations of mainstream "alternative" magazines like *Spin* and *Blender* would spiral towards irrelevance, *Pitchfork* would continue to grow—to over 100,000 hits a day by 2005, and over 200,000 hits a day by 2010—in the process becoming a powerful alternative to fossilized mainstream rock criticism.

Rockism

While Radiohead's *Kid A* was revealing the rock establishment's inability to assess artistically adventurous rock music, an equally devastating critique of the rock establishment was beginning to gain momentum in some critical and academic circles. The roots of this critique were in the university, where the traditional canons of both literature and visual art had been under siege for decades. Beginning in the late 1960s—following the lead of European philosophers like Theodor Adorno, Jacques Derrida, and Michel Foucault—a growing number of American critics and scholars had been exploring the (heretofore largely ignored) sociological, economic, and political factors which had influenced traditional assessments of art. Under the umbrella term "Cultural Studies," these scholars and critics were soon deconstructing the traditional canons of literature, music, and visual art according to feminist critiques, Marxist critiques, multicultural critiques, LGBT critiques, etc. All of these critiques shared a discontent with the way that traditional assessments of art tended to bolster existing power structures while marginalizing the challengers to those structures, leading to canons disproportionally populated by rich, white, Western, heterosexual males.

By the time rock's critical establishment began moving towards solidifying a canon for rock music, sociological assessments of art had already become the norm in academia. And as the rock canon began to come into clearer focus around the turn of the millennium, it made an easy target for deconstructionists of all stripes; after all, the emerging rock canon was—even more than the traditional canons of literature, music, and visual art—made up of predominantly white, heterosexual males. In addition, the fact that the rock establishment had long since jettisoned artistic substance as a necessary requirement for admission to its pantheon of greats made the rock canon even *more* susceptible to critique. For instance, where the defenders of the traditional literary canon could at least argue that the works of white males like Shakespeare or Milton were canon-worthy due to their artistic merit, it was hard for those within the rock establishment to argue that vacuous heavy metal acts like Black Sabbath and AC/DC had been admitted to the rock pantheon thanks to the depth of their artistic substance. Thus, rock establishment claims that rock music was somehow *inherently* more important and authentic than other popular music genres became increasingly vulnerable to the simple question: "Why?" Why, for instance, did the rock establishment deem dim-witted 70s metal acts more "important" than their (far more culturally diverse) contemporaries in the disco scene? It didn't take much imagination for deconstructionists to conclude that the rock establishment's embrace of heavy metal and its disdain for disco was due to the simple fact that disco had largely been music for women, gays, and people of color, whereas heavy metal had been music for white, heterosexual males. Thus, the rock establishment's canon-building efforts could be characterized as little more than a thinly veiled attempt to consolidate the white, heterosexual male power structure while dismissing the voices of the marginalized (and countless academic papers from the early 2000s would do just that).

The reality, however, was a bit more complicated. On the one hand, there really were those within the rock establishment whose aesthetic was blatantly misogynistic, homophobic, and racist, as typified by Joe Carducci's 1990 book *Rock and the Pop Narcotic*, which associated rock with "dragging balls" and "a hard cock," and used the terms "faggot" and "femmy" as the ultimate put-downs. For this group of rock fans and critics, the use of the (artistically arbitrary and conveniently vague) question *"Does it Rock?"* as the primary means of assessing music had been the not-so-imaginative rationale behind the marginalization of non-rock music—such as disco—being made outside the world of white, heterosexual males. And over the years, the rock establishment's myth-making campaign had granted these kinds of prejudicial rock-centric assessments greater and greater influence in order to justify the self-perpetuating expansion of the rock canon to include commercial behemoths like Led Zeppelin and Black Sabbath.

But rock criticism hadn't always been embodied by rock-centric stylistic assessments; early rock criticism had embodied a very different aesthetic. Rock criticism had *not* been founded in order to defend rock's particular style, sound, or social demographic, but rather as a reaction to the sudden proliferation of artistic substance in rock music in the mid-60s. Unlike heavy rock apologists like Joe Carducci, early rock critics had appealed to independent standards of art and authenticity which existed outside the insular rock world, allowing these critics to embrace artistically substantive music from across the sociological and sonic spectrum: from Otis Redding to Joni Mitchell, David Bowie to Aretha Franklin, and even not-very-rocking white, heterosexual males like Simon & Garfunkel. At the same time, rock criticism's appeal to independent standards of artistic substance and authenticity had allowed early rock critics to lambaste rock acts like Led Zeppelin and Black Sabbath who failed to live up to those standards. And so, when most rock critics had dismissed disco in the 1970s, it wasn't because disco failed to conform to rock's stylistic requirements, but rather because disco was perceived to lack the requisite artistic substance for serious critical consideration, and it was thought to be too much a product of the commercial entertainment industry to exhibit an authentic artistic voice. In short, Donna Summer's music wasn't dismissed by early critics because she failed to "rock" as hard as white, heterosexual males, but because songs like "Hot Stuff" were seen as the trivial byproducts of an increasingly commercial entertainment industry. These were the very same criticisms, incidentally, with which the same critics dismissed the vapidity of blatantly commercial rock acts like Black Sabbath and Kiss. All this to say, the aesthetic of most early rock critics was clearly *very* different from the *"Does it Rock?"* aesthetic of heavy rock enthusiasts like Joe Carducci.

But when the rock canon began to elicit widespread criticism from deconstructionists around the turn of the millennium, rock's detractors failed to make any distinction between these two distinct aesthetics. Instead, millennial revisionists lumped them together under the pejorative designation "rockism," a term which had been coined and used half-humorously by a few British music critics in the early 80s before being revived in the early 2000s as a catch-all term used to dismiss "rock-centric" assessments of music. According to the opponents of "rockism," rejecting rock mythology's rock-centric stylistic prejudices also necessitated a rejection of early rock criticism's appeals to standards of authenticity and artistic substance, even though these two distinct aesthetics were only tangentially related (and were more typically diametrically opposed to each other). And this basic misunderstanding would lead the opponents of rockism into some dubious leaps of logic. For instance, Kelefa Sanneh's 2004 *New York Times* manifesto "The Rap Against Rockism" argued that the rock establishment's racist, misogynist, and homophobic aesthetic meant that all of the attributes valued by early rock critics must also be dismissed *en masse*: countercultural independence (as opposed to industry compliance), the ability to write one's own songs (as opposed to relying on industry songwriters), focusing on artistically expansive full-length albums (as opposed to disposable singles), the ability to sing one's songs live (as opposed to lip-synching), the willingness to give listeners the uncomfortable truth (as opposed to pandering to their tastes), and on and on. According to Sanneh, all of these preferences needed to be rejected as inherently compromised. But his logic was fatally flawed; Sanneh didn't seem to understand that the rock establishment's prejudicial, rock-centric mythmaking had gone hand in hand with the *rejection* of early rock criticism's appeals to independent standards of artistic substance and authenticity, not the *application* of those standards. And thus his argument that the prejudices of rock mythology necessitated dismissing any and all appeals to standards of authenticity or artistic substance just didn't hold up.

Nevertheless, the rejection of so-called "rockist" assessments of music led to a very specific result for many critics writing in the early 2000s: a wholehearted embrace of blatantly commercial pop music. For instance, Sanneh's *New York Times* piece argued that the appropriate response to rockists was to embrace "the inclusive possibilities of a once-derided term: pop." This embrace would eventually come to be called "poptimism." The central tenet of poptimist ideology was the idea that traditional rockist assumptions were the result of *elitist* claims to artistic substance and authenticity, whereas mainstream pop music was the *populist* music of the masses. This idea found its most fully realized expression in poptimist critic Carl Wilson's 2007 book *Let's Talk About Love: A Journey to the End of Taste*, which cites Celine Dion's massive popularity as all the evidence necessary to conclude that the Canadian pop singer had been wrongly dismissed by elitist critics. "Dion has sold 175 million albums," writes Wilson. "She has five recordings in the Recording Industry Association of America's list of the Top 100 albums by sales... She is beloved by people from Idaho to Iraq, who trade news and debate favorites on Internet message boards like any other group of fans. They cook, work out and date to her music, and when weightier events come, her songs are there, for first dances at weddings and processions at funerals." Wilson argues that looking at what the masses choose to listen to is a far more democratic way to assess music than listening to the recommendations of elitist critics. You want the populist assessment rather than the elitist assessment? Just look at the *Billboard* sales charts.

While such arguments played to Western democratic sympathies (according to Wilson, Celine Dion "stinks of democracy"), the plain fact was that—by the 1990s, especially—the assertion that mainstream pop music was somehow populist or democratic was simply untenable. Sales figures had never been a particularly accurate indicator of popular taste; payola schemes, radio hype campaigns, and major label marketing clout had been stacking the deck in favor of some artists over others since the dawn of the music industry. And by the 1990s, the consolidation of music industry control in a small handful of multinational corporate conglomerates, the astronomical sums being spent on promotional campaigns, and the top-down sales strategies being employed by the major label machine made it impossible for anyone with even the slightest knowledge of the music industry to plausibly assert that sales figures were some sort of populist indicator of mass taste. Not only were the major labels exerting more and more control over the creation and production of the music itself, their huge promotional budgets and marketing campaigns had become the determining factor in what music the public would be exposed to.

For example, the late 90s ascendance of pop music sales and decline of rock sales cited by poptimists as evidence of pop music's "populist" appeal hadn't been a reflection of a sudden shift in popular tastes; it had been the direct result of a fundamental shift in major label marketing strategies. Thanks to market research, which had revealed the massive buying power of the teen market, the music industry machine had begun pumping tens of millions of dollars into the launch of pop albums at the expense of rock albums. For instance, in 1999 Sony had spent $14 million launching actress-turned-pop-singer Jennifer Lopez's debut album *On the 6*, roughly *forty times* the promotional budget allotted for the rock band Wilco's critically-acclaimed album *Summerteeth*, which was released by Warner Bros. that same year. For most casual music fans, the "choice" to purchase Lopez's *On the 6* over Wilco's *Summerteeth* was hardly a choice at all. Even though both albums had been released by major labels, the gaping disparity between the promotional budgets for the two albums all but guaranteed that Lopez's album would be hugely popular while most people wouldn't even be aware that a rock band called Wilco existed. And even though *Summerteeth* actually sold more albums per promotional dollar spent than *On the 6*, Warner Bros. subsidiary Reprise

211

would cite Wilco's "lack of popular appeal" when they dropped the band from the label two years later. Meanwhile, thanks in large part to Sony's multi-million dollar promotional efforts, "J-Lo" would go on to become a ubiquitous mainstay of the early 21st Century pop culture landscape.

Much like Jennifer Lopez, the international popularity of Celine Dion's music had been the direct result of an unprecedented promotional campaign by her record label, Sony. In an unparalleled move for the time, Sony had tied the release of every (English-speaking) Dion album released in the 1990s to the release of a major motion picture, all of which featured a Dion song on their soundtracks. Not only did these tie-ins only allow Dion to benefit from the marketing campaigns for the movies themselves (including the movie-themed music videos for *Beauty and the Beast*'s title song, *Sleepless in Seattle*'s "When I Fall In Love," *Up Close and Personal*'s "Because You Loved Me," and—most famously—*Titanic*'s "My Heart Will Go On"), they allowed her to reach a global audience with her Oscar performances. In fact, thanks to the *Titanic* tie-in, Sony executives bragged that Dion 1997's album *Let's Talk About Love* was the biggest ship-out in the company's history; Sony was able to ship over 10 million copies of *Let's Talk About Love* to record stores *before the record-buying public had chosen to purchase a single copy of the album*. In addition to the movie tie-ins, Sony also engaged in an extraordinary international marketing campaign on behalf of Dion, arranging promotional tie-ins in countries around the world (most notably in France, Japan, and Latin America) while releasing different versions of her albums—and employing different marketing strategies—which had been tailored to specific foreign markets. The campaign was so extensive that even Dion herself, a paragon of world-conquering ambition, balked. "I didn't want to do the Spanish song," she told *Time* in 1996. "What to do they want me to do next? Learn Japanese?" In fact, yes. And so, in 1999, Dion recorded a song in Japanese for a tie-in with a Japanese soap opera. One highlight of the international promotional campaign came in 1996, when Sony arranged for Dion to be the only non-American performer at the opening ceremonies for Atlanta's 1996 Summer Olympics in front of a global audience of three-and-a-half *billion* people. These unprecedented international efforts were combined with more traditional—though equally lavish—promotional efforts, such as the $845,000 kickoff party for *Let's Talk About Love*, which included a transatlantic video hookup from Dion in Montreal to fans and media in London, Paris, and Cologne (the cost of the kickoff party alone was more than twice the entire promotional budget allotted most major label rock albums). Taken together, Sony's globally synergized promotional efforts ensured that Celine Dion would be the most hyped recording artist in the history of humankind. If ever there was an artist who was inescapable, it was Celine Dion in the 1990s, as virtually anyone who lived through that era will attest. This meant that whatever populist "demand" there may have been for her music was impossible to separate from the tens of millions of dollars Sony and its corporate partners had spent marketing Dion throughout the decade. In this sense, the commercial success which poptimists attributed to Dion's "populist" appeal could just as easily—and probably more accurately—be attributed to simple capitulation to commercial marketing forces. And what Carl Wilson described as "elitist" contempt for Dion's music could alternatively be attributed to a simple aversion to the ubiquity of those same commercial marketing forces.

In his book *Let's Talk About Love*, Wilson attempts to bolster his claims about Celine Dion's populism by devoting thousands upon thousands of words to Dion's personal narrative, emphasizing those aspects of her story which cast her as an outsider or underdog: her meager small-town upbringing as the youngest of fourteen children, her affiliation with the marginalized *Quebecoise* of French-speaking Canada, her unrefined looks and garish lack of style. In short, Wilson argues that the populist appeal of her music is that Dion, too, is an outcast, just like the masses who revere her. But the problem with using Dion's personal narrative to explain her popular appeal is that what the public receives as the *product* "Celine Dion" is only tangentially related to the *person* Celine Dion. For starters, unlike more independent "guitar-and-a-song" artists like Neil Young, Bob Dylan, or Joni Mitchell (the kind of artists who tend to be favored by "rockists"), the songs that a pop singer like Dion sings are not the result of her own creative vision; her hits have been written by a who's who of industry insiders, from Glen Ballard (of Wilson Phillips and Alanis Morissette fame) to Jim Steinman (Meat Loaf) to Diane Warren (LeAnn Rimes, Faith Hill, Aerosmith) to Max Martin (Backstreet Boys, Britney Spears, Taylor Swift). Surely, the people who write the actual songs have something to do with the "appeal" of Dion's music, begging the question: If Wilson is really interested in getting to the bottom of Celine Dion's appeal, why doesn't his book also include the personal biographies of James Horner and Will Jennings, the men who wrote Dion's most popular song, *Titanic*'s "My Heart Will Go

On?" And then there's the fact that the songs Dion sings aren't even necessarily the result of her own personal choices, but rather the market research influenced choices of the corporate executives at her record label. For instance, Dion famously *hated* "My Heart Will Go On" and had to be pressured by Sony executives into recording it. Given how much the choice of that particular song had to do with her popularity, shouldn't the biographies of the corporate executives who choose what songs Dion sings be included in Wilson's exploration of her popular appeal, too? Similarly, Dion's public image is curated by a meticulous team of professional handlers. Even her basic appearance is not entirely her own; it was her manager (and eventual husband) Rene Angelil who insisted that Dion have her teeth capped, eyebrows plucked, and undergo a comprehensive makeover before embarking on a career as an adult pop singer. Where are the biographies of her husband and handlers? Are they not relevant to Dion's appeal? All this to say, the "appeal" of a modern pop singer like Celine Dion is not the result of an individual creative vision, but rather the manufactured result of the painstaking efforts of a team of thousands: songwriters, producers, handlers, managers, fashion advisors, PR teams, market researchers, international liaisons, corporate executives, and on and on. And so, for Wilson to ignore this fact and lean exclusively on the personal biography of a commercial pop icon like Dion in order to explain her appeal was an exercise in mythmaking every bit as egregious as anything the rock establishment had engaged in on behalf of rock music. Only, in the case of poptimists like Wilson, the perpetuation of pop mythology was undertaken on behalf of the multi-billion dollar corporate music industry machine, a far more supreme and formidable power structure than the "elitist" rock critic establishment had ever been. In reality, Wilson and his fellow poptimists were—wittingly or not—completely subverting the anti-establishment sensibility which had been the impetus for the entire Cultural Studies project in the first place. As Rob Horning wrote for *PopMatters* in 2006, "Nice of the poptopian to do the marketers' work for them and expand the reach and provide the ideological justification for the hegemony of the big commercial music manufacturers. ('Buy what records they've already decided to manufacture the most of; this will make you a positive optimist. Don't reject what's already been prepared for you; that's so last year. It's your patriotic duty to support blockbusters.')"

The theoretical framework for the dismissal of "rockist" claims to artistic substance—as well as the subsequent "poptimist" embrace of commercial pop culture—had been laid by sociologist Pierre Bourdieu's hugely influential 1979 study *Distinction: A Social Critique of the Judgment of Taste*. According to Bourdieu, it was not just the canonizing efforts of "elitist" critics whose aesthetic assessments were the result of claims to social and economic power, but *all* aesthetic assessments, by everyone everywhere. Surveys conducted in Bourdieu's native France revealed conspicuous similarities in taste between those in similar economic and social strata, and he used these similarities to argue that what we call aesthetic assessments are simply symbolic associations which we use to create distinctions between ourselves and those whose social ranking we feel is beneath us (even though, as Celine Dion's massive popularity demonstrated, the fact that, in a commercial society, people in similar social strata are subjected to the same commercial marketing campaigns seemed to offer an equally plausible explanation for their similarities in taste). For Bourdieu, however, his findings proved that class structures didn't just influence artistic assessments of substance and quality, there was *no such thing* as artistic substance or quality; the primary function of *all* aesthetic judgments was the perpetuation of existing class structures.

Bourdieu's attempt to see art through the eyes of class was not new; attempts to tie art to class stretch at least as far back as Karl Marx's pioneering work in the mid-19th Century. But Bourdieu's particular contention that "taste" was based on purely sociological factors rather than artistic assessments was hugely influential on the poptimist critics of the early 2000s. Carl Wilson's book on Celine Dion—which is tellingly subtitled *A Journey to the End of Taste*—devoted an entire chapter to Bourdieu. Similarly, cultural critic Chuck Klosterman paraphrased Bourdieu in a 2002 *New York Times* article in order to argue that there is no substantive difference between "good" music and "bad" music, while dismissing anyone "who honestly believes the concept of 'good taste' is anything more than a subjective device used to create gaps in the intellectual class structure." And in his 2003 book *Sex, Drugs, and Cocoa Puffs: A Low Culture Manifesto*, Klosterman parlayed Bourdieu's assumptions into a poptimist embrace of commercial pop culture. "The goal of being alive is to figure out what it means to be alive," he writes. "And there is a myriad of ways to deduce that answer; I just happen to prefer examining the question through the context of Pamela Anderson and *The Real World* and Frosted Flakes. It's certainly no less plausible than understanding Kant or Wittgenstein."

Klosterman's faith in the revelatory powers of plastic supermodels, reality television, and corporate brands begged the question: Why would anyone need art? If the traditional belief in the experience of art as *transcendence*—what Kant called the *sublime*, what Lester Bangs called *illumination*, what Paul Simon called "the deep truths that artists speak"—was nothing more than an illusion disguising self-interested class assertions, why couldn't purely commercial products be every bit as valuable to the human experience as the unique creative visions of individual artists? In fact, from this perspective, corporate commercialism was even *more* valid than individual artistic creativity because it didn't pretend to be important or authentic; instead, unabashed corporate commercialism embodied what Cultural Studies sociologist Lawrence Grossberg called "authentic inauthenticity" and Carl Wilson called "genuine fake." According to Wilson in *Let's Talk About Love*, since "all art is fake," the fans and critics who accept and embrace commercial products are simply "savvy enough to realize image-construction is an inevitability and just want it to be fun." On the flipside, any artist or critic who makes either explicit or implicit claims to the transcendent aesthetic possibilities of art can be reflexively dismissed as "pretentious" and "elitist." And thus, by marginalizing any and all appeals to artistic standards, poptimists severely weakened the place of traditional criticism, which had long functioned as one of Western society's few remaining bulwarks against the purely commercial domination of popular culture.

In the end, the poptimist efforts in the early 2000s resulted in a devaluation of the place of art and artists in society. And in their place, pop apologists were relentlessly endorsing commercially-driven, celebrity-centric pop culture as a valid substitute. In fact, during the first few years of the new millennium, poptimist revisionism was working in concert with both rock establishment mythology and corporate commercial marketing in order to marginalize the perceived importance of the unique creative visions of individual artists. While influential cultural critics were busy spreading the "poptimist" belief in the value of commercial pop music and disparaging the "rockist" values of artistic substance and authenticity, rock establishment stalwart *Rolling Stone* was unveiling its list of mythological "Immortals" and movies like *Detroit Rock City* (1999), *Almost Famous* (2000), *Rock Star* (2001), and *School of Rock* (2003) were likewise emphasizing the importance of rock's mythology over its artistic substance. And, of course, the corporate music industry machine was spending hundreds of millions of dollars each year trying to convince the record-buying public that its commercial approximations of art had rendered individual creative visions obsolete. It was in this hostile environment that a fragile group of independent music labels and artists was coalescing into what would come to be known as the "indie" music scene.

PART IV

ROCK MUSIC FOR A NEW MILLENNIUM

Chapter Fifteen

Little Pockets All Across America

Merge Records, Napster, and a
New Generation of Independent Music

The Roots of a New Indie Scene

For roughly 30 years—from the arrival of Bob Dylan on the rock scene in the mid-1960s to the ultra-consolidation of the mainstream music industry that culminated in the mid-1990s—the major label system had proved willing to bankroll the creative visions of artistically substantive rock artists, from Bob Dylan to U2, Joni Mitchell to Tori Amos, Neil Young to R.E.M, The Clash to Nirvana. As Warner Brothers executive Mo Ostin had famously said, "If you believe in the artist, if you believe in his talent, if you believe he speaks the truth, then you have to be supportive of him... You have to encourage the artists to do whatever they think is right." The willingness of executives within the mainstream commercial music industry to advocate artistically substantive rock artists had helped transform rock into a unique musical genre. Thanks in part to major label patronage, rock music had achieved the potential to be both artistically substantive and commercially popular at the same time.

But in the 1990s, as a result of unprecedented media corporatization and consolidation, the mainstream music industry began moving away from Ostin's pragmatic admonition that music executives "Follow the artist, follow the music." The ultra-consolidation and hyper-commercialization of the mainstream media industry in the 1990s cemented a new industry paradigm where the corporate structure of the major labels themselves all but guaranteed the dominance of purely commercial aspirations. And as the major labels became more and more corporatized and consolidated throughout the 90s, there were countless musicians who, feeling themselves completely alienated from the mainstream, came of age with no aspirations to mainstream commercial success. In little pockets all across America, tiny, unique scenes were emerging, made up of artistically adventurous musicians who had little or no expectation of reaching an audience beyond their local communities.

In 1989, Mac McCaughan and Laura Ballance founded Merge Records in Chapel Hill, NC in order to release music by the bands they were playing in—Wwax, Metal Pitcher, Bricks, Superchunk—as well as some of their friends' local bands. "Originally, we started the label so that we could document all the cool stuff happening here," Ballance told *Spin* in 2013. In the early days, Merge focused on releasing music from the North Carolina "Triangle"—Chapel Hill, Raleigh, and Durham—on 7" records, a cheap, short-playing vinyl format with a long and storied indie-punk history. McCaughan and Ballance would borrow the money to make a record, package the record themselves at a "sleeve-stuffing party," sell as many copies as possible, and then pay back the loan with what they made on the record. When the records made more money than they had borrowed, that simply meant they'd be able to borrow less in order to make the next one. Even after their band Superchunk started making a name for itself outside of North Carolina—the band signed to New York-based indie label Matador Records, who released Superchunk's self-titled debut full-length album in 1990—McCaughan and Ballance continued to keep Merge active, releasing 7" records by local bands throughout the early 90s.

During that time, a buzz was starting to build around Superchunk. "It's this offering by Chapel Hill, NC quartet Superchunk that really gets my blood boiling," raved the *Chicago Tribune*'s Greg Kot about the band's full-length debut on Matador in October of 1990. "Sure the distorted guitars, bludgeoning bass, and snarling vocals are de rigueur at the moment, but these 10 songs offer something more than postmodern nihilism: unwashed melodies and gobs of genuine feeling." Then, in early 1992, on the heels of Nirvana's mainstream breakthrough, the call came from Danny Goldberg, manager of both Nirvana and Sonic Youth, and a new senior executive at major label subsidiary Atlantic

Records. Superchunk's subsequent meeting with Goldberg was a lesson in major label charm. "At one point the secretary buzzed in and says, 'Danny, Bonnie Raitt is on the phone,'" says McCaughan in the 2009 oral history of Merge Records, *Our Noise*. "And Danny says, 'Tell her I'm in a meeting with Superchunk.' I was like, really? She really called? It would be normal if she called, I guess. But did the secretary really tell her he was in a meeting with Superchunk? Would Bonnie Raitt have any idea who Superchunk was?" In the same oral history, Superchunk guitarist Jim Wilbur adds, "It was comical. [Goldberg] said, 'I'm gonna make you the center of my world! We don't even have to put the Atlantic logo on the records! I want to use you to look cool. All I want is to be associated with you, and not be a dick.' He actually said that." In the end, the band decided not to sign with Atlantic. According to McCaughan:

> Those guys are real good talkers, so sometimes you start thinking, 'Oh, maybe he's right. It could be really cool.' We listened to what he was saying… But if you think about it long enough, where are the examples of a band like us being happy or successful on a major label? Husker Du signed to Warner Brothers, and I thought the records got worse. And then they broke up. Maybe they would have made the same records on SST, but it's easy to look at and say, 'That's what happens when you work with a major label.' Same thing with The Replacements. I like *Tim*, but those Sire records got progressively worse. Is that because they were on a major label? I don't know… but it always seems to happen. If our records are going to sell less and less, I'd rather have them sell less and less in a creative situation—a cool situation— than a depressing one where it's just a job to do.

Ballance summed it up more succinctly, "I had grown up with that whole concept of, 'Dude, so and so sold out! That's not cool!' And the fact that Nirvana had done it didn't make me want to do it. When the industry folks would come around, I would leave the room." However, in 1993, Superchunk's label Matador decided to sell a 49 percent interest to Goldberg's Atlantic label. Matador's deal with Atlantic was part of a larger trend; by the mid-90s, most of the iconic independent labels of the 1980s had either folded or made deals with major labels. Influential British indies Rough Trade and Factory Records filed for bankruptcy in 1991 and 1992, respectively. Minneapolis-based Twin/Tone Records closed up shop in 1994, New York's Homestead Records folded in 1996, and Greg Ginn's legendary Southern California-based SST label went into hibernation around the same time. Most of the indie labels that did survive, both in America and abroad, did so by making deals with major labels. UK-based 4AD signed an exclusive distribution deal with Warner Brothers in 1992 and, in a deal similar to Matador's, Sub Pop sold a 49 percent interest to Warner Brothers in 1994.

Facing the prospect of releasing their subsequent albums through a major label subsidiary, the members of Superchunk made the bold decision to leave Matador in order to release all of their upcoming material on Merge. Superchunk drummer Jon Wurster, whose previous band The Right Profile had been signed to major label subsidiary Arista Records, explained his rationale in a 2013 *Spin* interview:

> Going through that major label thing, where you can't do *anything* yourself, makes you realize you're dependent. You become dependent on this guy OK'ing this, this person OK'ing this. Then you get to make your record, and they judge whether or not that's OK or releasable. The thrill of going from *that* to Superchunk and Merge, where we did everything ourselves, was so refreshing. It's kind of an amazing story when you think about it: That two people in the band went on to form one of the greatest, most successful record labels of the past 20 years. I mean, it couldn't have worked out any better for the band—we're probably not going to get dropped.

Once the fates of Superchunk and Merge were firmly intertwined, McCaughan and Ballance began throwing themselves into signing and releasing more and more bands and albums. They cultivated their relationship with Corey Rusk, the head of veteran indie label Touch and Go Records, and they soon formed a lasting partnership; Touch and Go would go on to distribute Merge Records releases for the next 13 years. And as they toured with Superchunk, they began to come in contact with musicians from all around the country who felt similarly alienated from the major label system.

Little Pockets All Across America

In the 1980s, Ruston, Louisiana—a small town of 20,000 located roughly 40 miles east of Shreveport—wasn't exactly an indie music hotbed, but that didn't stop childhood friends Jeff Mangum, Robert Schneider, Bill Doss, and William

Cullen Hart from making music. "In school I was surrounded by racist, sexist jocks," said Mangum in a 1998 interview. "From an early age, my friends and I all felt like we didn't belong there. We all kind of saved ourselves from that place. The little world we had there was beautiful." Mangum and his friends wrote songs, formed bands, dissolved bands, and documented their creations on crudely recorded cassettes. "We took our recordings very seriously," said Schneider in *Our Noise*. "But it was for each other. I don't think we even considered ourselves musicians. That involved some sort of long hair, or leather pants or something."

Once the friends hit their twenties, they began to go their separate ways, and in the early 90s they set up little outposts from Athens, Georgia to Denver, Colorado. But they continued recording, exchanging tapes across the country which bore the logo "Elephant 6 Recording Co." even though no such company existed anywhere but in their minds. Schneider ended up in Denver, where he started a band called The Apples in Stereo and made a short-lived attempt to turn Elephant 6 into an actual label. Mangum occasionally played bass in Schneider's band, but an emerging nomadic streak soon took him to Los Angeles and then Seattle, where a tiny local label called Cher Doll agreed to put out a single of one of his solo songs called "Everything Is" in 1994, under the name Neutral Milk Hotel. In the spring of 1995, Mangum re-united with Schneider in Denver in order to record a full-length Neutral Milk Hotel album in Schneider's 4-track home studio. "Jeff wanted to make something really meaningful," said Schneider in 2009. "A classic that would blow people's minds. That even if nobody hears it, it's going to be a classic."

Unbeknownst to Schneider or Mangum, the "Everything Is" single had found its way into the hands of Merge's Mac McCaughan and music business attorney Brian McPherson, both of whom became instant fans. McPherson sought out Mangum, appointed himself Mangum's attorney, and when the full-length Neutral Milk Hotel album was completed, he sent a copy to Merge. "Brian sent us a copy," says McCaughan in *Our Noise*. "It had a handmade paper cover. And who knows how many generations from the original this tape was. I was just, like, 'Whoa!' There were trombones, all kinds of crazy stuff. It was crazy-sounding, but so cool." Merge agreed to put out the album, now titled *On Avery Island*, and it was released in the spring of 1996. The album sold only 5,000 copies, but Merge convinced Mangum to put a band together and go on a national tour playing the Neutral Milk Hotel material. According to

Schneider, "The band was never, in any way, what you would call tight or polished. They were like, if you took a carnival, and you played it on an AM radio, and then you stuck it in a bucket with a microphone and recorded it, and then played it on a Victrola, and then rolled it down the stairs, and there's someone there to catch it—that's a Neutral Milk Hotel show."

Shortly before recording *On Avery Island*, Jeff Mangum had picked up a used copy of *The Diary of Anne Frank*. Frank's story haunted Mangum, he began having nightmares, and he eventually began writing songs about them. When Mangum returned to Schneider's Denver studio in the summer of 1997 to record his next album for Merge, he was armed with his full touring band and a notebook full of songs inspired by the young victim of a Nazi concentration camp. It was an unlikely genesis for what would become one of the most highly acclaimed albums of the indie era. The songs that would come to make up *In the Aeroplane Over the Sea* were indeed haunted, and whether they struck listeners as strangely beautiful or uncomfortably intimate, there was little disputing that they were the product of a creative vision completely cut off from everything else going on in popular music at the time. Merge Records initially pressed only 5,500 copies of the album, but it would be championed by the emerging music blogosphere—including *Pitchfork*, which gave the album an impressive 8.7/10.0 rating—and in the coming months and years, the album would find an enthusiastic cult following.

Jeff Mangum himself would find the growing attention unsettling. "He hated it," says Schneider in *Our Noise*. "That sort of mainstream business-y culture has always been repulsive to all of us, but to Jeff especially. He's really sensitive about what's pure in his music." Following the tour for *In the Aeroplane Over the Sea*, Mangum would retreat from the public eye, disbanding Neutral Milk Hotel and refusing any and all interviews that came his way. But the music he and his Elephant 6 friends from Ruston, Louisiana had created would leave a lasting impression on like-minded musicians around the country. In addition to Neutral Milk Hotel, Robert Schneider's Apples in Stereo would carve out a modest but influential career for themselves on the emerging indie circuit. The same was true of their Ruston, Louisiana friends Bill Doss and William Cullen Hart's band Olivia Tremor Control. And by the late 90s, there were similarly independent local scenes popping up all over the country.

Though significantly larger than Ruston, Louisiana, Omaha, Nebraska was almost as unlikely a locale for an independent music scene. Located in the center of "red state" middle-America, Nebraska's largest city was equally cut off from the mainstream music industry hubs of New York, Los Angeles, and Nashville. But in 1993, a couple of music fans named Mike Mogis and Justin Oberst started Lumberjack Records as part of a college class on entrepreneurship. In need of material for their "label," the duo tapped Oberst's younger brother, 13-year-old Conor, to record for them. Once the college assignment was completed, Lumberjack changed its name to Saddle Creek Records and commenced efforts to document the burgeoning Omaha music scene. In 1995, Conor Oberst, now 15 years old, formed the band Commander Venus. Though the band was short-lived, its members would go on to found the acts—Cursive, The Faint, and Bright Eyes—that would become the core of both Saddle Creek's roster and the growing Omaha scene. Oberst's solo project Bright Eyes would become particularly influential; his cracked, plaintive vocal delivery and experimental folk instrumentation would become touchstones for numerous indie acts. And by the turn of the millennium, Bright Eyes and Saddle Creek were starting to draw out-of-town acts like Now It's Overhead, Azure Ray, and Spoon into the expanding Omaha orbit.

Meanwhile, in the Pacific Northwest, a whole slew of small independent labels were following in the footsteps of local indie legends Sub Pop, C/Z, and K Records. As singer-songwriter Neko Case—who came of age in the vibrant music scene in Vancouver, BC—pointed out in a 2002 interview, "It was an incredibly good time for music in the Northwest. There were a lot of clubs, a lot of bands, a lot of people coming through, a lot of all-ages stuff—it was a very exciting time to live there." Case played in numerous Vancouver bands in the 90s, most of which were signed to local indie label Mint Records, which would eventually release Case's first solo albums as well as those of The New Pornographers—an influential "collective" which started as a side-project for Case and fellow Vancouver scenesters Dan Bejar (of the band Destroyer) and Carl Newman. Just down the coast from Vancouver, Seattle-based Barsuk Records—which, like Merge, had initially been launched in order to release the music of its founders Christopher Possanza and Josh Rosenfeld—was making a name for itself as the home of Death Cab for Cutie and Rilo Kiley. And further down the coast in Portland, the Kill Rock Stars label was documenting the feminist punk Riot Grrrl movement typified by acts like Bikini Kill and

Sleater-Kinney, as well as the less abrasive sounds of acts like Elliott Smith and The Decemberists.

At the same time, a new scene was taking shape throughout the Midwest around the "alternative country" genre inspired by the Belleville, Illinois-based band Uncle Tupelo. Even though Tupelo's first three albums on the tiny independent Rockville Records imprint had failed to crack the mainstream, their combination of the indie-punk sensibility with American roots music proved powerful, especially once the band's founders Jay Farrar and Jeff Tweedy split and formed their own bands, Son Volt and Wilco, both of which landed major label deals under the Warner Brothers umbrella. By the late 90s, the scene had its own independent magazine—titled *No Depression* in honor of Uncle Tupelo's first album—and a handful of small independent labels dedicated to promoting the alt-country genre. One of these labels, Chicago-based Bloodshot Records, would make a name for itself with releases by acts like The Old 97s, The Bottle Rockets, and Ryan Adams. These alt-country acts would join with Americana revivalists like Gillian Welch, Lucinda Williams, and Fred Eaglesmith in expanding the borders of "Americana" music, introducing a new generation of independent music fans to America's country and bluegrass roots.

Yet another unique artistic sensibility trickling into America's late-90s indie consciousness was the largely instrumental "post-rock" music being created by bands like Canada's Godspeed You! Black Emperor, Scotland's Mogwai, and Iceland's Sigur Ros. Sigur Ros's 1999 sophomore album *Agaetis byrun* was particularly influential, combining aspects of rock, classical, and traditional Icelandic music into a soaring, ambient soundscape that won independent critical accolades—*Pitchfork*'s glowing 9.4/10.0 review called them "the first vital band of the 21st Century"—and inspired dozens of American bands. One of those was the Austin, Texas-based quartet Explosions in the Sky, who formed in 1999 and began molding the various elements of the instrumental post-rock template into a reflection of their native Texas landscape. The band would go on to become a vital part of the eclectic Austin, Texas music scene, which was itself another influential hub of independent music activity.

While these unique, independent scenes were popping up across America, Merge Records remained busy signing a string of soon-to-be iconic indie acts; in addition to Neutral Milk Hotel, the label would sign Rocket from the Crypt, Lampchop, Archers of Loaf, and The Magnetic Fields. And by the end of the decade, Merge had amassed an impressive discography while—like all of the disparate independent scenes of the late 90s—remaining a strictly underground phenomenon (no Merge album would enter the *Billboard* 200 album chart until 2004). But technological changes in the way music was being discovered, acquired, and listened to would soon blast the doors off the mainstream music industry and help all of these independent music scenes to reach a much wider audience. As *Pitchfork*'s Eric Harvey would later write, "Coupled with peer-to-peer, not only did [mp3s] quickly make music replication and distribution cheap and fast, but turned something that used to be a distant, industrial process into an accessible and easy thing anyone could do. In other words, it's not only unsurprising that a sustainable independent music industry took shape along with mp3s. Looking back, it's unthinkable for things to have happened any other way."

The mp3 Revolution

In 1988, the International Organization for Standardization—a Switzerland-based regulatory agency that sets international standards for everything from screw threads to railroad tracks—commissioned a new body called the Moving Picture Experts Group (MPEG) to create standards for digital video and audio, which were expected to become necessary in the near future. The initial group was headed by Italian engineer Leonardo Chiariglione and didn't include a single person associated with the music business. "Some of them came later, when the group became larger," Chiariglione told *The Atlantic* in 2000. "But at the time—well, nobody *knew*, you see. Nobody, I promise you, had any idea of what this would mean to music."

Up until the work of MPEG, the typical digital files created by converting film and music into code were far too large for most existing computers to use. But during the 80s, researchers had invented ways of shrinking the size of music files without losing their identifying qualities by omitting the range of tones that human hearing generally fails to perceive. Using this method, a German group called the Fraunhofer Institute for Integrated Circuits had managed to shrink music files by a factor of twelve or more with little noticeable loss of quality. In 1992, Chiariglione's Moving

Picture Experts Group completed its first audiovisual standard, called MPEG-1, which consisted of three layers: two for high-performance applications, and a compressed third layer (known as Layer 3)—based on the work of the Fraunhofer group—which was intended for use on the slower computers and systems most people were using at the time. The source code for converting audio into MPEG-1, Layer 3 files—or mp3 files—was stored on a computer at Bavaria's Fraunhofer Institute, from which it was downloaded by a Dutch hacker named SoloH (a presumed *Star Wars* fan), who repurposed the source code to create software capable of converting the audio files on CDs into compact and listenable mp3 files. "This single unexpected act," wrote *The Atlantic*'s Charles C. Mann in 2000, "undid the music industry." Within mere months, the software for "ripping" CDs into mp3 files—an application that Chiariglione and his MPEG team hadn't even considered—had been disseminated around the globe, and before long there were websites all around the still-fledgling internet featuring thousands of free mp3 files available for download.

In the mid-to-late 90s, these sites were still scattershot and of varying dependability, but soon additional sites emerged that were devoted to promoting the more reliable mp3 download sites. One of these aggregators, an 18-year-old McDonald's employee who went by the online handle "Blex," had pointers to thousands of songs, and by 1997 he had more than 10,000 daily visitors to his website. Major label representatives were astonished by the popularity of Blex's site, and the countless others like it. As *The Atlantic*'s Charles C. Mann pointed out in his 1998-2000 series of articles on digital technology, "None of the big music studios had imagined that tens of thousands of high school and college students with Pentium PCs would be willing to spend hours downloading music and playing it on their computers. But there were. Only in 1997—as people on five continents eagerly sought out mp3 information from the Blexes of the world—did the [major record labels] launch a campaign against illicitly copied music on the internet." Soon, the Recording Industry Association of America (RIAA), a trade group which represents the interests of the major labels, was issuing warnings, sending out nasty letters, and filing a few lawsuits against file traders.

The majority of those at the major labels, however, remained skeptical of the impact of mp3 websites. "What are they going to do?" asked Jeffrey Neuberger—an attorney who represented multiple major labels—in Mann's

1999 *Atlantic* piece. "Present you with an undifferentiated mass of music, most of which is garbage, and let you browse through it, on the theory that you might find something you like?" But another of Mann's interviewees, John Perry Barlow of the Electronic Frontier Foundation, believed the eventual impact of mp3s would be transformative. As Mann wrote in 1998, "In the future, Barlow told me, people will be able to download music and writing so easily that they will be reluctant to take the trouble to seek hard copies, let alone want to pay for them… the Internet is not just full of people who scoff at copyright but [it is] also, as a practical matter, too large to police." The real test of both Neuberger and Barlow's assessments would come sooner than either anticipated.

In November of 1998, a Northeastern University freshman by the name of Shawn Fanning began soliciting advice on the Internet Relay Chat forum (IRC) under the moniker "napster" about an idea he had for creating a global internet community, with access to every music file on every hard drive, everywhere. Fanning's proposal met with both excitement and skepticism within the IRC community, but a number of the forum's members—including eventual Napster co-founder Sean Parker and eventual Napster architects Jordan Ritter and Ali Aydar—took enough interest in the idea that Fanning was inspired to drop out of school and work on the idea full-time. With the help of his IRC chatmates, Fanning had an operational platform for Napster up and running by early 1999, at which point he simply uploaded it to the internet and waited for a response.

The idea of "peer-to-peer" (P2P) file sharing was not a new one; in fact, P2P networks had been used by military and university infrastructures since the infancy of the internet. But the idea of an open, global network for file sharing was truly revolutionary. As Napster co-founder Sean Parker said, "We were going to build the world's first decentralized file system." The widespread use of such a network, however, was far from inevitable. One of the primary obstacles was technological: In the dial-up era of the late 90s, it often took hours to transfer a single a music file, when such transfers were successful at all. Another obstacle was psychological: Would people actually give strangers the access to their personal hard drives necessary for widespread, anonymous P2P file sharing?

Fanning was convinced that the potential benefits of a trusted platform for sharing music files would win out. "One of my [college] roommates was into mp3s and he would skip class and sit at home and download music. He was always complaining about how unreliable the technology was," Fanning said in a 2001 interview. "He was complaining a lot and that sort of signaled to me that there was a potential, that there was a problem that could be solved. And I just looked into it and came up with the solution, which ultimately became Napster." Sean Parker was excited enough about the idea to agree to help Fanning seek investment capital in order to realize his idea, and they met in person for the first time in order to attend a meeting with potential investors. As investment money started to come in, Fanning and Parker moved Napster to Silicon Valley—the hub of the ongoing internet revolution—and opened a low-rent office above a bank in San Mateo, CA. They were soon joined by a few of their technologically-inclined friends and IRC cohorts and went about expanding the functionality of the Napster framework with an eye towards facilitating a truly global P2P network. By mid-summer 1999, the Napster website had 30,000-40,000 active users. Then, on Aug. 13, an article about Napster appeared on the internet news site *ZDNet*, which kicked off an explosion of growth that would increase Napster's user base to over 20 million in just a few short months, thanks primarily to word-of-mouth on college campuses. Indiana University, for instance, would soon ban the use of Napster, claiming that use of the file-sharing website—*which comprised 61 percent of all internet activity on the campus*—was clogging the campus internet network. The idea that users would be hesitant to grant access to their personal hard drives had proved to be unfounded, and by the end of 1999, virtually every song ever committed to CD was available as a free download through Napster. Not only that, but the increasing speed of internet connections was making it easier and easier to download them.

It soon became obvious that the Napster phenomenon would have profound, far-reaching implications for the way that music was discovered, shared, experienced, and purchased. According to Parker in the 2012 Napster documentary *Downloaded*:

> We were trying to create a platform that would allow music to be shared more widely—on a global scale—than ever before, that would galvanize enormous excitement, that would re-energize the conversation about music, and ultimately that would lead to a golden age of music… It was one of the first times in history where you had this sort of pure youth revolution: young,

inexperienced, relatively unsophisticated—but smart—kids could create something entirely out of nowhere and revolutionize an industry that they frankly knew nothing about and had no relationships in… I think 6 months passed before we had a conversation with anyone in the industry. And it wasn't because we didn't *want* to have a conversation with anyone in the industry; we just didn't *know* anyone in the industry.

In September of 1999, just a few months after Fanning had uploaded the Napster platform, the RIAA set up a meeting with Napster to discuss what the major labels perceived as an egregious case of music piracy. Even though Napster was facilitating rather than providing the music being shared over its network, RIAA spokeswoman Hilary Rosen pointed out that "[Napster] is a company that is building a business. They've got venture capital money. They're out on Wall Street looking for financing. This isn't, you know, some sweet young guy just looking for fun in his college dorm room. They're building a business by facilitating the stealing of artists' music."

The ensuing meetings between Napster and the RIAA were later characterized very differently by the two parties. According to Parker in the *Downloaded* documentary, "Ultimately, we were going to have to figure out a revenue model. And by the time we started talking with labels, we were more than happy to turn the whole thing over to the labels and basically become their digital distribution service. We always wanted that." But RIAA Chairman and CEO Cary Sherman saw the meetings differently. "We had serious conversations in September of 1999," he recalls in the same documentary. "And when it became clear that they were just stringing us along and that they had no intention of actually negotiating licenses, we filed a lawsuit in December." The Napster contingent was taken completely off guard by the lawsuit; they saw Napster's meteoric rise as proof that a massive technological shift was clearly underway, and they assumed that the labels would inevitably want to make some kind of deal in order to capitalize on it. "We're pretty confident that there are so many wins with digital distribution," said Fanning in late 1999, "that ultimately, once we have the opportunity to work with artists and work with the labels to discuss what models are viable and what are not, that we can come to a conclusion and a model that works." And according to Napster investor Ron Conway in *Downloaded*, Napster's attitude was, "'You can't stop technology. Tell us what you want us to do. We want to cooperate.'

And guess what, nobody really cooperated and it never got resolved. It's still not resolved. It's 12 years later, and that's pretty pathetic."

After filing suit against Napster in December of 1999, the RIAA embarked on a massive PR campaign in order to brand Napster as a group of copyright thieves who were knowingly encouraging illegal internet piracy. But the reaction among actual musicians at the time was more mixed, as documented in *Downloaded*. According to Chuck D of the rap group Public Enemy, "Napster—and downloadable distribution—is the biggest excitement since disco, rap, and The Beatles. It's like new radio." And according to Billy Corgan of Smashing Pumpkins, "There's no doubt in my mind that the future of music is free. You're not going to be able to stop fans from trading music on the internet. Even if it's not through a company or a website, fans are going to trade music on their own. There's no stopping it. This revolution has already taken place." Some musicians, however, were simply more comfortable with the status quo. "I thought the way that people got music for the last 50 years worked," said Noel Gallagher of the rock group Oasis. "You went to the record shop, you bought the record, you took it home, you played it, you loved it, you went to see the artist live, everybody lived happily ever after." But there were also musicians who echoed the RIAA's damning characterization of Napster as nothing more than common thieves. Singer-songwriter Sheryl Crow stated bluntly that, "Napster is an evil, evil, evil place to go." And other artists were even more blunt. "Napster is bullshit," summed up popular rapper Eminem, and his mentor Dr. Dre's mantra on the subject was "Fuck Napster."

But it would be the popular metal act Metallica that would come to embody the opposition to Napster. On May 22, 2000, Metallica drummer Lars Ulrich arrived at the Napster offices in San Mateo with a truckload of boxes filled with documents listing some 260,000 Napster users who had shared Metallica songs. Ulrich held a press conference on the front steps, asking Napster to use the information he had delivered in order to stop the illegal sharing of Metallica songs. The young Napster founders—Fanning was still 19 years old at the time and Parker was only 20—looked on in bemusement at the spectacle, star-struck by Ulrich's presence on their doorstep, yet convinced that Napster was protected under the "safe haven" provisions of the 1998 Digital Millennium Copyright Act.

Eventually, two competing narratives would vie for public opinion, both of which painted the issue in black and white terms. On one side was the

RIAA, which pressed the legal side of the issue in order to paint music artists and labels as victims of unabashed copyright theft. On the other side were the technological innovators, who pressed the philosophical side of the issue in order to paint the major labels as an archaic, self-interested power structure bent on stifling the democratic impulses of both artistic and technological creativity. Both narratives had high-profile advocates. "I'm all for technology," said Nine Inch Nails' Trent Reznor in a 2000 MTV interview. "And it's interesting, the exchange of music. But the way that it's set up right now is theft, basically, pure and simple." Soundgarden's Chris Cornell disagreed, "I think the aspect of technology is really gonna bring a lot of different angles of life and commerciality out of the corporate world and give it back to the individuals." Or, as Public Enemy's Chuck D put it, "For the first time, the audience has gotten to the technology before the industry, before the music business. The record companies are afraid because they'll be forced to share."

Meanwhile, the lawsuit against Napster dragged along, even as Napster continued trying to negotiate a settlement. According to Napster strategist Ricki Seidman, "From the moment that [Napster CEO] Hank [Barry] came in, he was looking at making deals [with the record labels]. He did everything but turn cartwheels on Hollywood Boulevard." But Napster's reported asking price for a settlement—$2 billion, according to former Universal CEO Edgar Bronfman, Jr.—was a non-starter for an industry which was negotiating from a position of strength; worldwide music industry revenues had hit an all-time high of $27 billion in 1999, the year that the RIAA filed suit against Napster. And no one in the industry had any idea that those revenues might be *cut in half* in the coming years (annual industry revenues would drop all the way down to $14 billion by 2012). In retrospect, given those numbers, acquiring Napster—even at Napster's hefty asking price—in order to corner the download market in its infancy might have been a bargain for the major labels. According to Island Records founder Chris Blackwell in *Downloaded*, "I think Napster had 60 million customers at one time, or people that were getting their music through Napster. And that seemed like an incredible opportunity. But because the major labels couldn't come to terms with them, they essentially burned it down."

Finally, in February 2001, San Francisco's Ninth District Court ruled against Napster, ordering the company to prevent the sharing of copyrighted material on its website or face immediate shutdown. "What happened yesterday is the effective shutdown of Napster," said Gene Kan of the P2P website Gnutella. "And what that's going to do is give birth to 1000 of Napster's spawn, and these children are going to be much better bred." The years following Napster's demise did indeed see the proliferation of thousands of file sharing sites: Gnutella, Limewire, Kazaa, The Pirate Bay, and on and on. And unlike Napster, few of these sites had any interest in negotiating a deal with the major labels in order to honor existing copyright law. As a result, a clear divide would emerge between the mainstream music industry and an entire generation of music fans who had come of age downloading mp3s—and had no attachment whatsoever to the music industry's old business model. The divide between the major labels and young music fans would only be exacerbated when the industry began prosecuting its own consumer base; the RIAA would file over 18,000 suits against rank-and-file music traders in the wake of the Napster ruling. By the early 2000s, this growing divide would create the space for the new generation of indie labels to move in and create a sustainable market for music being created outside of the major label system.

Chapter Sixteen

Music for People who Love Music

The Bands, Blogs, and Business of Indie's Golden Era

A Millennial Shift

In 1999, major label attorney Jeffrey Neuberger had asked of mp3 download sites, "What are they going to do? Present you with an undifferentiated mass of music, most of which is garbage, and let you browse through it, on the theory that you might find something you like?" Even though Neuberger's perspective seems painfully shortsighted in retrospect, he did have a legitimate question; the glut of mp3s created by Napster and other download sites cried out for reliable music filters.

For decades, major labels had functioned as filters for music listeners—one of the reasons the majors purchased smaller, iconic labels was in order to cultivate a brand identity that music fans would trust—but by the turn of the millennium corporate consolidation had reduced the majors to little more than interchangeable dispensers of commercial product. Similarly, mainstream music publications like *Rolling Stone* had once functioned as trusted filters, but by the time mp3s exploded onto the scene, *Rolling Stone* had long-since abandoned its role as a reliable new music filter, and its erstwhile descendants like *Spin* and *Blender* were well on their way to similar irrelevance. The indie labels and fanzines of the 1980s had been seen as reliable filters by a small but dedicated group of music fans, but by the late 90s most of those fanzines and labels had closed shop or been co-opted by larger corporate entities. And thanks to the digital nature of the mp3 medium, independent record stores—which had long functioned as filters for dedicated music fans—would soon be on their way out, as well. In short, mp3s demanded a whole new filter system.

The thousands upon thousands of online music blogs that emerged in the early 2000s were more than just an inevitable outgrowth of internet culture; they were a response to a very real demand for reliable filters for new music. "It's no coincidence," wrote *Pitchfork*'s Eric Harvey in 2009, "that mp3 blogs would emerge as an eclectic network of music fans as the decade opened." And Harvey also blithely noted that "*Pitchfork*'s own rise coincided with the mp3 market glut." Since its humble beginnings in the mid-90s, *Pitchfork* had been reviewing albums from the far-flung independent scenes and labels popping up across America. And by the time its review of Radiohead's *Kid A* went viral and put the online magazine on the map in the fall of 2000, *Pitchfork* was primed to step into the filter vacuum by helping to connect these previously disparate music scenes with each other.

The independent music scenes that emerged in the 1990s had been all over the map both geographically and stylistically, ranging from the American Southeast to the Pacific Northwest, from Riot Grrrl punk to twangy alt-country. For most of the decade, in fact, the only unifying principle among these independent rock scenes had been their shared separation from the increasingly commercialized alternative rock genre that had become the template for mainstream rock. As Nitsuh Abebe would later write in *Pitchfork*, "The kinds of alt-rock that got popular tended to be very straightforward: fuzzy, glossy rock songs; brash, masculine grunge... It's probably no accident that if you look at the things the 'indie' world turned toward over the following years, a lot of them can be read as straight-up reactions to those qualities." Even so, independence from the mainstream alt-rock template was a broad enough umbrella to encompass widely divergent styles and attitudes. For instance, many devotees of the emerging indie scene saw the "We don't give a shit" slacker ethos of New York-by-way-of-Stockton-California rockers Pavement as the embodiment of the definitive indie template. To these fans, the band's overt sloppiness—out of tune guitars, off-key vocals, tossed-off lyrics, loose rhythm section (the band had to employ an additional percussionist in order to compensate for its timing-challenged drummer)—represented a refreshing corrective to the increasingly slick production and anguished over-earnestness of mainstream alt-rock bands like Live, Matchbox Twenty, and Creed. As

Pitchfork would retrospectively note in 2003, "In comparison with the dead art foisted on the proletariat by any number of status quo cadres disguised as rock bands, [Pavement's debut full-length album] *Slanted* [*and Enchanted*] is a radical, liberating document." And in the Pavement documentary *Slow Century*, Sonic Youth's Thurston Moore describes how a record store clerk's judgment that Pavement was "unlistenable" had the opposite of the intended effect on the indie icon. Rather than scaring him away from Pavement, the record clerk's "unlistenable" warning, said Moore, "sold me right away."

At the other end of the spectrum from Pavement's tossed-off slacker ethos was the fragile sincerity of a singer-songwriter like Will Oldham. Under his "Palace" and "Bonnie 'Prince' Billy" pseudonyms, the smothering intimacy of Oldham's music—which was distributed by Chicago-based indie label Drag City—was also miles away from the manufactured arena-scale melodrama of mainstream alt-rock. As *Pitchfork* would write in 2001, the 1999 Bonnie "Prince" Billy release *I See a Darkness* was "almost shocking in its confessional honesty… wrought with all the prayer and fear and wonder that goes into the most perfectly recited psalm."

And yet the tastemakers at *Pitchfork* would embrace both Oldham and Pavement. Oldham's *I See a Darkness* garnered a rare 10.0/10.0 rating and was ranked #9 on the online magazine's retrospective "Top 100 Albums of the 90s" list. Similarly, Pavement's first two full-length albums—*Slanted and Enchanted* and *Crooked Rain, Crooked Rain*—both made the Top 10 on the same list, clocking in at #5 and #8 respectively. By avoiding stylistic homogeneity and embracing virtually any music that seemed to stand in opposition to the mainstream alt-rock template, *Pitchfork* was helping to create a loose but identifiable "indie" umbrella.

In this sense, the millennial indie music scene was a much more direct descendant of the wide-ranging 80s *alternative* scene than it was the smaller and more rigid 80s *indie* scene; where 80s alternative music had encompassed wide-ranging stylistic diversity, the much smaller 80s indie scene had generally opted for minimalist post-punk stylistic fidelity. And the way that the millennial indie scene was starting to come together also echoed the emergence of the alternative scene in the mid-80s. The alternative scene hadn't coalesced into a cohesive phenomenon until MTV's *120 Minutes*—which debuted in 1986—had begun tying its disparate local scenes together. Similarly, beginning around the year 2000, the power of the *Pitchfork*-led music blogosphere was exposing independent music to an increasingly national and international audience, in the process tying its far-flung iterations into something approximating a cohesive scene.

Pitchfork's advocacy of Neutral Milk Hotel, for instance, would help introduce the band's music to an expanding audience. After an initial pressing of just 5,500 copies, *In the Aeroplane Over the Sea* would eventually sell an astonishing 250,000 copies—helping Jeff Mangum's intimately crafted songs influence countless indie acts, from Bright Eyes to The Decemberists. Similarly, *Pitchfork*'s glowing 9.0/10.0 review of alt-country singer-songwriter Ryan Adams' *Heartbreaker*, which had been released on the independent Bloodshot label in the fall of 2000, catapulted Adams into the national underground consciousness, where he would remain an influential touchstone for the rest of the decade. *Pitchfork*'s positive review of Bright Eyes' 2002 release on tiny Saddle Creek Records, *Lifted (or The Story is in the Soil, Keep Your Ear to the Ground)*, was enough to help land the album on the *Billboard* 200 album chart (albeit at the modest peak of #161). And the online buzz that the album generated led *Rolling Stone*—which hadn't bothered to review *Lifted* upon its initial release—to belatedly jump on the bandwagon, including the album in its year-end Best of 2002 list. And when *Pitchfork* gave the experimental Portland, Oregon-based band Menomena's *I Am the Fun Blame Monster* an enthusiastic 8.7/10.0 "Best New Music" review in 2003, it almost singlehandedly lifted the band out of obscurity. According to Menomena's Brent Knopf in a 2013 *Mule Variations* interview, "At the time, we were selling the record on CD Baby, and we were monitoring the sales, 'Oh, hey, we sold two CDs today!' And then one day we sold 300 CDs, and we were like, 'What the hell happened!?' We couldn't figure it out, until someone said, 'Hey, *Pitchfork* wrote about it' … It made a really big impact." In a relatively short period of time, *Pitchfork* had gained the power to make or break albums all by itself.

In addition to *Pitchfork*'s increasingly towering influence, the collective power of smaller blogs was becoming just as influential. As *L.A. Weekly*'s Alec Hanley Bemis would write in 2005, "The digital landscape has been laid; the critical apparatus necessary to govern its borders is settling into place. It's a hierarchy of Web zines, MP3 blogs, podcasts, and message boards with peculiar names like *Music for Robots, Coolfer, Stereogum, Brooklyn Vegan,* and *Tracks Up the Tree.* An artist can make or break a career via a thousand different sites that are insignificant on their own, but together quite powerful." The smaller scale on which each individual blog operated meant easy access for indie acts and labels, minimizing the disadvantages that they had traditionally encountered in trying to gain the ear of mainstream behemoths like MTV or *Rolling Stone*. And as the decade wore on, aggregators like *Hype Machine* and *Metacritic* would take the far-flung opinions of the blogosphere and reconstruct them into a decipherable critical consensus, functioning as a perfect shortcut for underground music fans who lacked the time or interest necessary to peruse dozens of individual blogs before deciding whether to check out or purchase a new album. While the ability to launch multi-million dollar promotional campaigns and garner mainstream media coverage would always give the major labels a leg up on indies, the music blogosphere was now providing an alternative promotional network that could be won over without the help of a deep-pocketed benefactor.

The Expanding Definition of "Indie"

While the music blogosphere was quickly coming of age, the turn of the millennium would also see a blurring of the lines between major and indie label affiliation, eventually expanding definition of the term "indie" itself. During the early 2000s, the term indie was increasingly being used to describe the more artistically adventurous acts operating within the major label system. For instance, indie veteran Calvin Johnson's Olympia, Washington-based K Records had experienced a late 90s resurgence thanks to its work with local experimental rock band Modest Mouse, who would go on to become icons of the emerging indie scene in the coming years, even after they signed to major label subsidiary Epic Records. Around the same time, long-slumping Sub Pop Records began moving towards resurgence on the strength of releases by The Shins and The Postal Service, even as Sub Pop remained under Warner Brothers' major label umbrella.

The Shins, in particular, would become a flagship act of the emerging indie scene. Albuquerque, New Mexico-based singer-songwriter James Mercer had formed The Shins in the late 90s out of the ashes of his previous band Flake Music, and the positive local response to the band's first EP *Nature Bears a Vacuum* was enough to encourage them to go on the road in support of it. In 2000, while on tour in San Francisco opening for their friends Modest Mouse, The Shins' Mercer was approached by Sub Pop's Jonathan Poneman, who eventually agreed to release the band's first single, "New Slang," and first full-length album, *Oh, Inverted World*, in 2001. The album's combination of 60s-inspired melodies (The Beach Boys and Simon & Garfunkel were commonly cited influences), inventive instrumentation, and Mercer's distinctive vocals would become a benchmark for musicians throughout the budding indie scene. The Shins would also help Sub Pop regain some semblance of the indie credibility it had lost during a protracted late 90s slump. But it would be another Sub Pop act that would solidify the label's resurgence.

A key factor in Sub Pop's early 2000s renaissance was a lesson it had learned from the financial difficulties it had experienced in the late 90s. "We were lucky that we were going bankrupt two years before everybody else in the music business," Sub Pop's head of A&R Tony Kiewel would later tell the *L.A. Times*. "We fixed everything two years ahead of everybody else. If we spend only $5,000 recording an album, we can afford to keep doing records with artists that we truly love." Sub Pop's newfound thriftiness helped make a project pitched to Kiewel by his former college roommate Jimmy Tamborello particularly attractive. In 2001, Tamborello—an electronic musician who performed and recorded under the name Dntel—had collaborated with Death Cab for Cutie frontman Ben Gibbard on a song called "(This Is) the Dream of Evan and Chan" for the Dntel album *Life is Full of Possibilities*. The response to the collaboration was so positive—*Pitchfork*'s Matt LeMay called it "one of the best songs of 2001"—that Tamborello and Gibbard had begun working on a full-length album together. And thanks to the music's electronic backbone, recording costs for the album would essentially be equal to the cost of a computer hard drive, making the project an easy sell for Kiewel and Sub Pop. Even so, no one at the label expected the album to become Sub Pop's biggest seller since Nirvana's *Bleach*.

Gibbard and Tamborello chose the name The Postal Service for their collaboration due to the process by which they wrote songs together. Tamborello would create instrumental electronic tracks and mail them to Gibbard, who would then write lyrics and add vocals to the tracks before mailing them back to Tamborello for additional edits. Having cobbled together a full album's worth of material over a period of months, they delivered the final product to Sub Pop, who released *Give Up* in February 2003 to positive critical reception, including an 8.0/10.0 rating from *Pitchfork* and 4-Star stamp of approval from *Rolling Stone*. But the combination of Tamborello's clean electronic soundscape and Gibbard's confessional vocals struck an unexpected chord with listeners. *Give Up*'s peak at just #114 on the *Billboard* album charts belied the album's cultural reach and influence; by March of 2005 it had sold 500,000 copies in America alone, and it would continue to sell consistently in the coming years, eventually going platinum in 2012. The impact of The Postal Service's *Give Up*, coupled with the critical and commercial success of The Shins' 2003 follow-up release *Chutes Too Narrow*, placed Sub Pop squarely at the center of the burgeoning indie scene, where it would remain for the rest of the decade. The Postal Service's success would also help Ben Gibbard's primary band Death Cab for Cutie reach a wider audience; Death Cab's 2003 release on the independent Barsuk imprint, *Transatlanticism*, would soon join *Give Up* on the *Billboard* charts and go on to sell over 500,000 copies, in the process becoming a staple on college campuses across the country.

During the early 2000s, the common classification of Sub Pop's artists as "indie"—even as the label remained under Warner Brothers' major label umbrella—was indicative of the way artistically adventurous major label acts were now being classified. For instance, Oklahoma City-based rock veterans The Flaming Lips—who had achieved one-hit wonder success with their unlikely single "She Don't Use Jelly" in 1993—built a second career as indie trendsetters on the strength of 1999's *The Soft Bulletin* and 2002's *Yoshimi Battles the Pink Robots*, both of which garnered rave reviews at *Pitchfork* and became integral parts of the indie landscape, even though they were released through major label Warner Brothers.

Similarly, the band Wilco had shed its mid-90s alt-country roots in order to pursue a more expansive level of sonic sophistication on its 1999 album *Summerteeth* and—even more noticeably—on its critically-acclaimed follow-up *Yankee Hotel Foxtrot*, which earned a rare perfect 10.0/10.0 rating from *Pitchfork*. The major label travails involved with the making and release of *Yankee Hotel Foxtrot*—documented at length in the 2002 film *I Am Trying to Break Your Heart*—became symbolic of the rapidly fading artistic ambitions of major labels, as well as their fiscal idiocy. Warner Brothers subsidiary Reprise had dropped Wilco rather than release what it deemed to be the "non-commercial" *Foxtrot*, only to have fellow Warner subsidiary Nonesuch subsequently agree to release the album, meaning that the Warner Music Group had essentially blundered its way into paying Wilco for the same album twice. The widely publicized story managed to simultaneously paint the major labels as artistically tone-deaf buffoons and elevate Wilco to the status of indie folk heroes, even though the band remained, at least for the time being, signed to a major label subsidiary.

Thanks to major label bands like The Flaming Lips, Wilco, Radiohead, and Modest Mouse—and the willingness of indie tastemakers like *Pitchfork* to embrace them—the term "indie" was becoming less tied to strict label affiliation and, much like the term "alternative" in the 1980s, was increasingly being used to refer to any artistically credible rock music perceived to exist outside the rock mainstream, which had come to be dominated by vacuous commercial behemoths like Nickelback and Linkin Park. And much like the growth of the alternative scene in the 80s, the indie music umbrella would slowly expand in the first few years of the new millennium, spawning more new bands and winning more new fans with each passing year.

Arcade Fire and the Growth of the Indie Scene

In the spring of 2004, Merge Records' co-founder Mac McCaughan received an email from Montreal-based friend Howard Bilerman:

> hello hello… i've been put in a slightly uncomfortable situation here by the band i'm drumming in called the arcade fire… uncomfortable only 'cause i'm really shy & clumsy about these things. basically we're recording a record right now, and are in the process of figuring out who will put it out… win (singer/songwriter) has been asking me about merge, partly 'cause he loves so much of the stuff on the label, and partly 'cause he knows I know you… anyhow, I want you to know that there are no strings attached here. if you are completely uninterested in the music, i will take no offense, and you can still crash at my place next time you roll into town.

The record Bilerman and his band were working on would eventually be called *Funeral*, and it was destined to become Merge's first album to hit the *Billboard* 200 album chart. But in the spring of 2004, nobody knew that. When Merge agreed to put out *Funeral*, they pressed 10,000 copies, a larger than usual number—at least by Merge standards—for a debut album by an unknown band.

Then, on September 13, 2004, the day before the album's scheduled release, *Pitchfork* published a glowing 9.7/10.0 review. According to *Pitchfork*'s David Moore, *Funeral* was nothing less than the embodiment of a generational ethos:

> How did we get here? Ours is a generation overwhelmed by frustration, unrest, dread, and tragedy. Fear is wholly pervasive in American society, but we manage nonetheless to build our defenses in subtle ways—we scoff at arbitrary, color-coded 'threat' levels; we receive our information from comedians and laugh at politicians. Upon the turn of the 21st century, we have come to know our isolation well. Our self-imposed solitude renders us politically and spiritually inert, but rather than take steps to heal our emotional and existential wounds, we have chosen to revel in them. We consume the affected martyrdom of our purported idols and spit it back in mocking defiance. We forget that 'emo' was once derived from emotion, and that in our buying and selling of personal pain, or the cynical approximation of it, we feel nothing. We are not the first, or the last, to be confronted with this dilemma. [Talking Heads singer-songwriter] David Byrne famously asked a variation on the question that opens this review, and in doing so suggested a type of universal disaffection synonymous with drowning. And so The Arcade Fire asks the question again, but with a crucial distinction: The pain of Win Butler and Régine Chassagne, the enigmatic husband-and-wife songwriting force behind the band, is not merely metaphorical, nor is it defeatist. They tread water in Byrne's ambivalence because they have known real, blinding pain, and they have overcome it in a way that is both tangible and accessible. Their search for salvation in the midst of real chaos is ours; their eventual catharsis is part of our continual enlightenment… So long as we're unable or unwilling to fully recognize the healing aspect of embracing honest emotion in popular music, we will always approach the sincerity of an album like *Funeral* from a clinical distance. Still, that it's so easy to embrace this album's operatic proclamation of love and redemption speaks to the scope of The Arcade Fire's vision. It's taken perhaps too long for us to reach this point where an album is at last capable of completely and successfully restoring the tainted phrase 'emotional' to its true origin. Dissecting how we got here now seems unimportant. It's simply comforting to know that we finally have arrived.

Pitchfork's review single-handedly opened a floodgate of demand for *Funeral*. Merge and their distributor Touch and Go had trouble printing copies of the album fast enough. According to Touch and Go's Ed Roche in *Our Noise*, "We sent out one hundred advance copies to mom and pop stores prior to that review, and across the board nobody really cared… And then, literally, that review hit within a few days of the release date, and within hours, everybody who had thought that the record was okay now thought it was the greatest record of all-time. And we sold out of everything immediately. There was no magic happening until that review happened, and then all of a sudden everybody reevaluated. *Pitchfork* was powerful enough to scare stores into making sure they had it; it just steamrolled after that."

Suddenly, Arcade Fire was the "it" band at that October's CMJ Festival in New York, playing a sold out showcase that attracted the attention of heavyweights like the *New York Times*, who wrote, "The debut Arcade Fire album, *Funeral*, was released barely a month ago, on Sept. 14, by the indie label Merge, based in North Carolina. Enthusiastic reviews were written, even more enthusiastic blog entries were posted, mp3s circulated. It used to take months of touring and record-shop hype for an underground band to build a cult, but now it takes only a few weeks. 'I'd like to thank the Internet,' Mr. Butler said, and he wasn't serious, but he also wasn't wrong… Even so, the seven members of the Arcade Fire managed to exceed all expectations." And the attention kept coming. The band was soon asked to share the stage with the likes of David Bowie and Bruce Springsteen, and then, in November of 2005, Arcade Fire was tapped to play three nights in a row opening for U2, just one year removed from playing small clubs in Montreal.

The ability of an independent magazine like *Pitchfork* to break a band on an indie label like Merge, without the help of a major label promotional campaign or the mainstream music press, was something altogether new. As John Cook pointed out in 2009's *Our Noise*, "The attention paid by *Pitchfork* and by regular folks' blogs turned the Arcade Fire into a hit before most people had heard [*Funeral*]. Overnight success is nothing new in the music business, but it is usually mandated by a deep-pocketed label's publicity campaign in concert with glossy magazines like *Spin* and *Rolling Stone*. Because *Pitchfork* is independent, as are most of the labels whose bands it reviews, the traditional corporate publicity machinery is totally short-circuited. A decade ago, a review of a Merge band in *Rolling Stone* would have been a coup; in 2004, no one even noticed when *Rolling Stone* played catch-up and reviewed *Funeral* (giving it four stars) in December, three months after *Pitchfork*." Within the blogosphere, three months was an *eternity*.

While indie labels like Merge worked within their limited means to sell as many records as possible, they still wanted to be able to put out music that they liked, and the fickle nature of what constituted commercial success was a generally perceived as a secondary concern. "You can put out the best record in the world, and it doesn't mean shit," said Merge co-founder Laura Ballance in *Our Noise*. "If the timing is wrong, or the right people don't notice it—I cannot explain what makes a record happen big. Not that it matters. I love putting out good records. And I don't care if it sells 500 copies or 250,000." It was the continuing focus on "good records" that set labels like Merge apart from the increasingly bottom line-oriented world of major labels. "I think it goes back to the amount of trust they put in their artists," said Merge artist M. Ward of his label in *Our Noise*. "They've been, and continue to be, in our shoes. And they understand that if you need a label executive to help you do what you're doing... then maybe you shouldn't be doing it... They rely on the strength of the music, not the strength of the marketability of somebody's face, or clothes. And I'm really happy to be working with people that have the faith that the public responds well to music that sparks their imagination, as opposed to bad publicity photos that spark the darker recesses of your mind."

At the same time, in the tradition of former Warner Brothers president Mo Ostin's assertion that following the artist would "lead you to the money," indie labels' trust in their artists was leading to greater and greater commercial success. Even in the midst of a decade-long downturn in music revenues—with international sales plummeting, big name retailers like Tower Records and Sam Goody going out of business, and major labels blaming mp3 file-sharing for their ills—Merge's Mac McCaughan was upbeat about his company's future at the 2007 Future of Music Coalition's annual policy summit. "Business is great for us," he told a room full of industry insiders. "The last few years have been our best ever. People may be buying fewer bad records, but I don't see them buying fewer good records." As McCaughan explained further in *Our Noise*:

> We've managed to create the business that works for the way we want to do business. Our customers are music fans. Even though we have some records that have sold a lot of copies, we've always seen ourselves as a niche brand. It may be a large niche at times, but at bottom, it's people who love music. And in the record industry, that is a niche. If you ask someone who works for Sony, 'Who do you want to sell records to?' They'll say they want to sell them to everyone who has access to a Best Buy. But for us—that's great if

those people want what we have. That's awesome and we want them to be able to get it. But we're not swinging for the fences in that way.

In other words, the commercial success of indie music had the potential to be sustainable. The most popular bands associated with the mid-2000s indie sensibility—Arcade Fire, Death Cab for Cutie, The Shins—had achieved, according to traditional measures, only modest commercial success. According to indie label standards, Arcade Fire's *Funeral* may have "steamrolled," but its roughly 400,000 sales between 2004 and 2009 was a far cry from the commercial ubiquity enjoyed by previous rock stars, for whom multi-platinum record sales had been commonplace. After all, *Funeral* had peaked at just #123 on the *Billboard* album charts, hardly a smash hit by traditional rock standards, and thus the album's success remained primarily an underground phenomenon. The same was true for other iconic indie acts like Death Cab for Cutie; their 2003 album *Transatlanticism* may have been a staple on college campuses, but its success didn't translate into mainstream sales in the same way that previous generations of rock acts had; much like *Funeral*, *Transatlanticism* peaked at just #97 on the *Billboard* 200.

By the middle of the 2000s, the indie scene had achieved an unlikely combination: artistic freedom, modest but potentially sustainable commercial success, and relative mainstream anonymity. It was an excellent situation for indie artists. The artistic freedom afforded by indie labels encouraged artists to follow their individual creative visions, while the modest commercial stakes minimized the distracting fantasy of world-conquering rock stardom. As a result, the coming years would see an explosion of diverse, artistically substantive rock acts who would come to rival the creative output of any previous era in rock history.

Indie's Golden Era

In the years immediately following the release of their debut album *Funeral*, Arcade Fire would prove to be more than just emblematic of a new industry paradigm; the band's ethos—what *Pitchfork*'s *Funeral* review described as "embracing honest emotion"—would become a prominent thread tying the loosely affiliated indie music scene together. While there were still indie bands and fans who would continue to champion the tossed-off ironic posturing assumed by acts from Pavement to Wavves, it would be a string of artistically substantive and emotionally candid indie acts—from Sufjan Stevens to Neko Case to Explosions in the Sky to Band of Horses to Feist to Fleet Foxes to The National to Bon Iver—who would resonate with an increasing range of listeners, expanding the indie scene's horizons even as the music itself continued to defy stylistic categorization.

Singer-songwriter Sufjan Stevens embodied, perhaps more than any other indie artist of the era, the wide range of sonic approaches and textures that would come to fall under the "indie" umbrella during the 2000s. The Brooklyn-by-way-of-Michigan native's 2000 debut *A Sun Came*, self-released on his own Asthmatic Kitty label, wrapped eclectic ethnic influences and instrumentation—banjo, sitar, oboe, etc.—into something approximating a traditional folk album. His follow-up, 2001's *Enjoy Your Rabbit*, was an indulgent, experimental song-cycle based on the animals of the Chinese zodiac, which incorporated everything from 70s funk to traditional folk influences, all packaged in an expansive, electronic music-based sheen. For his next album, 2003's *Michigan*, Stevens settled into a more straight-forward songwriting approach, yet through the continued use of unique arrangements—plucking banjos, muted horns, choral backing vocals—he began defining a musical style that sounded more like a truly distinctive creative voice than just a scattered jumble of eclectic influences.

It was *Michigan*'s mythological promise, however, that most distinguished the album from its contemporaries in the growing indie music scene. At the time of its release, Stevens announced his intention to embark on a "50 States Project," through which he would write an album for each of the 50 American states, sparking listeners' enthusiasm about the prospect of one of the era's most promising songwriters making their particular state the subject of his next musical offering. *Michigan*'s geographical mythology also served as a platform by which Stevens could use the everyday minutiae of his home state to tap into his own personal experiences in an exploration of themes as various as childhood, poverty, spirituality, and urban social decay. The fifteen-track offering (twenty-one including the vinyl-only bonus tracks) was an ambitious undertaking, and though the self-released album would fail to crack the mainstream consciousness, it did attract the attention of *Pitchfork*, who gave the album an 8.5/10.0 "Best New Music" rating, concluding approvingly that,

"The record is stacked with impressive space for Stevens' shimmering geography, and it manages a melancholy beauty; *Michigan* is a frost-bound tone poem in which average people live out their victories and defeats with a shadowy, dignified grace." *Pitchfork*'s stamp of approval helped Stevens reach the growing underground network of indie music listeners for the first time; as *Stereogum* pointed out in an article marking the 10th anniversary of *Michigan*'s release, "[Stevens had] already released two albums before 2003, but barely anybody heard them."

2004's *Seven Swans* found Stevens scaling back the instrumentation even further, utilizing the intimacy of his least frenetic album yet to delve into a candid exploration his own spirituality. And it was a testament to Stevens' subtle artistry that an album which openly embraced his Christian faith and liberally quoted the Bible was able to avoid the dreaded "Christian music" stereotype and maintain Stevens' momentum within the predominantly secular indie music scene. *Pitchfork* awarded *Seven Swans* with a second consecutive "Best New Music" tag. And, as *Stereogum*'s Chris DeVille would later write, "Here was a guy who could earnestly pour out his heart to God without sounding like a desperately trite worship leader. People outside the Christian rock ghetto took [Stevens] seriously—as they should—and not because Sufjan toned down his faith to court a wider audience like so many youth group favorites desperate for a hit ('sup, Switchfoot?), but because those beliefs inspired such deeply human music... [His] tales of grappling with real-life problems still resonate whether you agree with Sufjan's solutions or not. Amen to that."

But the promise of both *Michigan* and *Seven Swans* still failed to anticipate the phenomenon that Stevens' next release—2005's *Illinois*—would become. *Pitchfork* gave the second installment of the "50 States Project" a glowing 9.2/10.0 rating, raving that, "in both theory and execution, *Illinois* is huge, a staggering collection of impeccably arranged American tribute songs." The album would go on to become, according to the aggregator *Metacritic*, the most critically-acclaimed album of the year. *Illinois* finds a supremely confident Stevens reveling in his diverse influences and unique musical sensibilities, meticulously tying them together into an anthemic, quirky modern-day opus. The playful verbosity of the songs' titles—which included such gems as "A Short Reprise for Mary Todd, Who Went Insane, but for Very Good Reasons" and "Out of Egypt, into the Great Laugh of Mankind, and I

Shake the Dirt from My Sandals as I Run"—were counterbalanced by the hushed, spare intimacy which characterized the album's lyrics as they swerved through subjects as various as childhood death, coming-of-age road trips, and even the notorious serial killer John Wayne Gacy, Jr. *Illinois'* ambitions were so all-encompassing that the whole project could have veered into incoherence if not for Stevens' single-minded vision, which tied the various moods and themes of the album into a listening experience that transcended the sum of its parts, expanding the mythology *Michigan* had established and creating expectations that would prove hard for Stevens himself to live up to in the coming years. But for the time being, *Illinois'* twenty-two tracks—especially when augmented by the twenty-one "outtakes and extras" released in 2006 as *The Avalanche*—were more than enough to satiate Stevens' growing fan base.

While Stevens' fan base was indeed growing, the fact that *Illinois* qualified as a "phenomenon" illustrated the continuing niche orientation of the indie scene. In a year which saw Mariah Carey and 50 Cent each sell 5 million copies of their new albums, Stevens' *Illinois*—like Arcade Fire's *Funeral* before it—would fail to achieve even gold record status, selling just 73,000 copies by the end of the year and stalling at #121 on the *Billboard* 200 album chart. And the fact that the year's most critically celebrated album would achieve such modest sales demonstrated the continuing commercial power of major label marketing campaigns relative to even the most universal underground critical consensus. Nevertheless, the modest commercial success albums like *Funeral* and *Illinois* had attained was more than enough to sustain a career, especially for an artist like Stevens, whose own Asthmatic Kitty record label allowed him to keep a far greater share of sales revenues than artists who recorded for major labels.

Much like fellow Brooklyn resident Sufjan Stevens' Asthmatic Kitty imprint, Aaron and Bryce Dessner (along with friend Alec Hanley Bemis) founded Brassland Records in 2001 in order to release the music of their own band, The National. Though founded in Brooklyn, The National's roots were in Cincinnati, Ohio, where the Dessner twins had been childhood friends with brothers Bryan and Scott Devendorf, who had played in a college band with fellow Cincinnatian Matt Berninger. Once they had all relocated to Brooklyn, Berninger and the two pairs of brothers formed The National, whose self-titled debut album became Brassland's first official release in October of 2001. *The National* was a promising, if uneven debut, straddling the line between alt-country and indie-punk over its 12 self-produced tracks. Their follow-up, 2003's *Sad Songs for Dirty Lovers*, continued to refine the band's sound—earning an impressive 8.4/10.0 rating at *Pitchfork*—but it was their third album, 2005's *Alligator*, that would resonate within the growing underground consciousness.

Prior to recording *Alligator*, The National had signed to veteran indie label Beggars Banquet (though Bemis and the Dessners would continue to keep Brassland active), guaranteeing the band wider promotion and distribution than tiny Brassland had yet been able to muster. And the album solidified what would become the band's distinctive combination of meticulously layered sonic songcraft and almost awkwardly confessional lyrics. Though *Alligator* failed to reach the *Billboard* 200 album chart, it slowly found a widespread listenership, generating a swell of underground anticipation for the band's 2007 release *Boxer*, which would become their critical and commercial breakthrough. Musically, *Boxer* dialed back *Alligator*'s occasional freneticism, slowing the pace in order to create its own self-enclosed world in which the slightest vocal tic, the most delicate guitar riff, the most subtle rhythm was suddenly recognizable and imbued with the optimum meaning and significance (an approach which their subsequent album, 2010's *High Violet*, would come scarily close to perfecting). The musical maturation evident on *Boxer* would land the album on dozens of year-end "Best of 2007" lists, generating enough interest for the album to peak at #68 on the *Billboard* 200. *Pitchfork*'s "Best New Music" review gushed, "These songs reveal themselves gradually but surely, building to the inevitable moment when they hit you in the gut. It's the rare album that gives back whatever you put into it." *Paste* magazine was even more enthusiastic, naming *Boxer* the best album of 2007. And *Rolling Stone*, late to the game as usual, finally gave the band a proper review, approvingly slapping *Boxer* with a 4-Star rating. By that time, The National, like fellow indie acts Arcade Fire and Sufjan Stevens, had already managed to build a sustainable career almost completely below the mainstream radar.

During the second half of the 2000s, while the mainstream music industry continued to see drastic declines in sales and revenue, the stories of modest but notable commercial success achieved by acts like Arcade Fire, Sufjan Stevens, and The National started to become commonplace for artistically substantive acts from across the indie spectrum. And in 2007-2008, a string of critically-acclaimed albums released on independent labels would reach the *Billboard* 200 while still managing to remain primarily cult phenomena: Arcade Fire's much anticipated follow-up *Neon Bible*, the more straightforward indie-rock of Band of Horses' *Cease to Begin*, the eclectic folk of Neko Case's *Fox Confessor Brings the Flood*, the expansive instrumental soundscapes of Explosions in the Sky's *All of a Sudden I Miss Everyone*, the Beach Boys-influenced harmonies of Fleet Foxes' self-titled debut, the sultry lyricism of Feist's *The Reminder*, the log cabin-recorded intimacy of Bon Iver's *For Emma, Forever Ago*, the catchy, syncopated world music homage of Vampire Weekend's self-titled debut. While none of these albums would achieve gold record status—which had traditionally been the baseline measure of a rock album's commercial success—they were able to reach an audience that would have been inconceivable for indie acts just a few years earlier. Thanks in part to the internet-based advocacy of a flowering underground infrastructure, the indie scene was, according to its own modest aspirations, a thriving enterprise. And for fans of substantive rock music who were willing to venture outside the mainstream, the second half of the 2000s was something approaching the "golden age of music" that Sean Parker had hoped Napster would spawn. Even an archetypal rock traditionalist like Nick Hornby—who had once disparaged Radiohead's trend-setting artistry and had repeatedly expressed skepticism of the mp3 generation—had been won over. In a 2009 *Guardian* article Hornby boldly proclaimed:

> I don't know how it will all pan out, who will pay the artists to make their lovely or ugly or scary music in a world that's increasingly beginning to expect everything for free… All I know is that if you love music, and you have a curious mind, there has never been a better time to be alive.

Chapter Seventeen

Commerce Strikes Back

Max Martin, American Idol, and the Commercial Marginalization of Art

The Continuing Consolidation of Popular Music

As the first decade of the new millennium came to a close, indie music was continuing to achieve modest commercial gains. And in the midst of a music industry whose overall sales had dropped every year from 2004-2010, albums released by indie artists were claiming higher and higher slots on the *Billboard* charts, almost by default. In 2010 alone, Sufjan Stevens' much anticipated album *The Age of Adz* debuted at #7 on the *Billboard* 200 album chart, Band of Horses' *Infinite Arms* likewise hit #7, The National's *High Violet* made it to #3, and Vampire Weekend's *Contra* and Arcade Fire's *The Suburbs* both went all the way to #1. However, the impressive chart numbers belied the extent to which indie music remained a niche market; none of the aforementioned albums managed to go platinum, and music released on indie labels still accounted for just 12% of overall album sales in 2010. In fact, when the sales numbers were tallied for 2000-2010, not a single act on an indie label made *Billboard*'s decade-end list of the top 50 selling acts. Even though independent labels had carved out a modest commercial niche for themselves in the 2000s, major labels still dominated the commercial landscape.

Meanwhile, the consolidation and corporatization of the mainstream music industry which had typified the 1990s continued at breakneck speed into the new millennium. Polygram Records—whose roots in the historic Decca Records label stretched all the way back to recorded music's 1920s infancy—was purchased by the Universal Music Group in 1999, reducing the number of major labels from six to five. Then in 2004, major label BMG—whose roots in industry innovator RCA likewise stretched back to the 20s—was absorbed by Sony, leaving just four majors. And in 2012, EMI's assets—including its venerable American arm Capitol Records—were split up and sold to Universal and Sony, leaving just three major record labels: Universal, Sony, and Warner Brothers. But by that time, the distinctions between the major labels had become essentially immaterial, at least as they pertained to the creation of popular music. Over the first decade of the new millennium, an increased focus on market research and a growing reliance on just a handful of professional songwriters had turned the major labels into largely indistinguishable dispensers of commercial product.

During the 2000s, major labels continued to move away from signing and promoting rock acts; *Billboard*'s decade-end Top 50 contained just *six* rock acts (none of whom—Nickelback, Creed, Linkin Park, Three Doors Down, Santana, and Matchbox Twenty—were exactly paragons of artistic substance). And the continuing move away from rock music was increasingly freeing the major labels from having to follow and promote the creative visions of individual artists, allowing them to rely on a smaller and smaller group of industry insiders to craft the songs which they would release. As a result, the vast majority of the hit songs of the 2000s would be written by a remarkably small cadre of writer/producers, leading to such a complete homogenization of mainstream popular music that the traditional boundaries between popular music genres would begin to disappear altogether.

Popular songwriters who wrote in multiple genres for multiple labels weren't a new 21st Century phenomenon. For instance, popular songwriter Desmond Child got his start all the way back in the early 1980s as a "song doctor" for creatively challenged rock acts, co-writing hits for Kiss, Aerosmith, and Bon Jovi (including the latter's #1 hit "Livin' on a Prayer") before moving on to write hits for non-rock acts like Cher, Michael Bolton, Hansen, and Ricky Martin (including Martin's mega-hit "Livin' la Vida Loca"). Over roughly the same period, the similarly prolific songwriter Diane Warren wrote huge hits for acts as various as the rock band Starship ("Nothing's Gonna Stop Us Now"), pop singer Celine Dion ("Because You Loved Me"), country singer LeAnn Rimes ("How Do I Live"), R&B singer Toni Braxton ("Un-break My Heart"), the rock band Aerosmith ("I Don't Want to Miss a Thing"), and country diva Faith Hill ("There You'll Be").

But the extent to which the major labels would come to rely on a small cadre of professional songwriters in the 2000s was something altogether new. During the first decade of the new millennium, writer/producers like Christopher "Tricky" Stewart (who co-wrote songs for Rihanna, Katy Perry, Mariah Carey, Jennifer Lopez, Britney Spears, Beyoncé, Snoop Dogg, and Justin Bieber, among many others), "Dr." Luke Gottwald (Ke$ha, Britney Spears, Flo Rida, Katy Perry, Adam Lambert, Miley Cyrus, Pink, Kelly Clarkson, Avril Lavigne), and John Shanks (Michelle Branch, Sheryl Crow, Keith Urban, Hilary Duff, Ashlee Simpson, Santana, Bon Jovi, Jewel, Miley Cyrus, Goo Goo Dolls) had their fingerprints on so many hit singles in so many different genres that they became difficult to keep track of, resulting in striking musical and lyrical similarities between songs from across the shrinking spectrum of popular genres (for instance, the uncanny sonic similarities between Ke$ha's 2009 hit "Tik Tok" and Katy Perry's 2010 hit "California Gurls"—which resulted in countless deprecating YouTube mash-ups of the two songs—could be traced to writer/producer "Dr." Luke Gottwald's participation in the creation of both).

Perhaps the most influential pop figure of the era, however, was Swedish writer/producer Max Martin. Following a decade-long stint in the Swedish glam metal band It's Alive, Martin turned his attention to songwriting and production in the 1990s, earning his first notable production credits on Swedish pop group Ace of Base's sophomore album before landing a gig as a writer/producer for the boy band Backstreet Boys in 1995. Martin would go on to write and produce a string of hit singles for the group, including all of the singles from the band's multi-platinum 1999 release *Millennium*. He would also help put Britney Spears on the map, writing and producing Spears' 1999 breakthrough hit "…Baby One More Time" and many of her other early singles, including "Oops!...I Did it Again," "Stronger," and "I'm Not a Girl, Not Yet a Woman." During the same period, Martin would also co-write hits for 'N Sync and Celine Dion, solidifying his place as pop music's leading songwriter and producer. And his scope of influence would only increase in the new millennium. In 2004, Martin began working with fellow writer/producer "Dr." Luke Gottwald on Kelly Clarkson's sophomore album *Breakaway*, and their collaboration on Clarkson's chart-topping single "Since U Been Gone" would commence a commercially potent partnership. Through their work with Clarkson, Pink, Avril Lavigne, Katy Perry, Britney Spears, Christina Aguilera, and Ke$ha, Martin and Gottwald would almost single-handedly codify the sassy, sexy "bad-girl" template that would come to dominate the pop music landscape.

The increased reliance of the major labels on such a tiny group of songwriting insiders inevitably resulted in a flattening of the scope of mainstream music. The criticisms leveled against pop music's formulaic tendencies were typified by Greg Kot's review of Katy Perry's 2010 album *Teenage Dream*. "The Frankenstein-like productions—the latest gleaming assembly-line product by usual suspects Dr. Luke, Max Martin, Tricky Stewart, and StarGate, among others—sap the music of personality, presence, surprise," wrote Kot for the *Chicago Tribune*. "There's nothing subversive about *Teenage Dream*. Perry's notion about how teenage girls behave—or what they want from their pop music—is pretty depressing. It shares a lot in common with the major label executive who once said he signed Britney Spears so he could market her not just to the overdriven libidos of adolescents but to the dirty imaginations of older men. In Katy World, teens spend 'Last Friday Night' this way: drinking shots, streaking, skinny-dipping, breaking unnamed laws, engaging in three-way sex and then passing out, determined to do it again next week. 'Peacock' repurposes the beat from Toni Basil's 'Hey Mickey' into a naughty metaphor that barely qualifies as an off-color joke, let alone a song... With music as rigidly formulaic as this, no wonder the teens in her songs want to party until they blank out."

And because the era's most prolific songwriters wrote songs across genres—pop, rock, country, hip hop—the unique characteristics of the genres themselves were beginning to disappear. By the end of 2013, *Grantland*'s Steven Hyden was able to say:

> In 10 years, all pop music genre classifications will be obsolete. I feel 100 percent confident in predicting this. The only reason I'm reluctant to state this belief publicly is that it almost seems self-evident... I'm sure there will still be 'rock' music and 'country' music and 'rap' music in 2023. I just don't

think there will be discernible musical differences between them (at least when it comes to the most commercial versions of those genres). The only way people will be able to distinguish between different kinds of artists is by the types of hats and pants they wear. If any aspect of what I've theorized proves to be incorrect, I suspect it will be the part about the process taking 10 years. In fact, it's possible that I haven't really 'predicted' anything—there's plenty of evidence to suggest that what I've described has already happened. A cursory survey of contemporary hits supports the idea that all forms of pop music now sound like all forms of pop music.

The Power of American Idol

Given the industry-wide consolidations of the 1990s and 2000s, it was hardly surprising that the mainstream pop music of the new millennium was displaying an unprecedented level of homogeneity. What *was* surprising was the way that more and more mainstream music critics were buying into the flawed logic of "poptimism" in order to defend the increasingly monotonous pop music emanating from the corporate major label machine, often at the expense of the burgeoning indie music scene. And what was even more surprising was that the primary catalyst for the critical legitimization of blatantly commercial pop music would be a major TV network reality-singing competition.

On June 11, 2002, *American Idol* made its television debut, inaugurating a decade-long run of ratings dominance; for eight consecutive years, from 2003-2011, the show would rank #1 in U.S. television ratings, the longest run of any show in American television history. In addition, the show's runaway success would spawn a long line of commercially successful performers. Season 1 winner Kelly Clarkson's debut album *Thankful* debuted at #1 on the *Billboard* 200 album chart in 2003, paving the way for the platinum-selling success of future *Idol* contestants like Clay Aiken, Carrie Underwood, Jennifer Hudson, Chris Daughtry, and Adam Lambert. In 2012, *Billboard* determined that *American Idol* alumni had notched an astounding *three hundred and forty-five* #1 songs and albums on its various charts since the show's 2002 debut.

Thanks to all of the contestants' exclusive contracts with *Idol*-affiliated management company 19 Management, the *American Idol* franchise profited from each successive hit song and artist. And the show's countless commercial tie-ins—which included the successful "Karaoke Revolution" video game series and Disney World's "The American Idol Experience" attraction—helped turn the *American Idol* franchise into a multi-billion dollar corporate empire by the end of its first decade.

While *American Idol*'s staggering commercial success was indisputable, initial reactions to the show's artistic merits were more dismissive. Shortly after *Idol*'s 2002 debut, *Entertainment Weekly*'s Ken Tucker surmised that, "As TV, *American Idol* is crazily entertaining; as music, it's dust-mote inconsequential. Whoever survives the show's grueling winnowing-down process will doubtless be so eager to sell out, his or her recording debut will likely be another piece of corporate product." The *Chicago Sun-Times* likewise dismissed the show as a "giant karaoke contest." And music historian Michael Feinstein argued in *USA Today* that "*American Idol* isn't really about music. It's about all the bad aspects of the music business—the arrogance of commerce, this sense of 'I know what will make this person a star; artists themselves don't know.'" Feinstein's observation was particularly prescient, in that the show was nothing if not a celebration of the age-old industry artist development model, where artists were signed according to their voice and/or look and then an all-powerful major label would provide songs for them to perform and record, songs which had been written by professional songwriters according to tried and true commercially successful formulas. In addition, *Idol* enhanced the industry's growing reliance on market research; each *American Idol* episode essentially *was* market research, skipping the middle-man and allowing audience preferences to determine which artists *Idol*'s major label partners would sell back to them. From a strictly commercial point of view, it was a stunningly efficient process, but it was also a complete subversion of the rock era's trust in the independent creative visions of individual artists.

Slowly but surely, however, the normalizing ubiquity of *American Idol* would prove powerful enough to start changing the critical consensus about the show's artistic merits. "At a certain point, whether it's respectable or not, it just becomes undeniable," said music journalist Alan Light in a 2007 *Today* article titled "*American Idol*'s Music Cred Growing." In 2010, the *New York Times* published an article titled "Worshipping at the 'Idol' Church" in which critic Michael Slezak would unabashedly say, "Make no mistake: I'm not one of those *Idol* watchers who labels my enjoyment of the show as 'ironic' or protects my cool factor by passing it off as a guilty pleasure. Because for all its bloated, synthetic, product-shilling, money-making trappings, *Idol* provides a once-a-year chance for the average American to combat the evils of today's music business. Every time a major label tries to convince us it's a good idea to buy a pricey concert ticket to listen to an amplified backing track give voice to a glassy-eyed Britney Spears, *Idol* counters by introducing us to Carrie Underwood, the country diva whose M16 instrument obliterates the notion that major-label acts—especially the pretty blond ones—can't get the job done without Auto-Tune." The fact that a *New York Times* piece could paint the *American Idol*-bred and major label-promoted Underwood—who recorded for the very same major label as Spears (Sony)—as the cure for the "evils of today's music business" was symbolic of the extent to which *Idol* had re-legitimized the purely commercial top-down paradigm for music creation which had, up until recently, been marginalized by decades of major label trust in artistically independent rock artists.

By 2012, NPR's leading music critic Ann Powers—who described herself an "unashamed enthusiast" for *Idol*—was able argue that the show had "reshaped the American songbook... lend[ing] legitimacy to music previously dismissed as less than canonical. In a world dominated by *Idol*, the glitz of Queen makes a stronger impression than the grit of The Rolling Stones; craftsmen like Phil Collins count for as much as do visionaries like Stevie Wonder, and the interpretive art of selling a song again finds equal footing next to the introspective act of writing one." According to Powers, these weren't negative changes, but rather the vanguard of "a new way of viewing ourselves in relationship to mainstream popular culture... Because it was structured as a 'journey' for contestants whose interactions with the judges and others—stylists, celebrity mentors, the band—helped them focus a gift and turn it into a product, this updated version of the star search felt less like the kiss of a fairy godmother (or cranky Simon Cowell-esque godfather) and more like the reward for contestant's entrepreneurship."

Powers' choice of words—by which songs were "sold," musical gifts were turned into "products," and performers were rewarded for their "entrepreneurship"—was a telling indicator of the way mainstream music criticism was coming to use *commercial* terminology in order to assess *artistic* merit. This attitude was indicative of a decade during which the most revered public figures were not artists or politicians or athletes, but rather "visionary" corporate moguls like Microsoft's Bill Gates, Apple's Steve Jobs, Google's Larry Page, and Facebook's Mark Zuckerberg. Even those in other fields were increasingly being judged according to commercial measures; just as the singers on *American Idol* were judged according to their entrepreneurial skills, athletes like LeBron James and actors like Tom Cruise were being assessed according to how well they cultivated their "personal brands." And so it wasn't surprising that the acceptance of commercial terminology as a legitimate judge of artistic merit was starting to extend beyond the world of *American Idol* and into mainstream music criticism at large.

A Changing Critical Climate

Back in 1988, *Rolling Stone*'s Michael Azerrad had written that Bon Jovi's album *New Jersey* was "so purely commercial that it's practically beyond criticism (it would be more appropriate to evaluate its sales potential)." But by the second decade of the new millennium, evaluating an artist or album's "sales potential" had become one of the primary features of music criticism. Where previous generations of critics had pointed out and derided music industry "hype campaigns," such campaigns were now an accepted part of the popular music landscape, and part of a critic's job was to determine how effective such campaigns had been. For instance, the critical response to Taylor Swift's chart-topping 2012 release *Red* was almost singularly focused on Swift's commercial marketing acumen rather than the artistic substance of her music (or lack thereof). Jon Caramanica's complimentary *New York Times* review said that, "She is showing maturity less as an adult—though there is some of that—than as a strategist," praising Swift's savvy ability to "carve new territory: a nontransgressive, rose-colored female pop megastar, the likes of which haven't been seen in decades." *Grantland*'s Steven Hyden similarly praised Swift's ability to be "so preternaturally wise about making songs that are so good at being so popular," while paying far less attention to the traditional critical function of assessing whether or not her songs were simply "good." In fact, Hyden's review was so singularly focused on the phenomenon of "Taylor Swift: Commercial Brand" that the more traditional artistic assessments of the album tacked on at the end of the review seemed almost jarringly out of place.

The focus on Swift's savvy commercial acumen allowed respected mainstream media outlets like NPR and the *New York Times* (who would name *Red* 2012's second-best album of the year) to take her seriously as an artist, even though her music itself rarely ventured beyond the world of formulaic truisms intended for adolescents. In a rare dissent from the critical status quo, Swift's hometown *Nashville Scene* pointed out this incongruity in a review of the country-pop diva's September 2013 concert at Nashville's Bridgestone Arena:

> Swift is very aware that she's talking to kids a lot of the time. During her between-song banter with the crowd (which went on forever ever ever), she said things like 'When I was writing songs and thinking about feelings,' and 'I compare things to things, in analogies,' and 'These are what I call the crazy emotions.' She said that colors can also represent emotions (hence 'Red'), as if that weren't a fundamental concept in all human societies. She said 'We're never going to figure out love.' She was like the narrator of a 'Learning 2 Feel' CD-ROM.... Look, we get it. It's music for kids. It's emotions for beginners. We love that kind of stuff, and every generation of girls needs its hands held as it enters the weird world of adolescent sexuality. There is nothing wrong with that. It's a necessary part of pop culture. But Taylor Swift, for whatever reason, is given accolades from the wider adult world, and it's weird. David Cassidy didn't spend his career winning armfuls of Grammys. The romantic life of Debbie Gibson did not leak out of *Tiger Beat* and into *Time*.

Even on the rare occasions when mainstream critics actually stopped to consider *Red*'s artistic merits, they tended to completely ignore the implications of the corporate commercial realities involved in the music's creation. For instance, not a single major review of *Red* bothered to ask whether Swift's decision to collaborate with the formulaic hit-maker Max Martin on the album's lead singles "We Are Never Ever Getting Back Together" and "I Knew You Were Trouble" might have any compromising effect on the quality or authenticity of her art. Caramanica's *New York Times* review stated flatly that "Ms. Swift's work with the pop-production technicians Max Martin and Shellback [was] the clear choice for any singer looking for a loud pop splash." *Grantland*'s Hyden was similarly nonplussed by the choice of Martin, whom, he adds in his review of *Red*, "brings some Kelly Clarkson–goes–Skrillex mojo" to the album. And NPR's Ann Powers went so far as to argue that the Swift/Martin collaboration "We Are Never Ever Getting Back Together" established Swift as the new "Princess of Punk," tracing the song's roots to female punk pioneers Patti Smith and Blondie's Debbie Harry without stopping to consider whether Martin's involvement—with his recent string of similarly-themed songs for artists like Kelly Clarkson, Pink, Avril Lavigne, Britney Spears, Katy Perry, and Ke$ha—might more accurately place the song's thematic content in an entirely different tradition: the calculated co-option of formerly subversive themes as "brand identities" to be peddled by the mainstream corporate machine. While this latter tradition had a long history of *commercial* success—one that *Red*'s multi-platinum sales would continue—its *artistic* implications were far less rosy.

Nevertheless, by 2012 the vast majority of music critics were displaying an unquestioning acceptance of pop music's commercial aspirations, even as the system giving birth to the music was becoming more and more corporatized, commercialized, and homogenized. One telling example of the ongoing critical shift was the evolving critical response to Ke$ha, one of the many female pop singers who relied heavily on the writing/production duo of Max Martin and "Dr." Luke Gottwald and their hedonistic bad-girl formula. Ke$ha's 2010 debut *Animal* had been one of the most widely panned albums of the year, accumulating a paltry score of 54 on *Metacritic*'s review aggregator. "It's hard to remember the last time an album so flat and vacuous generated such a buzz," said James Reed in a *Boston Globe* review that was representative of the mainstream critical consensus. "That dollar sign in Ke$ha's name tells you everything you need to know about her debut, *Animal*, a shallow hodgepodge of 2009's tried-and-true formulas... Even though Ke$ha supposedly co-wrote all of these songs, her personality is completely missing from them. Reaching for attitude, she ends up sounding vapid and faceless, as if she doesn't even believe what she's singing."

But by the time Ke$ha released her follow-up album *Warrior* in 2012—for which the singer would again collaborate with Martin and Gottwald— the climate had already changed enough for the album to be met with more critical acclaim than dismissal (*Warrior* would notch a respectable score of 71 on *Metacritic*'s aggregator, a huge leap from *Animal*'s 54), even though it stuck to exactly the same tried-and-true Martin/Gottwald formulas which the team had employed on Ke$ha's debut. Veteran critic Simon

Reynolds set the tone for the critical shift in a serious-minded *New York Times* review, arguing that *Warrior* "caught the mood of embattled hedonism in post-crash America." Rather than connecting the dots between *Warrior*'s lyrical and musical themes and Martin and Gottwald's long line of startlingly similar work, Reynolds instead focused on the fact that Ke$ha "jointly writes her songs, supplying the lyrics and most of the vocal melodies," concluding that her hedonistic bad-girl persona "is her own creation." Reynolds' insistence on the independence of Ke$ha's creative voice was undercut, however, later in his own article. "'I went in [to the recording sessions for *Warrior*] really wanting to destroy with guitars,' [Ke$ha] recalled. But then she and her principal producer, Dr. Luke [Gottwald], had a sit-down. 'Luke said, 'If you want to be on pop radio, really what's dominating right now is dance.'" Not surprisingly, Ke$ha's guitar album idea was scrapped in favor of a dance sound that echoed virtually all of Martin and Gottwald's recent work. "[Ke$ha] wants to write uncompromising music that she loves," Gottwald tells Reynolds later in the article. "But at the same time she wants to have huge hits." And Reynolds lets the quote stand without raising the possibility that there might be any hint of conflict between the two goals.

Over at the popular website *Grantland*, Steven Hyden's praise for *Warrior* was even more effusive. Hyden begins his review with a nod to the legitimizing power of Reynolds' assessment in the *New York Times*. "Ke$ha is not only a crazy motherfucker," trumpets Hyden, "but according to the paper of record, she's also a crazy motherfucking spokesperson for a generation. As an early adopter [of Ke$ha], I find this gratifying." According to Hyden, "[Ke$ha] represents what pop music can deliver in its purest, most puerile form, which is pleasure outside the normal confines of taste, decorum, or 'goodness.'" Given pop music's preceding decade, Hyden's assessment was baffling. Not only was *Warrior*'s hedonistic "party like there's no tomorrow" ethos well within the confines of mainstream pop normality, its chillingly pure distillation of the Martin/Gottwald formula which had dominated pop music for the previous decade was the very *definition* of mainstream normality. The idea that *Warrior*—which was co-written with the tiny uber-establishment cadre of pop hit-makers, echoed both the canned lyrical themes and pervasive musical styles that dominated the pop charts, and was released and promoted to death by one of the three remaining corporate major labels—was somehow *subversive* or *anti-establishment* was laughable. Ke$ha's *Warrior* was the embodiment of the homogenized establishment status quo.

Ironically, Ke$ha's *Warrior* ended up being a commercial disappointment, selling just 300,000 copies despite the best efforts of its creators and corporate major label advocates. And in that sense, it was symbolic of the era. Even the most commercially-driven formulas crafted by writer/producers like Max Martin and Luke Gottwald hadn't been able to stem a growing tide of music industry losses. After averaging roughly a billion sales annually from 1994-99, American album sales had plummeted all the way down to 317 million in 2012, with annual worldwide industry revenues falling from a high of nearly $27 billion in 1999 to just $14 billion in 2012. While mp3s and file-sharing were commonly cited as scapegoats for the industry's widely publicized woes, the rising commercial fortunes of indie labels over the same period suggested that file-sharing wasn't the sole determining factor in the mainstream industry's rapid decline. Perhaps the major labels' abandonment of Mo Ostin's pragmatic trust in the creative visions of individual artists (which had led to three decades of steady growth in both sales and revenues) in favor of market research-driven formulas (which had coincided with a decade of unprecedented declines) hadn't been the best business decision. Maybe the record buying public could tell the difference between individual creative visions and homogenized corporate product after all.

Indie Backlash

Meanwhile, mainstream criticism's increasing advocacy of blatantly commercial pop music was beginning to lead to a backlash against indie music's countercultural tendencies. In an *Onion A.V. Club* article titled "The Winners' History of Rock and Roll" (which he would parlay into a sprawling, seven-part series for the pop culture website *Grantland* in 2013), critic Steven Hyden argued that, "Rock history, unlike regular history, is written by the losers. I define losers as people who liked music that wasn't popular in the mainstream, and had very little impact on pop culture at large... Because rock writers tend to love 'loser' music—punk, indie rock, alt-country, 'conscious' hip-hop, dance music that goes on forever without a hook—'loser' music is what gets remembered as history." According to Hyden, the rock narrative that had been constructed by "elitist" rock critics focused on "insurgents"—typified by countercultural elder statesmen like The Velvet Underground and modern-day indie bands like Arcade Fire—while "the rich and famous rulers of middle-of-the-road rock and roll are disregarded or flat-out ignored." For Hyden, this state of events necessitated an entirely new rock narrative which would eschew the artistic prejudices of the critical establishment in order to extend critical legitimacy to the multi-platinum rock acts—Led Zeppelin, Kiss, Bon Jovi, Metallica, Linkin Park, etc.—whose commercial exploits, in Hyden's view, reflected the will of the masses. In other words, the story of rock was best told through its "populist" commercial history rather than its "elitist" artistic history.

At its core, Hyden's "Winners' History" idea was essentially the same "poptimist" argument Carl Wilson had employed in his book *Let's Talk About Love*, which had argued that a critical reassessment of Celine Dion's music was necessary simply because she had sold millions of albums. And like Wilson's book, the primary flaw in Hyden's thesis was the assumption that commercial success in popular music was based on the "choice" of the populist masses rather than the multi-billion dollar marketing clout of the corporate major labels. For instance, in his "Winners' History of Rock and Roll" series, Hyden contrasts the 600,000 sales of Arcade Fire's 2010 album *The Suburbs* with the 3.9 million sales of Eminem's 2010 album *Recovery* in order to illustrate the "populist" appeal of the latter in relation to the former. But his comparison fails to take into account the fact that Arcade Fire's label Merge was a tiny company which averaged less than $2 million in annual revenue and was operated by a dozen employees, while Eminem's label Interscope was a subsidiary of Universal Music Group, which had 7,000 employees, generated $6 *billion* in annual revenue, and routinely spent more than Merge's entire annual budget in order to promote individual albums by its most popular artists like Eminem. In light of this reality, painting Arcade Fire's champions as "elitists" and Eminem's champions as "populists" would require swapping the very meanings of the terms "elitist" and "populist," a fact Hyden seems to acknowledge within the "Winners' History" series itself. "I stole this idea from Howard Zinn's *A People's History of the United States*," he says in a footnote. "Though I might've flipped the power structure."

As it happened, "flipping the power structure" was becoming a common theme in music criticism. For much of its history, rock criticism had championed the artistically adventurous rock music created by the outcasts, freaks, and underdogs who existed at the marginalized fringes of the mainstream—the 60s counterculture, the punk movement, the alternative scene, the indie scene—while simultaneously providing an independent outpost from which the mainstream commercial power structure could be openly criticized. But Hyden's advocacy of those within the commercial power structure and his bullying designation of those on the cultural fringes as "losers" was representative of an increasingly "poptimist" critical climate in which underground musicians were fair game for critical disparagement while the music being churned out by the corporate industry establishment was granted critical immunity because of its ostensibly "populist" commercial ubiquity.

A perfect example of this phenomenon was critic Carl Wilson's May 2013 article for *Slate*, in which he expresses his approval of poptimism's requirement that commercial pop music be granted critical immunity. "I have been a cheerleader for this shift to 'poptimism,'" he writes. "I've even written a whole book about why it matters not to be contemptuous of, say, Celine Dion." And by 2013, poptimism's chokehold on music criticism was so complete that Wilson could warn, "Dump on Kanye or Ke$ha or Justin Bieber and watch how quickly we critics will come back at you." However, Wilson concedes that, "In the end, it simply seems too repressive and stultifying to demand that we give up entirely on the fundamental pop pleasure of *taking a side*." And so Wilson argues that music fans should take a side—*against indie music*. The article, which is titled "Why I Hate The National: And How I Decided It's OK to Hate the Bands I Hate," goes on to attack what Wilson calls The National's "monotonous" lack of "eccentricity," which he characterizes as sounding like "thoughtful decision-making by a talented committee of professionals." Over the course of the article, Wilson insists on extrapolating his simple gut-level reaction to The National—"*I hate that goddamn band*"—into an assertion that "The National reflects the way social and economic stratification are narrowing the space for cultural free agency." The clear irony of Wilson's assertion is that all of the criticisms which he levels at The National—monotonous lack of eccentricity, decision-making by professional committee, narrowing the space for cultural free agency—were *far* more applicable to the cookie-cutter pop music being churned out by the corporate mainstream than they were to the music coming from the indie rock scene. But because poptimist ideology made criticizing mainstream pop acts like Ke$ha and Celine Dion decidedly off-limits, the only acts who were fair game for critical disparagement were those who—like The National and their fellow indie acts—existed outside the commercial mainstream. Thanks to poptimism's requisite defense of the mainstream power structure and marginalization of those outside it, "cultural free agency" was indeed being narrowed, but in a very different way than Wilson was arguing.

However, by the second decade of the 21st Century, the critical backlash against the indie scene was increasingly being overshadowed by concerns about its financial future. The more pressing question for virtually all recording artists had become: How much longer would there even be any recorded music industry at all?

Chapter Eighteen

Towards an Uncertain Future

Digital Hegemony, Shrinking Revenues, and the Future of Rock Music

Re-thinking Copyright in a Digital Age

By the second decade of the new millennium, the proliferation of digital music had completely reshaped the financial landscape in which rock music was being created and listened to. While there were isolated success stories like those of Merge Records and other independent artists and labels, the simple fact was that, over the first decade of the new millennium, less and less money was being spent on purchasing recorded music. And the drop in recorded music revenues was putting rock artists squarely at the center of a renewed discussion about the nature of the relationship between art and commerce. This discussion would hit the front pages in 2012, when an intern at NPR became the unlikely lightning rod for the ire of working musicians around the globe. But the terms of the discussion had been set in the 1990s, when the digital age was still in its infancy, and its roots stretched all the way back to the dawn of American copyright law. At the center of the discussion were a couple of age-old questions: Who is the rightful owner of a work of art? And who should have the right to make money from it?

While the answers to these questions seemed self-evident to many people, the issues at stake were actually quite nuanced. For instance, a certain ambivalence about the ownership of creative works existed at the very root of American copyright law. The American Founders had believed that, in Thomas Jefferson's words, the products of the human mind "cannot, in nature, be the subject of property." According to Jefferson's logic, unlike physical property, creative works like books and music could be used and disseminated without impoverishing their creators. As Jefferson explained, "He who receives an idea from me receives instructions himself without lessening mine; as he who lights his taper at mine receives light without darkening me." But even though Jefferson and the American Founders didn't believe that creative works were the property of their creators, they nevertheless decided that temporary ownership of creative works should be legally granted to their creators as an incentive for them to create. According to UC Berkeley intellectual property specialist Pamela Samuelson, the Founders regarded copyright protections as "a small evil done to accomplish a larger good." And thus, "intellectual property" rights for creators were included in the Constitution itself, and they have been an integral part of the American legal tradition ever since.

With the advent of recorded music in the late 1800s, music recordings were soon included among the creative works protected by copyright law. And throughout the 20th Century, a group of enterprising record labels would build a multi-billion dollar industry on the sale of copyrighted music recordings, even as periodic complaints from songwriters and performers alleged that the labels weren't sharing enough of the revenue generated by music sales with those responsible for the creation of the music itself. By the end of the century, a small handful of major labels were responsible for producing over 90 percent of the music purchased in the United States, and their increasingly corporatized infrastructure was wielding unprecedented power over music creation and distribution. But just as the major labels were consolidating their gains into record-setting recorded music revenues, the advent of mp3s threatened to break their decades-old grip on music creation and distribution wide open, in the process raising vital questions that went to the very foundation of copyright law.

The terms of the debate concerning digital music copyrights were set in the 1990s, even before the rise of Napster, and the interested parties eventually settled into two distinct camps. On one side of the debate were the defenders of intellectual property rights, who argued that copyright law had always been about protecting the interests of both creators and the public good. According to Charles C. Mann in his in-depth series on digital copyright for *The Atlantic* in 1998-2000, "[Copyright law's] real purpose is to foster ever more ideas and ever more innovation from ever more diverse sources. When in 1790, George Washington asked Congress to enact copyright legislation, he argued that it would increase the national stock of knowledge. And knowledge, he said, 'is the surest basis of public happiness.'" According to the defenders of intellectual property, enforceable copyright law was still vitally necessary in the digital age in order to foster creativity by ensuring that individual artists and creators would have the right to be compensated for their work, no matter whether that work was disseminated in physical or digital form. In fact, the proponents of copyright argued that intellectual property rights were more important than ever in the digital age, where the ability to digitally replicate creative works without a loss of quality—especially music—had eliminated the once-prominent cost barrier to widespread illicit piracy.

On the other side of the debate were the "free information" advocates, who echoed Jefferson's insistence that the products of the mind, including art, could not be owned, and should exist freely in the public square. According to Electronic Frontier Foundation co-founder—and former Grateful Dead lyricist—John Perry Barlow, copyright law had never really been about fostering creativity; rather, it had been enacted in order to compensate publishers for the costly printing and distribution of physical artifacts like books and record albums, and thus the internet's elimination of these costs had made the entire publishing industry—and the copyright law which protected it—obsolete. "While both the law and lawmakers continued to enshrine the incentivization of creators, the real focus of both was assuring the institutional preservation of publishers," he wrote in 1998. "Genuine creators, they knew, would create anyway. They have no choice. But publishers are rarely driven by any such mission." Barlow believed that the inevitable triumph of the internet would ultimately be beneficial for artists and creators, freeing them from the predatory publishing establishment—and its attendant copyright law—resulting in increased creative autonomy and financial rewards for artists by cutting out the middle-man between creators and consumers. "As a songwriter and essayist (who is highly motivated by greed, thank you), I have absolutely no economic interest in supporting either technical or legal efforts to protect the publishing industry, which has preyed on my kind for 500 years."

Meanwhile, there were others in the "free information" camp who believed the collective power of the internet as an aggregator of ideas had effectively rendered the interests of individual creators moot. According to author, musician, and virtual reality pioneer Jaron Lanier in his book *You Are Not a Gadget*, "Authorship—the very idea of the individual point of view—is not a priority of the new ideology." Rather, many at the head of the digital revolution, like *Wired* editor Kevin Kelly and Google founder Larry Page, believed that the information being shared over the internet had granted the web a distinct intelligence and collective consciousness which trumped the antiquated idea of individual creativity. According to this creed, said Lanier, "We technologists are turning ourselves, the planet, our species, everything, into computer peripherals attached to the great computing clouds. The news is no longer about us but about the big new computational object that is greater than us." Some digital revolutionaries, like Google director of engineering Ray Kurzweil, went so far as to suggest that the power of integrated computer systems had blurred the traditional lines between humans and computers, and would eventually result in a merging of human and computer intelligence into a super-intelligent hybrid dubbed "The Singularity." Whatever one thought of such concepts, it was clear that their inherent devaluation of individual human creativity would have a profound effect on the evolution of copyright protections for individual authors and creators, especially as the increased use of digital systems bestowed greater and greater power on the architects and advocates of those systems.

However, the high-minded rhetoric being bandied about by both sides of the debate surrounding digital copyright tended to obscure the fact that, behind all the rhetoric, there were powerful corporate interests for whom billions upon billions of dollars were at stake. And in the late 90s, most observers still assumed that the mainstream music industry's multi-billion dollar infrastructure would prevail in defending its long-standing intellectual property rights in order to cash in on the potentially lucrative financial spoils of the digital music age. As Charles C. Mann wrote in 1998, "According to the conventional scenario, the economic winners will be those who own the ones and zeroes, not those who make the equipment that copies, transmits, and displays them." At that time, the fledgling infrastructure of the internet was still in flux, and the champions of its revolutionary possibilities were still perceived as idealistic insurgents—whom Mann somewhat dismissively referred to as "a small but surprisingly influential cadre of libertarian futurists." But in the coming years, a convergence of factors would turn the tide in favor of the free information camp.

The first factor came from within the media establishment itself. In the late 90s, the media industry reacted to the digital threat to its intellectual property claims by seeking to strengthen its hand in order to strangle digital copyright infringement in its infancy. Among its proposed solutions were "copyright boxes" which would restrict the flow of information on the internet much like a V-chip for copyright, "copyright licenses" which would be required in order to view or listen to copyrighted materials online, and an intricate system of digitally "watermarked" content capable of self-limiting its ability to be shared online. Taken as a whole, these proposals met with widespread criticism, and they succeeded in alienating many of the most ardent and influential defenders of intellectual property. For instance, Harvard Law's Lawrence Lessig found the "suggestion that we erect a licensing regime to regulate the right to read" to be "chilling." "The legal scholar Julie Cohen has convincingly argued that our tradition should protect a right to read anonymously," he wrote. "I think that is right, and this proposal would be far removed from that tradition." Spooked by the prospect of an internet policed by an all-powerful corporate "Big Brother," most scholars and lawmakers decided that a wait-and-see attitude regarding the still-fledgling internet would be more prudent than stifling its growth by installing a bunch of potentially dangerous restrictions into its architecture. "We must watch and wait," wrote Lessig in 1998. "And remain vigilant." There would always be time—so the logic went—to enact more stringent legislation at a later date, when a clearer picture of the internet landscape had come into focus. And so the more draconian measures proposed by the mainstream media industry remained unenacted, and the philosophical arguments surrounding copyright faded into the background of the public discourse as lawmakers waited for direction from the development of the internet itself.

Meanwhile, as internet use was exploding in the first few years of the new millennium, the daily practices of internet users were gaining a legitimizing inertia that would be difficult to change or reverse by purely legal means. As free information advocate John Perry Barlow noted, "It is unusual for law to prevail against massively accepted social practice." And in the late 90s and early 2000s, the downloading of mp3s from illegal P2P sites was becoming exactly the "massively accepted social practice" Barlow had described. In addition, a protracted disagreement among the major labels about how to sell music online meant that a trusted, industry-wide online retailer for legal music downloads didn't even exist until Apple launched the iTunes store in 2003. By 2004, iTunes had become the trusted leader in digital music sales, but in the crucial five years between Napster's launch in 1999 and iTunes' market ascendance, millions upon millions of internet users—including the vital teenage demographic which traditionally drove music sales—had made free mp3 downloads an integral part of their internet experience. And convincing people to pay for something they had come to expect for free would be a monumental challenge for intellectual property advocates.

But the most decisive factor working in favor of "free information" was the ongoing consolidation of an online infrastructure dominated by a small cadre of influential corporations that were hostile to traditional copyright protections for artists and content creators. The meteoric rise of Google, in particular, would be instrumental in turning "free information" rhetoric into a thriving multi-billion dollar business with its own agenda that was at odds with the enforcement of traditional copyright law. Google's search engine website had been incorporated in 1998, and before the year was out *PC Magazine* was praising Google for its "uncanny knack for returning extremely relevant results." But like all the other dotcoms hitting the market in the late 90s, the company would have to come up with a way to monetize the traffic generated by its increasingly popular search engine. In 2000, Google began selling advertising space through its revolutionary AdWords auction system, inaugurating more than a decade of exponentially increasing revenues. And yet, because people weren't paying directly to use Google's search engine services, its business model remained entirely reliant on the attractiveness of the "complements" to its search capabilities. As Nicholas Carr explained in his 2010 book *The Shallows*:

> Complements are, in economic terms, any products or services that tend to be consumed together, such as hot dogs and mustard, or lamps and lightbulbs. For Google, everything that happens on the Internet is a complement to its main business. As people spend more time and do more things online, they see more ads and they disclose more information about themselves—and Google rakes in more money. As additional products and services have come

to be delivered digitally over computer networks—entertainment, news, software applications, financial transactions, phone calls—Google's range of complements has extended into ever more industries. Because sales of complementary products rise in tandem, a company has a strong strategic interest in reducing the cost and expanding the availability of the complements to its main product. It's not too much of an exaggeration to say that a company would like all complements given away. If hot dogs were free, mustard sales would skyrocket. It's this natural drive to reduce the cost of complements that, more than anything else, explains Google's business strategy. Nearly everything the company does is aimed at reducing the cost and expanding the scope of internet use. Google wants information to be free because, as the cost of information falls, we all spend more time looking at computer screens and the company's profits go up.

While "free information" was indeed free to consumers, Google's business model illustrated just how much money could nevertheless be made off of that information. For instance, every time someone performed a Google search for a free music download, the search results were flanked by the kinds of advertisements which provided the backbone of Google's revenue stream. Every time someone visited a free mp3 download site, the site was plastered with advertisements, many of which were powered by Google's massive affiliate program. And every time someone watched a free music video on YouTube, the video was preceded and/or flanked by advertisements, each and every one of which enriched Google, which owned the popular video streaming website. Throughout the 2000s, there were huge fortunes being made from free online content—particularly music—and virtually none of it was going the creators of that content. In a complete reversal of the predictions made by leading pundits like Charles C. Mann in the late 90s, the clear "economic winners" of the digital era were *not* the owners and creators of online content, but rather those who controlled the internet infrastructure which copied, transmitted, and displayed that content. Back in 1998, Harvard Law's Lawrence Lessig had argued that, even in the presumably wide open digital age, "a new 'middleman' is essential and inevitable." Even though the old media power structure typified by major record labels might disappear, Lessig had predicted that "cyberspace will have constraints of its own... Power will shift, not disappear." And by the end of the first decade of the new millennium, the new power structure of the digital age was coming into focus.

In 2014, Google grossed more than $66 billion, more than *four times* the revenue of the entire worldwide recorded music industry combined, meaning that Google alone had more than enough financial and legal power to compete with the mainstream media power structure on a level playing field in the arena of copyright law. By the time John Perry Barlow's Electronic Frontier Foundation and its allies—which Charles C. Mann had dismissively referred to as a small "cadre of libertarian futurists" just a decade earlier—were lining up to fight 2011's Stop Online Piracy Act (SOPA) and Protect Intellectual Property Act (PIPA), they were no longer the underdogs in the fight over copyright law. Instead, the list of the bills' opponents was a who's who of the world's most powerful and influential online corporations—Google, Yahoo!, YouTube, Facebook, Twitter, Reddit, Wikipedia and the Wikimedia Foundation—all of whom had a huge financial stake in keeping information "free." And the fact that neither SOPA nor PIPA even made it out of committee was indicative of the massive lobbying power of the deep-pocketed "free information" movement. By that time, it was clear that a formidable infrastructure of tech conglomerates had supplanted the mainstream music industry and its copyright-friendly allies in order to become the dominant power structure of the digital age.

A Renewed Debate

In June of 2012, a twenty-year-old intern at NPR's "All Songs Considered" named Emily White published a short article titled "I Never Owned Any Music To Begin With," inadvertently sparking a firestorm of controversy and re-kindling the debate about the nature of music copyright and ownership in the digital age. White's article—in which she claimed "I've only bought 15 CDs in my lifetime. Yet, my entire iTunes library exceeds 11,000 songs"—was seen as a shot across the bow by a whole host of working musicians, many of whom had never really been cool with file-sharing to begin with, had watched recorded music revenues fall consistently for an entire decade, and had always vaguely blamed young internet "pirates" who didn't pay for music. None of White's critics was more vocal than Cracker and Camper Van Beethoven singer-songwriter David Lowery, who penned a vitriolic 4,000 word "Letter to Emily White at NPR All Songs Considered" for the *Trichordist* website which garnered over half-a-million views in just 48 hours, galvanizing a disgruntled group of musicians for whom Emily White became the embodiment of their deepest fears and resentments. "I never went through the transition from physical to digital," said White in her article. "I'm almost 21, and since I first began to love music I've been spoiled by the Internet... As I've grown up, I've come to realize the gravity of what file-sharing means to the musicians I love. I can't support them with concert tickets and T-shirts alone. But I honestly don't think my peers and I will ever pay for albums."

White was simply expressing the prevailing sentiment among music listeners of her generation, but by the time her article appeared, David Lowery was waiting with a well-prepared ideological response. Lowery had become a guest lecturer on music business at the University of Georgia, and in February 2012 he had given a presentation at the SF MusicTech Summit called "Meet the New Boss, Worse than the Old Boss?" in which he argued that the digital music market had stabilized enough that its financial merits could now be assessed. And, according to Lowery, the emerging financial picture was not a rosy one for musicians:

> I was like all of you. I believed in the promise of the internet to liberate, empower and even enrich artists... But the music business never transformed into the vibrant marketplace where small stakeholders could compete with multinational conglomerates on an even playing field. In the last few years it's become apparent the music business, which was once dominated by six large and powerful music conglomerates, MTV, Clear Channel and a handful of other companies, is now dominated by a smaller set of larger even more powerful tech conglomerates. And their hold on the business seems to be getting stronger... In fact it is nigh impossible for me to pursue my craft without enriching Apple, Amazon, Facebook and Google... With exploitive record contracts The Old Boss tried to take your songs a dozen at a time and pay you pennies. The New Boss wants to take ALL of your songs, past present and future and pay you nothing.

Lowery's "Letter to Emily White" blamed White's apparent disregard for the financial concerns of artists on the "false choices" her generation had been presented by the "technological and commercial interests" of the "free culture movement," which was actively "attempting to change our principles and morality." According to Lowery, "The accepted norm for hundreds of years of western civilization is the artist exclusively has the right to exploit and control his/her work for a period of time… This system has worked very well for fans and artists. Now we are being asked to undo this not because we think this is a bad or unfair way to compensate artists but simply because it is technologically possible for corporations or individuals to exploit artists' work without their permission on a massive scale."

The viral reach of Lowery's letter to White immediately brought the debate about music copyright in the digital age back to the forefront of the public consciousness, generating more articles and public debate on the subject than any time since the Napster era. Countless musicians posted links to Lowery's article on their social media pages, including singer-songwriter Aimee Mann, who posted the link on Twitter with the comment, "For anyone who wants to know how me & most of the musicians I know feel about the current state of the music business." But not all musicians sided with Lowery. In a dismissive *Huffington Post* article, Travis Morrison of the critically-acclaimed indie band The Dismemberment Plan argued that the mp3 file-trading of White's generation was no different than the shoplifting, mix taping, radio taping, and library copying which had been rampant in his generation, essentially telling Lowery to get off of his high horse and leave White and her generation alone. For its part, the *New York Times* chimed in that, "Educating young people about the consequences of their economic decisions is a vital part of living in a free market and a democratic society." However, the venerable newspaper doubted that Lowery's article would have any real or lasting impact. "History has shown that heavy-handed moral arguments about music—or any other form of online entertainment, for that matter—are seldom effective."

The most tangible impact of Lowery's article, however, was the way it signaled to his fellow musicians that the time had come to assess the financial state of the music industry in the digital age, and the ensuing months would see a deluge of articles and social media posts from musicians who were dissatisfied with how things were shaking out financially, especially on the music streaming sites like Spotify and Pandora which were being hailed as the next generation of music consumption. As Lowery had argued in his letter to Emily White, "The problem with Spotify starts [with illegal file-sharing]. The internet is full of stories from artists detailing just how little they receive from Spotify. I shan't repeat them here. They are epic. Spotify doesn't exist in a vacuum. The reason that Spotify can get away with paying artists so little is that the alternative is [free downloading]. There is simply no market pressure. Yet Spotify's CEO is the 10th richest man in the UK music industry, ahead of all but one artist on his service."

On the heels of Lowery's article, the popular indie band Grizzly Bear took to Twitter in August of 2012 to tell fans that "Mog and Spotify do not help bands or labels or indie stores... Buying an album helps tenfold..." The following month, critic Nitsuh Abebe published a *New York Magazine* profile on the band titled "Grizzly Bear Members Are Indie-Rock Royalty, But What Does That Buy Them in 2012?" in which he details the relatively meager lifestyle that the digital era had afforded a band which had two Top 10 albums to its credit. "For much of the late-twentieth century, you might have assumed that musicians with a top-twenty sales week and a Radio City show—say, the U2 tour in 1984, after *The Unforgettable Fire*—made at least as much as their dentists. Those days are long and irretrievably gone, but some of the mental habits linger. 'People probably have an inflated idea of what we make,' says [Grizzly Bear's Ed] Droste. 'Bands appear so much bigger than they really are now, because no one's buying records.'" Even in the indie community, where, according to Abebe, "audiences can react badly to musicians who acknowledge a relationship with money," artists like Grizzly Bear were starting to speak out. As Abebe documents, "Droste will say that paying $9 for a digital download of an act's new album—the price of 'a fucking appetizer, a large popcorn at the movie theater, and you'll have it forever, and they took two years to make it'— matters more than people seem to think, and not just in terms of income. 'Maybe they'll get on the radio. Every record sold shows the industry your value.' Meanwhile, streaming the album from a service like Spotify nets the musicians almost irrelevantly small amounts."

In November of 2012, Damon Krukowski of the indie band Galaxie 500 wrote a lengthy feature article for *Pitchfork* detailing just how small the amounts being paid to artists by streaming sites like Spotify and Pandora were. According to Krukowski:

> Today it is no longer possible for most of us to earn even a modest wage through our recordings. Not that I am naively nostalgic for the old days—we weren't paid for [our] first album, either. (The record label we were signed to at the time, Rough Trade, declared bankruptcy before cutting us even one royalty check.) But the ways in which musicians are screwed have changed

qualitatively, from individualized swindles to systemic ones. And with those changes, a potential end-run around the industry's problems seems less and less possible, even for bands who have managed to hold on to 100% of their rights and royalties, as we have. Consider Pandora and Spotify, the streaming music services that are becoming ever more integrated into our daily listening habits. My BMI royalty check arrived recently, reporting songwriting earnings from the first quarter of 2012, and I was glad to see that our music is being listened to via these services. Galaxie 500's 'Tugboat,' for example, was played 7,800 times on Pandora that quarter, for which its three songwriters were paid a collective total of 21 cents, or seven cents each. Spotify pays better: For the 5,960 times 'Tugboat' was played there, Galaxie 500's songwriters went collectively into triple digits: $1.05 (35 cents each). To put this into perspective: Since we own our own recordings, by my calculation is that it would take songwriting royalties for roughly 312,000 plays on Pandora to earn us the profit of one—*one*—LP sale. (On Spotify, one LP is equivalent to 47,680 plays.)

In keeping with the traditional argument for copyright protections—which asserted that guaranteeing the right of artists to be compensated for their work was a spur to creativity—many artists saw the fading fortunes of the digital era as a bad sign for the future of artistic creation. In an article for the *Guardian* provocatively titled "The Internet Will Suck All Creative Content Out of the World," former Talking Heads singer-songwriter David Byrne argued that, "In the future, if artists have to rely almost exclusively on the income from [streaming] services, they'll be out of work within a year." And when Radiohead's Thom Yorke angrily pulled his solo material from Spotify in early 2013, he and Radiohead producer Nigel Godrich took to Twitter to explain that Spotify's miniscule payouts might be a nice little bonus for older artists who had already made money on album sales during the pre-digital era. But for new artists, whose income from album sales was decreasing rapidly, the tiny revenues from Spotify weren't a sustainable substitution. As Yorke succinctly put it, "New artists get paid fuck all with this model." And according to Godrich, "Streaming suits [back] catalogue. But [it] cannot work as a way of supporting new artists' work. Spotify and the like either have to address that fact and change the model for new releases or else all new music producers should be bold and vote with their feet. [Streaming services] have no power without new music."

In a July 2013 *New Yorker* article, Damon Krukowski likewise suggested that leaving streaming services altogether might be the right course. "What if we call their bluff? Maybe no one will end up being paid for recordings, in that case—but as it stands, musicians aren't anyway." But the question remained: What exactly would a mass exodus from Spotify accomplish? Other than the demise of Spotify? Musicians might be able to take some satisfaction in knowing that Spotify's executives were no longer getting rich off of artists, but if the demise of Spotify led to an increase in illegal downloading, that would simply mean that the owners of file-sharing sites—and their affiliates like Google—would see a spike in revenue. And how would that be any better financially for artists? Weren't there any better solutions on the horizon? By the mid-2010s, the road towards increased recorded music revenues in the digital era was looking like a massive dead end.

Reassessing the Digital Era

As compelling as the arguments of disgruntled musicians like David Lowery, Damon Krukowski, and Thom Yorke were, they were all grounded in commercial rather than artistic assessments of the current music climate. And as such, they tended to overlook the obvious benefit of the digital music era: increased artistic autonomy. As Lowery himself had pointed out in his SF MusicTech Summit presentation, "In many ways we have more freedom. Artistically this is certainly true... the 'new boss' doesn't really tell me what kinds of songs to write or who should mix my record." Whereas, as Lowery would be the first to admit, dealing with the major labels—the "old boss" in Lowery's parlance—had always been a trade-off; in order to get a shot at the possible financial spoils offered by the major label system, artists always had to give up a measure of creative freedom. In addition, the major label system had been, for most of its existence anyway, a *closed system*; it had been nearly impossible to record professionally—let alone reach a wide audience—without the say-so of the corporate major label machinery. Whereas, in the digital era, the advent of affordable recording software and free international distribution via the internet had given rock artists the ability to create, record, and share their music without corporate commercial interference. Given these realities, maybe Lowery and his ilk were assessing the situation from the wrong perspective. Perhaps a musical era should be assessed according to the quality of music that era produced rather than the financial standing of its artists. And from this perspective, the digital music era exhibited much less cause for distress than the complaints of doom-and-gloomers like Lowery would suggest.

In his letter to Emily White, David Lowery had argued that the pre-digital system of copyright-protected music curated by major labels had "worked very well for fans and artists." This was, at best, a debatable statement. In the years which immediately preceded the digital revolution, the system may have been working for fans and artists according to purely *financial* measurements (though, of course, it "worked" best of all for the major labels), but the system wasn't working very well according to *artistic* measurements. The late 90s were a "golden era" of revenues for the recorded music industry (Lowery used the year 1996 as his representative year of the "old" regime), with U.S. album sales averaging roughly 1 billion annually. But within the world of rock music, anyway, this period of peak profitability coincided with rock's lowest point creatively since its birth in the mid-1950s. Not only were the major labels trotting out vapid, cookie-cutter acts like Creed and Limp Bizkit, but the virtual monopoly the majors wielded over the rock industry in the wake of the co-option of alternative music had left precious little space for independent label alternatives to mainstream homogenization. By contrast, the declining music revenues of the 2000s—and the concurrent decline in the power of the major label system over the creation and distribution of music—had coincided with a widespread proliferation of independent labels and artistically adventurous rock artists. While the ongoing exploitation of free music content by Google and the other rulers of the digital infrastructure was anything but fair, the fact that rock music could thrive artistically during a period of declining revenues flew in the face of the idea that the economic incentives provided by copyright law inexorably led to greater artistic creativity. In fact, there was plenty of anecdotal evidence to suggest that the boom in recorded music revenues which culminated in the 1990s had resulted in excesses which served as a detriment rather than a spur to artistic creativity.

The stories of spending excesses at major record labels were legion: hundreds of thousands of dollars spent recording single albums, millions spent on failed promotional campaigns, countless thousands on executive jets and expense accounts, and on and on. According to former major label executive

Glenn Boothe in *Our Noise*, "When I worked at Sony, I used to have an $18,000 expense account. And I was expected to spend it. And a lot of times that meant me and my friends went out and ate sushi. Because it's got to be spent. I used to date this girl who worked for a label, and one day she told me, 'Yeah, I needed a Snapple so I had a friend messenger me one from her office.' So instead of going downstairs and buying a Snapple, she spent $20 or whatever to have it messengered." And according to music business attorney Brian McPherson, "For a short time, I was an executive at a major label. And a guy would need to come to L.A. for a show from New York, and he'd book himself a $4,000 first-class flight at the last minute. I'd think, 'Wow, I could have made three records for that $4,000.'"

Stories like these were rampant within the major label system, but the connection between major label spending and the creation of better art had always been tenuous at best. So why, then, all the wasteful spending? "Because it's not their money. That's why," said Merge's Karen Glauber in *Our Noise*. "You don't care. It's all about market share. So you have to spend whatever it's going to take to maintain or grow your market share. So you throw good money after bad and bad money after good. [Only] two percent of all major label records recoup." Glauber was referring to the blockbuster revenue model which had defined major label operations for decades, in which a few huge-selling albums allowed major labels to lose money on the other 98 percent of their releases. According to Win Butler, whose band Arcade Fire had been wooed by multiple major label imprints after its initial breakthrough, "Big labels are so based on a blockbuster model, the Mariah Careys and Jon Bon Jovis of the world end up footing the bill for a lot of stupidly wasteful spending. Like putting Arcade Fire up in hotels and taking them out to steak dinners. Thanks Led Zeppelin, for the steak dinner! But when you own your own business, you just can't do it that way."

Beyond the glaring inefficiencies of the major labels' blockbuster model, advancements in recording technology in the digital era had made the idea of spending a million dollars recording a rock album not just inefficient, but completely unnecessary. By the 2000s, the sound quality of even the most expensive rock recordings of the pre-digital era could now be achieved by any prominent indie label for a fraction of the cost (and the sound quality of most *indie* albums from the pre-digital era could be replicated by any talented, self-taught artist with a few quality microphones and access to ProTools recording software). In fact, according to Sub Pop's head of A&R Tony Kiewel, it had been a *reduction* in recording costs that had led directly to the label's early 2000s creative renaissance. "If we spend only $5,000 recording an album," said Kiewel, "we can afford to keep doing records with artists that we truly love." In addition, digital distribution via online mp3 sales was far less expensive than printing and distributing physical CDs, drastically reducing the costs of associated with releasing an album. Given all of these factors, the drop in recorded music revenues in the 2000s could be seen as little more than the inevitable market correction to the excesses of an unsustainable recorded music boom.

Music as a Profession or Vocation?

The fact that rock music had experienced a creative renaissance during a time of flagging music revenues—and diminishing prospects of rock stardom—also begged the question: Had there *ever* been a positive correlation between rock star opulence and creative artistry? Or had that opulence actually functioned as a detriment to the creativity of rock's most talented artists? Why, for instance, had the creative life expectancy of rock artists typically been so much shorter than that of artists in other creative fields? Authors, visual artists, and classical composers routinely enjoyed vibrant creative lives well into—and in many cases beyond—middle age, whereas rock artists who managed to maintain creative relevance into their twilight years were exceedingly rare. At least one possible explanation for the short creative life of rock artists was the way that the relative immoderation of rock star adulation separated them from a vital connection to reality. Critic Lester Bangs had suggested as much back in the 1970s when he said, "It's no news by now that the reason most of rock's establishment have dried up creatively is that they've cut themselves off from the real world as exemplified by their fans... The everlasting and totally disgusting walls between artist and audience must come down, elitism must perish, the 'stars' have got to be humanized, demythologized, and the audience has got to be treated with more respect. Otherwise it's all shuck, a ripoff, and the music is as dead as The Stones' and Led Zep's has become." And the creative implications of rock star adulation which Bangs was addressing didn't even take into account the long, long line of deaths readily attributable to the excesses of the opulent rock star lifestyle, from Elvis to Kurt Cobain.

For rock fans who reveled in the kind of other-worldly superstardom valued by an increasingly celebrity-centric popular culture, the idea of world-conquering rock stars would always maintain an undeniable attraction. But for those who looked to rock music for its substantive artistry, for its potential to speak to them on a human level and provide truths which illuminated their lives, it was possible that the entire rock star phenomenon had been a decidedly irrelevant and potentially destructive distraction. In this sense, the demise of rock star culture could be seen as a positive sign for rock's creative future, rather than a sign of its decline (as was often bemoaned by older rock fans who continued to see rock music and rock stardom as irrevocably intertwined).

But what about artists who had no aspirations to rock stardom, those simply looking to make a living wage? This question goes to the heart of the age-old discussion about whether the creation of art is more properly viewed as a vocation or a profession. Given how prevalent the notion of art as a profession has become in Western culture, it can be easy to forget that music existed for centuries before it was deemed "property" by the Western legal system and transformed into a saleable commodity. According to DJ and music blogger Jace Clayton, "What we saw in the 20th century was an anomalous blip when music had a physical form. That was very unusual in the course of human history and it will soon be unusual again. Music has this intrinsic pull towards the dematerial, the unbuyable. It's a slippery, ghostly thing."

Even within the long shadow of intellectual property law, the classification of music as property has remained a tenuous designation, one which—at least in some estimations—has had something to do with the cultural pervasiveness of mp3 file-sharing. As singer-songwriter Jonathan Coulton wrote in a 2012 *Billboard* magazine article, "I don't know that I can articulate it here to everyone's satisfaction why getting digital music for free is different from getting physical objects for free, but it is hard to argue that it is not, in some fundamental way, very different. Clearly, we all think it's different, otherwise we would be stealing as many laptops as we are mp3s. Mp3s are lying all over the ground waiting for us to pick them up, and no matter how many we pick up, there are always more."

Coulton's observations echoed Thomas Jefferson's centuries-old sentiment about the inherent differences between intellectual and physical property. And for countless generations—long before the advent of file-sharing, recorded music, or the idea of intellectual property—the vast majority of artists had written and performed their music without any claims to ownership of it. While the ability to earn a living afforded by commodification had lifted many a starving artist out of poverty—and into the larger cultural consciousness—the resulting conflagration of art and commerce necessitated the loss of a certain purity of intention, one which some non-Western cultures continue to see as anathema. As singer-songwriter Fred Eaglesmith was quick to point out in a 2011 *Mule Variations* interview, "The Sufi religion believes that if you craft your art for commercialism it's the gravest sin. *The gravest sin.* It's so disgusting to them; it's worse than being a pedophile. Of course, the rest of us believe there's a balance." Where, exactly, that balance should be struck has been a question for every culture in which art and commerce intersect. And there is some evidence that today's rock artists are approaching that question differently than many of their predecessors. In fact, the limited financial prospects for musicians in the digital age are making the view of art as a vocation rather than a profession something of a necessity. As Nitsuh Abebe wrote in his recent profile of the band Grizzly Bear for *New York Magazine*:

> When I go to a Williamsburg bar to meet Frankie Rose, veteran of a string of much-discussed rock bands, she's just back from touring a solo album—her first stint without a day job—and already talking to the bartender about finding work. 'I feel like if you're in this at all to make money,' she says, 'then you're crazy. Unless you're Lana Del Rey or something, it's a moot point. You'd better be doing it for the love of it, because nobody's making real money.' This isn't exactly news... But [it] also require[s] musicians to approach what they're doing as an art—something with authentic, organic connections to style, aesthetics, and youth culture—not a craft to be dutifully plied for a living... [Grizzly Bear's Ed] Droste doesn't expect a middle-class living, but he wouldn't mind one. 'I'd like to someday own a house, and be able to have children, and be able to put them through school, in an urban environment that one enjoys living in,' says Droste. 'A lot of people do it. And doing it through music is harder than doing it as a lawyer.' I ask him if Grizzly Bear, with all its success, offers the beginnings of that. 'No,' he says, very quickly. 'I'd have to keep doing this forever. But the biggest thing you can't do is focus on money.' I ask how he'd feel if it turned out that pursuing music had prevented him from accomplishing any of that other stuff—would

that be worth it? 'Totally,' he says, also very quickly. Even the way I've phrased it, as a sort of gamble, doesn't sit well with him. 'It's not a gamble. You're doing it because you love it. I'm not placing bets on it, like, 'I hope this works, because otherwise my unborn child …' I'm doing it because I really enjoy it.'

Droste's sentiment is not something new. If anything, it's more in line with traditional view of art as a vocation, which, when taken in the long view, tends to make rock music's five decades of assumptions about the codependent nature of art and commerce look like a blip on the radar. But it *is* something new for rock. And, to the extent that today's rock artists are renouncing rock's long-standing commercial aspirations in order to view artistic creation as a vocation, they are keeping at least some small tie to music's pre-commercial intentions intact. In short, it means that there is hope that vibrant rock music will continue to exist into the foreseeable future, regardless of its financial fortunes. And for fans of rock music, that is very good news indeed.

Afterward

Art in a Commercial Culture

During the time I was writing this book, I happened to watch a documentary on PBS called *Paul Simon's Graceland Journey: Under African Skies*. As the title suggests, the film looks back at the making of Simon's seminal 1986 album *Graceland*, as well as the controversy that accompanied its recording, release, and subsequent tour. As detailed in the film, Simon had broken a United Nations-sanctioned "cultural embargo" in order to collaborate with the South African musicians with whom he had written and recorded *Graceland*. In doing so, he had angered the African National Congress, the leading black political party in South Africa, who had instituted the cultural embargo as part of a larger strategy intended to put pressure on the oppressive white government to end apartheid. Throughout the film, Simon continues to defend his decision not to live by the rules of the embargo:

> There's a certain hierarchy. At the top are the politicians, and behind the politicians are mysterious people who have money and power. After that comes the warriors, then comes the economists who say this is how a structure must be. And somewhere down the list comes the artist. And when the artist comes in, the politician says, 'We really need you to come in and play for this fundraiser.' Or, 'We have a very important dinner, we'd like you to come and sing a few songs acoustically after dinner. Come and take the love and respect that people have for you, and by implication transfer that to this candidate by your support.' The artists are always treated as if we worked for the politicians... That was the flaw in the cultural boycott, saying 'We won't let you come over here to record and bring what you know to

intermingle with what we know so that we can grow, so that we *all* can grow, and so that we all can grow and speak the deep truths that artists speak.'

Of course, time eventually proved Simon right. Not only was *Graceland* an artistic and commercial success, it also introduced the world to South Africa's vibrant music, putting a human face on the struggle against apartheid and helping to hasten its demise. It also led directly to the creation of the "world music" genre, which has subsequently helped countless musicians from around the world gain a wider audience.

But what immediately struck me about the above quote is the extent to which Simon's underlying assumptions—that art is uniquely capable of telling "deep truths," and that such art can be created in the context of rock music— are no longer shared by most contemporary music critics. For most of today's critics, belief in the artistic possibilities of rock music—and music in general— has become attenuated in an era where the assumption that "all art is fake," in the words of critic Carl Wilson, has eroded the centuries-old belief in the distinct and transformative potential of art.

For the entirety of the Western tradition, all the way back to Ancient Greece, art has been viewed as a unique way of *knowing*, a distinctly valuable way of perceiving and communicating the truth of the human condition. This view of art—the idea that art is a uniquely human endeavor that had something to do with the apprehension of truth and wisdom—remained consistent for more than two millennia, even through massive shifts in artistic style and philosophical disposition. The Greeks may have attributed artistic knowledge and inspiration to the muses, the Christians may have attributed it to the divine, and the Enlightenment philosophers may have attributed it to human ingenuity, but they were all in agreement about art's unique value. For Aristotle, art was intimately tied up with "the nature of Wisdom." For Lucretius, it was the development of the arts that had been the distinguishing characteristic of humanity itself. For Aquinas, art was evidence of "the freedom of the soul." For Marx, what distinguished human behavior was the uniquely human capacity for artistic imagination. For Kant, art was a window into "the sublime," created by humanity with "a view to communicating themselves to one another as completely as possible," and was thus the best representation of the inner life of humankind. This view still held sway well into the 20th century, and early rock critics like Lester Bangs still believed that rock music was part

290

of "the great search, fueled by the belief that through these musical and mental processes illumination is attainable. Or may at least be glimpsed."

But the poptimist critical hegemony of the new millennium has relegated this view of art and music to the periphery by eliminating the once-prominent distinction between genuine art and corporate commercial product. That's not to say there isn't a time and place for the kind of entertainment-oriented music that typifies commercial pop music; I'm as much a sucker for a killer hook or infectious dance beat as the next guy. But to the extent that our culture comes to view art and commercial product as one and the same, it limits our openness to the transcendent possibilities which are unique to the experience of art.

To be clear, I don't think that the current critical and cultural climate poses an insurmountable problem for artists themselves. I'm among those who would argue that the indefatigable drive and vocation to create art is deeply rooted enough in the human race that it will continue to exist regardless of how our culture perceives and rewards artistic creation. But I do fear that our failure to make any distinction between art and commercial product could have negative consequences for our culture as a whole, creating a climate in which we lose our ability to recognize and experience the "deep truths" that art is uniquely capable of telling. This, to me, would be a great tragedy. After all, what does it say about a culture that fails to see any special value in art beyond its commercial entertainment potential?

In this sense, the larger issues that this book explores are not unique to rock music. If you've read this far, it's probably pretty obvious that I am a fan of a lot of rock music, but I don't think that rock possesses any special quality which makes it inherently valuable artistically. I *do* think that rock's relative musical simplicity has had a democratizing effect on artistic creation, helping to obliterate the longstanding high art/low art distinction while granting artists who lack access to formal music training or major label backing an outlet to express their unique creative visions. But beyond that, I don't think there's anything uniquely compelling artistically about rock music's sound or ethos. For every great rock song, there are countless awful ones. And so I have little interest in the celebration of rock for rock's sake. When I listen to music, I'm always listening for a unique artistic voice, a creative human consciousness at work, and that voice and consciousness can be communicated through an infinite number of musical styles, from rock to jazz to rap to classical to country. As far as I'm concerned, a genre or style is far less important than the creative voice speaking through it. And if anything, my goal in writing this book has been to contribute, in some small way, to a discussion that might rekindle our appreciation for the transcendent experience of those creative voices, regardless of genre. My life has certainly been enriched beyond measure by the transformative experience of music. And I can only hope that similar experiences will continue to be possible in our culture, even in the midst of powerful commercial and cultural powers which seek to deny them. As long as we maintain the ability to experience the unique transcendence of art, there is greater hope for us all.

Acknowledgements

I am incredibly grateful for the opportunity to publish this book, and I am forever indebted to all those who made it possible. Thanks to Philip Francis and the whole *Mule Variations* crew for giving me a platform from which to write about music publicly for the first time. Without that opportunity, this book wouldn't exist. And thanks to fellow *Mule* alum Kathleen Fulton for the beautiful illustration that graces this book's cover.

Thanks to Myrsini Stephanides at the Carol Mann Agency. I would never have embarked on this journey without your initial encouragement and enthusiasm. Thanks to Sven Birkerts. Your thoughtful criticism and encouragement were instrumental in getting this book to the finish line. Thanks to Nathaniel Gaede, Brock Dittus, and Ryan Leach for reading through all or part of this manuscript multiple times. Your feedback was incredibly helpful. Thanks to Kevin Auman and Montreat College for granting me the opportunity to teach from this text before it was even published.

Thanks to my brother Josh, who was a partner in this project long before it was even conceived as a book. Your wisdom, humility, and emotional generosity made you the ideal sounding board for a project that was in danger of going off the rails multiple times. Thanks for keeping me on track, and thanks for making this book far better than it would have otherwise been. Thanks to my parents Jay and Gail for raising me in an environment filled with excellent music and teaching me how to experience all that music has to offer.

Finally, thanks to my wife Annie. Your willingness to bear with me as I poured myself into this project for three and a half years was nothing short of heroic. And your counsel and patience were invaluable resources as we spent the last few years navigating the unknown waters of the publishing world together. (And thanks to James, Henry, and Lizzie for being understanding as your father had less time to spend with you due to his writing schedule; I'll do my best to make it up to you.)

Sources

Books

Azerrad, Michael. *Come As You Are: The Story of Nirvana*. New York: Doubleday, 1993.

Azerrad, Michael. *Our Band Could Be Your Life: Scenes from the American Indie Underground 1981-1991*. New York: Back Bay Books, 2001.

Bangs, Lester. *Psychotic Reactions and Carburetor Dung*. New York: Random House, 1987.

Cantin, Paul. *Alanis Morissette: A Biography*. New York: St. Martin's Griffin, 1997.

Carducci, Joe. *Rock and the Pop Narcotic: Testament for the Electric Church*. Centennial, Wyoming: Redoubt Press, 1990.

Carr, Nicholas. *The Shallows: What the Internet is Doing to Our Brains*. New York: Norton, 2010.

Cook, John. *Our Noise: The Story of Merge Records*. New York: Algonquin, 2009.

SOURCES

Cott, Jonathan, ed. *Bob Dylan: The Essential Interviews*. New York: Wenner Media, 2006.

Cross, Charles. *Heavier Than Heaven: A Biography of Kurt Cobain*. New York: Hyperion, 2001.

Draper, Robert. *Rolling Stone: The Uncensored History*. New York: Doubleday, 1990.

Footman, Tim. *Radiohead: Welcome to the Machine*. New Malden, UK: Chrome Dreams, 2007.

Goldberg, Danny. *Bumping Into Geniuses: My Life Inside the Rock and Roll Business*. New York: Gotham, 2008.

Goodman, Fred. *The Mansion on the Hill: Dylan, Young, Geffen, Springsteen and the Head-on Collision of Rock and Commerce*. New York: Random House, 1997.

Goodman, Fred. *Fortune's Fool: Edgar Bronfman Jr., Warner Music, and an Industry in Crisis*. New York: Simon & Schuster, 2010.

Klosterman, Chuck. *Fargo Rock City: A Heavy Metal Odyssey in Rural North Dakota*. New York: Scribner, 2001.

Klosterman, Chuck. *Sex, Drugs, and Cocoa Puffs: A Low Culture Manifesto*. New York: Scribner, 2003.

Klosterman, Chuck. *Killing Yourself to Live: 85% of a True Story*. New York: Scribner, 2005.

Kot, Greg. *Wilco: Learning How to Die*. New York: Random House, 2004.

Lanier, Jaron. *You Are Not a Gadget*. New York: Vintage, 2010.

Marcus, Greil. *Mystery Train: Images of America in Rock 'n' Roll Music*. New York: Penguin, 1975

Marcus, Greil, ed. *Stranded: Rock and Roll for a Desert Island*. New York: Knopf, 1979.

Marks, Craig and Tannenbaum, Rob. *I Want My MTV: The Uncensored Story of the Video Music Revolution*. New York: Penguin, 2011.

McCormick, Neil, ed. *U2 by U2*. New York: Harper Collins, 2006.

Sandford, Christopher. *Kurt Cobain*. Cambridge, MA: Da Capo, 1995.

Tate, Joseph, ed. *The Music and Art of Radiohead*. Burlington, VT: Ashgate, 2005

Udo, Tommy. *Brave Nu World*. London: Cromwell Press, 2002.

Wallace, David Foster. *A Supposedly Fun Thing I'll Never Do Again*: *Essays and Arguments*. New York: Back Bay Books, 1997.

Wilson, Carl. *Let's Talk About Love: A Journey to the End of Taste*. New York: Continuum, 2007.

Yarm, Mark. *Everybody Loves Our Town: An Oral History of Grunge*. New York: Random House, 2011.

Films

Berlinger, Joe. *Under African Skies*. Radical Media, 2012.

Clifton, Peter. *The Song Remains the Same*. Swan Song, 1976.

Crowe, Cameron. *Pearl Jam: Twenty*. Tremelo, 2011.

SOURCES

Espar, David. *Rock & Roll*. WGBH, 1995.

Goodman, Barak. *Merchants of Cool*. PBS Frontline, 2001

Guggenheim, Davis. *From the Sky Down*. Universal, 2011.

Hackford, Taylor. *Hail! Hail! Rock 'n' Roll*. Universal, 1987.

Hickenlooper, George. *Mayor of the Sunset Strip*. Caldera, 2003.

Lacy, Susan. *The Making of David Geffen*. PBS, 2012.

Markey, Dave. *1991: The Year Punk Broke*. Geffen, 1992.

Pennebaker, D.A. *Don't Look Back*. Pennebaker Hegedus Films, 1967.

Pray, Doug. *Hype!*. Lions Gate, 1996.

Reiner, Rob. *This Is Spinal Tap*. Embassy, 1984.

Schnack, A.J. *Kurt Cobain: About a Son*. Balcony, 2006.

Scorsese, Martin. *No Direction Home*. Spitfire, 2005.

Temple, Julien. *The Future is Unwritten*. Vertigo, 2007.

Winter, Alex. *Downloaded*. VH1, 2013.

Articles

Aaron, Charles. "125 Best Albums of the Past 25 Years." *Spin*. 15 Feb. 2012: http://www.spin.com/spin25/readers-poll-spin-25-results/?page=25

Abebe, Nitsuh. "The Decade in Indie." *Pitchfork*. 25 Feb. 2010: http://pitchfork.com/features/articles/7704-the-decade-in-indie/

Abebe, Nitsuh. "On the Far Slope of Uncanny Valley." *Pitchfork*. 25 Mar. 2012: http://pitchfork.com/features/why-we-fight/8796-on-the-far-slope-of-the-uncanny-valley/

Abebe, Nitsuh. "Grizzly Bear Members Are Indie-Rock Royalty, But What Does That Buy Them in 2012?" *New York Magazine*. 30 Sept. 2012: http://www.vulture.com/2012/09/grizzly-bear-shields.html

Adams, Jason. "Pearl Jam's Drunken MTV Debacle." Entertainment Weekly. 16 Sept. 2011: http://music-mix.ew.com/2011/09/16/pearl-jams-drunken-mtv-debacle-cameron-crowe-looks-back-an-ew-exclusive/

Adler, Brian. "Chris Cornell Interview." *Adlercast*. 20 May. 2010: http://www.youtube.com/watch?v=0yyNH7SUn5g

Appelo, Tim. "Seattle Night Fever." *Entertainment Weekly*. 30 Sept. 2005: http://www.ew.com/ew/article/0,,311785,00.html

Arthur, Charles. "Thom Yorke Blasts Spotify as He Pulls His Music." *Guardian*. 15 July 2013: http://www.theguardian.com/technology/2013/jul/15/thom-yorke-spotify-twitter

Associated Press. "American Idol's Music Cred Growing." *Today*. 11 Jan. 2007: http://www.today.com/id/16580946/ns/today-entertainment/t/american-idols-music-cred-growing/#.UuE8_rROm01

Azerrad, Michael. "Nirvana: Inside the Heart and Mind of Kurt Cobain." *Rolling Stone*. 16 Apr. 1992: p. 36

Bangs, Lester. "Captain Beefheart: Trout Mask Replica." *Rolling Stone*. 26 July 1969: http://www.rollingstone.com/music/albumreviews/trout-mask-replica-19690726

SOURCES

Barber, Nicholas. "The Great Pretender; Interview: Gavin Rossdale." *Independent*. 2 Feb. 1997: http://www.independent.co.uk/life-style/the-great-pretender-interview-gavin-rossdale-1276479.html

Barshad, Amos. "Is Anyone Willing to Defend Modern Rock?" *Grantland*. 6 Jan. 2012: http://www.grantland.com/blog/hollywood-prospectus/post/_/id/40422/is-anyone-willing-to-defend-modern-rock-n'-roll

Basye, Ali. "The Day that Grunge Became Glam." *On This Day in Fashion*. 3 Nov. 2010: http://onthisdayinfashion.com/?p=7759

Bevan, David. "Merge Country." *Spin*. 20 Aug. 2013: http://www.spin.com/articles/superchunk-merge-records-durham-north-carolina/

Brown, Jake. "12 Years of Album Sales." *Glorious Noise*. 4 Jan. 2012: http://gloriousnoise.com/2012/12-years-of-album-sales-2011-year-end-soundscan-data

Browne, David. "Alanis Morissette: Jagged Little Pill." *Entertainment Weekly*. 4 Aug. 1995: http://www.ew.com/ew/article/0,,298223,00.html

Byrne, David. "The Internet Will Suck All Creative Content Out of the World." *Guardian*. 11 Oct. 2013: http://www.theguardian.com/music/2013/oct/11/david-byrne-internet-content-world

Caress, Adam. "Feature Interview – Fred Eaglesmith." *Mule Variations*. 1 Jan. 2011: http://www.mulevariations.com/features/feature-interview-fred-eaglesmith-part-1

Caress, Adam. "Feature Interview – Buffalo Tom's Bill Janovitz." *Mule Variations*. 1 Mar. 2011: http://www.mulevariations.com/features/feature-interview-buffalo-toms-bill-janovitz-part-1

Caress, Adam. "Feature Interview – Brent Knopf of Ramona Falls." *Mule Variations*. 20 Mar. 2013: http://www.mulevariations.com/features/feature-interview-brent-knopf-ramona-falls

Caress, Josh. "In Rainbows: Radiohead Bridges the Centuries." *Mule Variations*. 2 Nov. 2010: http://www.mulevariations.com/features/rainbows-radiohead-bridges-centuries-part-1

Caroli, Carly. "WFNX is Being Sold to Clear Channel." *The Boston Phoenix*. 16 May 2012: http://blog.thephoenix.com/BLOGS/phlog/archive/2012/05/16/breaking-101-7-wfnx-is-being-sold-to-clearchannel-pending-fcc-approval.aspx

Carson, Tom. "The Clash: London Calling." *Rolling Stone*. 3 Apr. 1980: http://www.rollingstone.com/music/albumreviews/london-calling-19800403

Christman, Ed. "How Five Indie Labels Are Trying to Change the Indie Distribution Game." *Billboard*. 31 May 2013: http://www.billboard.com/biz/articles/news/digital-and-mobile/1565541/how-five-indie-labels-are-trying-to-change-the-major

Colapinto, John. "Eddie Vedder: Who Are You?" *Rolling Stone*. 28 Nov. 1996: http://www.rollingstone.com/music/news/eddie-vedder-who-are-you-19961128

Connelly, Christopher. "U2: Under a Blood Red Sky." *Rolling Stone*. 19 Jan. 1984: http://www.rollingstone.com/music/albumreviews/under-a-blood-red-sky-19840119

Considine, J.D. "U2: War." *Rolling Stone*. 31 Mar. 1983: http://www.rollingstone.com/music/albumreviews/war-19830331

Considine, J.D. "Motley Crue: Shout at the Devil." *Rolling Stone*. 16 Feb. 1984: http://www.rollingstone.com/music/albumreviews/shout-at-the-devil-19840216

SOURCES

Coulton, Jonathan. "Emily White, David Lowery, and Legos: Can't We Get Along?" *Billboard*. 27 June 2012: http://www.billboard.com/biz/articles/news/1084925/guest-post-emily-white-david-lowery-and-legos-cant-we-get-along-by

Crowe, Cameron. "Five Against the World." *Rolling Stone*. 28 Oct. 1993: http://web.archive.org/web/20070619084803/http://www.rollingstone.com/news/story/10560431/five_against_the_world

DeCurtis, Anthony. "Truths and Consequences." *Rolling Stone*. 7 May 1987: p. 26

DeVille, Chris. "Greetings From Michigan: The Great Lakes State Turns 10." *Stereogum*. 1 Jul. 2013: http://www.stereogum.com/1396241/greetings-from-michigan-the-great-lakes-state-turns-10/top-stories/lead-story/

DiCrescenzo, Brent. "Tool: Laterus." *Pitchfork*. 15 May 2001: http://pitchfork.com/reviews/albums/8104-lateralus/

DiCrescenzo, Brent. "Radiohead: Kid A." *Pitchfork*. 2 Oct. 2000: http://pitchfork.com/reviews/albums/6656-kid-a/

Dombal, Ryan. "U2: Achtung Baby." *Pitchfork*. 9 Nov. 2011: http://pitchfork.com/reviews/albums/16022-achtung-baby-super-deluxe-edition/

Eddy, Chuck. "Radiohead: The Bends." *Spin*. 1 May 1995: http://www.spin.com/reviews/radiohead-the-bends-capitol/

Edwards, Gavin. "Fortune Flows from Grungy Beginnings." *Los Angeles Times*. 8 Jan. 2012: http://articles.latimes.com/2012/jan/08/entertainment/la-ca-subpop-20120108

Elder, Sean. "The Death of Rolling Stone." *Salon*. 28 June 2002: http://www.salon.com/2002/06/28/rollingstone/

Fletcher, Gordon. "Led Zeppelin: Houses of the Holy." *Rolling Stone*. 7 June, 1973: http://www.rollingstone.com/music/albumreviews/houses-of-the-holy-19730607

French, Karl. "The A-Z of Spinal Tap." *The Guardian*. 21 Sept. 2000: http://www.guardian.co.uk/books/2000/sep/22/film.film

Frere-Jones, Sasha. "A Paler Shade of White." *New Yorker*. 22 Oct. 2007: http://www.newyorker.com/arts/critics/musical/2007/10/22/071022crmu_music_frerejones

Frere-Jones, Sasha. "If You Care About Music, Should You Ditch Spotify?" *New Yorker*. 19 July 2013: http://www.newyorker.com/online/blogs/sashafrerejones/2013/07/spotify-boycott-new-artists-music-business-model.html

Gehman, Pleasant. "Nirvana: Artist of the Year." *Spin*. Dec. 1992: p. 50.

Gross, Terry. "Fresh Air: Kiss's Gene Simmons." *NPR*. 4 Feb. 2002: http://www.cpworks.org/rotton_school/blog/TERRYGRO.HTM

Harris, Keith. "Lift Every Voice." *Village Voice*. 6 Aug. 2002: http://www.villagevoice.com/2002-08-06/music/lift-every-voice/

Harvey, Eric. "The Social History of the MP3." *Pitchfork*. 24 Aug. 2009: http://pitchfork.com/features/articles/7689-the-social-history-of-the-mp3/

Harvilla, Rob. "The Arcade Fire Get Serious." *Village Voice*. 4 Aug. 2010: http://www.villagevoice.com/2010-08-04/music/the-arcade-fire-the-suburbs/

Hiatt, John. "The Black Keys." *Rolling Stone*. 4 Jan. 2012: http://www.rollingstone.com/music/news/cover-story-excerpt-the-black-keys-20120104

SOURCES

Hilburn, Robert. "Working Their Way Out of a Jam." *Los Angeles Times*. 22 Dec. 1996: http://articles.latimes.com/1996-12-22/entertainment/ca-11456_1_pearl-jam-concert

Himmelsbach, Erik. "The Alternative Revolution." *Los Angeles Times*. 3 December, 2006: http://www.latimes.com/features/image/la-et-125kroq3dec03,0,103491.story

Hogan, Marc. "Noah and the Whale: Peaceful, the World Lays Me Down." *Pitchfork*. 6 October 2008: http://pitchfork.com/reviews/albums/12248-peaceful-the-world-lays-me-down/

Holmes, Tim. "Motley Crue: Theater of Pain." *Rolling Stone*. 12 Sept. 1985: http://www.rollingstone.com/music/albumreviews/theatre-of-pain-19850912

Hornby, Nick. "Beyond the Pale." *New Yorker*. 30 Oct. 2000: http://archives.newyorker.com/?i=2000-10-30#folio=104

Hornby, Nick. "The Thrill of it All." *The Guardian*. 5 Sept. 2009: http://www.guardian.co.uk/music/2009/sep/06/nick-hornby-mp3-record-shops

Horning, Rob. "Poptimism: the Death of Pop Criticism." *PopMatters*. 11 May 2006: http://www.popmatters.com/post/poptimism_the_death_of_pop_criticism/

Houghton, Bruce. "Indie Labels just 12% of U.S. Sales." *Hypebot*. 5 Jan. 2012: http://www.hypebot.com/hypebot/2012/01/indies-just-12-of-2011-us-music-sales-how-4-3-major-labels-divided-the-rest.html

Hyden, Steven. "The Winners' History of Rock 'n' Roll." *Onion A.V. Club*. 26 Feb. 2007: http://www.avclub.com/article/the-winners-history-of-rock-n-roll-15400

Hyden, Steven. "The Preternatural." *Grantland*. 23 Oct. 2012: http://grantland.com/features/taylor-swift-officially-assumes-pop-center-new-album-red/

Hyden, Steven. "Ke$ha, Warrior Princess." *Grantland*. 4 Dec. 2012: http://grantland.com/features/praising-kesha-warrior-princess-dirty-pop-star/

Hyden, Steven. "The Winners' History of Rock and Roll, Part 1: Led Zeppelin." *Grantland*. 8 Jan. 2013: http://grantland.com/features/the-winners-history-rock-roll-part-1-led-zeppelin/

Hyden, Steven. "One Direction Should Not Be Ignored." *Grantland*. 26 November 2013: http://grantland.com/features/one-direction-midnight-memories-review-end-genre/

Kaufman, Gil. "The Rolling Stone Pearl Jam Letters." *MTV*. 6 Jan. 1997: http://www.mtv.com/news/articles/508838/rolling-stone-pearl-jam-letters.jhtml

Kemp, Mark. "Radiohead: OK Computer." *Rolling Stone*. 10 July 1997: http://www.rollingstone.com/music/albumreviews/ok-computer-19970710

Klosterman, Chuck. "The Ratt Trap." *New York Times*. 29 Dec. 2002: http://www.nytimes.com/2002/12/29/magazine/29RAMONE.html

Kobel, Peter. "Smells Like Big Bucks." *Entertainment Weekly*. 2 Apr. 1993: http://www.ew.com/ew/article/0,,306055,00.html

Kornhaber, Spencer. "What Yankee Hotel Foxtrot Said." *The Atlantic*. 3 May 2012: http://www.theatlantic.com/entertainment/archive/2012/05/what-yankee-hotel-foxtrot-said/256320/#

Kot, Greg. "Radiohead: OK Computer." *Chicago Tribune*. 4 July 1997: http://articles.chicagotribune.com/1997-07-04/entertainment/9707040186_1_ambition-ugly-star

SOURCES

Kot, Greg. "Katy Perry: Teenage Dream." *Chicago Tribune*. 22 Aug. 2010:
http://leisureblogs.chicagotribune.com/turn_it_up/2010/08/album-review-
katy-perry-teenage-dream.html

Krukowski, Damon. "Making Cents." *Pitchfork*. 14 Nov. 2012:
http://pitchfork.com/features/articles/8993-the-cloud/

LeMay, Matt. "The Postal Service: Give Up." *Pitchfork*. 9 Feb. 2003:
http://pitchfork.com/reviews/albums/6432-give-up/

Lowery, David. "Meet the New Boss, Worse than the Old Boss?" *The
Trichordist*. 15 Apr. 2012:
http://thetrichordist.wordpress.com/2012/04/15/meet-the-new-boss-worse-
than-the-old-boss-full-post/

Lowery, David. "Letter to Emily White at NPR All Songs Considered." *The
Trichordist*. 18 Jun. 2012:
http://thetrichordist.wordpress.com/2012/06/18/letter-to-emily-white-at-npr-
all-songs-considered/

Mann, Charles C. "Who Will Own Your Next Good Idea?" *Atlantic*. Sept.
1998: http://www.theatlantic.com/past/docs/issues/98sep/copy.htm

Mann, Charles C. "Copyright Roundtable." *Atlantic*. 10 Sept. 1998:
http://www.theatlantic.com/past/docs/unbound/forum/copyright/intro.htm

Mann, Charles C. "The Mp3 Revolution." *Atlantic*. 8 Apr. 1999:
http://www.theatlantic.com/past/docs/unbound/digicult/dc990408.htm

Mann, Charles C. "The Heavenly Jukebox." *Atlantic*. Sept. 2000:
http://www.theatlantic.com/past/docs/issues/2000/09/mann.htm

Marks, Craig. "Let's Get Lost." *Spin*. Dec. 1994:
http://www.fivehorizons.com/archive/articles/spin1294.shtml

Marin, Rick. "Grunge: A Success Story." *New York Times*. 15 Nov. 1992: http://www.nytimes.com/1992/11/15/style/grunge-a-success-story.html

McCulley, Jerry. "The Roots of Spinal Tap." *Gibson*. 23 May 2008: http://www.gibson.com/en-us/Lifestyle/Features/therootsofspinaltapwith/

Mendelsohn, John. "Led Zeppelin I – Review." *Rolling Stone*. 15 Mar. 1969: http://www.rollingstone.com/music/albumreviews/led-zeppelin-i-19690315

Moore, David. "Arcade Fire: Funeral." *Pitchfork*. 12 Sept. 2004: http://pitchfork.com/reviews/albums/452-funeral/

Montgomery, James. "Lollapalooza Lookback 1992: Meet Pearl Jam." *MTV*. 2 Aug. 2010: http://www.mtv.com/news/articles/1644863/lollapalooza-lookback-1992-meet-pearl-jam.jhtml

Morrissey, Janet. "Battle of the Bands (and Egos) for the Rock Hall of Fame." *New York Times*. 3 Dec. 2011: http://www.nytimes.com/2011/12/04/business/in-rock-hall-of-fame-vote-a-battle-of-industry-egos.html

Naughton, John. "Apple's Patent Absurdity Exposed at Last." *The Guardian*. 30 Jun. 2012: http://www.guardian.co.uk/technology/2012/jul/01/apple-google-patent-case-john-naughton-comment

O'Neil, Luke. "How the Decemberists Ruined Indie Rock." *Boston Phoenix*. 26 Jan. 2011: http://thephoenix.com/boston/music/114581-how-the-decemberists-ruined-indie-rock/

Opus. "Why are Indie Labels Leaving Spotify?" *Opus*. 19 Nov. 2011: http://opus.fm/elsewhere/why-are-indie-labels-leaving-spotify

SOURCES

Ordonez, Jennifer. "Pop Singer Fails to Strike a Chord Despite the Millions Spent by MCA." *Wall Street Journal*. 26 Feb. 2002: http://online.wsj.com/news/articles/SB1014678641479060480?mg=reno64-wsj&url=http%3A%2F%2Fonline.wsj.com%2Farticle%2FSB10146786414 79060480.html

Osorio, Alexandra. "The History of Recording Industry Sales, 1973-2010." *Digital Music News*. 17 Feb. 2011: http://www.digitalmusicnews.com/stories/021711disruption

Pareles, Jon. "R.E.M. Conjures Dark Times on Document." *New York Times*. 13 Sept. 1987: http://www.nytimes.com/1987/09/13/arts/rem-conjures-dark-times-on-document.html

Pareles, Jon. "Review/Rock: The Barrage Method of Tweaking Taboos." *New York Times*. 10 Aug. 1993: http://www.nytimes.com/1993/08/10/arts/review-rock-the-barrage-method-of-tweaking-taboos.html

Pareles, Jon. "Nirvana, the Band That Hates to Be Loved." *New York Times*. 14 Nov. 1993: http://www.nytimes.com/1993/11/14/arts/pop-music-nirvana-the-band-that-hates-to-be-loved.html

Pareles, Jon. "Music Confers an Afterlife As Cacophony Lingers On." *New York Times*. 17 Apr. 1994: http://www.nytimes.com/1994/04/17/weekinreview/the-nation-music-confers-an-afterlife-as-cacophony-lingers-on.html

Petrusich, Amanda. "Sufjan Stevens: Illinois." *Pitchfork*. 4 Jul. 2005: http://pitchfork.com/reviews/albums/7514-illinois/

Phillips, Chuck. "Pearl Jam, Ticketmaster, and Now Congress." *Los Angeles Times*. 30 June 1994: http://articles.latimes.com/1994-06-30/entertainment/ca-10438_1_pearl-jam-merchandise

308

Phillips, Chuck. "Warner Music Chief Expected to Quit Today." *Los Angeles Times*. 3 May 1995: http://articles.latimes.com/1995-05-03/business/fi-61908_1_warner-music-group

Pond, Steve. "U2: The Joshua Tree." *Rolling Stone*. 9 Apr. 1987: http://www.rollingstone.com/music/albumreviews/the-joshua-tree-19870409

Powell, Alison. "Scene There, Done That." *The Guardian*. 4 Feb. 2005: http://www.guardian.co.uk/music/2005/feb/05/popandrock1

Powers, Ann. "The End of 'Idol.'" *NPR*. 23 May 2012: http://www.npr.org/blogs/therecord/2012/05/23/153316590/the-end-of-idol-there-are-no-more-songs-left-to-be-sung

Powers, Ann. "Taylor Swift, Princess of Punk?" *NPR*. 21 Aug. 2012: http://www.npr.org/blogs/therecord/2012/08/23/159559500/taylor-swift-princess-of-punk

Reynolds, Simon. "The Ghost of Teen Spirit." *Slate*. 23 Aug. 2011: http://www.slate.com/articles/arts/music_box/2011/08/the_ghost_of_teen_spirit.single.html

Reynolds, Simon. "Dancing Up a Storm, but Dying to Rock." *New York Times*. 23 Nov. 2012: http://www.nytimes.com/2012/11/25/arts/music/kesha-tilts-closer-to-a-rock-sound-with-warrior.html

Robbins, Ira. "Nirvana: Smells Like Teen Spirit." *Rolling Stone*. 28 Nov. 1991: http://www.rollingstone.com/music/albumreviews/nevermind-19911128

Rock and Roll Hall of Fame. "Induction Process." *Rock and Roll Hall of Fame*. http://www.rockhall.com/inductees/induction-process/

Rose, Charlie. "A Conversation with Cameron Crowe." *Charlie Rose*. 11 Sept. 2000: http://www.charlierose.com/view/interview/3522

Rosen, Jody. "The Perils of Poptimism: Does Hating Rock Make You a Music Critic?" *Slate*. 9 May 2006: http://www.slate.com/articles/arts/music_box/2006/05/the_perils_of_poptim ism.html

Ryan, Chris. "Overrated, Underrated, or Properly Rated: Ethan Hawke." *Grantland*. 6 June 2013: http://grantland.com/hollywood-prospectus/overrated-underrated-or-properly-rated-ethan-hawke/

Sanneh, Kelefa. "The News from Nebraska: Local Bands Make Good." *New York Times*. 23 Mar. 2003: http://www.nytimes.com/2003/03/23/arts/music-the-news-from-nebraska-local-bands-make-good.html

Sanneh, Kelefa. "A Draining Week in the Indie-Music Spotlight." *New York Times*. 18 Oct. 2004: http://www.nytimes.com/2004/10/18/arts/music/18band.html?_r=1&

Sanneh, Kelefa. "The Rap Against Rockism." *New York Times*. 31 Oct. 2004: http://www.nytimes.com/2004/10/31/arts/music/31sann.html

Schreiber, Ryan. "Radiohead: OK Computer." *Pitchfork*. 1997: http://web.archive.org/web/20010303103405/www.pitchforkmedia.com/rec ord-reviews/r/radiohead/ok-computer.shtml

Sherma, Laura. "The New Counterculture's Buying Power." *Forbes*. 1 Oct. 2008: http://www.forbes.com/2008/10/01/hipster-buying-power-forbeslife-cx_ls_1001style.html

Slezak, Michael. "Worshipping at the 'Idol' Church." *New York Times*. 14 May 2010: http://www.nytimes.com/2010/05/16/fashion/16Idol.html

Smith, Clyde. "Grizzly Bear Tweets: Buying Albums is the Best Way to Support Bands." *Hypebot*. Sept. 2012: http://www.hypebot.com/hypebot/2012/09/grizzly-bear-says-buying-the-album-is-the-best-way-to-support-your-favorite-bands.html

THE DAY ALTERNATIVE MUSIC DIED

Strauss, Neil. "Forget Pearl Jam, Alternative Rock Lives." *New York Times*. 2 Mar. 1997: http://www.nytimes.com/1997/03/02/arts/forget-pearl-jam-alternative-rock-lives.html

Strauss, Neil. "Pay-for-Play Back on the Air But This Rendition Is Legal." *New York Times*. 31 Mar. 1998: http://www.nytimes.com/1998/03/31/arts/pay-for-play-back-on-the-air-but-this-rendition-is-legal.html

Suddath, Claire. "How Pitchfork Struck a Note in Indie Music." *Time*. 15 Aug. 2010: http://content.time.com/time/magazine/article/0,9171,2007424,00.html

Sweeney, Joey. "Days of the N." *Salon*. 5 Apr. 2001: http://www.salon.com/2001/04/05/numetal/

Thompson, David. "Nirvana And Co. Are Carrying Punk's Torch." *Seattle Times*. 29 Mar. 1992: http://community.seattletimes.nwsource.com/archive/?date=19920329&slug=1483573

Tucker, Ken. "American Idol." *Entertainment Weekly*. 4 July 2002: http://www.ew.com/ew/article/0,,269319,00.html

Weisbard, Eric. "This Monkey's Gone to Heaven." *Spin*. Jan. 1998: p.64

White, Emily. "I Never Owned any Music to Begin With." NPR. 16 Jun. 2012: http://www.npr.org/blogs/allsongs/2012/06/16/154863819/i-never-owned-any-music-to-begin-with

Wilson, Carl. "Why I Hate The National." *Slate*. 28 May 2013: http://www.slate.com/articles/arts/music_box/2013/05/the_national_s_troubl e_will_find_me_reviewed_too_many_crescendos.single.html

Wolk, Douglas. "Like Our New Direction?" *Village Voice*. 3 Oct. 2000: http://www.villagevoice.com/2000-10-03/music/like-our-new-direction/full/

SOURCES

Wolk, Douglas. "Thinking About Rockism." *Seattle Weekly*. 9 Oct. 2006: http://www.seattleweekly.com/2005-05-04/music/thinking-about-rockism/

Woods, Scott. "Tom Carson Talks Straight." *RockCritics.com*. 2001: http://rockcriticsarchives.com/interviews/tomcarson/tomcarson.html

Yardley, William. "Post-Grunge, Seattle Rocks On." *New York Times*. 16 Sept. 2011: http://www.nytimes.com/2011/09/16/us/post-grunge-seattle-still-rocks-20-years-after-nirvanas-nevermind.html

Young, Charles. "Kiss: The Pagan Beasties of Teenage Rock." *Rolling Stone*. 7 Apr. 1977: http://www.rollingstone.com/music/news/kiss-the-pagan-beasties-of-teenage-rock-20120427

Additional Online Resources

The Recording Industry Association of America: www.riaa.com

Billboard Magazine: www.billboard.com

Radio Hit List: www.radiohitlist.com

Robert Christgau's Consumer Guide: www.robertchristgau.com

The *120 Minutes* Archive: www.tylerc.com/the-120-minutes-archive

Index

313

INDEX

314

315

INDEX

INDEX

INDEX

320

INDEX

INDEX

INDEX

CPSIA information can be obtained at www.ICGtesting.com
Printed in the USA
LVOW06s1555251115

464204LV00008B/825/P